# The National Question

## Decolonizing the Theory of Nationalism

James M. Blaut

with a Foreword by Juan Mari Brás

**Zed Books Ltd.**
London and New Jersey

*The National Question* was first published by Zed Books Ltd.,
57 Caledonian Road, London N1 9BU, UK, and
171 First Avenue, Atlantic Highlands, New Jersey 07716, USA,
in 1987.

Cover designed by Andrew Corbett.
Typeset by EMS Photosetting, Rochford, Essex.
Printed and bound in the United Kingdom
by Biddles Ltd., Guildford and King's Lynn.

**British Library Cataloguing in Publication Data**

Blaut, James M.
    The national question : Decolonizing the Theory of
Nationality.
    1. Nationalism
    I. Title
    320.5′4        JC311

    ISBN 0-86232-439-4
    ISBN 0-86232-440-8 Pbk

**Library of Congress Cataloging-in-Publication Data**

Blaut, James M. (James Morris)
    The national question.

    Bibliography : p.
    Includes index.
    1. Nationalism and socialism. 2. National liberation
movements.  I. Title.
HX550.N3B53  1987        320.5′4        87-13281
ISBN 0-86232-439-4
ISBN 0-86232-440-8 (pbk.)

# Contents

Dedicated to the memory of Rafi Cintrón, Rudy Lozano, and Ed Marksman, colleagues and compañeros.

# Acknowledgements

Four of the chapters in this book have been adapted from published articles; permission was kindly given by the following publications to reprint them here: *Science and Society* (Chapter 2); *Antipode: A Radical Journal of Geography* (Chapters 3 and 6); *Monthly Review* (Chapter 5); and the Puerto Rican pro-independence newspaper *Claridad* (the original version of Chapter 6). Many people contributed in important ways to the writing of this book and the ideas it contains (but not its errors). I wish to express my special gratitude to Abdul Alkalimat, José Alberto Alvarez, Ramon Arbona, Gini Blaut Sorrentini, the late Rafi Cintrón, Otis Cunningham, Horace Davis, Loida Figueroa, José López, Olga López, the late Rudy Lozano, Manuel Maldonado-Denis, Juan Mari Brás, Francis Mark, the late Ed Marksman, Robert Molteno, José and Mariana Navarro, Anselme Rémy, Antonio Ríos-Bustamante, Digna Sánchez, Chris Searle, José Soler, América Sorrentini de Blaut, Howard Stanton, David Stea, José Villamil, Dessima Williams and Ben Wisner.

**J. M. Blaut**

# Foreword

Good theory is the accurate generalization of practice. That is why there is no good theory, social, political or whatever, if it is not predicated on a profound and extended practice of the matter up on which one is theorizing.

This book is an outstanding contribution to Marxist theory concerning national struggle. The author is very well equipped for the task. In the first place, he has been for the last 15 years an activist in the liberation struggle of Puerto Rico. Thus, he has been practising national struggle in one of the last frontiers of colonialism in the world today. Secondly, as a professional geographer, he is sensible to the significance of physical location in affecting the course of social and historical processes. This is certainly most important in this case. The geographical factor springs from his definition of national struggle as "the form of political class struggle which is associated, in general, with states which are externally governed."

This volume constitutes a critique of past Marxist theories of national struggle, nationalism and, in general, Third World participation in international class struggle. The theories developed derive general concepts from particular experiences, as any piece of sound theory should. The particular experience here is the reflection of the debates and discussions in the Puerto Rican liberation movement, and specifically in the socialist current of this movement, as well as among the Puerto Rican emigrant community in the United States.

Based on these experiences, the author moves with great intellectual lucidity and honesty through some of the most controversial themes of Marxist theory: whether national struggle is something separate from class struggle or an integral and prominent part of it; and even when recognized as a form of class struggle, whether it should be understood as something associated mainly with the bourgeoisie as a class and with the period of early capitalism as a stage of social evolution.

In both cases, he proves his point in favour of a class struggle perspective and the universal significance of national struggle for the international working class. It is evident that Lenin has been, so far, the major theoretician for these propositions. Certainly, the political genius who led the first victorious socialist revolution in world history was himself a frontier man from a frontier nation, which made him particularly fitted for such a theoretical discovery. Probably one of his major accomplishments as a theoretician of the social evolution of human kind was his rupture with the Eurocentric conceptions of Marx and Engels inasmuch as it was necessary to translate Marxist theories into practice in a mostly non-European country like Russia.

Professor Blaut analyses the propositions mentioned above throughout his book. As for the discussions within the Puerto Rican Independence movement that led to these theoretical confrontations, they have, in my estimation, been largely transcended by history. It is now more evident than a few years ago for anyone, except those with very underdeveloped political minds, that the national liberation struggle of the Puerto Rican independence movement is of the essence of class struggle and that the achievement of independence for Puerto Rico is the major contribution that Puerto Ricans can make to the complete victory of socialism in the world. Yet, the theoretical elaboration of this fact, which some day will be self-evident, is still necessary. Few works can be as valuable as the present one for the full clarification of these points.

It is, however, in chapter seven of this volume that the author makes what I consider a real, outstanding contribution to Marxist theory. His ideas about Eurocentrism and geographical diffusionism as shortcomings of Marxist theory ought to be seriously considered and developed in the future by many other thinkers.

As a matter of fact, the creative, political focus of Marxist theory has moved substantially from Europe to the Third World throughout the present century. Little new is coming from Europe now to enlighten the theory of social evolution based on historical materialism during the next epoch. All the dissident varieties of current European socialist thought are rooted in the same theoretical paradigm caused by the basic defect of Marxism, which is its Eurocentric conception of the historical and social processes of class societies.

"These limitations of Marxist theory as a whole", affirms Professor Blaut correctly, "are, unsurprisingly, found also in the theory of nationalism or the national struggle."

I hope that this volume, and particularly the latter chapters, will bring further developments of the basic ideas discussed, and that it will stimulate new theoretical efforts from Third World scholars and militants of revolutionary action.

**Juan Mari Brás**

# Preface

## Purpose

In every national liberation struggle there is concern about the national question: the question of how the fight for political sovereignty is to be carried out and what role it should play in the larger struggle for social justice. The issues are always complex and difficult, and always there is a search for general principles, for theory, to provide some guidance for practice. I will argue in this book that the Marxist theory of national struggle can offer this kind of guidance, provided that we adapt the theory to the conditions that are faced in Third World liberation struggles: conditions of colonialism and neocolonialism. I will also defend the basic or classic theory, as it was formulated by Marx, Engels, and Lenin, against the charge that it is not relevant to national liberation struggles in the Third World of the 1980s, and against the charge that it somehow defines these struggles as reactionary or insignificant or out of date. Finally, I will contribute some new elements to the theory itself, and to historical materialism.

The book evolved as a series of separate essays, and I cannot claim for it the virtues of systematic organization. Each chapter is an essay, and each essay is a self-contained argument. Nevertheless the book as a whole has a single point of reference and a single argument. The reference point is the Puerto Rican independence movement. The national question is seriously debated within our movement and among its political and intellectual allies. Much of the debate centres on questions of theory. Is there a contradiction between national struggle and class struggle? Between a multi-class nation and an international working class? Are national struggles simply out of date? Those who believe in the existence and generality of such contradictions are prone to criticize the Puerto Rican movement or abandon it.

This book demonstrates, from the point of view of Marxist theory, that such contradictions do not exist in the conditions with which we are concerned; that struggles for national liberation in colonies and neocolonies are a vital, central part of the movement towards social justice in these countries and in the world. The argument is put forward at the level of theory, and I say relatively little about Puerto Rico itself (which I treat in another, forthcoming work: *La cuestión nacional en Puerto Rico*). But here, as elsewhere, theory is written for the sake of practice.

# Plan

Most struggles against colonialism and neocolonialism have a great deal in common with one another, and it will become clear as the argument proceeds that the problems confronted in this book are crucial issues for national liberation movements throughout the Third World; crucial also for theoretical, scholarly debates about colonialism, underdevelopment, uneven development, and imperialism. I can illustrate all of this by briefly recounting the way this book evolved.

Until the mid-1970s few Marxists questioned the axiom that anticolonial struggles are progressive and important. Debates about the national question in regard to colonized peoples tended to focus on a narrower issue: the problem of determining whether a given community was a nation (with the right of self-determination including secession) or merely a 'national minority' within some larger nation. This issue was central to the national question in Third World countries with serious internal secessionist movements (for example in Sri Lanka, Iran, or Ethiopia), in the South African and Palestinian liberation movements, and in the varying struggles of Third World minorities in the United States, one of these being the Puerto Rican community. (Two million Puerto Ricans live in the US; three million live in Puerto Rico.)

In the 1970s, the Puerto Rican national question concerned neither the existence of the nation itself nor the legitimacy and progressiveness of its independence movement. It concerned (mainly) the question of whether Puerto Ricans within the US were part of that nation or were a US 'national minority'. For Marxists, the latter position implied an obligation to use multinational, not national, forms of communal and political organization, and to give absolute priority to the task of liberating the US, not Puerto Rico. The main argument in favour of the 'national minority' position involved a Stalinesque interpretation of the Marxist theory of nations and minorities, an interpretation which posits the inevitability of national assimilation. Chapters 5 and 6 of the present book were written to combat this view of Marxist theory and of historical reality. They were written as contributions to the debate about Puerto Ricans in the US, but their arguments apply (and have been applied) to other debates about 'national minorities', and to scholarly debates about the theory of nationalism.

The national question became a much larger issue for Marxists in the mid-1970s. No longer was it considered axiomatic that national struggles against colonialism are legitimate, justified, progressive, and important. The axiom itself derived mainly from Lenin's classic argument that colonialism is a central feature of monopoly capitalism (or imperialism), that anti-colonial struggles are class struggles, that they are directed mainly against the imperialist bourgeoisie, and that they are crucial to the struggle for socialism. During the 1970s the Leninist analysis of these processes, and of imperialism as a whole, was coming under attack from a number of theoretical directions, and various competing world models were being proposed and defended by Marxists, some of whom considered themselves to be within the Leninist theoretical tradition, others outside it. Most of the models interpreted imperialism as, in essence, a diffusion of capitalism, a matter of uneven development or uneven 'modernization', and national liberation struggles were typically viewed as moments in the rise of capitalism (or of the bourgeoisie) in peripheral countries, not as struggles against metropolitan capitalism and to a significant extent against capitalism in general.

All of this led to a significant devaluation of national liberation: it was to be reduced to 'bourgeois nationalism', or 'narrow nationalism', or to some ideological and non-class force, a force sometimes equated with fascism. While the critique of Lenin's view of imperialism developed steadily throughout the the 1970s (and beyond), the derivative critique of nationalism became important mainly after the fall of Saigon, symbolically a birth date for New-Leftist and Neo-Marxist critiques of Third World revolutions from Vietnam to Angola to Cuba. It was in this atmosphere that a number of new theories of nationalism or national struggle were proposed and some old ones resurrected. Most of these theories fell into two groups. One group argued that national struggle is autonomous from class struggle. The other argued that national struggle is class struggle but it is associated mainly (or only) with one class, the bourgeoisie, and one stage of social evolution, the period of early or rising capitalism.

These two theories have had corrosive effects on the Puerto Rican liberation movement, and it is for this reason that I wrote the essays which form Chapters 2, 3, and 4 of the present book. The Puerto Rican movement had been very nearly crushed in the 1950s, but during the 1960s and 1970s it grew rapidly, and became explicitly socialist and Marxist in resonance with liberation struggles elsewhere in the Third World. For a time this rapid efflorescence of the movement led to over-confidence and illusionism about the timetable of liberation. When the expectations proved to be unrealistic, many Marxists reacted by questioning not only the illusions, and the errors made in the struggle, but also the basic legitimacy of the struggle itself. They reacted also to sobering events elsewhere in the region – the invasion of Grenada, the threat of invasion in Nicaragua – and to the larger atmosphere of the early 1980s period, when Reagan–Thatcherism was ascendant, when the socialist world was disunited, and when many newly independent countries were experiencing serious difficulties. In Puerto Rico it was asked: 'Is the independence movement merely "nationalist", or "bourgeois nationalist"? Is it out of date? Is there a "contradiction" between the struggle for independence and the struggle for socialism? Does the Puerto Rican nation still exist as a political reality, or has it, after eight decades of US colonialism, dissolved into the United States?' Since about 1980 these issues have been debated with increasing intensity, and part of the debate has focused on the Marxist theory of nationalism.[1]

Chapters 2, 3, and 4 of this book are efforts to demonstrate that national struggle *is* class struggle, however much its class nature may be obscured by ethnic and other complications; that the primary contradiction is the one between contending classes, exploiters and exploited; and that national movements are progressive and significant when their main class forces are the proletariat and other exploited and marginalized classes, as in struggles against colonialism. The essays were written as theory, and they criticized Marxist theoreticians, but their underlying purpose was to show that Marxist theory is a weapon of liberation, in Puerto Rico as elsewhere, and that it cannot be used to question the validity of national liberation struggles, in Puerto Rico or anywhere else.

The argument begins, in Chapter 2, with a theoretical demonstration that nationalism is not an autonomous force. Next, in Chapter 3, I criticize at length a theory of nationalism put forward by the British Marxist Tom Nairn, a theory which became, in Puerto Rico and elsewhere, an influential statement of the position that nationalism is something distinct from class struggle. Nairn's theory utilizes the classic non-Marxist argument that Third World national movements result from the diffusion, from Europe, of 'modernization', along with the argument that nationalism is akin to fascism and national liberation movements themselves are somehow akin to fascist movements. For these reasons, all of them relevant to the Puerto Rican debates, it seemed important to write a thorough critique of this one Marxist theory.

If national struggle, however, is class struggle, then which classes make use of it, in which historical epochs, and for which purposes? Chapter 4 is a critique of Eric Hobsbawm's influential theory that national struggles are appropriate only to the period of rising capitalism and national movements are strategies appropriate only (in essence) to the rising bourgeoisie; that, in the 20th Century, national movements are irrational and atavistic. Hobsbawm posits a second kind of contradiction between class struggle and national struggle: whereas Nairn and conservative theorists describe the two as different kinds of phenomena, Hobsbawm describes the latter as (in essence) a stage of the former, a stage that is now ended: national movements, including national liberation movements, are no longer rational. Hobsbawm's theory has a noble ancestry: it derives from the early 20th Century (mainly Luxemburgian) argument that all nationalism is bourgeois and that capitalism, having become international, no longer needs the nation state. The old view was attacked by Lenin and survived thereafter in the writings of very few Marxists. When Hobsbawm revived this view in the late 1970s, presenting it in a moderated and well-reasoned way, detached from the old 'all-nationalism-is-bourgeois-and-bad' dogmatics, and asserting it to be the essential Leninist position, the impact of his statement was considerable. In Puerto Rico it gave support to two pessimistic positions which emerged in the late 1970s: the view that independence is mainly a bourgeois objective, and the view that the independence movement has become an anachronism in a world that is now international, not national. I wrote Chapter 4 to counter Hobsbawm's view that national movements are mainly bourgeois and that national states are becoming outmoded, and to show that these conceptions are contradictory to Lenin's theory. This chapter, like the preceding one, is framed as a critique of one Marxist's writings on the theory of nationalism. But a critique of Hobsbawm's theory is also a critique of a range of important new Marxist theories which question the underlying legitimacy of national liberation.

The Marxist theory of national struggle needs to be placed more firmly within the larger theory of social evolution, of historical materialism, and Chapter 7 is an effort toward this end. Historical materialism is an incomplete theory where it deals with pre-capitalist history and Third World geography: it is still to some degree Eurocentric and diffusionist. In Chapter 7, I argue that class struggle has always had an external as well as an internal component; that struggles against external or foreign ruling classes are, themselves, class struggles; that they are as central to social evolution as are local class struggles. Under capitalism, external class struggles assume a qualitatively new form: they become national. But they evolved historically not as diffusions from Europe but as one of the primary forms of class relations and class struggle.

Chapter 1 lays out the six theoretical problems with which the book is mainly concerned: Is nationalism class struggle? Is it bourgeois class struggle or something larger? Did it diffuse from Europe? Is it akin to fascism? Are national states and national movements anachronistic? And what must be done to improve the Marxist theory of minorities? Chapter 8 simply closes the argument of the book and points to a few of the many problems which remain unsolved.

## Limitations

This book is not a comprehensive treatise on the Marxist theory of nationalism. It is an inquiry into those aspects of the theory which are of greatest concern for Third World liberation movements. Because the national question is a complex and contentious matter for Marxist theory and for Marxist (and non-Marxist) practice, I have to make clear at the outset of the discussion that the book has these limited objectives. It does *not* attempt to deal with most aspects of the national question. For example:

(1) The book focuses on national liberation struggles against colonialism and neocolonialism, struggles which are basically progressive. There exist many other sorts of national struggle, some progressive, some reactionary, and some ambiguous. Although I discuss the general theory underlying all forms of national struggle, I say very little about reactionary and ambiguous forms. This should not be construed as an indiscriminate argument in favour of all national movements, all struggles for state independence. In fact, the Marxist theory of national struggle, as I present it here, provides the best way (though not an infallible one) to find whether a given position on a given national struggle is, or is not, progressive.

(2) This book deals with theory. It applies theory to just one empirical category, national struggles against colonialism and neocolonialism, and one specific case: Puerto Rico. The book does not attempt to analyse, much less pass judgment on, any other concrete cases of the national question, elsewhere in the world. Theory will not solve these national problems, but it will help towards their solution.

(3) This book does not discuss the national problems which continue to exist in parts of the socialist world. These very real problems cannot be dismissed as bourgeois remnants, but they do reflect the fact that capitalism still rules over more than half of the globe. In the course of the book (Chapters 2, 7, and 8) I will show that, although national struggle is class struggle, in today's world it also affects societies in which exploiting classes have been deposed.

## Note

1. The present volume deals with the issues of theory involved in these debates: here, I will not venture a critique of positions taken by participants. (I do so in *La cuestión nacional en Puerto Rico*, forthcoming.) Anti-independence positions are

put forward by K. Santiago, 'La cuestión nacional: Algunas tesis ignoradas', *Proceso* (Puerto Rico) 4 (1981), and Colectivo Socialista de San Juan, 'Marxismo o independentismo socialista?', *Pensamiento Crítico* 5, 35 (1983). For a reply to the Colectivo position, see: Taller de Formación Política and others, 'Crítica a la ponencia del Colectivo Socialista de San Juan', *Pensamiento Crítico* 7, 36 (1984). The view that the nationalism of the Nationalist Party (which was strong from about 1930 to 1950) was not class struggle is held by a number of Marxists. A few of the latter identify the Nationalist Party with fascism: see, e.g., G. Lewis, *Puerto Rico: Freedom and Power in the Caribbean* (1963). Others who find a contradiction between this nationalism and class struggle include José Luis González, *El país de cuatro pisos* (1980) and Juan Angel Silén, *Pedro Albizu Campos* (1976). The opposing view, that (in essence) the nationalism of the Nationalist Party was a class struggle and progressive for its period – a time, we should note, when few anti-colonial movements in the Caribbean and elsewhere had developed Marxist ideologies – is put forward by, e.g., M. Maldonado-Denis, *Hacia una interpretación marxista de la historia de Puerto Rico y otros ensayos* (1977); Juan Mari Brás, 'Albizu Campos: His Historical Significance', in I. Zavala and R. Rodríguez (eds.), *The Intellectual Roots of Independence* (1980); and Taller de Formación Política, *La cuestión nacional: el Partido Nacionalista y el movimiento obrero puertorriqueño* (1982). Several Marxists see the independence struggle as, in varying ways and degrees, bourgeois (although they themselves are pro-independence). A. Quintero-Rivera for instance argues (in essence) that state-forming movements are appropriate to the period of early capitalism, the rise of the bourgeoisie; that Puerto Rico was not fully capitalist when the US invaded in 1898; that Puerto Rico, accordingly, experienced only an 'incomplete bourgeois revolution' and for this reason did not develop a strong independence movement comparable to other colonies (but no colony anywhere experienced a 'complete bourgeois revolution'): see his *Conflictos de clase y política en Puerto Rico* (1977) and 'Notes on Puerto Rican National Development: Class and Nation in a Colonial Context', *Marxist Perspectives* 3, 1 (1980). For a contrary view of Puerto Rican history, in which the independence struggle is seen as an evolving process, see M. Maldonado-Denis, *Puerto Rico: A Socio-Historic Interpretation* (1972), and J. Mari Brás, *El independentismo: su pasado, su presente, y su futuro* (1984). The view that Puerto Rico has been absorbed into the United States, following the logic of capitalism's development from a national to an international condition, is put forward by, e.g., F. Bonilla and R. Campos. See Bonilla's 'Ethnic Orbits: The Circulation of Capitals and Peoples', *Contemporary Marxism* 10 (1985). Bonilla argues, for instance, that nations are dissolving as capitalism becomes international: 'Puerto Ricans in the United States and Puerto Ricans in Puerto Rico', *Journal of Contemporary Puerto Rican Thought* 2, 2–3 (1975). See also History Task Force (Bonilla, Campos, and others), *Labor Migration Under Capitalism: The Puerto Rican Experience* (1979). I criticize these views in *La cuestión nacional en Puerto Rico* (forthcoming). The view that Puerto Ricans in the US are a 'national minority' is put foward, e.g., in Puerto Rican Revolutionary Workers Organization, 'National Liberation of Puerto Rico and the Responsibilities of the U.S. Proletariat', *Jour. Contemp. Puerto Rican Thought* 2, 2–3 (1975); for the opposing view, see, e.g., Partido Socialista Puertorriqueño, *Desde las entrañas* (1974); also see J. Blaut, 'Are Puerto Ricans a National Minority?' and 'El mito de la asimilación' (revised as chapters 5 and 6 of the present volume); for a reply to 'Are Puerto Ricans . . .' see El Comité, 'Crítica a una perspectiva nacionalista de la cuestión nacional', *Pensamiento Crítico 1*, 5–6 (1978). Several important works in English describe the Puerto Rican independence struggle: see, e.g., Maldonado-Denis, *Puerto Rico* . . .; L.L. Cripps, *Puerto Rico: The Case for Independence* (1974); L. Bergman et al., *Puerto Rico: The Flame of Resistance* (1977); and Zavala and Rodríguez (eds.), *The Intellectual Roots of Independence* (1980).

# 1. Introduction: Six Problems for the Theory of Nationalism

## The Theory of Nationalism and the Practice of National Liberation

The subject of this book is called 'the national question' when our concern with it is practical and political, and called 'the theory of nationalism' (or 'the theory of national struggle') when our concern is more general. Most of the topics dealt with here are in the realm of theory, and I hope that the work as a whole will make a useful contribution to the theory of nationalism. But social theory is not written for its own sake: the underlying purpose of this work is to fashion a set of theoretical tools to help us understand why some national struggles in the modern world are progressive and others are reactionary, and to help us win the first kind of struggle and defeat the second.

More concretely, this book has a definite focus on one kind of national struggle: the fight for national liberation in colonies and neocolonies. Most of the current and influential writings about the theory of nationalism have very little that is useful to say about this particular form of the national question, and much of the work tends to obscure and mystify it, misjudging its significance and failing to comprehend, much less explain, its progressive role in the fight for social justice. In the case of mainstream theory – by which I mean non-Marxist, generally conservative theory – the national struggles in colonies and neocolonies are incorrectly viewed as products of an autonomous ideology, not products of political and economic oppression, an ideology which is assumed to have diffused outward from Europe to the colonial world as part of a process of 'modernization', with colonialism itself being misidentified as a process that brought 'modernity', not poverty and underdevelopment. For those who are unfamiliar with this literature, my sweeping characterization of it may seem to be unfair and oversimplified. But in the following pages I will show that the mainstream theory of nationalism is very consistent in its misidentification of national liberation struggles and of colonialism. Indeed, until recently, most mainstream European writers about nationalism quite failed to notice anti-colonial struggles, and even today these are with great regularity thought to be simple products of the diffusion of 'civilized' European ideas to the backward folk of Africa, Asia, and Latin America.

Matters are somewhat better within the Marxist corpus of theoretical writings about the national question, as we would expect to be the case given the history of Marxist participation in and support of anti-colonial liberation struggles. Even so, we will find that Marxist theory about this form of the national question is far from satisfactory. Much of the current writing about this topic is virtually indistinguishable from the mainstream corpus, ascribing anti-colonial liberation struggles in the same way to a primordial ideology, not to the logic of resistance to exploitation and political oppression, and in the same way invoking the Eurocentric notion of the diffusion of 'modernization'. But even when we set aside this body of work which puts forward conservative theory under the Marxist banner, some very serious inadequacies can be seen in the Marxist corpus of writing on the national question, and most of these inadequacies reflect an imperfect conception of national liberation struggles in colonies and neocolonies.

This has two very unfortunate consequences, one for theory and the other for practice. That part of social theory which is supposed to deal with all forms of national struggle, that corpus of ideas which both Marxists and non-Marxists usually call the theory of nationalism, proves instead to be only a partial theory, applicable only to certain forms of national struggle and not to others – and not, most conspicuously, to the struggles of colonized and other oppressed peoples for state sovereignty. But this theory claims, nonetheless, to be fully general. Thus it misconstrues the nature of national liberation struggles. It forces them into theoretical categories which they do not fit. For instance, they are assimilated to the rise of the bourgeoisie, or to the bourgeois democratic revolution, as though the political struggles of the bourgeoisies of Europe against various archaic states were of a piece with, say, the struggle of Vietnamese workers and peasants a century later; as though Vietnamese revolutionaries today were bourgeois, not socialist, and Vietnam today were a capitalist country, not a socialist one. Again, national liberation struggles are declared to be a product of a peculiar and autonomous ideological force, the force of nationalism, not of political oppression and economic exploitation. And so on. What we have then is a theory of nationalism, of national struggle, which is badly flawed because one terribly important form of struggle (and epoch of struggle) is misconstrued, while at the same time we have formulae which 'explain' national liberation struggles in a grossly incorrect manner.

The problem for theory is in fact even more serious than this, because you really cannot understand the modern world as a whole if you do not understand the dynamic of that part of it which has endured and struggled against colonialism, the part known as the Third World. There can be no adequate theory of development, of imperialism, of accumulation on a world scale, and of much more beside, if there is not an adequate theory of national liberation, of national struggle in its anticolonial form. Failure to understand the causes and effects of this kind of struggle has led to serious errors in theories which describe capitalism as a single, essentially undifferentiated world system, one in which the difference between oppressor nations and oppressed nations is treated as an abstract or trivial matter, and in which national liberation struggles are treated as something other than class struggle or marginal to class struggle. Much rethinking needs to be done about the 'capitalist world-system', about capitalism as a diffusing mode of production which merely articulates with other modes at its edge, about uneven development as a more or less continuous process (or a many-linked chain) between an abstract centre and an equally abstract periphery, and about many other Marxist visions of the modern world – rethinking which can fruitfully begin with a fresh look at the national liberation process and the national question.

Theory of course has immense importance for practice. When theoreticians generalize about the nature and meaning of particular categories of social struggle, and sometimes about individual struggles in particular countries, this often influences the conduct of these struggles and the support given or withheld from them around the world. The majority of contemporary pronouncements about national struggle coming from Marxists, at least from 'Western Marxists', have an ambivalent if not negative tone towards national liberation struggles. They are 'bourgeois'. They are 'akin to fascism'. They 'neglect the domestic class struggle'. They are 'irrational' because the state is no longer of importance in a 'fully international capitalism' or in a 'world system'. And so on. Such pronouncements, as I will argue in this book, are wrong. They ignore the reality of struggles in colonies, neocolonies, and precariously free former colonies, and they are ignorant even of the main line of Marxist analysis regarding colonialism. These views have had a definite effect on liberation struggles, at times splitting movements, at times discouraging young people from participating in struggles which the pundits declare to be bourgeois or backward or irrational, at times obstructing work done in support of these struggles in other countries. I simply assert that an effort to clarify the theory of nationalism or national struggle, and to refute those views which are false, must have concrete value for the practice of national liberation.

In this introductory chapter, after a short discussion of the terminological difficulties surrounding such terms as 'nationalism' and 'the national question', I will enunciate six problems which have great significance for the theory of nationalism and the practice of national liberation and indicate how they are to be treated in the book. I will also indicate in which parts of which chapters each of the problems is to be dealt with, because each of the problems is discussed in more than one of the chapters. The six problems are as follows:

(1)   Is nationalism (here meaning the whole content of national struggle) a form of class struggle? Or is nationalism an autonomous force?

(2)   Is national struggle appropriate only to the bourgeois–democratic revolution and the bourgeoisie? Or is it a feature of class struggle in general?

(3)   Did nationalism diffuse from Western Europe to the rest of the world?

(4)   Does nationalism bear some special relationship to fascism?

(5)   Is national struggle now out of date? Is the national state an anachronism in the era of multinational capitalism?

(6)   What is the theoretical status of the concept 'national minority'? And why, in the present era, do many immigrant minorities remain unassimilated?

The six basic problems are completely general and theoretical issues, and I will deal with them as such. But they also happen to be matters of very intense political concern to everyone who is engaged in a struggle for the national liberation of a colony (like Puerto Rico) or a neocolony (like El Salvador) or a free but embattled former colony (like Mozambique). Each of the six points of theory is frequently used as a basis for criticism of such struggles, criticism which tries to argue that there is something inherently flawed, or reactionary, or atavistic, or trivial in these efforts to win or preserve national liberation – because they are 'nationalist'. Here are six familiar-sounding (though hypothetical) examples:

1) 'There is an inherent contradiction between class struggle and national struggle. Therefore progressives should not participate in or support national liberation struggles (or any other kind of national struggle) except, on occasion, tactically.'

2) 'National liberation struggles, being national struggles, are necessarily led by the bourgeoisie, not by the working classes (or by socialists), because all nationalism is bourgeois nationalism, and leads to the creation only of bourgeois states' (and so liberated countries like Cuba, Angola, Vietnam, etc., must be, by implication, capitalist countries, not socialist ones).

3) 'Nationalism in colonies and neocolonies is not a struggle by exploited classes against colonial oppression and exploitation. Such nationalism is merely the effect of the diffusion from Europe of "the idea of nationalism", an idea which originated in Europe and was thereafter brought by Europeans to the colonized people in a form of tutelage towards civilization.'

4) 'All nationalism appeals to primitive passions, to "blood" and "tribalism", and necessarily declares one's own nation to be better than all other nations. These features also characterize fascism. National liberation movements are of a piece with fascism.'

5) 'It is pointless to struggle for national liberation at a time in world history when capitalism is multinational, not national. Why fight to establish or defend a state if states themselves are no longer important?'

6) This argument pertains to groups which are minorities in other countries, as two million Puerto Ricans – about 40 per cent of the total population of their nation – are in the US: 'Emigrant groups, once they have left the territory of their own nation, automatically acquire the nationality of the host nation, even when the migration is a forced migration and a feature of colonialism. Therefore, minority groups like the Puerto Ricans in the US (and Tunisians in France, Palestinians in Lebanon, Koreans in Japan, etc.) should not dedicate themselves to the liberation of their homelands'.


Each of the six theoretical questions is distinct, but the answers form a single structure of argument. It may be useful to outline now the skeleton of this structure.

What is the root cause of national problems? Is it some autonomous force of 'nationalism' or 'nationality' or 'the nation'? Or is it class struggle? If it is *not* class struggle, then a theory of national struggle can go on to argue that there is a primordial 'nationalist ideology' and that this ideology either is part of some broadly democratic ideology of 'modernization', which diffuses outwards from civilized Europe to an uncivilized Third World, or is part of a more sinister, hate-driven ideology which embraces fascism, xenophobia, and the arrogance of nationality.

If, on the other hand, national struggle *is* class struggle, then the theory must ask: is it basically the struggle of one class, the bourgeoisie, to form or enlarge a bourgeois state? Or is it deployed by different classes, both exploiters and exploited, under differing historical and social circumstances? If national movements for an independent or enlarged state are appropriate only to the bourgeoisie, and to bourgeois states, it would follow that the era of mature capitalism, fully international capitalism, would be an era in which national movements no longer make sense, nationalism declines in importance, the national state becomes an anachronism, and bourgeois states commence to dissolve into a single international capitalist polity. And it would follow that Third World liberation struggles do not result from the exploitation and oppression associated with colonialism; that they reflect, rather, the efforts of a local incipient bourgeoisie to 'rise', to fight for power (and accumulation) against the foreign bourgeoisie. If this is the case, then other classes, including workers and peasants, are drawn into the national struggle illegitimately, because of 'false consciousness' – the transference of a 'bourgeois nationalist ideology' to non-bourgeois classes – or for some other reason that may be real and important like resistance to oppression or discrimination but is not part of the direct struggle against class exploitation and capitalism.

But national struggles are struggles for state power, and state power is sought by all classes in all class struggles. State power is the essential environment for exploitation. States cannot, therefore, decline in importance, and bourgeois nationalism survives as long as the bourgeoisie survives. But exploited classes also fight for state power, and when power is held by a ruling class which is partly or wholly external, 'foreign', then national struggle is just as appropriate for these classes as it is, under other circumstances, for the bourgeoisie.

This general argument takes on a special form in the case of colonies and neocolonies. Colonialism is the oppressive political mechanism which permits economic superexploitation – exploitation of workers at intensities not usually possible in autonomous capitalist societies – and the struggle against this political mechanism is a central part of the struggle against superexploitation. The colonial (foreign) bourgeoisie is at least part, sometimes the greatest part, of the ruling class in colonial and neocolonial societies. The struggle for national liberation, against colonialism, is therefore a struggle in which exploited classes play a central role. It is a struggle against capitalism itself, even though some local bourgeois sectors within a colony or neocolony participate in the struggle for their own separate class interests. Thus national liberation struggles against colonialism (in all its forms) are class struggles which are in large part anti-bourgeois. And anti-colonial struggles are, on a world scale, the most significant form of national struggle today. This form has evolved along with the evolution of capitalism, and today in most parts of the Third World it is a struggle against disguised colonialism, neocolonialism. Moreover, it has spread beyond the geographical Third World, because modern capitalism has forced many millions of Third World workers to migrate to the advanced capitalist countries, where most of them remain in ghetto communities and continue to experience superexploitation at a basically colonial level.

This book, in sum, is a contribution to the theory of nationalism or national struggle, and at the same time an attempt to answer false arguments drawn improperly from the theory of nationalism which have been used, not always with conscious intent, to attack national liberation movements in colonies and neocolonies. Such arguments have been used, also, to blur the vital and fundamental distinction between national liberation movements, on the one hand, and reactionary nationalism, on the other. No support will be given in this book to such reactionary nationalism, or to bourgeois nationalism, narrow nationalism, or trivial nationalism. National liberation is none of these.

## 'The National Question' and 'Nationalism'

This book deals with a definite kind of situation in social reality, something called 'the national question' or 'national struggle'. When this subject is discussed at the level of theory, a very confusing label is attached: it is conventionally called 'the theory of nationalism'. The confusion stems partly from the fact that the word 'nationalism' has several different meanings in English language discourse, and only one of the meanings is broad enough to embrace all aspects and forms of the national question, to be a plain synonym for 'national struggle'. Some of these problems of meaning will be discussed later; for now, I must make it clear that 'theory of nationalism' in this book means exactly 'theory of the national question'. Here are some of the common and well-known forms of the national question:

1) Efforts by one state to annex another state, or part of another state, to its own state territory, and counter-efforts to resist such annexation.
2) Efforts of some part of a state to secede from that state, and counter-efforts to prevent secession.
3) Efforts of a colony to win independence from the occupying colonial power, and counter-efforts by the colonial power to prevent the colony from gaining its independence.
4) Efforts of a country which is nominally independent but actually lacks real sovereignty – typically, today, this would be a neocolony – to win real sovereignty, and counter-efforts by the controlling state or states to deny sovereignty to the dependent state.
5) Efforts to form states by unifying previously distinct or partly distinct political entities, and efforts to prevent unification. In these situations states do not confront one another as organic individuals: some classes and groups within each political entity will tend to favour one position on the national question, some another.

There are of course additional forms of the national question, such as efforts to win autonomy short of independent statehood and counter-efforts to prevent this from happening, forms which are less typical but no less important. I have not tried to provide an exhaustive list.

What do all these forms of the national question, of national struggle, have in common? First, they are political struggles, struggles for state power. Second, they are complex: they comprehend a great range of social processes, including ideological elements (ideas, motives, values, etc.), social and economic phenomena and groupings, political movements, and much more. And third, they involve two or more opposing forces: they are 'struggles', 'conflicts', 'questions', not simple unidirectional social or historical processes. Marxists would add a fourth common characteristic of all national struggles: they are class struggles. But setting this last characteristic aside – we discuss it in Chapter 2 – the other three would seem to be acceptable without much controversy, to be almost self-evident. Yet they have implications which are indeed controversial, which cause great difficulty for some mainstream (conservative) theorists and a few Marxists.

1) Since national struggles are struggles for state power, it is the state, not the cultural (ethnic) region, which is their primary arena, and they have no necessary and invariant connection to cultural forces or factors or groups, nor even to individual 'nations' – a term I have not yet tried to explicate – since national struggles often involve multi-national states and movements.

2) Since national struggles incorporate a wide range of social phenomena, they cannot be reduced, as a matter of definition or meaning, to ideology alone.

3) Since they are struggles, conflicts, and contain opposing social forces, they cannot be adequately analysed or explained in terms of only one of the component forces, a practice employed by mainstream theorists when they describe an anti-colonial liberation movement as a product only of 'nationalist feelings', etc., as though the colonial power offers no resistance to decolonization.

We come then to the confusing word 'nationalism'. This word is a term of ordinary discourse in English and many other languages, and it has various alternative meanings. The important task is to show the several ways that it is used in Marxist theory. There are two principal usages. They differ not only as to semantic meaning, but in another and more crucial way as well. The first meaning designates a set of processes which are clearly evident to everybody: they are common, agreed subject matter for any explanatory theory. The second meaning, by contrast, is given *within* an explanatory theory, so that whenever we use words like 'nationalism' or 'nationalist' we are invoking that theory, knowingly or not.

The first meaning of 'nationalism' is broadly synonymous with the phrases 'national struggle' and 'the national question'. All three of these terms can be used interchangeably – grammatical considerations aside – to describe a definite kind of real-world situation, a 'national problem', whatever its origins, significance, outcome, or causal explanation. Among mainstream scholars and most (not all) Marxist scholars in English-speaking countries and some others, it is conventional to speak of 'theory of nationalism' in describing any sort of discussion about national struggles – about the kinds of situations which we discussed previously. I will follow this convention, too, although it would be better to call this kind of work 'theory of the national question' or 'theory of national struggle' precisely because the word 'nationalism' has other meanings, some of them tied to particular, often questionable points of view. In this book, any theory which tries to analyse a national struggle, or formulate strategy within such a struggle, will be called a 'theory of nationalism'. I stress this small point of terminology to avoid a source of confusion that plagues most writings about the Marxist theory of nationalism, confusion epitomised in the following comment: 'How can you describe this sort of thing as the Marxist theory of nationalism when you're theorising about *national liberation*, not *nationalism*?' We're theorising about national struggles in general, but with special attention to the kinds that liberate.

Before we turn to the second common usage of the term 'nationalism' it is important that we consider one very important source of confusion concerning the first meaning, the one which signifies only national struggle or the national question. Some writers give the word this meaning but then blur the picture in the following way: even though there are (at least) two contending forces in any national struggle, one side only is called 'nationalist'. What then do we call their opponents? 'Anti-nationalists'? The absurdity of doing so should be obvious. In general, there is the nationalism which is exhibited by the defending state or empire and the nationalism which is exhibited by those who fight for secession. Lenin made this point over and over again, writing about the 'great-nation nationalists', the 'Black Hundred nationalists' (Great Russian jingos), the 'oppressor-nation nationalists', and the like, and exhorting socialists not to look only at the nationalism of the small nation fighting for secession but also that of the large nation or empire fighting against secession, fighting to maintain its territory intact, and usually fighting for the privilege of continuing national oppression.

In a word: to oppose a national movement – that is, a secessionist or state-forming-movement – is not to oppose 'nationalism': it is to oppose only the one sort of nationalism, the one side of the national conflict. But it is so very easy to forget this point and thus to fall into a most serious theoretical and political error.

The error can be described rather starkly in the following way. A Marxist of the larger (capitalist) state or empire may imagine that his or her opposition to the secessionist movement of a part of the state or a colony of the empire is necessarily a resistance to 'narrow nationalism', and thus an embracing of 'proletarian internationalism' (etc.). But the politics of the larger (capitalist) state or empire is hardly likely to be infused with proletarian internationalism. This big state or empire is most probably pursuing its own sort of 'narrow nationalism', and any Marxist who defends this politics is defending nationalism, not internationalism. By the same token, those who struggle for secession, or for what we nowadays tend to call 'national liberation' in appropriate circumstances, may very well be infused with proletarian internationalism. Their sort of nationalism may well reflect a judgment that the only way to attain socialism in their territory is to fight for state sovereignty and against continued governance by a reactionary state. They are likely to view their national movement as one detachment in the world struggle for socialism, for a world in which capitalist states in general have disappeared, along with national oppression. And we know that in practice fighters for national liberation, before and after they gain victory, tend to help other struggles, elsewhere, as best they can. (For instance, Puerto Rican *independentistas* fought with Bolívar, Martí, Fidel, the Sandinistas, etc.) The error, then, is to believe that only one side in a national struggle is 'nationalist', and, worse yet, to believe that the other side must be 'internationalist'. Believing this, one can imagine that the subject matter of a Marxist theory of nationalism is the politics of secession, of what is correctly called 'small-nation nationalism'. The national politics of large states and empires then appears to reflect other sorts of causes, and to be the subject matter of a different sort of theory.

The second basic meaning of 'nationalism' describes a specific sort of political ideology, programme, and form of action, the one which we often describe as 'narrow nationalism'. The essence of this phenomenon is the belief – and the actions based on this belief: we are not discussing ideology alone – that the winning of a national struggle, the attaining of state sovereignty, is all that is needed to cure the main social ills of a given society. The most often-encountered form of this political phenomenon is the kind of small-nation nationalism which declares, usually in highly colourful language, that independence from the 'national oppressor' is all that is needed to solve the society's fundamental social problems. In practice, this position tends to be one of opposition to radical social change within the society itself, that is, within its internal class structure. When a socialist then argues that the fight is against all oppressors, domestic and foreign, he or she is likely to be denounced as a sower of social divisions, as one who undermines the (metaphysical) unity of the nation, and so on. This, then, is a form of nationalism which typically opposes socialism or is indifferent to it, and to which is attached a particular role: the (pure) nationalist.

Narrow nationalism is often also 'bourgeois nationalism', since most countries which fight for national independence are more or less capitalist societies (though their capitalism may be the distorted type characteristic of colonies), and the nationalists' goal may be to achieve an independent capitalist state, with the native bourgeoisie replacing a foreign ruling class. The 'nationalism' which characterized eastern and central Europe in the last century was another form of 'bourgeois nationalism', a form which was, for its period, progressive: it involved national struggles led by the local bourgeois classes and aimed at creating independent states within which these classes would hold state power and have unhindered opportunities to accumulate. Another kind of 'bourgeois nationalism', on the other hand, is thoroughly reactionary today, as it was in the last century. This is the expansionism of powerful bourgeois states, sometimes in the direction of annexing neighbouring states, sometimes in the direction of acquiring colonies overseas. But not all nationalism is 'bourgeois' or 'narrow', much less 'reactionary'. There is, for instance, a democratic form of anti-colonial struggle which dislodges foreign rule without consolidating the local bourgeoisie, either because the movement is strongly influenced by socialists or because the class forces behind it are not primarily bourgeois. For Marxists, the victory achieved by this sort of democratic nationalist movement is only a way-station towards later socialist transformation. But so far as it goes, this kind of nationalism is progressive.

Much more needs to be said by way of unsnarling the terminological confusion which surrounds words like 'nationalism', 'nation', and 'minority' (as in the problematic phrase, 'national minority'). There will be some further discussion of these matters in Chapter 4 and elsewhere in the book.

# First Problem: Is Nationalism a Form of Class Struggle?
## Some Conservative Views

All theories of nationalism are directly or indirectly concerned to explain a particular kind of concrete and observable process, something called a 'national struggle', or a 'national problem', or a particular instance of 'the national question'. There is, for example, a very salient 'national problem' in Puerto Rico, and theorists would want to understand, among other things, the nature of the national movement which struggles for the independence of Puerto Rico: to understand its strategy, its social base, its activities, the kind of society it proposes to create, and so on. But by no means all theorists would consider this instance of national struggle as having, apart from and opposed to the independence movement, an *anti-independence* component, a force fighting to *prevent* Puerto Rico from gaining its independence.

Some conservative scholars would simply define the anti-independence forces as being irrelevant for the theory of nationalism, if indeed they even noticed these forces. For these scholars, 'nationalism' as subject matter only embraces the national movement, the people fighting for independence or secession, and not the people who seek to prevent this national movement from accomplishing its goals. This is much more than a matter of convention or definition. It reveals a fundamental inadequacy of the mainstream theories of nationalism.

Conservative social scientists tend to accept, axiomatically, the idea that modern bourgeois democratic states like the United States are in some absolute sense right and rational, hence that any secession movement from these states, or from their colonial empires, is a curiosity, a self-generated phenomenon which is given the name 'nationalist' and is thought to have arisen for reasons which have little or perhaps nothing to do with the great power from whose territory they seek to secede. So a theory of nationalism in this tradition would tend to find the origin of a national independence movement in some realm that has little to do with the conditions imposed by the larger state: usually in something abstract and ideological called perhaps 'the idea of nationalism' or 'the idea of self-determination'. For colonies of European powers the conventional form for these theories is to suppose that the idea of nationalism or self-determination diffused to the colony from the colonizing power; hence, that it is the receipt of this infectious idea, rather than the fact – not acknowledged as such by conservative theorists – of social and political oppression and economic exploitation, which explains the phenomenon of nationalism and the rise of a national movement in the colony. In sum: most, though not all, conservative theories of nationalism tend to see as nationalism only the secessionist movements, and to ignore, or even deny the existence of, what others call 'great-power nationalism'. They tend also to find the source of these 'nationalist', that is, secessionist, movements in the realm of ideas, not the realm of economic or political struggle.

The thrust of my argument here can be conveyed rather well with an example from the work of Louis L. Snyder, one of the leading conservative theorists about nationalism in the United States. For Snyder, nationalism is 'first and foremost a state of mind' and one which tends in our time to be irrational and xenophobic.[1] His well-known book, *The Meaning of Nationalism*, opens its first chapter with a quotation from the document which was written by the Puerto Rican nationalist Lolita Lebron as she set out in 1954 for Washington with three of her Nationalist Party comrades to oppose, with arms, the imposition of a law declaring Puerto Rico to be an inseparable part of the US.[2] Snyder quotes these words: 'Before God, and the world, my blood claims for the independence of Puerto Rico. My life I give for the freedom of my country. This is a cry for victory in our struggle for independence.'[3] To Puerto Ricans this is a historic and eloquent pronouncement by a national heroine. Snyder, however, mockingly calls it a 'pencilled suicide note'. Then he uses the document, and the incident, to make his crucial argument: nationalism today 'is a destructive force' which tends to be imbued with 'hatred of the foreigner'. The incident in Washington, he asserts, was a 'completely irrational act (if the majority of Puerto Ricans had wanted independence, they could have had it)'.[4]

My point here is not Snyder's ignorance about Puerto Rico and his unawareness of the fact that the United States government has never so much as asserted that Puerto Rico could have independence if the people wanted it, or the fact that since 1898 the United States has tried unceasingly to suppress the Puerto Rican independence movement, often by force of arms and by assassination, or the fact that there has never been a legitimate plebiscite on the matter of independence. My point, rather, is to call attention to Snyder's naive conviction that this nationalism is exclusively Puerto Rican; that the colonial power, the United States, displays no nationalism here at all – in fact could not care less about the status of Puerto Rico ('if the majority of Puerto Ricans had wanted independence, they could have had it'). I doubt whether most mainstream, conservative, North American scholars of nationalism are as ignorant about Puerto Rico as is Snyder, but certainly the majority of them would agree with his assertion of subject matter: nationalism is inherently an idea (and an irrational one), and nationalism is displayed mainly, or only, by those who fight for independence, not by those who fight to defeat secessionist movements and to maintain the territorial integrity of a state or empire. Nationalism in colonies, like Puerto Rico, is just another manifestation of the old European urge towards national independence, 'self-determination'. It does not confront an opposing nationalism. It is not struggle.

Mainstream theories of nationalism are concerned with many kinds of nationalism beside the colonial struggles for independence (which, in fact, hardly interest them at all). But the basic subject matter of most of these theories tends to correspond fairly closely to Snyder's view. Nationalism is inherently a process in which groups of people work towards the creation of an independent state for themselves, a nation state, or towards the enlargement of such a state. It is a concrete, observable, social or socio-political process, but its cause, or source, or mainspring, or motor, is an idea or ideology. This idea is itself uncaused; or rather it sprang forth in France and Britain 200 years ago as simply the logic of advancing civilization, of creating a modern nation state; and then the idea diffused to the rest of Europe and eventually the colonies. Note, therefore, that the idea is primordial; save perhaps in the original West European 'homelands' it arises for no local geographical or historical reason, no reason of economic impoverishment, political oppression, or whatever. It results only from the diffusion of an idea.

Given this foundation theory – the diffusion of a causally efficacious idea – it is easy to take the next step and argue that nationalism itself is just an idea, and thus to forget the concrete social process and pay attention only to the putative cause, itself uncaused, the 'idea of nationalism'. Karl Marx and Friedrich Engels asserted long ago in *The German Ideology* that conservative social theory and philosophy dissolve all social processes into ideas, which are in turn treated as primordial facts needing no explanation. Most Marxist scholars, I among them, would argue today that a more sophisticated and less mystical form of this conservative doctrine still prevails in most (not all) social theory: the idea remains prior to the social fact. Certainly this is true of the great majority of conservative theories of nationalism.

The question, 'is national struggle a form of class struggle?' is therefore very easily disposed of in the ambience of conservative or mainstream social theory. Class struggle is admitted into this kind of social theory, if at all, as an effect of what is usually called the 'factor' of class: this factor, acting through class struggle, produces certain effects. The 'factor' of nationalism (ultimately the idea of nationalism) produces other effects. And so on. Class may on occasion produce national struggle, as when an impoverished society of one nationality is ruled by a class of another nationality and the natives grow restless – recall Snyder's stereotyping comment about 'hatred of foreigners' – but basically there is no important relation, in most of these theories, between national struggle and class struggle. The question is scarcely asked.

## The Problem of Colonial and Anti-Colonial Nationalism

One more generalization about mainstream, conservative theories of nationalism needs to be entered here before we turn to the Marxist theory. Modern mainstream theories should be divided into three temporal groups: those written before the rise of Nazism, those written between 1933 and the 1950s, when anti-colonial struggles were becoming very intense, and those written after about 1960. The early theories tended to look almost exclusively at the way in which the 'idea of nationalism' had spread across Europe in some (much-debated) association with the pre-existing nationalities. The outcome of this process was a seemingly natural pattern according to which some of the nationalities formed themselves into nation states, or shared such states with perhaps one or two other major nationalities, while the remaining peoples dissolved into 'national minorities' which did not and could not play a role in state formation. Thus, it was postulated, there was just one kind of nationalism and national movement, a kind which seeks to form nation states. It led either to the formation of nation states or to the ill-starred, romantic but rather pitiable, movements within 'national minorities' whose destiny it was to disappear from the map or dissolve into one of the great empires or (after Versailles) one of the new national or multinational states. It is true that attention was sporadically paid, particularly during wars, to another form of nationalism, the expansionism of great powers within Europe, but this category was never of much interest prior to the rise of Hitler. Nor was colonial expansionism considered in general to be a form of nationalism.[5]

After 1933 the naked expansionism of Nazi Germany forced theorists to seriously consider for the first time this form of nationalism, one characterized by the aggrandizement of the territory of one's own 'civilized' neighbours. Thereafter, and notably in the important analysis of nationalism by Britain's Royal Institute of International Affairs in 1939, German-style (and also Italian- and Japanese-style) expansionism came to be treated as a specific aberrant form of nationalism: a transmutation of what had been the normal organic growth of nation states into a cancer-like overgrowth.[6] Nationalism was still seen as an idea. It was the rational idea underlying efforts of certain communities ('nations') to strive for a state of their own, the irrational idea underlying efforts by certain other communities (some of the lesser 'national minorities') to strive for independence when this goal was for them unrealizable, and, finally, the truly irrational aberration of the idea of nationalism by which great states like Germany, Japan, and Italy sought to enlarge their territory at the expense of other great states.

Finally, starting perhaps around 1960, conservative theorists of nationalism began to pay attention to what seemed to be a relatively new phenomenon: efforts to gain the independence or liberation of colonies. I say 'seemed to be' because colonial peoples had been struggling for liberation throughout the colonial period, but this was scarcely noticed by European scholars until the map of the world began to change before their eyes, in very dramatic ways, with the appearance of an independent India, Pakistan, Indonesia, and so on. Now this was a time when many pro-independence struggles were taking the form of ugly, bloody, confrontation with the colonial power, as in Indonesia, Puerto Rico, Algeria, Vietnam, Kenya, Angola, and many other places. The colonial powers were not simply giving independence when it was asked for.

Thus emerged two rather new questions for the mainstream theory of nationalism, a theory propagated mainly in the very countries which were fighting to hold on to their colonies. The first question was: How do you conceptualize the colonial independence movement? Do you assimilate it to the older forms of nationalism? And second: How do you conceptualize the colonizing power's resistance to an independence movement? Is this, too, nationalism? Is there, then, a form of nationalism which fights to acquire other peoples' territory and thereafter hold on to it, a form which embraces not merely the aberrations of Nazism and fascism but also the external politics of self-consciously democratic states like Britain, France, and the USA?

I am not trying here to write a history of conservative theories of nationalism. I am trying simply to show their basic inadequacies. One such, as we saw, is the tendency to reduce national processes to ideology: to view nationalism as inherently and aboriginally an idea, not a direct or indirect outcome of social processes and social struggles. A second is almost total blindness toward the phenomenon of colonialism. The act of acquiring colonies and the act of suppressing or trying to suppress independence movements in colonies are not seen as moments of nationalism, but rather as a completely natural dimension of the modernizing, civilizing process. Therefore, the answer to the second of the two new questions was: democratic capitalist states simply do not engage in territorial aggrandizement, and the acquisition and retention of colonial empires simply is not national aggrandizement – not comparable to the expansionist nationalism of the Nazi Germans, the Italian fascists, the Japanese 'imperialists'. It is, rather, the benign and perhaps divinely guided spread of 'civilization' to the uncivilized. This same answer serves for the other of the two new questions: the act of struggling for independence in colonies is, indeed, a new form of the old, 19th Century European state-building nationalism. It is a kind of natural acquisition of nationalism as the modern, democratic, 'idea of nationalism' diffuses outwards from Europe to the farthest corners of the world as part of the spread of 'civilization' and 'modernity'. So anti-colonial liberation struggles are not a response to colonialism but a kind of social and intellectual growing up.

Perhaps these limitations of the typical mainstream theories of nationalism do not seem very important. I will try to prove otherwise.

## Conformity and Compatibility of the Mainstream Theories

It seems to me that there is a very clear reason for the limitations of mainstream (conservative) theories of nationalism. All social theory tends to be shaped or constrained by the society which produces it, and this occurs in two main ways. First, there is a constant vetting of hypotheses by means of which those which might disturb the social fabric are, in many different and often subtle ways, discouraged, while those which strengthen the social fabric are encouraged, often to the extent that they are accepted without test or evidence. We may call this the constraint of 'conformity'. Secondly, each new hypothesis is screened to determine whether it is compatible with existing conformist social theory, a constraint which can be called 'compatibility'.[7] Both constraints have helped to shape the mainstream theory of nationalism in many ways, among them the following.

First, it has been vital to the ideology of capitalist society to conceptualize colonialism, a process in which colonized peoples are forced to work and generate profit (surplus value) for the colonizers, as a process which benefited the colonized peoples instead of harming them. Thus colonialism was not a matter of exploitation, underdevelopment, and cultural suppression, but rather one of 'tutelage' – the colonizer's favourite word – towards 'civilization' and 'modernity'. Why was this vital? One reason from the start was the need to persuade the citizenry in the colonizer's country to support a policy of imperial aggrandizement. Another was the need to manufacture and sustain an ideology in the colony itself, one in which submission would seem right and sensible. For both these reasons it was crucial to be able to deploy theories which conceptualized colonialism itself as a civilizing, modernizing process, not one of selfish – and nationalistic – expansionism and domination of colonial peoples for the purpose of bringing wealth to the colonizer. As to the conformism of the idea that nationalism is a natural process in colonies as elsewhere, this idea was so counter-conformist that books which put it forward were sometimes suppressed in colonies, right down to the time of independence.[8]

But recent times have seen a new set of conformist imperatives. Decolonization occurred much against the colonizer's will, and often in spite of his armed efforts to hold on to the colony. I will deal later in this book (Chapter 4) with the false thesis that decolonization was a voluntary gift from the colonizer. When independence movements were not opposed, this in all cases reflected a calculated strategy, in the face of more or less anti-colonial pressure, to smooth the transition to neocolonialism, that is, to a continuation of colonial economic relations after formal independence had been obtained. The first imperative for the colonizer was to smother the colony, during and after the decolonization process, with an ideology according to which the colonial economic structure would be seen as beneficial to the colonized, so that persistence of the same structure after decolonization – with modifications to accommodate some local class interests – would seem beneficial as well. An important part of this ideology was the tenet that decolonization itself was merely a step in the ordinary process of social evolution; that the colony was gaining its independence because it had reached maturity, no longer needing tutelage, and thus quite naturally had reached the stage where nationalism would arise and be followed in due course by state independence, in the same evolutionary-diffusionist process which had previously brought nation states to Europe. Independence was not, therefore, a fruit of struggle. It was a graduation ceremony.

Appropriate theories of nationalism were (and are) needed as well to form compatible sub-assemblies within a global social science model describing the metropolitan capitalist countries, the former colonies and other Third World countries, and the relations and transactions between the two sectors. This model depicts the world, minus its socialist sector, as a world of equal capitalist nation states, with the poorer states benefiting from the greatest possible intercourse with the richer states, the result of which will be economic development for the poorer states. Institutional changes will result from economic development and from other influences emanating from the richer countries, changes called in aggregate 'modernization'. Thus the model depicts the diffusion of economic and social advance – providing, of course, that the receiving countries place no obstacles in the way of this diffusion.

Although purveyors of this model genuinely believe in it, it is nonetheless profoundly deceptive. The states in the system are not equal. The substance which diffuses towards the poor countries is not economic development and modernization: it is political dependency and neocolonial exploitation. In fact the real diffusion is the flow of wealth in the opposite direction, from poor capitalist countries to rich ones. But the model has important ideological functions. In the advanced capitalist countries it legitimizes the continued expansion of multinational capitalism along with the terribly costly politico–military infrastructure needed to support it, and more particularly needed to try to prevent poor countries from opting out of the system and choosing socialism. In the neocolonies it legitimizes continued dependency and acceptance of multinational (and domestic) capitalism.

The theory of nationalism which is compatible with this global model is the idea that the classical, European, bourgeois, nation state, or something very like it, is the natural and necessary political framework for the promised economic development and social modernization, and that the diffusion of classical European nationalism (of the normal, not cancerous, sort) is the mechanism by which the nation state, the 'modern state', arrives in a given Third World space. Thus the colonial liberation movements are declared to be natural components of the overall diffusion process. Although conservative theories of nationalism differ among themselves as to how the diffusion process is to be described and explained, even whether or not it can succeed in taking place throughout the Third World, yet all the currently popular theories seem to argue this way.[9] I will expand on this as we proceed, even though my principal concern is with Marxist views on nationalism, not mainstream views.

## Class Struggle Theories

Marx, Engels, Lenin, Luxemburg, and most other Marxists past and present have argued that national struggle is a part or form of class struggle. The essence of the argument is remarkably simple. The sharpest and most crucial kind of class struggle is the struggle for state power; for control of the state; for the power over society without which exploitation cannot take place. National struggle is one form of this struggle for state power. There are instances of the struggle for state power in which the ruling group, the class or class fraction with state power, is in some sense foreign or external to the classes that are ruled. (See Chapter 7.) There are ambiguous cases, of course, but the great majority of instances and types of the national question are quite clearly defined.

Colonial rule, and the resistance to it, is one such type. Another involves a social group which lies within a larger state, is territorially distinct, and, usually, is also different in culture from the holders of power. In this type, the minority group may or may not be an oppressed minority, oppression here implying either suppression of its culture (most frequently its language) or exploitation of its working popula-tion at a more intense level than is found in other parts of the state, or (typically) both at the same time. If this is an oppressed minority, there may or may not be a struggle to wrest state power from the 'foreigners'. If there is such a struggle, it is national struggle, a case of the national question. Even if there is a struggle for some degree of autonomy short of complete state independence, that, too, is a national struggle, provided that autonomy in this case implies the transfer of real authority to the minority community. Other forms of the national question could be added if we wished to compile an exhaustive list.

The crux of the Marxist theory is that all national struggles are at root class struggles. They are examples of the class struggle for state power. They are class struggles because the engine which drives them is the exploitation of one or several classes – in a few very small societies, it can be the entire population – by a ruling class. This basic fact underlies, and ultimately accounts for, all the particular arenas of conflict, such as language, religion, wages, social conditions, and the rest. Like all class struggle, it is, or ultimately becomes, political: a fight for state power.

A class struggle for state power assumes the national form under certain conditions. Crudely stated – we will discuss them more precisely in Chapters 2 and 7 – these are conditions of spatial and social separation (or externality, or 'foreignness') between the main sector of the ruling class and those classes which are nationally oppressed or threatened with national oppression. Spatial or territorial separation is usually complete, and it must become so, of course, when an independence struggle is successful (because two states cannot occupy the same territory at the same time). Social separation or difference is a more complex question. In its classical formulation, among both Marxists and conservatives, national struggles were presumed to be, normally, conflicts between 'nationalities', a 'nationality' being what today we would call a spatially discrete 'culture'. But national struggles can also engage social communities which are not very different from one another: witness the case of Northern Ireland, in which the only major cultural difference is religion, while social separation is nonetheless fairly distinct, except at workplaces. Certainly there is no necessity that the social units engaged in national struggles be 'nations', or that the word 'national' implies that the issues are matters of culture. They may or may not be cultural, but they are always political.

The class struggle theory of national struggle, or nationalism, is the majority view among Marxists today, and it was the view of Marx, Engels, Lenin, and Luxemburg. There have been dissenters, among them Otto Bauer at the beginning of this century and a number of neo-Marxists today. But it is fair to say that the question of whether national struggle is a form of class struggle is one of the fundamental points of disagreement between Marxism and conservative social thought.

## The Argument of This Book

The thesis that national struggle is indeed class struggle, that it is a form of the class struggle for state power and is not an autonomous force – an 'idea', a sociological 'factor', or whatever – is the central argument of this book, and is expanded in the next two chapters.

It occupies all of our attention in Chapter 2, 'Nationalism as an Autonomous Force'. In that chapter I show that the class-struggle theory of national struggle represents the main line of Marxist thinking since Marx, and I try to refute a number of arguments that have been put forward in recent years by Marxists and Neo-Marxists who have tried to show that nationalism – by which they mean national struggle – is, indeed, something other than class struggle. The argument continues in Chapter 3. This chapter is a critique of one such 'autonomist' theory, a theory which was developed by an influential British Marxist and which is, in all probability, the best-known and most fully elaborated statement of this position that one can find in contemporary Marxist writing.

The argument of Chapter 2 begins by examining 19th Century European theories about nation states and national struggles. The important conservative theories postulated that one or another sort of metaphysical 'will' or 'idea' underlies the struggles to create independent states and to enlarge them. Marx and Engels showed in some of their earlier writings that the state is not an idea or a metaphysical superorganism (with its own 'will'), that struggles for state power are class struggles, that the state itself is not prior to but rather a product of these struggles, and that, accordingly, all of the political struggles concerning the state, including most particularly fights for state independence and efforts at Prussian-style territorial aggrandizement by imperial states, are at root class struggles.

Marx and Engels also showed that the rising bourgeois class found it necessary to control the state, therefore to transform existing states and form new ones, and that a large and linguistically uncomplicated nation state was the most appropriate political form for bourgeois rule; for capitalism. But Marx and Engels also showed, using Ireland as their main example, that national liberation struggles need not be essentially bourgeois in nature and part of the politics of the rising bourgeoisie; that exploited classes might in some few cases (like Ireland) take the lead, and fight to create a socialist state, not a capitalist one. In sum, the basic theoretical argument that national struggles are class struggles was made by Marx and Engels. Thereafter Lenin and other 20th Century Marxists elaborated the argument and updated it, but the basic position required no change.

When we argue that national struggle is 'at root' class struggle, we have to be able to show that the many dimensions of national struggle, some of them matters of language rights, some matters of religion, of civil equality, of equal opportunity, and so on, are embraced within the idea of class struggle; for it is clearly true that national struggles sometimes seem to be far removed from direct class conflict. In Chapter 2 I try to make this point. Marxism does not 'reduce' the national struggle to something which excludes the manifold dimensions of human culture; it conceives these latter to be forms and arenas of class struggle. Most critically, Marxism does not reach behind or under class struggle to find some other, more basic, force or phenomenon, something like an eternal 'nation', an 'idea of the nation state', a 'principle of nationalities', a pseudo-biological principle of 'territoriality' or 'aggression', or the like, something supposedly autonomous from class struggle and more deeply rooted in 'human nature'. Some few Marxists have argued that way. For Bauer, Renner, Poulantzas, and Debray, national processes emanate from 'the nation' as a primordial (and Hegelian) entity.[10] For Tom Nairn, nationalism is rooted in the human psyche (it is akin to 'dementia' and 'infantilism'). Even Horace Davis, who is perhaps the best modern Marxist scholar on the national question, accepts the mainstream thesis that nationalism is an autonomous idea, one of the great liberating ideas of Enlightenment Europe. In the concluding sections of Chapter 2, I dispute these and other arguments. I try to show that nationalism, national struggle, is class struggle.

One form of the 'autonomist' position which is quite dominant among conservative writers on nationalism is the theory of 'modernization' applied to national phenomena. Supposedly, nationalism arose as a component of Europe's modernization in the early 19th Century and then diffused throughout the world as part of the package of 'modernizing' or 'civilizing' ideas bestowed upon backward peoples by Europeans. This theory requires us to believe that colonialism was a 'civilising' process, not one of oppression, underdevelopment, and in some places genocide. And it claims, of course, that the diffusion of 'modernization' is also, necessarily, the diffusion of capitalism. For these and other reasons, the theory of 'modernization' is not popular among Marxists who have an understanding of the Third World, colonialism, and imperialism, and this holds true most definitely for the theory that Third World national struggles are products of Europe and 'modernization'.

One Marxist, however, who does accept this theory is Tom Nairn. Chapter 3 of our book is a critique of the 'modernization' theory of nationalism, and of the Eurocentric diffusionism embedded in this theory. But this general doctrine is one of the major bodies of conservative thought, and one cannot deal with it adequately in a few pages. So I have chosen to direct the critique at one writer, Nairn, partly because he is a perfect stand-in for the many conservatives who hold this general view, and partly to show that the 'modernization' theory of nationalism cannot be reconciled with the kind of Marxism which takes proper account of colonialism and national liberation.

It is true that one cannot refute the entire array of autonomist theories of nationalism by criticising only the Marxist versions of this theory. Still, all the major mainstream theories of nationalism seem flawed and invalidated by the same fallacious arguments made by certain Marxists and criticised in Chapters 2 and 3 of this book. I seek to show, altogether, that theories of nationalism are wrong if they do not reduce national struggle in the last analysis to class struggle. And I have yet to encounter a non-Marxist theory which gives causal weight to class struggle.

## Second Problem: Is Nationalism Appropriate Only to the Bourgeois-democratic Revolution?

### The Dogma
Marxist theory has more than its share of dogmatic notions, and one of the worst of these is what is usually referred to as the 'stage' theory of history. This is the dogmatic belief that (1) there is a definite, known sequence of stages in social development, (2) each stage has certain invariable characteristics, and (3) each society or social formation must pass through the same dreary sequence of stages that other societies have already endured. This three-part dogma has been criticized by many modern Marxist theorists, who have shown, among other things, that the stage theory was not really adhered to by Marx, Engels, or Lenin, as dogmatists have contended. But it so happens that the stage theory has spawned a very influential theory of nationalism or national struggle, and this has not been adequately criticized as yet. And so long as we accede to a stage theory of national struggle, we shall not have an adequate theory of nationalism.

The stage theory of national struggle argues as follows. Nationalism, considered to be the effort to forge a sovereign state – one that is relatively uncomplex in cultural terms, a nation state, and as part of this effort a body of nationalist ideology, a national movement, and so forth – all of this is appropriate only to one stage in social development: the stage of capitalism. It is appropriate, in fact, only to one sub-stage: the period called that of 'rising capitalism', the time when the bourgeoisie is, so to speak, getting its act together: fighting free of feudalism, beginning to accumulate, and so on. This argument is extrapolated from the Marx–Engels description of the role of the state in the rise and consolidation of capitalism. That description is valid but the extrapolation is not.

Marx and Engels showed that state power is crucial to all forms of class society, not least the capitalist form, and thus the rising capitalist class, the bourgeoisie, must seek to seize power in an existing state or create a state of its own. Then Marx and more crucially Engels argued that a relatively large state and one in which there is a common language, thus a nation state, would be the most useful state form for capitalism. It would not be the only state form. Marx and Engels did not deny that there had been pre-capitalist states. Nor did they argue that the bourgeoisie is the only class that has an interest in, and can lead, a struggle for state power. They wrote most fully about the bourgeois form of the national struggle, about the bourgeois state, and about bourgeois nationalism, but they also wrote sparingly about other forms. For instance, they argued that the Irish national struggle, which they clearly saw as an anti-colonial struggle, was more urgent for the exploited classes than for the bourgeoisie, and they felt that the exploited classes could and perhaps would lead that struggle. (See Chapter 5.)

The post-classical period of Marxist thought, the time between the death of Engels and the beginning of the First World War, was a period when Marxist theory went through many forms of distortion and dogmatization, not least in the matter of nationalism. It may be true that every major thinker during this period believed that national movements were on the decline because they were appropriate only to the period of rising capitalism, a period which seemed to be ending as capitalism matured. Even Lenin argued that nationalism, overall, was declining, although national movements would still be on the agenda of history in backward parts of the world like Russia and the colonial world. After 1914, Lenin produced a very different analysis, now arguing, as part of his magisterial theory of imperialism, that nationalism is actually a dominant characteristic of advanced capitalism; that national struggle does not decline as capitalism matures into its imperialist stage; that great-power nationalism becomes more pervasive than ever while the nationalism of colonies and other oppressed countries intensifies as well. (These matters are discussed in Chapters 4 and 5.) But these arguments came later. Before 1914, it seemed almost self-evident that 'the stage of nationalism' was pretty much coterminous with 'the stage of youthful or "rising" capitalism', a stage now basically ended.

This doctrine received its strongest expression in the writings of Rosa Luxemburg and in a famous and influential article written by Joseph Stalin in 1913. Stalin equated national movements with the emergence of nations, and the latter he declared to be associated only with the stage of rising capitalism. (See Chapters 2 and 5.) Luxemburg went much farther. Writing in the years 1898–1908, she declared that the stage of nationalism was strictly associated with the rise of the bourgeoisie, was therefore bourgeois nationalism, and that this stage was now over. Nationalism was strictly a feature of rising capitalism; that stage is now over; so nationalism is dying.

This all-nationalism-is-bourgeois theory has had immense influence on Marxist theory and practice in more recent times. Its influence has been largely negative. True, it has had the positive effect of sensitizing Marxists to the real dangers of bourgeois nationalism. But the theory has led very many Marxists to believe, incorrectly, that any national struggle in our own time is necessarily bourgeois in its goals and its leadership, hence that anti-colonial struggles in countries like Vietnam and Angola cannot be struggles for socialism: they must be examples of the bourgeois revolution, not the socialist revolution. And if a Marxist party in a colony, like Puerto Rico for instance, fights for independence as a component of the struggle for socialism, why, then, it must be a bourgeois party with bourgeois nationalist goals, because a fight for state independence is simply nationalism, and all nationalism is bourgeois. At the level of theory, the all-nationalism-is-bourgeois view has led many Marxists to lose sight of, and at times to deny the validity of, the basic Marxist theory of nationalism as developed by Marx, Engels, and Lenin. And this view does preclude any further development of the theory.

## The Argument of This Book

I confront the all-nationalism-is-bourgeois theory at various points in this book, but always as part of a larger argument. In Chapter 2, I describe somewhat briefly the position taken by Marx and Engels on national struggle and show that they did not equate all national struggle with the bourgeoisie and the rise of capitalism. In Chapter 5, I criticise Stalin's theory of nations, which is closely tied to the theory that national struggle is strictly associated with what Stalin called the 'epoch of rising capitalism', and strictly associated with the rising bourgeoisie. But the more crucial arguments against the all-nationalism-is-bourgeois theory are given in Chapter 4, in which I criticise a new and somewhat moderated form of this theory put forward by Eric Hobsbawm, and in Chapter 7, in which I try to generalise the theory of national struggle to classes and modes of production other than the bourgeoisie and capitalism.

Chapter 4, 'Hobsbawm on the Nation-State', is a critique of a theory of nationalism, Hobsbawm's, which is in many respects an improved and modernized version of the all-nationalism-is-bourgeois theory, and which argues towards a bleakly negative judgment of national struggles, including national liberation struggles. Hobsbawm maintains that nationalism, meaning the national struggle to create something like a nation state, was rational in the 19th Century but no longer is so. He presents the classical arguments according to which the rise of capitalism called for the creation of nation states. But, says Hobsbawm, capitalism no longer needs the nation state, hence national movements in the present century are irrational; are, in effect, atavistic. From here he goes on to criticize all modern forms of national struggle, including the anti-colonial forms. While Hobsbawm does not deny that some modern national struggles have aimed at and achieved socialism, he considers this to be a rare sort of outcome, much less significant in the modern world than the creation of what he views as frivolous mini-states and reactionary or simply irrational social movements.

I offer three broad arguments against the theory that all national struggle is 'bourgeois nationalism'. First, in Chapter 4, the critique of Hobsbawm, I display some of the evidence that classes other than the 'rising bourgeoisie' have had it in their interest to fight for state power in national struggles. National aggrandizement, including colonial expansion, has been a strategy of the mature, full 'risen', bourgeoisies of imperial states for a very long time, and in the present century this kind of great-bourgeois nationalism has been a basic characteristic of the age and a cause of world wars. By the same token, the internationalization of capitalism, and most recently the growth of multinational corporations, has not (as Hobsbawm claims) led to a decline in the importance of the national state. Capitalism needs state power, today as yesterday, and therefore the national struggles over sovereignty for colonies and neocolonies are as important in the present age of international capitalism as they were in prior ages; probably more so. But the most telling evidence against the all-nationalism-is-bourgeois theory comes from the working classes. Workers, poor peasants, and marginalized petty-bourgeois segments, and parties reflecting their class interests, have played major roles in most national liberation struggles against colonialism and neocolonialism. In many of these struggles, as in Vietnam, Angola, and Cuba, the working classes have played a leading role. And the states they have created are not bourgeois but socialist.

The second argument against the all-nationalism-is-bourgeois view concerns the history of Marxist theorizing about the national question, a matter dealt with at length in Chapter 4 and briefly in Chapters 2 and 5. Neither Hobsbawm nor the other writers whom I criticize seem to be aware that Lenin, in the period 1914–1921, refuted the belief that national struggles are necessarily bourgeois, that he refuted the older view (associated mainly with Luxemburg), and in fact developed an essentially new theory about the national liberation struggles against colonialism, showing why these are (partly, at least) working-class struggles and are part of the 'rise' not of capitalism but of socialism. He also refuted the theory that modern, international capitalism has less need of the state and that national liberation struggles are passé; he even gave this latter theory a name, 'imperialist economism', fully a half-century before the theory became popular among Marxists. It is clear today that anyone who maintains that national movements are necessarily bourgeois, and that national liberation always leads to capitalism, not socialism, is arguing against a long established and quite solid body of Marxist theory. And against the facts.

Chapter 7, 'Class Struggles across a Boundary', is an attempt to broaden or generalize the Marxist theory of nationalism. It presents another argument against the all-nationalism-is-bourgeois theory, because it tries to show that the conditions underlying national struggle are characteristic of class society in general, not only of capitalism. In all forms of class society since ancient times, though not in all specific societies, there exist two sorts of class exploitation, an *internal* and an *external* sort, the latter involving members of a producing class in another society which the first society's ruling class has conquered or otherwise come to dominate. I argue that the two sorts of exploitation entail two somewhat different forms of class struggle, particularly as regards the struggle for state power. I conclude that the struggle to control the state when it is in the hands of a class which is external (from the point of view of the local producing class) is the specific form of class struggle which in modern times becomes national struggle. This is not an argument that nationalism, or national struggle, is as old as class society itself; it is merely an argument that nationalism today is situated in a form of class struggle, external class struggle, which itself is as old as class society and is therefore a fundamental category for historical materialism. It hardly needs to be added that this argument is incompatible with the thesis that national struggle is strictly a trait of early-bourgeois society and strictly a strategy of the rising bourgeoisie.

## Third Problem: Did Nationalism Diffuse from Western Europe to the Third World?
### Eurocentric Diffusionism: A Capsule View
Just about all conservative social theory and much Marxist theory is afflicted with Eurocentric diffusionism, the explicit or implicit view that social evolution in general occurs first in Europe, or western Europe, or the West, and then diffuses outwards to the rest of the world. I pointed out earlier that diffusionism is a crucial, central part of mainstream capitalist thought; it is the basic rationale for

colonialism and neocolonialism. The foundation of capitalist ideology is the set of beliefs which rationalizes capitalist class relations and the exploitation of labour, and diffusionism is the first ideological storey built upon this foundation: it rationalizes the external portion of capitalism, the political dominance of Third World areas and the superexploitation of Third World labour.

In Marxist thought, by contrast, diffusionism contradicts Marxism's foundations. For one thing, it assumes a basic inequality among the peoples of the earth as regards their potentialities for social evolution. For another, it inserts in Marxist theory the belief that the spread of capitalist traits from the advanced (core) sector is, somehow, evolutionarily natural and progressive, a part of the 'Enlightenment'. Thirdly, it wrongly attributes some basic historical processes of Third World countries to diffusion from Europe. One of the most important of these processes is the national movement for state independence. Therefore a diffusionist version of the Marxist theory of nationalism must be theoretically invalid and politically troublesome. An important task of this book is to combat diffusionism.

It can hardly be denied that European political and economic control spread out over the Americas in the 16th to 18th Centuries, that most of Asia and Africa were conquered in the 19th Century, and that this process of colonial and semi-colonial expansion produced not only a flow of wealth inwards, towards Europe, but also a reciprocal flow in the outward direction, a flow of European populations, European colonial political forms, and European commodities. All of this is real diffusion, in both directions, and it needs to be explained. But the explanation need not invoke some innate progressiveness of European culture, such that it would be considered somehow natural to believe that Europe was more advanced and was progressing more rapidly than the non-European world at each epoch in world history and down to the present. This belief is Eurocentric diffusionism. I have argued elsewhere that Europe was no farther along in social evolution than Africa or Asia (painting on a continental-sized canvas) at any time prior to 1492.[11] In my view the single advantage which Europe's mercantile-maritime communities enjoyed over the competing mercantile-maritime communities of Africa and Asia was location. European centres were some 5,000 miles closer to the New World than any competing non-European centre, hence were much more likely to make contact with New World places and peoples first, and were thereafter certain to monopolize the immense fruits of plunder and exploitation. I argue further that these New World sources of wealth explain the more rapid rise of mercantile capitalism in Western Europe than elsewhere, and thus the bourgeois political revolutions of the 17th Century.[12] And after capitalism had taken power in its 'home' countries and thus could exploit a potential proletariat both at home and in the colonies, it is not hard to see why Europe then entered a period of autonomous progress and simultaneously squelched the economic and political progress of other parts of the world.

Other writers have developed other historical models which explain Europe's rise without conceding any special qualities of progressiveness to Europeans. But it is nevertheless true that many Marxists and nearly all conservatives continue to believe in a fundamental Eurocentric diffusionism. They believe, first, that Europe did indeed have progressive qualities lacking in other societies in ancient times –

they coopt ancient Egypt, Palestine, etc., as 'Europe's cultural hearth' – or in medieval times, or perhaps always. They believe, next, that the colonial expansion of Europe was innately a process of diffusing civilization, not a process of gathering in all forms of wealth and diffusing only the infrastructure needed to obtain further wealth (along with relative surplus population). This particular belief tends to form itself into the fairy tale that Europe bestowed 'the Enlightenment' on the rest of the world within the framework of colonialism, and that the main ingredient of diffusing Enlightenment was a diffusion of what are called 'the idea of freedom' and 'the idea of democracy' (which, be it noted, are the very antithesis of colonialism).

Finally, and most crucially, these writers believe that the current relationship between the capitalist European countries (including former European settler colonies, like the United States) and the Third World is predominantly a continuing diffusion of this same Enlightenment. For some Marxists, it is merely the spread of enlightening capitalism to areas falsely thought to be primitive and 'traditional', or the (mythical) spread of industrialization and of the high living standards of advanced capitalism itself. For these Marxist scholars, and for just about all non-Marxist scholars, all of this is part of a single process, most often called 'modernization'. Europe's advanced capitalism is engaged simply in the altruistic diffusion of modernity.

## Diffusionist Theories of Nationalism

One of the supposed dimensions of 'modernization' is the 'modern state'. Sometimes this is expressed in nakedly ideological terms: Europe, having given birth to the 'idea of freedom', the 'idea of democracy', etc., is now diffusing these modern ideas to non-Europe. And the ideas of freedom and democracy are considered, in this same ideologically determinist argument, to be the roots of nationalism. More concretely: nationalism is a process generated by the European idea of freedom, that is, the idea that people should govern themselves in a sovereign state; and it is the diffusion of this idea which then causes the rise of national movements in non-European areas. Therefore colonies, in this formulation, become nationalistic and develop independence movements, not because their inhabitants are oppressed and superexploited, but because their colonial rulers brought them Enlightenment.

I stated earlier in this chapter that every one of the modern conservative theories of nationalism of which I am aware employs some form of this diffusionist doctrine. Europe invented nationalism, for whatever reasons – it is on this question of reason that conservatives debate one another's theories – and, having invented it, they then diffused it outwards to the other peoples of the world. If one rejects this formula, as I do, how does one go about refuting it? The problem is that this bundle of theories is riding piggy-back on the much more robust doctrine of Eurocentric diffusionism, and one cannot readily get at the one without first getting at the other.

## The Argument of This Book

In this book I cannot dispose of diffusionism, one of the deepest, most pervasive, and most crucial world-models in Western conservative thought. So I have had to content myself with a more accessible target: Tom Nairn's presentation of one form of the theory of nationalism as the diffusion of European 'Enlightenment' and 'modernization'. Nairn proclaims his view to be Marxist, and this provides the excellent opportunity to criticize, not simply the diffusionist view of nationalism, but also the contention that this view is somehow compatible with Marxist theory. Hence Chapter 3.

The diffusionist theory of nationalism put forward by Nairn and conservative writers makes a number of assertions about the past and present world which I try to refute as misstatements of fact. First, colonialism did not bring the ideas of freedom, national self-determination, etc., to the colonial subjects. On the contrary, such ideas were suppressed, because colonialism as a system was (and still is in places like Puerto Rico) totally undemocratic and the colonizers of necessity taught submission and obedience, not the Rights of Man. Second, anti-colonial struggles were (and are) not simply the bourgeois–democratic revolution diffusing outwards from Europe to the wider world. There were bourgeois elements, but the basic motor in these struggles was, and is, intense exploitation and the resistance to that exploitation, and at the same time intense oppression to permit this exploitation to take place and again the resistance to oppression. Third, and very much a derivative of the foregoing argument, national liberation struggles do not simply spread capitalism to the outer world, via a bourgeois–democratic revolution led by a 'rising bourgeoisie'. They are a new form of social struggle which may, certainly, bring into existence a novel form of bourgeois-dominated society (as in Iran and many typical neocolonies) but may, and frequently does, bring into existence a socialist society. Nairn, along with the Neo-Marxists who put forward the same or similar arguments, and along with most conservatives, completely denies the fact that socialist countries exist in the Third World, and the diffusionist theory of nationalism provides perhaps the crucial ideological prop for this political position.

A very different critique of the Eurocentric diffusionist theory of national struggle and some related doctrines is put forward in Chapter 7. Here I develop a theoretical position which views national struggle as the product of what I call 'external class struggle', that is, the kind of political struggle which takes place when part or all of the ruling class is in some sense 'external' or 'foreign' vis-a-vis the producing classes. States, as organized political systems governing masses of people and definite territories, have been in existence since the dawn of class societies. So has exploitation of external producing classes, and so, too, has class resistance to this peculiarly intense form of exploitation. This was not properly 'national struggle' until recent centuries, but it was an autochthonous form of class struggle in all historical epochs and class modes of production. Thus national liberation struggles against colonialism and neocolonialism are responses to the diffusion of European colonialism and its form of capitalism, but the national struggle is generated by the colonized people themselves; it is not simply a product of an idea of nationalism which diffused outwards from Europe. On a wider canvas, Chapter 7 tries to respond to the much larger doctrine that the only place where social evolution originates is Europe and its planted settlements in other continents.

# Fourth Problem: Does Nationalism Bear Some Special Relationship to Fascism?

## Ideologies of Nationalism and Fascism

If nationalism is a form of the class struggle for state power, then we should not expect it to be associated with one specific ideology, because each class or class combination in each kind of national struggle would have an ideological position of its own, and these would moreover differ for different historical epochs and geographical circumstances. This argument holds true even if we limit the use of the word nationalism to efforts to create new sovereign states and efforts to enlarge existing states, and do not describe as nationalist the opposing efforts to prevent secession or resist annexation. Even in this restricted usage, it would be incorrect to assimilate to one ideological position such differing national movements as, for instance, the 19th Century small-nation bourgeois national movements, the 19th Century colonial (including settler-colonial) expansions of large bourgeois states, the bourgeois nationalism of imperialist states in the present century, the anti-colonial liberation movements which are narrowly nationalist (that is, contemplate no major social change after independence), and the anti-colonial liberation movements which are Marxist in ideology, are grounded in exploited classes, and, as in Vietnam, carry a national liberation movement forward to the point of creating a socialist society. There are many kinds of national struggle, many class positions, and many ideologies.

Nevertheless, it is widely believed that there is a single, characteristic ideology of nationalism, and this view leads into all sorts of speculation about the relationship between nationalist ideology and other ideologies, most notably those of socialism and fascism. Among Marxist writers there is anything but unanimity on this question of the singularity and specificity of nationalist ideology. Those Marxist scholars who have a good understanding of national movements in the modern Third World are unlikely to consider the attendant ideologies of national liberation to be homologous with, for instance, the wildly mystical doctrines of some European national movements of the last century, or with other equally dissimilar nationalist ideologies. For example, Horace Davis, one of the foremost Marxist scholars of nationalism, speaks strongly against the tendency to lump national movements and their ideologies together and render a single moral judgment on all of them. Nationalism, he points out, is a neutral tool which can be used as a weapon of destruction or an implement of progress, depending on who picks it up and uses it – and, as I would add, depending on which classes use it at which times and places and for which purposes.[13]

Those Marxists who accept the all-nationalism-is-bourgeois theory are inclined, on the other hand, to accept the notion of a specific, singular, nationalist ideology: it is simply part of bourgeois ideology. This argument is seductive, because there certainly is a characteristic family of closely related ideologies which we correctly call the ideologies of 'bourgeois nationalism'. Even within this restricted family, however, there is much variation. The bourgeois nationalism of, for instance, the 19th Century national movements of the Greeks, Czechs, Serbians, Norwegians, Latin Americans, Chinese, etc., is very different from the bourgeois nationalism of the expanding colonial empires and different as well from the bourgeois nationalism associated with later fascist movements.

Eric Hobsbawm makes the case, which I confute in Chapter 4 of this book, that nationalism really is a singular social entity and its characteristic ideology was appropriate to some, though not all, of the 19th Century national movements of rising capitalism, but is no longer appropriate to anything. This ideology in today's world is simply – Hobsbawm's word – 'irrational'. I am sure that Hobsbawm considers the nationalism of insignificant Ruritanias to have a different sort of irrationality from that of fascist Italy or Nazi Germany, although he does not address this point. But his basic argument remains clear: nationalist ideology arose in connection with the rational state-forming national movements of rising 19th Century capitalism, and this same ideology today, when state formation is no longer (in his view) rational, has itself become irrational. Anti-colonial liberation movements are not specifically excepted from this judgement.

An altogether different argument is made by the neo-Marxist Tom Nairn and by the conservative theorists of nationalism (notably Ernest Gellner) whom Nairn follows rather closely, as we will see in Chapter 3. For these theorists, nationalism arose once, in one place, and a distinctive nationalist ideology was not only associated with it but served as its historical motor. Then nationalism diffused to the rest of the world and so too did its ideology, which we now see popping up in the farthest corners of the Third World with an appearance not unlike that of its European forebears.

There are two main forms of this model, each associated with its own kind of postulate as to the nature of the original European nationalism, and each leading to a very different conclusion about the nature of nationalist ideology and its relationship to other ideologies, notably fascism. The more widely accepted of the two forms considers nationalism to be simply the logic of early capitalist democracy, the product of what Hobsbawm has called the 'dual revolution' (political and industrial). Given this conception, the diffusing ideology of nationalism is likely to be seen as the diffusion of the quite benign ideology of democracy, freedom, and modernity, from its supposed British and French hearth.

But the other form identifies original nationalism, not with democratic Britain and France, but with undemocratic Germany. In fact it focuses on something which is sometimes called the 'Germanic theory of nationalism', using the word theory to mean both an operant ideology and an analytical structure. As I show in Chapter 2, there were two sets of originating circumstances for early German nationalism. One was the political effort to unify the German states into a cohesive nation state; the other was the ideology which supported this political programme. The ideology was a quite mystical doctrine, deriving from Herder, Fichte, Hegel, and some others, according to which the German nation is a superorganism with a 'will' and 'spirit' of its own, and the German citizen is someone not at all free as to will and rights, but merely a cell or component part of the state organism and subject to its superordinate 'will'. (I discuss this theory in Chapter 2.) It is evident that this doctrine is very distant from the doctrine of the Rights of Man, of democracy and freedom, although attempts to combine the two doctrines were sometimes made, as by Herder and Mazzini, and a democratic variant of the Germanic doctrine became significant in the later 19th Century. The Germanic doctrine tends to romanticize the unity of the civil community, using language as the most important common and unifying trait of that community, and denies both the real freedom of the individual and the existence of internal conflicting classes.

The original Germanic doctrine acquired a strong flavour of expansive nationalism with the addition of Ratzel's theory of *Lebensraum*, 'living space', during the Bismarck era, the theory according to which the German national organism, like all other organisms, has the inherent need, and therefore somehow the inherent moral right, to grow and thus to expand. It is unclear, however, whether this portion of the Germanic theory diffused to the wider world along with the rest of the doctrine. One must add also that the rise of the *Lebensraum* doctrine in Germany owed at least as much to pragmatic Bismarckian efforts to emulate British and French colonial expansion as it did to Hegel and the other mystic theorists of German nationalism. In any event, the Germanic or (as I describe it in Chapter 2) Hegelian ideology diffused into many parts of Central and Eastern Europe, and into Italy, sometimes with a democratic cast, sometimes not, but always retaining the mystical idea of the higher spiritual unity of the nation and its inherent right and need to have a sovereign state of its own.

Among conservative writers about nationalism today, it is a very common error, traceable perhaps to the old Germanic theory, to confuse two very different bodies of ideas: analytical theories about nationalism and ideological doctrines which are propagated and used by national movements and their spokespeople. This confusion is allowed, and probably explained, by the fact that the underlying theory which these writers accept itself asserts that ideology is primordial, autonomous, and determinative. What this typically leads to in practice is a tendency to imagine that the Germanic theory of nationalism in fact *is* nationalism. Consider, for instance, the following definition of (supposedly real-world) nationalism by a well-known, influential, and very conservative theorist about nationalism, Elie Kedourie:

> Nationalism is a doctrine invented in Europe at the beginning of the 19th century. It pretends to supply a criterion for the determination of the unit of population proper to enjoy a government exclusively its own, for the legitimate exercise of power in the state, and for the right organization of a society of states. Briefly, the doctrine holds that humanity is naturally divided into nations, that nations are known by certain characteristics which can be ascertained, and that the only legitimate type of government is national self-government.[14]

Kedourie simply dismisses all theories of nationalism which allude to exploitation and oppression as causal forces, and he ignores all national movements which fight for the establishment of multinational states and other such non-national units. And referring specifically to anti-colonial movements, Kedourie claims that the underlying force, or motor, or cause of such movements is the doctrine or theory quoted above.

A variant of this approach, with like confusion between operant doctrine and theory, is employed by the neo-Marxist Tom Nairn in his presentation of what he wants to call a Marxist theory of nationalism, the theory which is criticized in

Chapter 3 of this book.[15] He, too, believes that ideology is the motor of national movements, and that nationalist ideology in general is simply the Germanic theory, with its mysticism, its idea of higher unity, and so on, and that all of this diffused around the world and, in the arid atmosphere of underdevelopment, kindled the various national movements. Nationalism, for Nairn, is the diffusion of the Germanic theory around the world, while, back in Germany, this same theory nurtures fascism.

So we come to fascism. Nairn is by no means alone in bracketing fascism with nationalism, connecting both at the level of ideology or doctrine and assuming that each doctrine then has a similar outcome: fascist movements are thus like national movements and vice versa. Nairn considers fascism to be a much-intensified form of nationalism, but this caveat does not alter his basic equation of the two. Along with others who argue this way, Nairn makes essentially two arguments to support the supposed homology of nationalism and fascism. The first one flows directly from the model according to which the Germanic doctrine of nationalism is, in fact, nationalism, or at least causes national processes and national struggles. We are simply provided with the standard historical account of the rise of the ideology of Nazism (the example of fascism under discussion) out of early German nationalism, Bismarckian expansionism, and the German nationalism of the First World War. I need not repeat the account; it is substantially correct and is not very controversial as a description of the forerunners of Nazi ideology. But Nairn goes much farther: he claims that this ideological history is the true cause of the rise of Nazism, instead of pointing to non-ideological processes which led to the acceptance of this ideology, and to all the rest of the Nazi horror.[16] In sum: nationalism is declared to come from the same historic root as Nazism; therefore both are common branches of a single tree, the root of which is ideological.

The second argument purports to be empirical. It points out that the Nazis engaged in real territorial aggrandizement, in real expansionist nationalism, and used an extreme form of the older Germanic doctrine to justify Nazi aggression against other states. Thus Nazism both deployed expansionist nationalism and justified it with a theory of nationalism. None of this is in dispute. But Nairn's argument then goes on to infer that the use of nationalist practice and doctrine turns Nazism itself in essence into a case of nationalism.

But the Germanic doctrine does not underlie most national movements, past and present, and certainly not the movements of national liberation in colonies. Whatever mysticism and romanticism and emotionalism we find in these movements betrays no homology with Nazism; indeed it is hardly different from the romanticism and emotionalism and, yes, mysticism we find in most social movements, including socialist movements. (Would these have gained any victories had they eschewed emotionalism? Can any socialist or trade unionist who has ever walked a picket line honestly claim that socialism is unemotional – is pure cold rationality?)

Furthermore, fascism as a category is much larger than Nazism as a category. I think it cannot be established that, for instance, the Italian and Spanish forms of fascism were rooted, even ideologically, in the Germanic doctrine. As to the empirical evidence, Nazism indeed engaged in aggressive, expansionist national struggle, but so did the democratic states in their colonial expansion. Interestingly, the Nazis employed quite ordinary colonialist ideology as part of their ideology of expansion; they claimed the right to win back a colonial empire.[17] Mussolini's fascism engaged in expansive nationalism in an almost classically colonialist manner, even though the declared aim was to rebuild the Roman Empire. And Franco's fascism did not place much emphasis on enlargement of the state as cardinal policy. Again we are reminded of the truth of Horace Davis' observation that nationalism is a tool which can be picked up and used in many ways, progressive and reactionary. Expansive nationalism, state-forming nationalism, defensive nationalism, anti-secessionist nationalism, and all the other forms of national struggle are utilized and engaged in by a great number of different social formations, and the fact that Nazism and some other fascisms make use of national struggle does not permit us to argue that there is homology between fascism and some of these other nationalisms, least of all with the anti-colonial movements for national liberation.

## The Argument of This Book

Chapter 3, which criticizes Nairn's theory of nationalism, is the vehicle for my argument that fascism bears no inherent relationship to nationalism. A section of that chapter ('Nationalism and Fascism') deals specifically with Nairn's attempt to connect the two, but equally relevant are the parts of that chapter which criticize Nairn's thesis that classical Germanic nationalism, doctrine and practice, is in fact the one nationalism, and that it was this model that diffused around the world.

The critique focuses mainly on Nairn's contention that 'modernization', because it proceeds unevenly, sets up a psychological frustration-reaction in the elite groups of any given 'modernizing' area, a subconscious, even psychopathological explosion akin to dementia and this is nationalism. When extremely violent, it emerges as fascism (which, for Nairn, is the 'archetype' of nationalism). To attack this theory one must analyse separately each of three contentions. First, there is the contention that both nationalism and fascism can be explained, historically, in terms of an ideological prime cause which is declared to be autonomous, a cause uncaused except in some indefinable way by a frustration-reaction to 'modernization'. I argue that neither nationalism nor fascism can be explained as an effect of a free-floating ideology; they are profoundly complex social phenomena in which ideology plays a part, but by no means a determining part. Second, there is Nairn's contention that both fascist and nationalist movements are ultimately led and used by ruling classes. Quite often this is not the case in nationalist movements, in some of which the crucial role is played by exploited classes, and by the ideology of Marxism, which is hardly comparable to the ideology of fascism. And third, Nairn contends that both nationalism and its 'archetype', fascism, emerge in each part of the globe at just the appropriate time in relation to the arrival of 'modernization'. I show that no space–time correlation exists to justify this argument. In fact, Germany and Italy became modernized, in every valid sense of that term, a half-century or more before the rise of fascism. What we correctly call 'nationalist ideologies' span a great range of social referents, only one of which is fascism.

## Fifth Problem: Is National Struggle Out of Date? Is the National State an Anachronism in the Era of Multinational Capitalism?

### Conservative Views of the National State

Earlier in this chapter I noted that conservative theorizing about nationalism went through a signal change around 1960 when theorists began seriously to conceptualize decolonization and the anti-colonial national movements, and sought to find a place for these processes in the general theory of nationalism. The outcome of this change was the wide acceptance of a formulation, really part of the 'modernization' doctrine, which can be called the evolutionary–diffusionist theory of the national state.

This is a two-part argument. First, a certain number of original national states – Britain and France for some theorists; these two plus Germany and perhaps Italy, the US, and one or two other countries for other theorists – emerged quite naturally during the 19th Century. Then, second, this original form of state diffused outwards to the rest of the world: to eastern Europe before and after the First World War; to Asia, Africa, the Caribbean, etc., after the Second World War. The people of these receiving areas were seen as evolving towards the level of political maturity earlier attained by 'the West', the level at which they would adopt the national state as their political form. We noted earlier that this theory served an important ideological purpose in explaining decolonization as a moment in the supposedly natural, benign, and smooth evolution of colonies from the condition of colonial 'tutelage', through the graduation ceremony of decolonization, to the mature, adult, condition of dependency and neocolonialism. The theory rationalized post-colonial economic and political dependency as continued evolution toward 'modernity' and as the only road to economic development.

The evolutionary-diffusionist theory of the national state seems now to be losing favour among conservative scholars. Some of them, at least, are putting forward a very different theory, one reminiscent in many ways of a theory which was widely accepted before the period of decolonization. This new theory considers the national state to be a characteristically Western institution, something that cannot diffuse to other areas and peoples. This view is of a piece with colonialist ideology in its earlier incarnation. E. H. Carr, for instance, in 1942 deplored the fact that the principle of self-determination of nations as enunciated by the Wilsonians in 1919 was now being extended to the non-European world. Said he, 'the days of the small independent national state, the embodiment of the ideals of 1919, are numbered'.[18] And quite consistently he described the idea of decolonization as 'reactionary'.[19] Alfred Cobban, another British authority on nationalism, asserted in 1944 that 'the more backward peoples . . . should be trained to operate a system of local autonomy . . . Self-determination does not mean giving peoples power they do not want and cannot use', this in a book of his entitled *National Self-Determination*.[20] The general position, then, was that small and new states, mostly colonies, could not viably exist in the coming (post-war) world; that the principle of self-determination and the absolute right of sovereignty had to be subordinated to some system by which a few great states would manage the affairs of the rest, presumably to the latters' benefit. This would of course mean a perpetuation of the principles of colonial and semi-colonial rule, along with the counterpart of this as practised by the United States, namely, gunboat diplomacy and periodic invasion and occupation of small neighbouring states plus a dollop of ordinary colonialism in countries like Puerto Rico.

The evolutionary-diffusionist theory has not proved to be a very good predictor of the modern world of states. Decolonization did not produce the expected landscape of stable, developing, capitalist states. Some former colonies chose socialism. The rest could not be maintained in an economically neocolonial (hence profit-generating) status without a great deal of interference in their internal affairs, part of it economic, part of it political, part of it overtly or covertly military. The kind of state which capitalism wants and needs in the Third World simply does not arise naturally, in accordance with evolutionary–diffusionist principles. Deliberate intervention is needed, and does not always work. Compounding the problem is the fact that the majority of the member states of the United Nations no longer support the powerful capitalist states. In the 1950s and 1960s, when these powerful states controlled automatic majorities in the General Assembly and the Security Council, there was scarcely any concern over the fact that many member states were small and weak. But as voting patterns changed, as, for instance, majorities began to vote for resolutions demanding self-determination for Puerto Ricans and Palestinians, Western politicians and mainstream scholars began to condemn loudly the so-called 'mini-states', and also to condemn the not-properly-integrated-and-so-not-truly-national states of the Third World which were certain to decompose due to their supposed non-viability (but hardly ever decompose in reality), and eventually to condemn the United Nations itself.

Hence the need for and supply of a new theory. Or at least the proliferation of arguments, some old, some new, denying that true national states have diffused to the Third World and asserting the virtues of limited sovereignty as supposedly being best suited for the majority of the new states. Part of this formulation has been a critique of the concept of the national state itself. (I use 'national state' instead of 'nation state' because the emphasis in the present discussion is on matters relating to power and sovereignty, not on questions of nationality and the like. More on these concepts in Chapters 4 and 5.) Supposedly the world is now going through a dual process, both tendencies working against the continued significance of the national state. On the one hand, it is argued, we see ethnic or nationality groups demanding some form of autonomy or independence in even the large and powerful Western countries, thus a tendency towards decomposition of the traditional national state. On the other hand, it is argued, we see the growing importance of multiple-state alliances, like NATO (but not like the UN), which are emerging as the true centres of power, the modern counterparts of the old colonial and continental empires. I need hardly add that the transformation is viewed as functional not only for controlling troublesome Third World countries but also for preserving world capitalism itself.

Not all problems can be tackled, much less solved, in one book on the national question. My perspective is Marxist, and my main concern is with points of view and theories expressed and debated within the Marxist corpus of writings on nationalism and the national question. But quite a few Marxists and neo-Marxists have recently joined their conservative colleagues in arguing that the national state is out of date. Marxists, however, cannot deal with this question unless they deal with another one as well. They have always supported national liberation struggles in colonies and neocolonies. Now some few Marxists and a flock of neo-Marxists question even these struggles, arguing also that national struggle in general is out of date. This thesis must claim our attention.

**Marxists and Neo-Marxists on the Decline of the National State and National Struggle**

The idea that national states are declining in importance, or never have been important under modern capitalism, is being advanced in various forms these days by a number of neo-Marxists, including Nairn, Wallerstein, and Arrighi, and by at least one traditional Marxist: Hobsbawm. If states are becoming or soon will become unimportant and perhaps will wither away under capitalism, it would follow that national movements, even national liberation movements, are now passé and irrelevant. Some argue that the formerly progressive movements have now become reactionary, and they are fond of quoting Rosa Luxemburg's famous comment about the Polish independence movement:

> [Knowing] the objective movement of history . . . we are protected . . . from mistaking, as revolutionary activity, aspirations that have long since been transformed by the forces of social evolution into their reactionary opposites.[21]

Obviously the truth or falsity of this argument is of considerable significance for the theory of nationalism. Obviously also, it is of significance for all the national struggles in which Marxists are today engaged. For example it is clear that, although Puerto Rican Marxists were virtually unanimous until recently in their conviction that the fight for socialism in Puerto Rico requires a fight for independence, for national liberation, as an absolutely necessary step in the path to socialism in that country, voices are now, for the first time in recent memory, being heard to suggest that the fight for independence may not be a proper fight for socialists. Why? Because this, supposedly, is the era when states are dissolving, and national struggles have become passé. (One or two voices add: 'All national struggle is bourgeois!') Thus the issue is important for practice as well as theory.

To understand this issue it is helpful to see it in historical perspective. I will go into the history of the question in Chapter 4, but a few words here will not be out of place. In the post-classical period of Marxist thought, after Engels' death and before the First World War, it was conventional wisdom that capitalism had become, or was quickly becoming, international, outgrowing the national state and rendering national struggles out of date, at least in the centres of advanced capitalism, while the proletariat was of course internationalist in the nature of things. The national state was not thought to be dissolving, but it was of declining importance. New states would not emerge (for Luxemburg) or would emerge only in relatively backward regions (for Lenin). Nationalism was a declining force. And all capitalist states would in any case soon disappear in the impending world revolution. A time of optimism. When the First World War broke out, however, it became startlingly evident that most of the proletariat of the warring countries was not yet ready for internationalism, while the capitalists themselves were pursuing their own sort of internationalist aims through the use of very national armed forces.

Among those Marxists who opposed the war unconditionally, two strikingly different positions emerged and were debated. One was Lenin's, a view informed now by his analysis of imperialism and its relationship to national struggle. Nationalism, he said, is a central feature of the era of imperialism or monopoly capitalism. Bourgeois nationalism of the great power sort becomes intensified by the cannibalistic struggle of great capitalist states to steal one another's colonies and other sources of raw material, markets, and the like. And national liberation struggles become more intense than ever, in colonies and other sorts of oppressed nations.

Ranged against Lenin were the Luxemburgians, Bukharin, Radek, Trotsky, and others, who insisted – in the midst of the World War – that national struggles and the national state are of declining importance. Said Trotsky, 'The War heralds the break-up of the nation-state'.[22] Said Radek, 'Imperialism represents the tendency of finance capital *to outgrow the bounds of a national state*'.[23] Said Pyatakov, independence for the colonies is 'unachievable' under capitalism.[24] And so on.

Thus Marxists were debating the issue of the decline of national states and national struggle nearly seventy years ago. And they are doing so still. Meanwhile, states have not disappeared from the political map of the world and remain as important as ever, while national struggles go on with unabated intensity from El Salvador and Puerto Rico to Namibia and Timor.

Between the time of the Russian Revolution and the 1960s, the idea that national states are declining and national struggles are passé was not, as far as I can tell, of much currency among Marxists. In the last decade or so, however, there has been a resurgence of the old national-states-and-national-struggles-are-out-of-date position and other views not unlike it, some representing cross-fertilization from the conservative decline-of-the-national-state theories discussed previously. Apart from Eric Hobsbawm and perhaps one or two other traditional Marxists, the exponents of this general position tend to be neo-Marxists (a term which designates – and usually self-designates – writers who have one foot in Marxism and the other planted safely in some non-Marxist body of social or philosophical thought). Among the neo-Marxists, three broad currents of ideas seem to agree in arguing the decline of the state.

One of these currents of ideas is merely an updated form of the old tendency called economism, the view that political processes in general are not of critical importance in capitalist society and political institutions do not deserve serious attention. The original 'economists' in turn-of-the-century Russia advocated economic struggles and downplayed political struggles. In the later debates with the Luxemburgians, Bukharin, and others who, during the World War, proclaimed the decline of states, Lenin labelled their point of view 'imperialist economism', meaning economism suited to the new era of imperialism or monopoly capitalism: it claimed that, since capitalism in its imperialist stage is now fully international, the merely national state is losing its significance, and struggles focusing on this target, such as national struggles, are declining in importance.

Today's economism makes a strikingly similar argument. To begin with it resurrects the old formula about capitalism having become international, not national. Second, it focuses on the activities and significance of multinational corporations and argues that these corporations, which it considers to be the characteristic entities of present-day capitalism, are able to function in all capitalist states and to cross state boundaries at will; hence they somehow reduce the state to insignificance. Thirdly, a link-up is made with the original economism by describing the geography of the entire world as, in essence, a uniform surface, not really divided up into discrete political spaces. Political boundaries in no way inhibit the flow of multinational economic processes. Thus there is now a world-space in which economic distance alone governs the relationship between the centres of advanced capitalism and the peripheral regions.

There is some irony in the fact that Lenin's term, 'uneven development', is now the code for this purely economic model of the world: ironic because Lenin more than any other theorist in 20th Century Marxism underscored the political component in world capitalism of the imperialist epoch. Uneven development, for neo-economism, is on the one hand a static concept denoting the unevenness of the landscape of development, and on the other hand a purely diffusionist concept of steady flows outwards from the centres of advanced capitalism, flows in which distance, not political differentiation, determines the rate and direction of change. Thus what was once a slope of decreasing development within a single capitalist country, as, a century ago, from industrial southern England to northern Scotland or from western Russia to Siberia, is now a slope extending out to the opposite ends of the earth, and the intra-state spatial expansion described for Britain by Marx in *Capital* and for Russia by Lenin in *The Development of Capitalism in Russia* is supposed to have extended itself onto a world scale. This ignores or even denies that there is a difference between uneven development within a country and uneven development across state boundaries. And the activities of multinational corporations in the farthest corners of the earth today are supposed by neo-economism to be merely a scale enlargement of the activities of intra-national corporations in the farthest corners of their own countries yesterday. So the political forms in the peripheral parts of the world today – classical colonialism as in Puerto Rico, new-style colonialism as in South Africa and Timor, and neo-colonialism as in most other countries of the Third World – are considered to be irrelevant, or nearly so. For the neo-economists, the political map of the world no longer holds any interest.

A thorough critique of neo-economism is much needed, but it cannot be ventured in the present volume. It is needed because this is an important strain of radical thought which denies the relevance of political processes to the extent that it tries to construct nominally Marxist theories in which political processes are suppressed. Sometimes it employs such theories to downplay the importance of political action and to inject pessimism into such action, suggesting that this kind of struggle cannot accomplish much so long as the real bastions, the multinational corporations and related economic structures, remain unconquered. A critique of this position would incorporate, among other things, the following arguments (some but not all of which are sketched in Chapter 4 of this book): first, capitalism cannot function without state power; such power is no less critical to its activities today than it was in the past; and such power resides in the state and basically nowhere else. Second, multinational corporations today, like the international and colonial corporations of prior times (the East India Companies, United Fruit, Lever Bros., etc.), are based in the advanced capitalist states: they are multinational only in their scale of accumulation, accumulation which very largely flows back to the home office and its surrounding state – a state which also plays a very powerful political role in the corporation's work, as the US did for ITT in Brazil and Chile. Third, the activities of capitalism on a world scale cannot accurately be analysed if we imagine that spatial relations and locations have only an economic significance; that uneven development is the basic dynamic; and that imperialism, with its political characteristics like colonial and neocolonial states and politico–military interventions, is erased from our mental map of the world.

A second national-states-are-out-of-date position is associated with metaphysical neo-Marxists like Giovanni Arrighi, Immanuel Wallerstein, and the latter's associates at the Fernand Braudel Center for the Study of Economies, Historical Systems, and Civilizations, of the State University of New York. This position, or family of related positions, mystifies, or re-mystifies, capitalism, so that it becomes something different from and greater in scale than all the merely empirical processes taking place on the earth's surface.

Wallerstein's group employs what it calls 'world system analysis'. This is a form of neo-Marxism distinguished – I employ caricature here, but not unfairly so – by its insistence that the capitalist world system, at the global scale, determines all partial processes, such as politics, and all part-regions, such as states. This is very close to pure Hegelian holism. The capitalist world-system is not defined by its parts and their interrelations. Rather, this system is something greater than parts and relations, and it determines their nature, behaviour, and historical evolution. 'It' is not empirically identified, and thus closely resembles Hegel's undefinable 'world spirit' (and other undiscoverable entities of romantic philosophy, like the 'life force'). Marx's critique of Hegel's mystical and holistic theory of the state as 'spirit' might serve also as a critique of the metaphysics of 'world-system analysis'.[25]

In any event, the 'world-system' school puts forward some empirical propositions which supposedly derive from the higher 'world-system' processes, and which have concrete and troublesome meaning in the real world, not least for national liberation struggles. First, since the capitalist world system maintains in some mysterious way a hegemonic control of political processes throughout the world, no state exists outside its sphere of control, and no state in the entire world, therefore, is really socialist.[26] Second, sovereignty is an illusion, since the overarching world system controls all states.[27] Third, decolonization did not result from liberation movements, nor these from the peculiarities of colonial oppression and superexploitation; rather, decolonization occurred simply when the capitalist world-system had entered a cyclic phase – Wallerstein believes firmly in repetitive historical cycles – in which 'informal empire' seemed more desirable than colonies.[28] Fourth, and by the same token, all anticolonial revolutions, without exception, have failed to achieve fundamental social change.[29] And finally, as a kind of summing-up of all of the foregoing, the state is not of fundamental importance and struggles for state-sovereignty are somewhat frivolous.[30]

A related position is Giovanni Arrighi's peculiar 'geometry' of world processes under capitalism. Arrighi is an admitted Kantian, and he believes that the basic forces determining the historical trajectory of the modern world are ultimately spatial, in an absolutist, Newtonian or Kantian sense. Thus he deduces what he calls the 'crisis of the nation-state', the latter seen as a mere spatial cell in the geometry of the world. In this geometry, scalar forces like imperialism – Hobson's concept, not Lenin's, which Arrighi dismisses – are seen as acting independently of other scalar forces like capitalism.[31] The 'crisis of the nation-state' derives from these world-scale absolute-spatial forces, which seem likely soon to erase states from the geometrician's blackboard. In sum, these are two forms of neo-Marxism which postulate not empirically observable processes, but world-embracing metaphysical forces, as the explanation for what one theorist (Arrighi) believes to be the decline of the national state and the other (Wallerstein) the insignificance of the state and of struggles to control it.

A third point of view argues, somewhat paradoxically, that the national state is declining because nationalism is on the increase. This view is widely held among conservatives and is best represented among neo-Marxists by Tom Nairn, whose theory of nationalism is criticized in Chapter 3. This general position really goes back to conservative theories of nationalism and to one early Marxist position, that put forward by Otto Bauer before the First World War. (I discuss Bauer's theory briefly in Chapter 2.) Nationalism is seen as an ethnic force, even a psychological force (in the Germanic sense of 'folk-psychology'), and not as a form or product of class struggle nor even as a force that is in some other way a vector of political, social, and economic processes. Ethno-psychological nationalism is supposed to operate autonomously to create national struggle and (Bauer dissenting here) to fight for and create nation states, that is, states coincident with culturally defined nationalties, in a process, real or mythical, which is sometimes called the 'principle of nationalities'. This is the principle that each nationality must have its own state and each state its own nationality. But, the argument continues, this same ethnic nationalism has the power to destroy states which are multinational or complex in ethnic terms, and it is this latter force which predominates today. Most of the large states of the world are, we are told, being broken up by ethnic nationalism, because all of them are to one extent or another multinational, or culturally complex. Witness the separatist movements within Canada, Britain, France, Spain, and the new states of the Third World.

But this argument fails for two reasons: facts do not support it and theory does not render it reasonable. Most states of the world were not created by ethnic groups acting alone, and relatively few liberation struggles, past and present, have been grounded in one culture or nationality. It is really a myth of conservative ideology that typical national struggles are, or were, rooted in the 'folk', their 'mythology', their 'traditional leaders', and the like. (By this I do not mean that cultural issues and struggles are unimportant in liberation movements. The fight to retain the Spanish language, for instance, has been a crucial part of the struggle in Puerto Rico.) National movements typically arise either in some combination of a rising bourgeoisie and one or more oppressed producing classes or, in modern times, a struggle by one or more oppressed and superexploited classes fighting to remove the burden by gaining control of the state in a process of national liberation. In either case the most basic forces impelling the national movement are class forces, not ethnic forces. However, the national movements may cleave along ethnic lines, for any number of well-known reasons, and this is easily misinterpreted as evidence that ethnic conflicts *per se* are at the root of the struggle.

I am of course oversimplifying, and there indeed are national conflicts which are grounded in ethnic conflict, although ordinary capitalist oppression and exploitation is almost always behind the ethnic conflict. But ethnic nationalism is not typical, and when it occurs it is rarely the basal force. Moreover, no one has ever produced a defensible theory to explain why cultures, ethnic groups, nationalities, should, in fact, invoke the 'principle of nationalities' – that is, why they should demand their own states instead of accepting equal membership in a democratic multinational state, unless exploitation and oppression against them and not against some other community impels them to go it alone. Tom Nairn tries to produce such a theory, and much of my Chapter 3 is devoted to showing that theory to be invalid.

Finally, we come to the position put forward by Eric Hobsbawm, a respected Marxist historian who believes that national states are crumbling under the pressure of 'fissiparous nationalism', that states in general are losing their importance, and that national struggles for state power are now, quite simply, irrational. Hobsbawm's argument is many-faceted and subtle, and it gains special strength from his thorough command of modern European history. It is now considered by some to be the most serious endeavour by a Marxist, using Marxist theory, to attack all modern nationalism, including the reactionary and the silly forms of nationalism, but including also the national liberation struggles of our times. All these are declared to be irrational.

Hobsbawm's argument will be analysed in detail in Chapter 4. For now, I will summarize it very superficially in a few words. Hobsbawm means by 'nationalism' the process of state-formation and the process of state-enlargement by aggrandizement of neighbouring territory, but not colonial aggrandizement which he appears to consider a different process. Nationalism includes a political movement, a concrete national struggle, and a nationalist ideology. The ideology may be democratic or undemocratic, realistic or unrealistic, but it is a quite definite ideological message, one that extols the national collective, invokes the idea of national unity, and considers other nations to be inferior to one's own.[32] This definite sort of social process was a rational part of the overall development of capitalism in 19th Century Europe. It was not just 'bourgeois nationalism' but it was indeed associated with the rise of the bourgeoisie and – crucially, for Hobsbawm – the formation of states which were appropriate to a certain scale of economy, the 'national economy'. But now, in the 20th Century, the economy of capitalism is international, not national, and national states no longer have the crucial tie to a national-scale economy. Hence the existing states are in danger of splitting up under the pressures of ethnic nationalism, and those which were born via decolonization tended to be 'mini-states' because, again, of the irrelevance of size to the present-day form of capitalism. And, finally, national movements which are fighting today to form new states are irrational. This is the central thread of

Hobsbawm's theory, though it is much more complex and subtle than I have conveyed.

Yet in the last analysis Hobsbawm's view is not entirely different from the old First-World-War views that were criticized by Lenin as 'imperialist economism', and the view epitomized in Luxemburg's comment about 'aspirations that have long since been transformed by . . . social evolution into their reactionary opposites'. Hobsbawm does not say that national liberation movements are 'reactionary', but he questions their 'rationality'. Yet he is, withal, a strong socialist and no friend of colonialism or neocolonialism. These and other contradictions will claim our attention in Chapter 4.

**The Argument of This Book**

It is pertinent here to repeat some of the words of the paragraph which opened this chapter. Most of the topics dealt with in this book are in the realm of theory, but theory is not written for its own sake, and the underlying purpose of the present work is to fashion a set of theoretical tools to help understand why some national struggles in the modern world are progressive and others are reactionary. Those who maintain, whether from a conservative, a Neo-Marxist, or a Marxist perspective, that national struggle is out of date and the national state is, or is fast becoming, an anachronism, are suggesting that *no* national struggle in the modern world is truly progressive, and that *all* are simply outmoded and insignificant; and whether or not they make this sweeping judgment, their theoretical positions make it for them.

Of all the theoretical positions about nationalism which have an impact on practice, on struggle, this one is probably the most critically important. It erodes support for anti-colonial national struggles, like the struggle in Puerto Rico. It renders more difficult the fight for true independence in neocolonies and the fight to preserve true independence in free but embattled countries like Nicaragua and Angola. And, paradoxically because it is overtly anti-nationalist, it removes the theoretical tools we have for identifying, analysing, and then opposing the truly reactionary nationalisms which dot the world's landscape, simply because it lumps all national movements together as neither progressive nor reactionary but, rather, as anachronistic.

I try to answer the national-struggles-and-national-states-and-national-movements-are-anachronistic position – it is really a galaxy of positions – at various places in this book. The most fundamental response is this: national struggle is one very important form of the struggle for state power. Capitalism, like every other class mode of production, must control the state in order to organize and police the behaviour of classes, the class relations of production, the process of production, the accumulation and disposal of surplus, and much more besides. When capitalism ceases to control the state it ceases to exist. Or, stated differently, when the capitalist state dissolves, it will not dissolve into a stateless 'capitalist world-system' or a capitalist world economy. It will transform itself into the socialist state or dissolve into barbarism.

The concrete arguments are laid out in detail in Chapters 3 and 4. Chapter 3 is a critique of Nairn's view of nationalism which supports his thesis that Great Britain is breaking up under the tensions of ethnic nationalism, and that modern states in general are threatened by this irrational force. My response is to question the theory behind these assertions. I show how it is grounded in the broader theory of the diffusion of 'modernization', which I criticise. It is essentially a psychological theory of nationalism which disengages the political process from class struggle. Finally, Nairn's argument relates how it supposedly came to pass that the centrifugal diffusion of 'modernization', and its discontents, somehow reversed direction and brought nationalism back into Britain and other advanced-capitalist states, there to 'break them up'. This argument I attack in its turn, simply showing that none of this happened.

But the strongest and most consequential statement of the general position that national struggles are passé is Hobsbawm's, and all of Chapter 4 is devoted to an analysis and critique of his view. He puts forth four main theses. The first is the assertion that national movements were rational in the last century but are so no longer. I raise the question whether 19th-Century national movements really did work towards 'rational' nation-states, of the appropriate size for a 'national economy', showing that mini-states existed then as they do now, and that state-making tended to be essentially conjunctural and pragmatic. Even the classic nation-states were in fact seats of huge empires, which were their own 'national economies'. Finally, I reject Hobsbawm's interpretation of the decolonization process as one which created mini-states: it created states roughly congruent with pre-existing colonies, and what mini-colonies existed became mini-states, for a reason that had very little to do with judgments about economic rationality.

Hobsbawm's second thesis asserts that sovereignty has lost much of its importance in the present environment of internationalized capitalism. I reply by showing that present-day capitalism needs the state as much as ever it did before, and that neocolonial states in particular need to be strong to play an appropriate policing role in Third World class relations to ensure the continued flow of super-profits.

Hobsbawm's third thesis is that struggles against neocolonialism are not national struggles; that the elimination of most classical colonies means the virtual end of genuine national liberation struggles. I reply that neocolonies do not have real sovereignty, and part, though not all, of their liberation must consist in fighting free of external political domination and economic control, this being a national struggle.

Hobsbawm's fourth thesis concerns the history of Marxist ideas on the national question. He maintains that Marxists have always tended to relate to national movements in a 'pragmatic' way, that Lenin's policies on the national and colonial questions were indeed 'pragmatic', and that Lenin in fact had no theory of national struggle: merely a set of morally and politically sound but nonetheless 'pragmatic' judgments. In responding to Hobsbawm I develop at length an analysis of Lenin's theory and show that pragmatism had nothing to do with it. In fact, Lenin developed the skeletal structure of the modern Marxist theory of national struggle, the theory which has been put into use as a principled (not 'pragmatic') basis for literally all Marxist-informed national liberation struggles in the modern world. I show that Lenin entirely reversed the pattern of thought characteristic of post-classical (or 'Second International') Marxism. He showed, first, that national struggles intensify, instead of declining, as capitalism enters its imperialist, fully international, phase; and second, that national liberation struggles are part of the world struggle for socialism, and not, as previously thought, merely belated bourgeois-democratic revolutions which must eventuate in capitalist states or (as Luxemburg and Bukharin, among others, argued) must fail altogether.

In Chapter 7 of this book I return to the same argument. Lenin's theory of national struggle has been misunderstood by many modern Marxists besides Hobsbawm. It is important that we set the record straight: that we understand the theory and understand also why it has proven so powerful in the liberation of Third World countries. Beyond this, those who either misunderstand this theory or neglect it are essentially the same critics who assert, with Hobsbawm, Nairn, Debray, Ehrenreich, and many others, that there *is* no Marxist theory of national struggle – of nationalism. One of the aims of this book is to prove them wrong.

## Sixth Problem: What is the Theoretical Status of the Concept 'National Minority', and Why Do Some Immigrant Minorities Remain Unassimilated?

### Traditional Beliefs, Conservative and Marxist

It is very difficult to understand what is happening in the various types of minority communities in the capitalist world today, and to develop progressive practice in and relating to these communities, without an adequate theory. But the most widely accepted theories in both the conservative and Marxist traditions do not at all suffice. This holds true for minorities of all types, but it is painfully true for minority communities which are formed, and thereafter sustained, by colonialism. Colonialism, for Marxists, is the use of political oppression to enforce a situation in which abnormally high profits can be extracted from the labour of a colonized people, or from their lands and natural resources. Marxists have no difficulty identifying the minority communities which exist in this condition, communities in ghettos, 'native reserves' (or 'reservations'), 'bantustans', migrant-labour camps or barracks, and so on. But Marxists have not really learned how to conceptualize these communities in political terms, and this means, above all, understanding the content and importance of their demands for political self-determination; in sum, the national question. Conservatives, for their part, do not usually recognize colonialism in most of its manifestations, and their theories about these minorities (and others) tend to be far off the mark.

In this book I will put forward a Marxist theory applicable to minorities created and sustained by colonialism. The basic theory was outlined by Marx and Engels in their analysis of the Irish community in England, and it was developed further and generalized to the colonial world by Lenin. However, a sharply different theory of minorities was laid down by Stalin, and this theory – it is now universally called the theory of national minorities – has gained much wider circulation among Marxists today. Stalin's theory badly distorts the character of minorities formed and sustained by colonialism, but this fact has not been clearly understood; nor is it realized that another and more applicable theory exists. In Chapter 5 I will discuss both theories and show why the one is essentially useless and the other is very powerful. Chapter 6 then focuses on one kind of colonialism-related minority, the ghettoized communities of immigrant workers, mainly from Third World areas, which are now found in every advanced capitalist country of the world. In Chapter 6 the emphasis is on empirical characteristics of these communities and the nature of the national struggle within them. The case of Puerto Rican migrant communities in the United States is the main focus of both chapters: an example, and also a case of great importance in its own right. For all of these cases I will show why the theory of 'national minorities', and the related theory of 'assimilation', are quite inappropriate.

In conservative European thought of the 19th and early 20th Centuries, a 'national minority' or 'minority nationality' – the two terms were usually considered synonymous – was a linguistically and culturally distinct minority within a given state. Conservative scholarship in these matters tended to be very close to policymaking, and in none of the great European states of the last century was there any policy of granting independence to these minorities, under any circumstances whatever. (Sweden's granting of independence to Norway at the turn of the century was a partial exception.) Therefore, discussions about national minorities either concerned issues such as civil equality and rights governing the use of the minority's language, or they concerned the threat of secession. Minorities tended to be called 'national', instead of merely 'tribal' or 'cultural' or 'linguistic', when they seemed to have political palpability; when they invoked, or threatened to invoke, the 'principle of nationalities', which demands state independence under the slogan 'each nationality its state, each state its nationality'. While partisans of secession tended to invoke theories showing why their 'nation' warranted independence, the mainstream theoreticians of the states concerned tended to put forward theories explaining why the community concerned was merely a 'national minority', not a 'nation', and therefore was undeserving of independence. In a word, the theory of national minorities was implicitly the theory of non-nations, the theory which justified the denial of the right of self-determination and put forward alternative policies regarding the governance of any given minority.

The creation of new states in Europe after the First World War was the first important instance in which policy-makers discussed how to turn national minorities into self-governing nation states, and during and after this period there was a lot of scholarly concern about the right of self-determination for these European national minorities. However, as I will explain in Chapters 3 and 4, the post-war state-making process was not primarily a matter of the national question, nor was the famous Wilsonian principle of self-determination put into play as a purely ethical, democratic principle. The new states were created out of defeated and disintegrated empires: Germany, Austria–Hungary, Turkey, and the western part of formerly Tsarist Russia. Therefore new states of one sort or another had to be created in any case, given that the old imperial governments were not to be restored and the empires reconstituted. While there were serious attempts – aided by serious scholarship – to make the new states congruent with cultural communities, this seems to have been motivated mainly by a concern to create states which would be sufficiently stable to render them immune to Bolshevism. So conservative theorizing about national minorities remained essentially a matter of internal state organization, not of self-determination, and it remains so today.

A completely different theory of minorities emerged in the US and the other advanced capitalist countries into which large numbers of immigrants were flowing. This was the famous doctrine of the 'melting pot', the explicit theory that all immigrants would be assimilated into the host nationality in all important respects, including language. (The theory was simply not invoked for African slaves, Mexicans, and other non-Europeans.) Underlying the theory, today as in the past, are a number of crucial assumptions about why people migrate and about the social environment in the host country. Non-Marxist social theorists, with rather few exceptions, adopt a view of human decision-making which Marxists label 'voluntarism'. Applied to the theory of minorities, this becomes a pair of basic propositions. First, democratic capitalist societies create enough opportunity so that anyone can achieve any reasonable life goal which one wills for oneself; and failure is due, conversely, to a lack of will. Second, people immigrate to this kind of society voluntarily. They do so for the obvious reason that life is better here than it is in the home country. These are not forced migrations. Following from these propositions is the prediction that each individual migrant will undergo – voluntarily – an assimilation process, and at the aggregate level, communities of immigrants will only temporarily remain nationally distinct. The ghettos, in other words, will dissolve or will serve as receptacles for successive national groups of immigrants.

The theory of assimilation cannot cope with the huge modern migrations of workers, mainly from Third World areas, into the cities of the advanced capitalist countries. In no case has one of these in-coming national communities become assimilated, and the ghettos in which each was initially forced to live are still, in almost all cases, filled with the same nationally distinct group (except where there has been forced relocation as a result of gentrification or apartheid). The liberal form of this theory invokes the explanation that racist ideology accounts for the lack of assimilation of these groups, but racism itself is deemed a transient, curable condition, so that the inevitable assimilation will soon occur, as predicted. Thus the theory of minorities which is applied to immigrants, as opposed to indigenous minorities, is merely a theory of the dissolution of minorities. And this explains why the struggles of minority groups for self-determination are rather consistently misunderstood. Self-determination is an irrational goal if a national community has immigrated voluntarily and with the intent of becoming assimilated.

Among Marxists, the theory of minorities which is most widely accepted today is a relic of the kind of Marxist thought which prevailed before the First World War and is now quite out of date. Like conservative theory, it is dominated by the idea of the 'melting pot', the theory of assimilation. Marxists in those times believed that modern capitalism is erasing national differences, absorbing minorities in the national states which contain them, assimilating immigrant workers into the host nationalities, and, overall, blending all nations together into an international capitalist world in which neither the bourgeoisie nor the proletariat would be seriously divided by nationality. The Bolsheviks shared this world view but with an important reservation: in backward and oppressed areas like Russia and the colonial world there would still be viable and progressive national movements. Therefore they demanded, in their party programme, that the nations in the Russian empire be granted the right of self-determination, of secession. This demand occasioned some Olympian polemics among Russian revolutionaries, mainly pitting Leninists against those who (with Luxemburg) opposed the right of self-determination and those who (with the Bundists) demanded, not state independence, but national autonomy within the empire and, more vexing still, organizational autonomy for all national sectors within the party.

The main polemical salvo against national-autonomism was an article written by Stalin in 1913, 'Marxism and the National Question'. It needs to be said of this article that it is considered to be an important theoretical statement by all Marxists, including those who have nothing favourable to say about Stalin, and by many non-Marxist scholars as well.[32] But contained in this article is an assimilationist theory of minorities whose validity depends on the larger validity of the theory that national differences are weakening, nations are inter-blending, and that nationalism is disappearing – a theory disproven by events in 1914 and renounced by Lenin in his later writings on the national question. It is this out-dated theory, conveyed down to our own time in Stalin's authoritative (for many reasons) essay, 'Marxism and the National Question', which is the single most serious problem for the Marxist theory of minorities today.

Stalin argued, in essence, that the Bolsheviks recognized only two categories in the national question: nations and non-nations. Nations had the right of secession, and, given this potential trajectory towards independent statehood, they had the right (which, hopefully, they would not exercise) to organize their revolutionary party as a separate entity, a national movement. But groups which were not real nations had no such rights, and could demand no form or degree of autonomy. (Later, in the Soviet Union, many kinds of partial autonomy for national groups were recognized, but this tends to be forgotten by those whose dogma is the 1913 Stalin.) To defend this position, Stalin put forward two arguments. The first was his definition of a nation. The second was his characterization of non-nations, which he called national minorities (a common term in those days). In defining the nation he asserted that it was something which appeared, historically, in only one period: the time of early or rising capitalism. This meant that a 'national minority' in 1913 could not grow into a nation. Like all national minorities, it would become assimilated into the host nation, at least to the extent that it could claim no political autonomy. This, then, was the Stalinist theory of national minorities. Any nationally distinctive community which is not a nation can expect to become, in all politically important respects, assimilated, in the course of the general world-wide process of internationalization under capitalism.

Marxists have compiled a very good record on the national question. Not often have they supported reactionary nationalism and not often have they failed to support genuine movements for national liberation.[33] But this has been accomplished largely in spite of Stalin's theory of nations and national minorities. My point in discussing it here is to explain why the theory needs the kind of thoroughgoing analysis and criticism which I attempt to give it here (mainly in Chapter 5). Its most serious and fundamental flaw, from the point of view of the discussion in the present work, is that it perpetuates the very wrong ideas about minorities which were held by Marxists and conservatives alike in the period before the First World War (a war which in any case disproved the myth that nations, nationalism, and national struggles are disappearing in modern capitalism). The pre-war period was a time when it was thought that most minority problems, like most other national problems, were solving themselves through the universal solvent of modern 'international' capitalism. This has not happened.

Marx and Engels' very different view of minorities did not at all assume assimilation to be the inevitable or normal outcome of events. It was elaborated somewhat by Lenin in his theoretical writings about the national question after 1914 and in his practical and theoretical work in fashioning the Soviet Union. But this alternative theory is not widely known, and most Marxists (at least in capitalist countries) believe, or simply assume, that the Stalinist 'melting pot' theory is the classical formulation. And when they fight for minority rights, as they usually do, they tend to imagine that it is a matter of setting aside theory in the name of 'realism'. But theory should be a guide to practice, not a hindrance.

The Stalin view is still a very serious hindrance to Marxist practice in certain kinds of national problems involving minorities. It has interfered with an understanding of the struggle of native peoples, including native Americans, for self-determination. It has hindered theory and practice in another category of problem associated with the kind of minority created by long-distance labour migration from the colonial and neocolonial world to the centres of advanced capitalism, a total of perhaps forty million worker-migrants, including two million Puerto Ricans in the US. In Stalin's theory, all such minorities are doomed to assimilation: the melting pot. Such assimilation has not occurred, however. Rather the opposite has tended to be the case, with ghettoized immigrant minorities fighting successfully against the destruction of their communities and their cultures, and fighting as well for the liberation of the colonial or neocolonial country which is their homeland. An important example is the case of Puerto Ricans who have been forced to migrate from the colony of Puerto Rico to the cities of the US. Other instances stretch around the world: for example, Mexicans in the US, Algerians in France, Turks in West Germany, Koreans in Japan. Minorities of this sort, in Stalin's 1913 theory, have lost their membership in their own nation, and to struggle as members of that nation, and for the liberation of that nation, must somehow give evidence of 'narrow nationalism', or 'Bundism'. But to apply this dogma is to use Marxism against, not for, the liberation of oppressed peoples – a contradiction in terms.

### The Argument of This Book

Chapter 5 of this book deals with the Marxist theory of national struggle as it applies to minorities in general and to one minority in particular: the Puerto Ricans in the United States. The point of departure is a disagreement among Marxists as to the nationality of two million Puerto Ricans who now live in the United States. Some Marxists argue that this community is no longer part of the Puerto Rican nation. It is, they say, a 'national minority' (using Stalin's term) and thus an integral part of the North American nation. Therefore it should not organize itself in political and community forms of struggle which are explicitly Puerto Rican: this is 'national exclusiveness', 'narrow nationalism', etc. The reply is: there is no valid argument, from Marxist theory or from the facts surrounding the colonized Puerto Rican nation and the forced migration of 40% of its people to the United States, which justifies the judgment that Puerto Ricans in the United States have lost or are losing their Puerto Rican nationality. Therefore there is no valid principle which decrees that this community should give up its national forms of struggle, and its integral participation in the struggle to liberate Puerto Rico. This is an issue of theory with immense political implications. And it is an issue that has been debated in many other cases of this general form, in France, Japan, and elsewhere.

To resolve issues of this sort one must have a defensible theory which describes the dynamics of minorities in general. The argument of Chapter 5 is an attempt to show that Stalin's theory does not serve; that another Marxist theory does do so; and that this latter theory does not employ the idea of 'national minorities' as a special form of community which must, necessarily, dissolve through assimilation into the surrounding or host nation. I show that Stalin's theory is rooted in two propositions which are invalid. The first asserts that there is an absolutely general and invariable definition of 'nation', such that one can explicitly judge all communities as to whether they are indeed nations or merely fall in the residual category of 'national minority', the category which, for Stalin, forbids not merely self-determination but national forms of struggle. I show that Stalin's concept of nation, accurate for turn-of-the-century European nation-states, is not applicable to the majority of present-day nations, least of all to colonial nations. Stalin's second proposition is the historical principle that national minorities are undergoing an inevitable process of dissolution, of assimilation. I point out that this was true at the beginning of the century under many circumstances of developing capitalism (such as long-distance labour migrations to European and North American industrial centres), but not in all circumstances then, nor in many circumstances today.

We then turn to the alternative theory which, by contrast, relates minority dynamics to the historical processes of the 20th century, the era of imperialism. This is Lenin's theory of national struggle, which is a sub-assembly of his theory of imperialism and contains its own sub-assembly: a theory of minorities. Marx and Engels had shown much earlier that British colonialism led to the strengthening, not weakening, of the national struggle in Ireland and among the Irish in England who, said Engels, remained Irish in nationality. Lenin then built the general model. Imperialism leads not to a decline of national struggle, nations, etc., but to intensified national struggle, including inter-imperial national struggle and colonial liberation struggles. The arena of colonial struggles is not determined by a pattern of capitalist nations and 'national minorities', but by colonialism, which creates new national forms. In particular, said Lenin, forced migrants are 'foreign workers', not immigrants of the older (European) sort. Today we can thus argue that Puerto Ricans in the United States, like many other groups forced to migrate, under colonial or neocolonial conditions, to centres of advanced capitalism, tend to retain their nationality in the ghettos, reservations, and barracks in which they live.

Chapter 6 builds an empirical theory to explain and describe the condition of ghettoized minorities and to show precisely why they do not dissolve through assimilation. The argument begins, in essence, where Marx, Engels, and Lenin left off. It shows that monopoly capitalism in the 20th century, but particularly in the period after 1945, finds it necessary to greatly intensify the importation of 'foreign workers' as a modern evolution of the process of imperialism in general and colonialism in particular. Colonialism is a political environment for super-exploitation, that is, artificially low-wage labour, and modern capitalism finds it to be as necessary to maintain a massive super-exploited labour force at places central to the system as it does in peripheral regions, that is, the world of colonies and neocolonies. I argue then that the ghettos and comparable spaces of segregation (South African townships, migrant-labour camps, etc.) are maintained through a political control process akin to colonial rule though not identical to it – this is not literal 'internal colonialism', except in South Africa – but nonetheless a process serving the colonial function of maintaining a population of workers in a condition in which they are forced to accept super-exploitation. This process is central to modern capitalism, so we can assume that forced migration will continue, ghettos will not disappear, and nationally distinct populations of super-exploited workers will remain or grow larger. Assimilation will not take place because, for capitalism to continue super-exploiting this worker-population, it must enforce spatial and cultural segregation. This leads to forced culture change of a non-assimilative sort (even if a language change occurs, as it often does under colonialism). And resistance to it is always a struggle for self-determination: a national struggle. In cases like that of Puerto Ricans in US cities, the national struggle in the ghetto is part of the larger struggle for the liberation of the national territory. The final step in this argument is to show that the struggles in ghettoized communities are, indeed, part of the struggle for workers' rights and for socialism in the host country.

This book does not try to pronounce upon the myriad kinds and cases of the national question which are to be found in the world today. This holds true for minority struggles as for other national struggles. Our main concern is the underlying theory and its application to one struggle: that of Puerto Ricans in the United States and in the colony of Puerto Rico. But what we will have to say about the theory of minorities has important implication for many kinds of minority struggles in many parts of the world, struggles of indigenous communities (including Native Americans) as well as immigrant communities. This is one of the 'six problems for the theory of nationalism' whose solution should lead to more progressive and more effective practice on the national question.

# Notes

1. L. Snyder, *The Meaning of Nationalism* (1957).
2. The law was passed by the US Congress in 1950, ratified in an artificial plebiscite – independence was not on the ballot and *independentistas* boycotted the process – in 1952, and accepted as 'self-determination' by the UN in 1953 (under strong US pressure). In 1954 Lolita Lebron and three others from the Nationalist

Party attacked Congress to bring world attention to the situation. See M. Maldonado-Denis, *Puerto Rico: A Socio-Historic Interpretation* (1972).

3. Snyder, *Meaning of Nationalism*, p. 3.

4. *Ibid.*

5. A partial exception was the treatment of the intensified expansionism of the period 1870–1914, and particularly the so-called scramble for Africa. Conservative scholars often view this process as something rooted in ideology, an irrational or whimsical desire to extend the power and prestige of one's nation by territorial expansion, a kind of nationalism. See, e.g., Carlton Hayes, 'Nationalism', in E. Seligman (ed.), *Encyclopedia of the Social Sciences* (1933). See also Royal Inst. of International Affairs, *Nationalism* (1939).

6. Royal Institute, *Nationalism*.

7. I discuss these constraints in 'The Dissenting Tradition', *Annals Assoc. of Amer. Geographers* and in 'Some Principles of Ethnogeography', *Philosophy in Geography* (1979).

8. For example, anti-colonialist writings of George Padmore were banned during the 1950s in the British West Indies and perhaps in all British colonies.

9. See, for instance, A. Smith. *Theories of Nationalism* (1971), for a review of many such theories (including Smith's own). See also: K. Deutsch, *Nationalism and its Alternatives* (1969); E. Gellner, *Thought and Change* (1964); E. Kedourie, *Nationalism in Asia and Africa* (1970); H. Kohn, 'Nationalism', in *International Encyclopedia of the Social Sciences*, 2nd ed. (1968), p. 11; K. R. Minogue, *Nationalism* (1970).

10. The period I call 'post-classical' in this book is usually considered to be the period of the Second International. However, the Second International has survived in one form or another down to the present, so the periodicity is ambiguous. More crucially, I think, the beginning of the First World War, in 1914, and the development of Lenin's theory of imperialism, in 1914–16, seem to mark a decisive break-point between the post-classical and modern periods in Marxist thought. The 'classical' period, of course, is the time of Marx and Engels, and ends with Engels' death in 1895. The outbreak of the World War demonstrated that many post-classical theoretical doctrines were invalid (or were no longer valid), while Lenin's theory of imperialism provided the foundation for an understanding of capitalism as it had become by 1914. For the theory of nationalism in particular, as I will argue throughout this book, there is a clearly demarcated post-classical period with its own dominant theoretical position, or family of related positions. Lenin's theory of imperialism contained, as I show in Chapter 5, a comprehensive theory of nationalism, distinctively different from Lenin's earlier view, and the core of the mainstream Marxist theory of today.

11. I criticize the Eurocentric-diffusionist view of history in 'Where Was Capitalism Born?' *Radical Geography* (1977). The argument is summarized in Chapter 7, below.

12. See my 'Where Was Capitalism Born?' and J. Blaut, 'Imperialism: The Marxist Theory and Its Evolution' *Antipode* 7, 1 (1975).

13. H. Davis, *Toward a Marxist Theory of Nationalism* (1978). Also see his now classical work, *Nationalism and Socialism: Marxist and Labor Theories of Nationalism to 1917* (1967).

14. Kedourie, *Nationalism*, p. 28.

15. T. Nairn, *The Break-Up of Britain* (1977).

16. *Ibid.*, pp. 345–348.

17. See M. Townsend, 'Hitler and the Revival of German Nationalism', in E. Earle (ed.) *Nationalism and Internationalism* (1950); also Y. Goblet, *Political Geography and the World Map* (1955).

18. E.H. Carr, *Conditions of Peace* (1942), pp. 63–64.

19. *Ibid.*

20. A. Cobban, *National Self-Determination* (1951), p. 133.

21. 'Foreword' to the anthology *The Polish Question and the Socialist Movement* in H. Davis (ed.), *The National Question: Selected Writings of Rosa Luxemburg* (1976), p. 94.

22. Quoted in Davis, *Toward a Marxist Theory of Nationalism* p. 84.

23. Quoted in *The National Question: Selected Writings of Rosa Luxemburg*, p. 303.

24. Quoted in V. I. Lenin, 'A Caricature of Marxism and Imperialist Economism', *Works* 23, p. 37.

25. K. Marx, 'Contribution to the Critique of Hegel's Philosophy of Law,' Marx and Engels *Works* 13. For instance, Marx witheringly criticizes Hegel's practice of inverting subject and predicate so that empty or mystical categories, like the Hegelian 'idea', 'spirit', 'will' etc., seem to have genuine empirical attributes: 'Instead of conceiving them as predicates of their subjects, Hegel gives the predicates an independent existence . . .'(p. 23); 'He does not say "the monarch's will is the final decision", but "the will's final decision is the monarch". The first proposition is empirical. The second perverts the empirical fact into a metaphysical axiom' (p. 25). Compare Wallerstein: 'The unfolding of the institutional structures of the world-system – the classes, the states, the peoples, the households – has been reflected in the cultural mosaic of the world-system,' in 'Patterns and Prospectives of the Capitalist World-Economy', *Contemporary Marxism* 9 (1984). p. 66. A mild example of world-systemist reification is my colleague Peter Taylor's assertion that the scale of the world economy is 'the scale of reality', in contrast to the state or nation which is 'the scale of ideology' and the city which is 'the scale of experience', in 'Geographical Scales within the World-Economy Approach' *Review* 5 (1981). pp. 3–11.

26. Wallerstein, 'Crisis as Transition', in *Dynamics of Global Crisis* (1982), p. 51.

27. Wallerstein, 'Patterns and Prospectives', p. 27.

28. Wallerstein, 'The Future of the World-Economy', in *Processes of the World System* (1980), p. 175.

29. *Ibid.*

30. Wallerstein, 'Crisis as Transition', pp. 48–49.

31. 'The current crisis of the nation-state . . . is manifested both in the tendency to multinational and/or multistate aggregations and in the parallel process of internal decomposition of nation states into ethnically more or less homogenous regional entities', Giovanni Arrighi, *The Geometry of Imperialism* (1979), p. 110. No evidence is given in support of this assertion, possibly because Arrighi believes, with Kant, that '[there] is no innate characteristic in things themselves' (p. 30).

32. See, for instance, E. H. Carr, *A History of Soviet Russia: The Bolshevik Revolution, 1917–1923* (1951), vol. 1, pp. 421–422; Boyd C. Shafer, *Nationalism: Myth and Reality* (1955). p. 41.

33. In this connection see Davis, *Toward a Marxist Theory* Chaps. 4–9.

# 2. Nationalism as an Autonomous Force

If class struggle is the motor of history, as Marxists contend, then what is the role of national struggle, or nationalism? The traditional Marxist answer to this question is quite straightforward: national struggle is simply a form of class struggle. This view was expounded by Marx and Engels, was elaborated by Lenin and more recent theorists, and is accepted by the great majority of Marxists today. It is rejected, however, by a number of Marxist and neo-Marxist scholars, among them Nicos Poulantzas, Regis Debray, Tom Nairn, John Ehrenreich, and Horace Davis. For these scholars, nationalism is not a form of class struggle nor even a product of class struggle. It is an autonomous force: a second motor of history.

In this chapter I will try to show that nationalism is not a force autonomous from class struggle. I will present the traditional Marxist view – that national struggle is one form of the class struggle for state power – and I will defend this view against some of its Marxist critics. It is true that the class struggle view of nationalism has frequently been distorted into one or another dogmatic and simplistic argument about the national question, and these positions certainly do need to be criticized. For instance, national movements for state independence are not simply political strategies of one class, the bourgeoisie, against another class, or of one bourgeois class group against another. And the class struggle view should not lead to an underestimation or neglect of culture, nationality, or of ideology (in the mistaken belief that ideology is something different from class struggle). But one can criticize these and other distortions of Marxist theory without discarding what must surely be the most crucial pillar of Marxist theory itself, the position that political and social struggles – including national struggles – are ultimately class struggles.

If one were trying to construct a Marxist theory of nationalism step by step, the first step would be to show that nationalism is a form of class struggle, not an autonomous force. This step must be taken also if one is to demonstrate that national liberation movements against colonialism and neocolonialism are, in principle, part of the class struggle against capitalism.

There are two preliminary issues. The first is a matter (again) of terminology. The argument that nationalism is a form of class struggle extends to three important but different meanings of the word nationalism: nationalism as a synonym for national struggle; nationalism as the national movement or the side of any national struggle which fights for, not against, state independence; and, finally, nationalism as 'narrow nationalism'. In other words, nationalism in all of these senses is class struggle.

The second issue has to do with the Marxist concept of class struggle. For conservative theorists, class struggle is treated (if at all) as one of many discrete factors to be blended together in some great factor–analytic attempt at explanation. Nationalism is a second of these isolated factors. Religion is a third, and so on. In this formulation, the factor or force of nationalism is autonomous from that of class, almost by definition. For Marxists, however, class struggle is bound up with culture; it is not an isolatable factor. Putting the matter simply: in all class societies without exception, and in classless societies (so-called 'tribes') which are under external pressure from class societies, the primary source of conflict – that is, of oppression, resistance, and ultimately change – is the struggle between, on the one hand, a ruling class which is trying to exploit, amass surplus, and retain its power and possessions, and, on the other hand, a producing class which is resisting exploitation and trying to seize political power for itself. This, as I say, is the primary source of conflict and change, though not the only one.

For our purpose, the crucial point is that this process of class struggle makes use of all traits and institutions of culture as its instruments and arenas of exploitation and resistance. Therefore religious conflicts, educational struggles, work place struggles, and all the other, including national, struggles, do not function parallel to class struggle but are themselves mechanisms of class struggle. It is for this reason that Marxists can assert that class struggle is the motor of history without falling into some narrow determinism, economic or otherwise. So to sum up the traditional position: political struggle, the effort of given classes to seize state power, is a crucial arena of class struggle, and nationalism, or national struggle, or the national question, is one form of this political struggle to seize state power. It is, to be sure, a very distinctive form. But it is not an autonomous force.

## The Classical Critique

The theory of nationalism as an autonomous force was criticized by Marx and Engels in some of their earliest writings. This critique was in fact the first stage in the formulation of a distinctively Marxist theory of nationalism.

In Germany in the 1840s two conservative theories of nationalism were prominent. Both derived mainly from Hegel's concept of the state, or more properly the nation state, as a super-organic, metaphysical entity, a whole which was, on the one hand, substantial and corporeal, and, on the other hand, spiritual – what Hegel described as 'spirit', 'will', and 'idea'. Hegel's corporeal nation state, deployed with Herder's and Fichte's thesis that a nation is defined by its culture and principally its language, provided the theoretical and ideological foundation for the typical German nationalist view, that all German-speaking people and the land upon which they reside form a metaphysical whole, an organic nation, destined to become a unified and sovereign German state.[1] Hegel himself, however, was a Prussian nationalist, not a Germanic or pan-Germanic nationalist, and his concept of the super-organic nation state had been rather carefully constructed to provide a philosophical argument that the true, real, and rational nation state was Prussia, including both its German-speaking and non-German-speaking territories, and capable also of imperial expansion as and when the government saw fit.[2] This purpose was served by conceiving the nation state to be not a corporeal but a spiritual entity, an 'idea' identified with the monarch, such that it was the 'will' of the monarch which conferred nationality upon his subjects.[3]

This theory of the nation as idea was eminently suited to multinational and imperial states. It was the ideological basis for arguing that the empire, not the local cultural group, was the true source of nationality and the true object of national loyalty; this theory accordingly became the primary theory of nationalism used by apologists for colonialism and empire from Acton to Toynbee. The other Hegelian theory in turn formed the basis for the much better known but much less important theory of nationalism based on language, or more precisely on language as the indicator for a corporeal, super-organic nation. This latter theory came to be known as the 'principle of nationalities', the principle that each language group, however small, somehow has the right, duty, and destiny to become a sovereign state.

A third conservative theory of nationalism emerged later in the 19th Century out of Hegel's theory of the nation state as an idea. For Hegel the idea and will of the nation were truly and rationally expressed by the monarch. In bourgeois democratic thought, however, the idea and will of the nation were supposed to be present in the heads of all citizens, not merely the governing elite. Thus emerged the partly Hegelian, partly neo-Kantian idea that the nation is collective consciousness; that the 'idea of the nation' truly *is* the nation. The importance of this view is that it underlies the most important conservative theories of nationalism today. These theories argue that the idea of the nation emerged first in western Europe, realizing itself in the nation states of Britain and France, and then diffused, mainly through the distributive agency of colonialism, to the outer realms and more backward peoples, where this idea, this gift from the Europeans, transformed itself into the frenetic demand by colonial peoples for independence and a seat in the United Nations. According to this widely accepted theory, national liberation movements did not arise as a response to exploitation and oppression; they were merely the after-effects of the diffusion of the European idea of the nation.

Marx and Engels did not have occasion to criticize this third theory of nationalism. (It was, however, disputed by Kautsky, Lenin, and Stalin when, much later, it entered Marxist discourse through the writings of Otto Bauer.) The pure Hegelian theory of the super-organic and metaphysical nation state was powerfully attacked in Marx's early critique of the Hegelian philosophy of law.[4] Soon afterwards, in *The German Ideology*, Marx and Engels attacked the complementary notion that the state is an idea, an intellectual product; and this classical demonstration is still perfectly usable today for an attack on the diffusionist theory of nationalism with its contention that the idea of the nation spreads of its own accord, and thus creates new nations, for no material reason.[5] By 1848, Marx and Engels had definitely established the position, in the *Manifesto*, that struggles for state power are class struggles, and that the state is not prior to society, class, and class struggle but is a product thereof.[6] In later writings, Marx and (mainly) Engels disposed of the second Hegelian theory, that there is some immanent nationalism in language groups. Although Marx and Engels firmly, indeed actively, supported the German unification movement, on the grounds that it would benefit the working classes, they rejected the mysticism of language-based German nationalism. There is not one state in Europe, said Engels, in which only one language is spoken.[7] He thereby rejected the idea that nation states are associated one to one with languages, and in so doing he, and Marx also, rejected the 'principle of nationalities'.

In the *Manifesto* we see the beginnings of a second stage in the emergence of a distinctively Marxist theory of nationalism. Here and in later works it is argued that a rising class must seize or form a state in its struggle for power, and that in the specific case of the rising bourgeoisie this class finds best suited to its economic and political needs a rather large state and one not seriously fissured by internal cultural and political boundaries. Such a nation state, the size perhaps of Britain or France or a unified Germany, seemed the best vehicle for the development of capitalism and the simultaneous development of proletarian class struggle. However, Marx's and Engels' theory of state viability – it was, by the way, the closest they came to a theory of nations – was a matter of tendencies, not rigid rules. A nation as small as Ireland was considered to be viable, and grossly large imperial states, like Austria–Hungary and Turkey, were on the whole treated as unviable, as likely to decompose.[8] Size, or concentration, was not, therefore, seen as always and necessarily progressive. But the formation of new, viable states, whether through unification, as in Germany, or through secession, as in Poland, was, indeed, progressive. Thus national struggle was itself progressive under specifiable conditions.

In the third stage of Marx's and Engels' theory of nationalism, they argued that not only the bourgeoisie but also the working class needs to struggle for state power, and thus not all nationalism is what today we call bourgeois nationalism. Stated differently: there is also national struggle in the fight to overthrow capitalism and realize socialism. Marx and Engels did not fully develop this argument, no doubt because they expected, or at least hoped, that the proletarian revolution would spread very rapidly across the world and thus render all class states obsolete. But they made the argument quite forcefully in the cases of Germany, Poland and Ireland. For Ireland in particular, it was argued that the exploited classes formed the core of the national liberation movement, and the foreign – that is, British – bourgeoisie formed the main (though by no means the only) class enemy.[9]

It was left for Lenin and later Marxists to generalize the relationship between national struggle and the proletarian struggle for socialism. This part of the Marxist theory of nationalism is exceedingly important, not least for an understanding of the character and importance of national liberation struggles in countries like Vietnam, Cuba, and Puerto Rico. But this matter does not concern us in this chapter. Our concern is with the way Marx and Engels disposed of the two essentially Hegelian forms of the theory of autonomous nationalism, theories which treated the nation or state as an autonomous entity, in the one case corporeal and in the other spiritual, in the one case the expression of the metaphysical unity of a culture, in the other that of an imperial state. Marx and Engels showed that national struggle is, and can only be, a form of class struggle.

## Post-classical Variations

The theory of nationalism as an autonomous force entered Marxism at the beginning of the 20th Century. Otto Bauer and Karl Renner, theoreticians of the

Austrian Social Democratic Party, put forward highly philosophical arguments in defence of their party's position on the national question in the Austro-Hungarian empire.[10] The position proclaimed the right of all national groups within the empire to civil equality and a measure of autonomy in cultural matters, but rejected the right of self-determination – that is, the right of secession – and thereby upheld the territorial integrity of the empire.[11] The core of Bauer's (and less consequentially Renner's) argument was the neo-Kantian and ultimately Hegelian proposition that nations are in essence ideas, forms of consciousness. They are very old and deep in the human psyche. They have little or nothing to do with class struggle and the state, these being evolutionary features of class society. Therefore national struggles are not class struggles, not struggles for state power, for independence. National struggles aim only at protecting cultural rights, such as the right to use one's own language in schools and local government. It follows that social democrats should uphold such rights but should not support struggles for national independence, because state power is a goal of class struggle, not of national struggle. The state, as Karl Renner put the matter, 'is quite indifferent to the nation'.[12]

The Austrian theory penetrated Russia and became an ideological weapon against the Bolshevik position that all nations within the Russian empire had the right of self-determination, that is, of secession. Both Lenin and Stalin attacked the Austrian theory. Lenin called it, correctly, an 'idealist theory', one in which national phenomena were in essence reduced to consciousness.[13] Stalin countered it in his important 1913 essay, 'Marxism and the National Question', in part by criticizing its metaphysics and in part by proposing a theory of nations of his own, a theory in which nations were explicitly stated to be products of class struggle, and more especially products of the political struggles of the rising bourgeoisie.[14] Lenin, for his part, offered no definition of the nation; it can even be argued that he did not have a fully formed theory of nations in this pre-First World War period, although just a few years later, in the course of developing his theory of imperialism, he put forward a corollary theory of nationalism, nations, and national liberation in the imperialist epoch, a theory which remains today the basic Marxist position.[15] For present purposes I need merely note that Lenin, in the pre-war period, argued strongly and repeatedly that national struggle is class struggle and that the idea of the nation cannot be divorced from the idea of the state and the struggle for state power.[16]

The theory of nationalism as an autonomous force did not, to my knowledge, have a direct influence on Marxist thought from about the time of the Bolshevik revolution to the early 1970s. The theory did, however, have an indirect influence, mainly through the survival in reified (or petrified) form of two pre-revolutionary arguments, one stemming from Luxemburg and the other from Stalin. Luxemburg had argued that national struggle indeed is class struggle, but it is the class struggle only of the bourgeoisie and only of the period of early or rising capitalism. That period having passed, said Luxemburg, national struggle is now out of date. New nation states are most unlikely to be formed. Thus workers should not support national movements because these are no longer progressive and are unlikely to succeed. Wherever workers do support such movements, this is to be considered an atavistic attitude, a survival.

Perhaps a hundred new nation states have been formed since Luxemburg enunciated this position, quite a few of them through the efforts of the working classes, yet some Marxists today continue to advance the Luxemburgian position. They claim that there is a contradiction between class struggle and national struggle, that class struggle no longer takes the national form, and if it still occasionally assumes that form, this can only be a belated episode of the old bourgeois revolution. Moreover, we are told, national struggle is out of date because nations, and indeed states, are dissolving: capitalism is becoming international. All of these arguments were basically answered some 65 years ago by Lenin.[17] And today we notice that national struggles against colonialism and neocolonialism are still raging from Puerto Rico to Timor, while gorilla regimes and fascist movements prove by their proliferation that the state is as important to capitalism today as ever it was in the past. There is no contradiction between national struggle and class struggle. The contradiction is not between the forms of struggle but between the contending classes.

The second way in which the theory of autonomous nationalism has influenced modern Marxism involves a reification of Stalin's 1913 definition of the nation (which we discuss in Chapter 5, below). Stalin listed four attributes which all nations must have: common territory, common economy, common language, and (in essence) common culture, plus an historical criterion: nations arise only during the 'epoch of rising capitalism'. All of the attributes must be present, according to Stalin, or the candidate is not truly a nation. Stalin himself admitted later that his definition had been appropriate only to one part of the world and to the pre-war era, and that Lenin's analysis of imperialism had thoroughly changed the terms of the question. He referred to multilingual states like Czechoslovakia and Yugoslavia as 'national states'. He worked with Lenin to build new nations in the Soviet Union. And so on.[18]

Yet many Marxists continue to believe that all true nations conform to the 1913 definition. This gives the theory of autonomous nationalism a chance to slip back into Marxism through the back door. It does so in two ways, both of which involve converting the nation into a corporeal, almost Hegelian entity. First, if one believes that a genuine nation is not present unless all the attributes are observable, one argues in effect that behind these external attributes there is a definite entity, an essential nation, much as we identify a particular species of bird by its attributes of plumage yet we always assume that beneath the plumage there is the real, essential bird. This essentialist approach leads one towards the Hegelian argument that the nation itself is an entity, an active subject in history, autonomous not merely from class struggle but from social processes in general.

The second problem relates to the key attribute of the nation: common territory. Lenin, Stalin, and Kautsky all argued, in opposition to Bauer, the Bundists, and others, that a nation must possess territory, and they were absolutely right. But there are two utterly different ways in which it can be said that a nation possesses territory. What I would describe as the Leninist way is a straightforward political thesis. If any national community proposes to win for itself a sovereign state, that state must have territorial expression: must have defensible borders; must have space over which it exercises political control; must appear on the political map of the world. Stated differently: our interest in nations is political, a matter of self-determination and thus of the potential for forming independent states. But such self-determination is meaningless unless the future state can claim a specific territory, for there can be no state without territorial expression.

The other way in which territory can enter into the definition of the nation is plainly metaphysical. In this sense, territory is thought somehow to be an actual part of the nation. The nation thereby becomes a strange super-organism, partly human or social and partly environmental or territorial – exactly what Herder and Fichte thought it to be in their notion of the German national organism. If nations possess territory in this sense, they cannot be moved from one territory to another. National boundaries must remain fixed (they are part of the nation, like the skin of an organism). Dispersed or fragmented minorities cannot be reassembled into compact territorial communities and given sovereignty within that territory. Native American nations which have been spatially displaced or dispersed under US capitalism would be unable to reclaim national territory, and national sovereignty, in a future socialist society (although their right to full sovereignty is an indelible part of the socialist agenda). And so on. If we employ this concept of the nation as people-fixed-to-territory, we again elevate the nation into an entity independent of class processes and class struggle. If this concept appears in Stalin's 1913 essay, it is mainly because at that time it seemed to Marxists that nations were, indeed, artifacts of an earlier era, even if some national movements might still struggle successfully to form states, and the territorial expression of nations seemed quite fixed. 'Since when', asked Stalin in his 1913 essay, 'have Social Democrats begun to occupy themselves with "organizing" nations, "constituting" nations, "creating" nations?'[19] Yet five years later Lenin was beginning to do precisely that in the emerging Soviet Union.

## The Modern Theory and its Critics

During the mid-1970s there appeared a rash of articles and books attacking the traditional Marxist theory of nationalism. There have always been such attacks from conservative social thinkers, and from odd little political sects which try to keep alive the Luxemburgian view that all national struggle is bourgeois and reactionary. But the attacks I am referring to represent a new and different trend. These are Marxist theorists attacking their own theory. John Ehrenreich calls our understanding of nationalism 'shallow' and declares, 'It's time to admit that as Marxists we simply have no adequate understanding of the phenomenon'.[20] Tom Nairn proclaims the theory of nationalism to be 'Marxism's great historical failure'.[21] And so on. The attacks come from a number of theoretical and political perspectives, and it is not my intent to review them here. I propose to discuss three specific formulations, all of which are serious theoretical arguments and all of which contend that nationalism, or national struggle, is a force autonomous from class struggle.

The first formulation is Nicos Poulantzas's argument that the nation is something autonomous and substantial (in a Hegelian sense), something which acts on history independently of class processes. The second is Nairn's argument, put forward as Marxist yet hardly distinguishable from the standard conservative position, that nationalism is an autonomous ideological force, a product of 'modernization' and 'uneven development' but hardly connected at all to class struggle. The third formulation is Horace Davis's argument, a serious and scholarly one but nonetheless mistaken, that national struggle and class struggle are in essence complementary, closely interconnected but quite distinct. Brief mention will also be made of Régis Debray's position, which substantializes the nation even more than Poulantzas's does, and of Ehrenreich's elaboration of the Nairn theory to the point where class struggle disappears from the picture entirely.

The late Nicos Poulantzas was engaged, in the period just before his death, in constructing a theory of politics which paid lip-service to Lenin yet was profoundly anti-Leninist. Class struggle remained, for Poulantzas, the titular motor of history, but the contending classes dissolved into a swarm of ambiguous 'class fractions', among which it was hard to tell who was struggling with whom. More relevant for us was Poulantzas's parallel effort to show that the state is not the agent of class rule and the direct object of class struggle that Leninist theory makes it out to be, but is, rather, a distinct and separate entity. No Marxist would deny some institutional distinctness, even partial autonomy, to the capitalist state, but Poulantzas went much further. In his last book, *State, Power, Socialism*, the state was reified into a substantial object, something which Poulantzas proposed to deal with 'from the standpoint of its materiality'.[22] But how does the state acquire its 'materiality'? From the nation.

Poulantzas's nation is very much akin to Hegel's nation state. It is corporeal, implicitly super-organic, as old as if not older than class society, yet likely to persist 'even after the withering away of the state'.[23] It is an 'object both theoretical and real'.[24] It possesses what Poulantzas calls 'transhistorical irreducibility'.[25] As if all of this were not sufficiently metaphysical, Poulantzas finally grounds the nation – here he is Kantian, not Hegelian – in pure space and pure time.[26] The nation, therefore, is a truly basic, truly autonomous entity, something 'transhistorical', and something which obviously cannot be reduced to class processes and class struggle. This rock-of-ages nation serves as the mooring for Poulantzas's state. The state is substantial, material, and autonomous because it is anchored in the nation – is, in the last analysis, a nation state. The state's specific autonomy from class struggle is explained in the same way: the state is rooted not in class but in a deeper and more abiding substance, the nation.

Poulantzas does, it is true, argue that the nation changes its form with each successive mode of production, and this in turn facilitates the transformation of the state from, for instance, its feudal form to its capitalist form. But his arguments on this and related matters need not detain us. It is the central argument which is of concern, and this can be summarized as follows: the nation is not fundamentally a product of class struggle: it is prior to, more basic than, and autonomous from class struggle. It somehow underlies the state, giving the latter its materiality and partial autonomy from class struggle. By implication, all national struggle must somehow be derived, not from class struggle, but from the historically and logically prior phenomenon, the nation. Poulantzas of course realized how far all this departs from traditional Marxist theories of nationalism and the nation. 'We have to recognize', he said, 'that there is no Marxist theory of the nation'.[27]

Régis Debray substantializes and reifies the nation to an even greater extent, in fact to the extent of absurdity. 'It was the nation', he said in an interview, 'which first led me to question Marxism seriously'.[28] 'We must locate the nation phenomenon within general laws regulating the survival of the human species . . . against death. Against *entropy*'.[29] The nation comes from the need for 'an enclosure rendering the collectivity *organic* . . . a delimitation between what is *inside* and what is *outside*'.[30] 'The proletariat against the nation is like wood against iron'.[31] In a manner reminiscent of Hegel, Debray moves freely between the super-organic and the psychic, between the nation as thing and as idea: there is, for Debray, a 'national instinct', etc.[32] He is asserting that nationalism, embodied in the nation, is not only autonomous from class struggle but ultimately more important.

Tom Nairn, having dismissed the traditional Marxist theory of nationalism as 'Marxism's great historical failure', proceeds, with much chest-thumping, to provide us with what he proclaims to be a new and better theory. I will have a great deal to say about that theory in Chapter 3, but it is important in the present context, and at the expense of some repetition, to summarize Nairn's argument that nationalism (meaning all of national struggle) is autonomous from class struggle and is, in essence and origin, an idea.

Nairn begins with what is essentially the typical non-Marxist view of nationalism today. The point of departure is the supposed emergence of the idea of the nation state, hardly distinguished from the idea of freedom, from French and British society two centuries ago. The idea of the nation state, or nationalism, is then supposed to have diffused outwards to the rest of the world as part of the package of European ideas labelled 'modernization'. This theory of the spread of nationalism is thus merely a component of the larger theory of Eurocentric diffusion. (See Chapter 3.) Just in passing we may note how curious it is to be told that ideas like freedom and national sovereignty were spread around the world by European colonialism – their absolute negation.[33]

Tom Nairn accepts this basic theory with only two modifications, both essentially cosmetic. First, the theory of modernization is recast into the Marxist lexicon: diffusion becomes 'uneven development', and the like.[34] Second, the spread of nationalism is not simply described as the spread of the idea, nationalism. Rather, the unevenness of development stimulates, in the backward regions, an unconscious and irrational attitude – Nairn gets very pseudo-Freudian at this point – resulting from envy, rage, and frustration over unfulfilled expectations. This irrational outburst seizes upon the idea of nationalism and emerges as nationalist ideology, the national movement, etc.[35] The actors in this process are the elites of backward areas: it is they who are frustrated and envious, and who therefore decide to fight for state sovereignty, for an independent nation state, in order to speed the development process, mobilizing the necessary mass support for this effort by means of ideological trickery.

That is the entire explanatory model. Nationalism remains the idea of independence, of freedom (learned, we suppose, under the lash). Nationalism does not reflect exploitation, or oppression of the masses (who play no active role in the theory), or, for that matter, imperialism. Nairn seems not to believe in imperialism, preferring the conservative model of the world in which the prevailing centre-periphery relation is the outward spread of 'civilization', 'modernity', 'rationality', and 'enlightenment' – all Nairn's words – along with the spread of progress: progress under capitalism. None of this has much to do with Marxism.

Nairn's theory of nationalism, like so much of what is currently called 'Neo-Marxism', is in essence conservative thought fitted out in Marxist garb. The effect here, as elsewhere, is somewhat silly. Unfortunately, conservative theory itself is not silly: much of it is, after all, the ideology of exploitation. And Nairn's theory is by no means silly in its deduced consequences. Nationalism for him is at root instinctive, unconscious, even a 'dementia'. When this explosive psychological reaction to modernization occurs in strong countries, it produces fascism. Fascism, says Nairn, is the essence, the 'archetype', of national struggle, and fascism is therefore implicit in all national movements, all national liberation struggles. Nairn can argue this way because he has carved national struggle away from class struggle, and because national liberation does not reflect for him a political response to colonial and neocolonial exploitation, but instead is merely a sort of psychosis of modernization, and one which occurs in the elite, not the workers. I need hardly point out that expansionist nationalism, national struggle for conquest, is not always associated with fascism; it is more characteristically a feature of classical colonialism: 'manifest destiny', 'the British raj', and so on. I will say nothing more at this point on the subject of the relationship between nationalism and fascism (we return to the problem in Chapter 3) except to observe, first, that national struggle viewed as class struggle will necessarily be associated with all sorts of social formations, fascist ones included, and second, that you will find hardly anyone who has worked in or supported any genuine national liberation struggle, anywhere, who would agree with Nairn that fascism is implicit in that struggle.

A second consequence of Nairn's theory emerges from the judgement that national struggle is unrelated to exploitation, class struggle, and the working classes. This leads him to defend the legitimacy of Protestant separatism in Northern Ireland and also the nationalism of Israelis and white South Africans.[36] All of this follows from his thesis that nationalism is not associated with working class struggle. Oddly, Nairn claims the authority of Lenin for this view. In reality, Nairn's position is an amalgam of Luxemburg's argument that all nationalism is bourgeois, the Hegelian and neo-Kantian argument that nationalism is merely an idea, and the simple conservative theory of 'modernization'. It is not Leninist or for that matter Marxist.

John Ehrenreich takes the same basic argument a step farther along the same road. In a recent article (which he rightly calls 'a work of destruction, not of creation of new theory'[37]) he claims that 'Marxists have failed in their efforts at incorporating the reality of nationalism into their theoretical understanding, and . . . this failure is deeply rooted in the nature of Marxist thought itself'.[38] Indeed, the 'theoretical constructs of Marxism and the reality of nationalism have not been shown to be compatible'.[39] For Ehrenreich, the driving force in the modern world has been the autonomous ideological force of nationalism, not class consciousness or class struggle or even class itself. Marxists have been wrong not only in their analysis of nationalism but also, and more fundamentally, in their analysis of class. Marx was wrong about the proletariat. The working class does not make history. National struggle and class struggle are distinct, but neither of them brings us closer to socialism. Ehrenreich is a socialist and a more-or-less Marxist, but he sees no way out of this theoretical blind alley. He simply declares himself to be a pessimist.[40]

A number of other Marxist theorists have taken the position that nationalism is an autonomous force which is basically ideological and not, like class ideologies, derived from class processes and class exploitation. Horace Davis is perhaps the only one among the theorists holding this basic position who presents a truly thoughtful and scholarly argument, and his argument therefore deserves careful attention. The main statement is in his important book, *Toward a Marxist Theory of Nationalism.*[41] Davis is also the author of an earlier, very valuable study of pre-First World War Marxist views on the national question, and he edited and wrote an introduction to a volume of Luxemburg's writings on this subject.[42] In none of these three works does Davis really try to define, or describe in precise detail, what he means by 'nationalism', and the few relevant passages lead us back towards the traditional thesis that nationalism is a European idea and movement of the early 19th Century which has diffused to the rest of the world.[43] In his new work, Davis directly challenges the view that nationalism is a form of class struggle.[44] The challenge takes two forms.

First, Davis reinterprets the views of Lenin and Luxemburg and argues that both of them viewed nationalism as, at root, an idea, and more precisely a moral idea or precept. Using this interpretation, Davis returns to the classic debates and concludes that Luxemburg and Lenin were indeed in basic agreement: both insisted on an end to national oppression. Davis then argues that Lenin's main difference with Luxemburg, namely his defence of, and her attack on, the principle of the right of self-determination of nations, was a relatively unimportant disagreement, because national oppression could be attacked effectively without demanding state sovereignty.[45] In sum: the moral position taken by the two revolutionary thinkers was the same; the strategies were different; but Lenin's strategy was not fundamentally more efficacious than Luxemburg's. Davis then makes the curious assertion that Lenin's strategy, that of upholding the right of self-determination, was actually rejected by the majority of Bolsheviks at their Eighth Congress in 1919.[46]

Space permits only a brief rejoinder to this argument. First, Lenin's principal argument in 1903 and thereafter was that national oppression cannot be ended or even controlled under capitalism without an insistence on the right of self-determination. Luxemburg's strategy would not succeed because it sidestepped the crucial issue of state power. Second, by underestimating the difference between the Luxemburgian and the Leninist positions, Davis arrives at a conception of the Leninist position which is not at all Leninist, because, while it incorporates the strategy of general struggle against national oppression, it abandons the strategy of insisting on the right of self-determination. Davis is led by this position to define as Leninist some positions on the national question which are hardly that. (Surely it is inaccurate to describe China's nationality policy as 'Leninist' when China refuses to accord the right of self-determination, of secession, to her internal minority nations).[47] Third, Davis is wrong in claiming that Lenin's position on self-determination was defeated at the 1919 party congress. It is true that the phrase 'the right of self-determination' was deleted from the party programme at that congress. But this was done at Lenin's suggestion. He maintained that the phrase 'the right of self-determination' was dangerously ambiguous, and he had been arguing since 1917 (perhaps earlier) that it should be replaced in the party programme by the unequivocal phrase 'right of secession'. This view prevailed. Lenin was not defeated.[48]

Davis's second challenge to the class-based theory of nationalism calls attention to three different kinds of national struggle in which, he believes, class struggle is not or was not significantly involved. First, Davis cites Amilcar Cabral, I think inappropriately, to the effect that class struggle cannot be the motor of history since there will continue to be a history after class society has given way to classless society, and since, implicitly, there was history before classes emerged.[49] Cabral did indeed discuss the presumptive motor of history before and after the period of class society, but he did not deny the authority of class struggle for the period in between.[50] And in fact it was Engels who first pointed out that the operative sentence in the *Manifesto*, 'The history of all hitherto existing society is the history of class struggle', refers only to what he called 'written history', meaning the history of societies with classes.[51] As to the classless future, Davis does not (and would not be able to) present a case that national struggles will persist when class struggles have ended on a world scale. In a classless world, nations will no doubt persist as cultural, not political, entities. But what will they have to fight about?

Next in logical order, Davis argues that the class-based theory of nationalism cannot account for the fact that national struggles occurring in our own time sometimes involve classless 'tribal' societies, such as those in Africa (the area discussed in connection with this question).[52] This is an important and complex problem, and I do not have the space to show here precisely why national struggles in this category are also, at root, class struggles. Three propositions will have to suffice. First, the fact that a small society is internally classless does not imply that it is not integrated into a system of class exploitation. Surplus value has been extracted, under colonialism and neocolonialism, in countless ways and in great amounts, from essentially all the so-called tribal societies, in Africa and elsewhere, and the resistance of these people has been a form of class struggle. Second, most of the so-called tribes are indeed class-stratified societies, and for most of the remainder, in places like Africa, it is arguable that they were, in fact, class societies before the early colonial period, which truncated feudal political structures, destroyed proto-capitalist city states, and drove many peoples to form closed corporate communities in defence against slave-raiding and other manifestations of class exploitation, direct and indirect. Third, while it is certainly true that the overall environment of imperialism produces many very serious intercommunal stresses of the sort called 'tribalism', the plain fact is that very nearly all of the anti-imperialist struggles which won through to independence, to state sovereignty, were multicultural, not tribal. The independent states of Africa and the rest of the Third World typically possess the spatial boundaries of former colonies, not of tribes.

There remains one other form of category of national struggle which, according to Horace Davis, is something other than class struggle. This is the type of national liberation struggle which, in Davis's view, is not class struggle because it is waged by all classes. He singles out Cuba for special attention. According to Davis the anti-Batista phase of the Cuban revolution was a nationalist struggle but not a class struggle. 'Fidel Castro . . . was a nationalist before he was a socialist'.[53] 'Castro and Guevara began with Cuban nationalism and a programme that was democratic in the conventional sense . . . Socialism was added later, forced on them by the logic of the situation'.[54] In a word, the anti-Batista struggle was purely nationalist. In addition, Davis believes that all classes in Cuba participated in the struggle. But we have the statements of Fidel and numerous other sources to show that these contentions are not correct. Fidel was a revolutionary socialist, and 'the logic of the situation' forced him to recognize that national liberation was on the direct route to socialism. Furthermore, we know that the revolution was waged by exploited classes – urban and rural workers and small peasants – plus marginalized sectors of the petty and middle bourgeoisie. The enemy was a largely (but not entirely) foreign bourgeoisie and local subaltern groups.[55] In Cuba as everywhere else, the national struggle is indeed a class struggle.

Davis is therefore quite wrong in claiming that countries like Cuba furnish proof that 'Lenin's analysis . . . of the class basis of nationalism is in need of reformulation'.[56] Lenin's theory needs no reformulation. What it mainly needs is to be brought up to date.

## Some Concluding Comments

Marxists tend to question their own theory when things are not going well in the world of practice, and that is as it should be. Until the mid-1970s national struggle seemed to be essentially as Lenin had described it: a form of the class struggle for state power, a form that would be progressive, reactionary, or merely diversionary depending upon the classes and class-combinations that were engaged in struggle. But the 1970s presented Marxists, and socialists in general, with some disquieting situations. Not all of the decolonization struggles had produced socialist states. Serious conflicts were appearing between socialist states and between national communist parties. In the advanced capitalist countries the class struggle was not advancing at a very impressive pace. And so on. All of this led to a rethinking of many portions of Marxist theory, and in particular to a widespread questioning of Lenin's basic models of imperialism and the national struggles which it generates. This is part of the explanation for the fact that the basic class struggle theory of national struggle began, in that period, to be questioned seriously. The theory that nationalism is some sort of autonomous force was dominant, indeed hegemonic, in scholarly circles, and it was to be expected that some Marxist scholars would try to replace the classical theory (as it had evolved from Marx to Lenin to Cabral and other modern theorists) with the mainstream theory or a syncretic merger of the two.

But another phenomenon was also contributing to the critique of the Leninist theories of imperialism and national struggle. In the 1960s and early 1970s, Marxist theory became widely accepted as an analytic framework among evolutionary socialists and anarchists in the capitalist countries, but theorists in these socialist traditions found it necessary to cleanse Marxism of its unacceptable Leninist attributes; to create a 'pure' Marxism. This seems to have been the main content of the process which is often called the 'renaissance of Marxist theory'. One could treat Lenin's models in either of two ways: re-interpret them or reject them. The first method was used by many theorists to claim, for instance, that Lenin's theory of imperialism was merely a theory of the diffusion (via 'uneven development' – the code word) of capitalism, not a theory positing superexploitation, national oppression, and national liberation for the Third World. Thus the implication of a qualitative difference between the two capitalist sectors and the argument that national liberation is a central part of the world-wide class struggle are avoided. Lenin's theory of national struggle was approached in a different way: it was distorted, then the distorted version was shown to be false and was rejected. Lenin – and more generally the class struggle theory of nationalism – was supposed to have held that nationalism was a declining force in the modern world; hence the theory was wrong. Lenin was supposed to have treated nationalism as necessarily bourgeois and reactionary; hence Lenin was wrong. And he was supposed to have considered class struggle itself to be something non-national, a simple confrontation between labour and capital in which ethnic or cultural considerations were irrelevant or reactionary; hence Lenin was wrong again. But the Marxist theory of nationalism based on class struggle did not make these arguments after about 1914. So the logical basis for these critiques is, in fact, erroneous. The Marxist theory of national struggle is in many ways imperfect, and needs to be brought up to date. But the basic theory is sound.

I will close this chapter with three bare comments concerning aspects of the Marxist theory of nationalism, or national struggle, which seem to me to need further work, in order to bring the theory up to date in terms of the present-day world and our knowledge of it. Bringing it up to date will not render it perfect or complete. But at the present juncture I think it is more important to recognize the strength, and essential adequacy, of our theory of nationalism than to worry about its imperfections. Be that as it may, my three suggestions – they will be elaborated in later chapters – are the following:

1. Although most Marxists today agree that national struggle is indeed class struggle, there still remains the subordinate yet very important question: class struggle by which class or classes? Many Marxists still believe, in the face of all the evidence, that the bourgeoisie is the only class for which nationalism has functionality in class struggle (because, supposedly, nations are only formed by the bourgeoisie in the course of its rise). We should, first of all, correct the record and show that this typically pre-First World War view, which has survived mainly because it has behind it the authority of Luxemburg and Stalin (of the 1913 essay), was answered very thoroughly by Lenin in his writings on the national question, and on imperialism, after 1914. We should then show, for each of many national liberation struggles, how the new theory's predictions proved to be correct, and more particularly how the national liberation struggle proved to be an inseparable part of the class struggle for socialism. This also applies to questions of strategy for struggles not yet won. In the case of Puerto Rico, for example, it needs to be clearly understood by all Marxists that the struggle for independence is not a separate

matter from the struggle for socialism, and cannot therefore be called 'narrow nationalism' or 'bourgeois nationalism' or somehow in 'contradiction' to the struggle for socialism. For Puerto Rico and, I suppose, every other colony, the achievement of independence, of state sovereignty, is an absolutely vital goal for the working class on its path to socialism.

2. We certainly should update our theory of nations. This, too, begins with a correction of the record. Stalin's 1913 essay does not present 'the' Marxist theory of nations. Lenin developed a much more adequate theory in the period 1914–1922, and Amilcar Cabral, among others, has expanded Lenin's theory. There still remain a number of practical problems, two of which deserve mention here. First, Stalin in 1913, and most Marxists at that time, believed that nations emerge only in the period of early, rising capitalism, and die or dissolve with the socialist revolution. But nations have been born since 1913 under all manner of circumstances, socialist as well as capitalist, and more crucially, nations can also be destroyed under capitalism itself. In the case of Puerto Rico, for example, we can have no illusions that the Puerto Rican nation possesses some metaphysical immortality. It will survive only if the people fight in defence of their culture and towards their freedom. The second practical problem has to do with that part of the 1913 theory which is often called 'the theory of national minorities'. In Stalin's essay, it is categorically asserted that minority communities formed by long distance labour migration are destined to become assimilated into the host nationality.[57] This was true in the pre-imperialist epoch, when rapidly expanding demand for labour led to long distance labour migration and something like a 'melting pot' at the end of the trip. But even in those days there was little assimilation under non-European conditions, as with the Chinese in Southeast Asia, East Indians in the Caribbean, and many other cases. Broadly speaking, migration in colonial circumstances did not lead to assimilation. Today, under imperialist circumstances, we have for example ghettos, migrant labour camps, reservations, bantustans, and the phenomenon known as 'guest workers' in Europe – all communities which were formed by forced migration of one sort or another under imperialism. As a matter of fact, both Engels and Lenin pointed out long ago that migrations of these sorts do not lead to assimilation.[58] We need a theory of minorities for the period of imperialism, the period when in-coming workers tend not to be melted down into the host nationality. To paraphrase Lenin: in the period of imperialism, the national question becomes more acute, not less so. Realizing this, we should find ways to forge greater unity of the working class in the imperialist centres.

3. National struggle is class struggle, but it is nonetheless a very distinctive form of class struggle. As I will argue in Chapter 7, it can be thought of as 'external class struggle'. It occurs when the social relations of production extend across a spatial boundary. I think its typical form involves a ruling class which is exploiting both an internal producing class and an external one, the latter consisting of people from a different society who, through conquest or some other means of political domination, have been forced to deliver surplus to this (from their point of view) external ruling class. I use the most general terms here because I think it has been a structural feature of all class modes of production – not, however, all specific social formations – since ancient times. Perhaps it reflects the crisis which must afflict

any society when incremental surplus can no longer be extracted from the internal or domestic producers without bringing on rebellion or mass famine. Given sufficient power, a ruling class may then turn to external workers for the incremental surplus. It may wipe out the external ruling class or extract tribute from it. It may establish any of a number of different relations of production with the external workers. (It may even wipe them out and send internal workers to farm their land.)[59] I suggest merely that this line of thought may lead towards a generalization of our theory of national struggle, making it a theory applicable to all cases in which class struggle takes the national form.


# Notes

1. See G. W. F. Hegel, *The Philosophy of History* (1956) and *Philosophy of Right* (1952); J. G. von Herder, *Reflections on the Philosophy of the History of Mankind* (1968); J. G. Fichte, *Addresses to the German Nation* (1922). For Hegel, nation and state are roughly synonymous.

2. See K. Löwith, *From Hegel to Nietzsche* (1967). As Löwith points out, Hegel, the State Philosopher of Prussia, 'elevates the reality of the Prussian State to a philosophical existence' (p. 238). Also see F. Engels' *Ludwig Feuerbach and the End of Classical German Philosophy* (1976), p. 5; and Hegel's *Philosophy of Right*, p. 208, and *Philosophy of History*, pp. 427, 437, 456.

3. Hegel, *Philosophy of Right*, p. 182. Also see Marx's important comment on this passage in his 'Contribution to the Critique of Hegel's philosophy of Law' in K. Marx and F. Engels, *Works* (MEW) 3, pp. 38, 72.

4. Marx, 'Contribution to the Critique', pp. 3–129, 175–87.

5. Marx and Engels, *The German Ideology*, in MEW 5. The term 'theory of nationalism' (or 'theory of national struggle') is a modern label for these subject matters; Marx and Engels dealt with them under different labels.

6. Marx and Engels, *Manifesto of the Communist Party*, in MEW 6.

7. Engels, 'What Have the Working Classes To Do with Poland?' in D. Fernbach (ed.), *Karl Marx: Political Writings* 3 (1974), p. 383.

8. See, e.g., Engels, 'What is to Become of Turkey in Europe?' in MEW 12, and 'The Beginning of the End in Austria', ibid. 6.

9. For Poland, see, e.g., Engels 'What Have the Working Classes To Do with Poland?' For Ireland, see the anthology, Marx and Engels, *Ireland and the Irish Question* (1971), esp. pp. 147, 162, 281, 285, 293, 302–4, 332. For Germany, see, e.g., Marx and Engels' 1848 work 'Demands of the Communist Party of Germany', MEW 7. The first of the 17 demands reads as follows: 'The whole of Germany shall be declared a single and indivisible republic' (p. 3). The sentence following the list of demands states, 'It is to the interest of the German proletariat, the petty bourgeoisie, and the small peasants to support these demands with all possible energy' (p. 4).

10. O. Bauer, *Die Nationalitätenfrage und die Sozialdemokratie* (1907), K. Renner, *Der Kampf der Österreichischen Nationen um der Staat* (1903), and other works. Small excerpts of Bauer's and Renner's writings on the national question are translated in T. Bottomore and P. Goode, *Austro-Marxism* (1978).

11. I refer here to the 1899 Brünn programme, quoted in full in Bauer, *Die Nationalitätenfrage*, pp. 527–528. Bauer's proposals for changes in this party programme (to insert 'cultural–national autonomy') are not relevant to the present discussion (but see Chapter 5 below).

12. Quoted in Bottomore and Goode, *Austro-Marxism*, p. 120.

13. V. I. Lenin, *Works* 20, p. 398; and 41, p. 315.

14. J. V. Stalin, *Works* 3.

15. See Chapter 5 below.

16. See, e.g., Lenin's 'Critical Remarks on the National Question', *Works* 20.

17. See, in particular, Lenin's 'A Caricature of Marxism and Imperialist Economism', *Works* 23, and 'Report of the Commission on the National and Colonial Questions', 31. Also see Chapter 4 of the present volume.

18. See the Stalin anthology, *Marxism and the National-Colonial Question* (1975), esp. pp. 121, 138, 155, 282–83.

19. Stalin, *Works* 3, p. 340.

20. J. Ehrenreich, 'The Theory of Nationalism: A Case of Underdevelopment', *Monthly Review* 27, 1 (1977), p. 57. Also see Ehrenreich, 'Socialism, Nationalism and Capitalist Development', *Review of Radical Political Economics* 15, 1 (1983).

21. T. Nairn, *The Break-Up of Britain* (1977), p. 329.

22. N. Poulantzas, *State, Power, Socialism* (1978).

23. Ibid., p. 93.

24. Ibid., p. 94.

25. Ibid.

26. Ibid., pp. 97–119. For instance: 'Territory and tradition . . . are inscribed in the . . . underlying conceptual matrices of space and time' (p. 97). 'The State does not have to unify a pre-existing "internal" market, but installs a unified market by marking out the frontiers of what thereby becomes the inside of the outside' (p. 106). 'The modern nation makes possible the intersection of [the spatial and temporal] matrices and thus serves as their point of juncture; the capitalist State marks out the frontiers when it constitutes what is within (the people–nation) by homogenizing the before and after of the content of this enclosure. National unity . . . thereby becomes *historicity of a territory and territorialization of a history*' (p. 114). 'The territory and history crystallized by the State ratify the dominance of the bourgeois variant of the spatio-temporal matrix over its working-class variant' (p. 119). And so on, and on, and on . . .

27. Ibid., p. 93.

28. R. Debray, 'Marxism and the National Question: Interview with Régis Debray', *New Left Review* 105 (1977), p. 25.

29. Ibid., p. 27.

30. Ibid., p. 28.

31. Ibid., p. 33.

32. Ibid., p. 35.

33. The reader may consult A. D. Smith's *Theories of Nationalism* (1971), in which just about every (non-Marxist) theory of nationalism is briefly described, to appreciate how few of these theories depart from what I call here the typical form (diffusion of a modernizing idea).

34. Nairn, *The Break-Up of Britain*, pp. 334–41. I criticize Nairn's theory in detail in Chapter 3.

35. Ibid., pp. 96–104, 335–59. 'To say that the assorted phenomena . . . of nationalism have a "material" basis and explanation is akin to saying that

individual neurosis has a sexual explanation . . . "Nationalism" is the pathology of modern developmental history, as inescapable as "neurosis" in the individual, with a similar built-in capacity for descent into dementia, rooted in the dilemmas of helplessness thrust upon most of the world (the equivalent of infantilism for societies), and largely incurable' (p. 359).

36. Ibid., pp. 188–89, 216–55. See Chapter 3 of the present volume.

37. Ehrenreich, 'Socialism, Nationalism and Capitalist Development', p. 29.

38. Ibid., p. 1.

39. Ibid., p. 4.

40. Ibid., pp. 5–9, 28–29, 32.

41. H. B. Davis, *Toward a Marxist Theory of Nationalism* (1978).

42. H. B. Davis, *Nationalism and Socialism* (1967), and R. Luxemburg (H. B. Davis, ed.), *The National Question: Selected Writings of Rosa Luxemburg* (1976).

43. Davis, *Nationalism and Socialism*, pp. ix–xiv, and *Toward a Marxist Theory of Nationalism*, pp. 3–13, 22–25, 28–29.

44. In *Toward a Marxist Theory of Nationalism*, Davis refers to 'one of the favourite dogmas of Marxism, that the class struggle is the motor force of progress' (p. 223). 'Marxists, who have stressed class exploitation as almost the only form of exploitation, have come to recognize at long last that national exploitation can be just as serious and long-lasting as class exploitation' (pp. 159–60). 'Lenin . . . took the crucial step of incorporating national exploitation alongside of class exploitation' (p. 246). Also see pp. 27, 66, 83, 200, 205, 229.

45. Ibid., pp. 54–65.

46. Ibid., pp. 54, 68–69, 90.

47. Ibid., p. 18. ('In China, the Leninist nationality policy has been an outstanding success', p. 181.)

48. See Lenin's *Works* 24, p. 472, and 26, p. 175. This interpretation is widely accepted among left historians, including some who are unsympathetic to Lenin. See, e.g., F. Claudín, *The Communist Movement: Part 1* (1975), p. 254; and C. Bettelheim, *Class Struggles in the USSR, First Period* (1976), p. 420.

49. Davis, *Toward a Marxist Theory of Nationalism*, pp. 220–28.

50. A. Cabral, 'Declaration of Principles', in *Portuguese Colonies: Victory or Death* (1971), esp. pp. 110–17.

51. Engels' footnote to the 1888 English edition of the *Manifesto*. See Marx and Engels, *Works* 6, p. 482.

52. *Toward a Marxist Theory of Nationalism*, pp. 202–40. Davis also devotes considerable attention in this book to another contemporary form of (ultimately) classless society: the socialist countries. (I will not, nor does Davis, enter into the question of whether remnant classes exist in these countries. Obviously they do exist in some of them.) Davis shows that much progress has been made towards solving the national question in the socialist part of the world. He would perhaps agree with me that persistence of national conflicts there is attributable in the final analysis to external pressure from the capitalist world, leading, for instance, to the survival of non-socialist ideologies whose political expression may be a demand for autonomy or secession (along national cleavage-lines) from the socialist states; leading also to tensions between socialist countries which would not exist (or at any rate remain serious) in the absence of a capitalist threat to each country's revolution. These matters are outside the scope of the present essay. I merely need to point out that the survival of such national conflicts in a (still largely capitalist) world is interpretable within the class-based Marxist theory of nationalism.

53. Ibid., p. 189.

54. Ibid., p. 191.

55. Ibid., p. 192. For a Cuban view of these matters, see the Report of the Central Committee of the First Congress of the Cuban Communist Party, 1975, in *First Congress of the Communist Party of Cuba: Collection of Documents* (1976), pp. 16–62 ('Historical Analysis of the Revolution').

56. Davis, *Toward a Marxist Theory of Nationalism*, p. 200.

57. Stalin, *Works* 3, p. 339. Lenin held similar views in the pre-war period, but his views later changed dramatically as I show in Chapter 5.

58. Engels, in Marx and Engels, *Ireland and the Irish Question*, pp. 302–4 and 408–12; Lenin, 'The Socialist Revolution and Self-Determination', *Works* 22, p. 151, and 'Revision of the Party Programme', 26, p. 168.

59. National struggle in pre-capitalist modes of production need not imply the existence of nations. However, when the rigid identification of the birth of nations with the rise of capitalism has been discarded, we begin, inevitably, to think about the existence of pre-capitalist nations. The Vietnamese consider their nation to be very old indeed. (See, e.g., Nguyen Khac Vien, *Traditional Vietnam: Some Historical Stages*, 1970, esp. pp. 5 and 151–52.) The political, cultural, and economic fragmentation of medieval Europe tends to blind us to the fact that politically, culturally, and economically well-integrated and territorially demarcated societies were in fact rather common in other continents, and from very early times. On these matters, see Chapter 7.

# 3. Diffusionism and the National Question

'The theory of nationalism represents Marxism's great historical failure.' With this stern indictment, Tom Nairn begins his essay 'The Modern Janus', an essay designed to explain this failure (which was 'inevitable', he says, but 'can now be understood') and to provide us at last with a truly adequate theory of nationalism.[1] But the essay itself is a failure. The theory of nationalism which it attacks has not been widely held by Marxists since 1914. And Nairn's theory is anything but adequate. It is an attempt to construct a Marxist version of what is today the typical mainstream position: national struggles are not class struggles but are effects of an autonomous ideological force, nationalism, which diffused from Europe to the darker corners of the earth.[2] Nairn's theory is diffusionist and idealist. But it has become very influential as a Marxist theory of nationalism, and as a theory which explains Third World liberation movements in terms of the ideology of diffusing capitalism (mislabelled 'uneven development'). For these reasons it warrants a detailed critique. The critique can also be generalized to most other theories of nationalism as an autonomous ideological force. And, as I will suggest in the concluding section of this chapter, it raises questions about a peculiarly elitist sector of neo-Marxist thought.

'The task of a theory of nationalism', according to Nairn, is 'to see the phenomenon as a whole'.[3] Everything should be seen as a whole, of course, looked at from all points of view, and so on, but Nairn means to be taken literally. Nationalism for him is a whole phenomenon, a discrete process, a separate and autonomous force in history. Like the two-faced Roman god Janus, it has two aspects, one progressive and one reactionary, but these are merely facets of a single indivisible entity. This entity, nationalism, is not a form or part of class struggle nor even an outcome of class struggle, and viewing it as such has been the undoing of the Marxist theory of nationalism, the reason why it is 'Marxism's great historical failure'.[4] Marxism, says Nairn quite correctly, remains wedded to the view that class struggle is the motor of history. Not so, says Nairn. Nationalism does not emerge from class struggle: it is an autonomous force. Nationalism and class struggle have jointly fashioned the modern world and, of the two, nationalism has been the more important factor. It has been, says Nairn, 'the dominant contradiction'.[5]

Class struggle is also, as it happens, two-sided (or, if you prefer, Janus-faced); and we can usually tell roughly who are the exploiters and who the exploited. But for Nairn the two faces of nationalism have nothing much to do with exploitation or contending classes. One face points forwards to an ill-defined sort of 'liberation', something consisting mainly in freedom from 'domination'. The other points backwards to fascism.

Fascism, says Nairn, is one of the two faces of Janus. Nationalism is a single, whole phenomenon, and fascism is part of its very nature. Fascism is in fact the 'archetype' of nationalism.[6] It is 'a central sector of the phenomenon'.[7] It is therefore in some sense present in every national movement, every liberation struggle. It is literally part of the struggle.

No Vietnamese, Cuban, or indeed anyone else who has fought in or supported a national liberation struggle is likely to take kindly to a theory which brackets such struggles with Nazism and fascism, and which moreover insists that the class enemy is not the political enemy unless it is so by accident. And few Marxists anywhere will take kindly to a theory which relegates class struggle to a secondary role, which denies, as Nairn's does, that class struggle is the motor of historical change. Still, views of this sort are common in various sectors of progressive thought, even in certain corners of Marxist thought – in the advanced capitalist countries if nowhere else – and they cannot be dismissed out of hand and without comment. Nairn in fact defends his view with a reasoned, though faulty, argument, and it is important to examine that argument and refute it. I will try to do so in the following pages. Most of the attention will be devoted to the essay 'The Modern Janus'. This essay later reappeared as a chapter in Nairn's book *The Break-Up of Britain*, where it supplied theoretical ammunition for an argument to the effects that nationalist forces in Scotland, Wales, and Northern Ireland (among Protestants) are rising to success: are breaking up Britain.[8] Some of our attention will also be devoted to other chapters of Nairn's book, not for the purpose of commenting on the national question in any part of the British Isles – that is not our concern in the present book – but because Nairn's theoretical position is elaborated in various parts of *The Break-Up of Britain*.

## Nationalism and Diffusion

The first question to be asked about Nairn's theory, as about any theory of nationalism, is precisely what it deals with; what its subject matter is; what empirically identifiable entity or process it proposes to describe and explain. It is clear that Nairn wants to use the word 'nationalism' in primarily an ideological sense, as denoting such things as the ideas people have of the nation state, the psychological impulse to form an independent state, the political idea or doctrine which embodies that goal, and also a complex of truly deep psychological processes which Nairn associates with this idea, goal, and doctrine: processes which he labels with words like 'instinct', 'compulsion', and even 'dementia'. But Nairn is not concerned to construct a theory about the ideology (or ideologies) of nationalism as such, and his theory is not simply a topic in the history and geography of ideas. (Let it be noted that a theory about nationalist ideologies would in itself be a valid scientific contribution, provided it stopped short of explaining all the important phenomena of national struggle as mere effects of an ideological prime cause.) Nairn does indeed focus his attention mainly on matters of ideology and psychology but he moves smoothly and easily from this realm to a set of social and political processes which he clearly considers to be invariant effects of nationalist ideology. Nairn thus views his subject matter as embracing both a set of ideological processes and an entailed set of social and political processes, the former in some sense explaining the latter.

But his theory does not postulate ideology as a prime cause. Unlike many other theorists about nationalism, Nairn makes very clear what he considers to be the social – he calls them 'historical' – processes which engender nationalist ideology. The problem is that these processes have very little to do with matters of class, class struggle, or economic exploitation. Nairn reaches behind all such social, political, and economic facts to something more fundamental, something which he calls 'the crudest dilemma of modern history'. This is nothing less than the alleged diffusion of progress.

Nairn's concept of progress is completely in the classical tradition of Eurocentric diffusionism. He subscribes to the three basic tenets of this position and in fact uses them as tacit assumptions for his theory of nationalism. The first tenet holds that the important traits of progress, or civilization, or modernization, have always appeared first in Europe (or, for the present millennium, in Western Europe), that this pattern will apply in the future as it has in the past, and these traits of progress diffuse outwards from Europe to the rest of the world, arriving at any given place at a later date and often in damaged condition. The second tenet holds that these traits are ultimately matters of the ideological realm: they are 'ideas', 'inventions', and so on, and thus the priority of Europe is in the last analysis an intellectual priority, a matter of quicker and better thinking, or, as diffusionists since Max Weber have consistently expressed it, a matter of greater 'rationality'. The third tenet holds that centrifugal diffusion is the dominant process by which the European centre interacts with the extra-European periphery, and therefore that the outward spread of progress, modernization, civilization, and so on, is far more significant in every sense (including the moral one) than the centripetal processes, such as the infusion of surplus value, technology, and labour from the periphery to Europe. (In the old days colonialism was often justified with the diffusionist argument that no amount of wealth drawn out of the colonies could possibly repay the Europeans for their gift of 'civilization'.) The third tenet, in short, denies the importance of economic imperialism, past and present. What happens in the peripheral countries is not imperialism and underdevelopment but, on the contrary, progress and modernization.

Marx himself was something of a diffusionist, although he was less Eurocentric than any other European thinker of his time. But a survival of diffusionism into late-20th Century Marxist thought is something else entirely. Marx did not have access to information about extra-European civilizations, past and present: we do. Marx lived at a time and place where the most advanced thinkers still believed that agriculture, metal working, and even the human species itself had appeared first in Europe: we know better. In Marx's time, scholarly work was so entwined with Christianity that it seemed implausible that autonomous progress, or even rationality, would be found in non-Christian lands: we have sloughed off such prejudices. Today the Marxist tradition of thought has largely freed itself from Eurocentric diffusionism, though not entirely so (see Chapter 7 of this book), and if a Marxist proposes to defend such a diffusionist position today he or she must ground it, not in Marxism, but in conservative thought. This holds true most pointedly for Tom Nairn. His theory of nationalism owes more to Weberian theories of European rationality, along with more recent conservative theories of 'modernization', than it does to any tradition in Marxism. Let me now explain.

The key concept for an understanding of nationalism, according to Nairn, is uneven development. But Nairn gives this term a very special meaning. It is to be contrasted, first of all, with 'even development'. This too, has a special meaning. It does not carry the ordinary implication of geographical evenness or uniformity. Nairn is a diffusionist: development begins in Europe and spreads outwards; even development is simply smooth, even diffusion, with each part of the periphery acquiring the modernizing traits at the appropriate time. In sum: orderly progress on the periphery in a direction prefigured by the centre. Uneven development, by contrast, is, for Nairn, the condition which occurs when diffusion is disrupted, deflected, or frustrated; when peripheral regions are, as it were, anticipating the orderly, on-time arrival of the traits of modernization and development, but the traits fail to arrive.

Nairn says rather little about the causes of uneven development, that is, the reasons why diffusion fails to proceed as predicted and why peripheral regions experience the frustration of unsatisfied expectations. He blames it in part on the pernicious influence of the countries of advanced capitalism, whose domination of the peripheral countries, today as in the past, tends to hinder and distort their development. This is a familiar Marxist thesis, but what is important about Nairn's presentation of the thesis is the limited use he makes of it. There is some discussion of domination and dependency but scarcely any mention of exploitation or even, for that matter, colonialism. Occasionally peripheral countries are described as 'oppressed', but this seems to be merely a synonym for 'dominated', and to have little if anything to do with exploitation. But if exploitation is left out of the picture, we are no longer dealing with the Marxist theory of imperialism in any of its variants. This theory argues that peripheral societies, colonies and neocolonies, have experienced and are experiencing exploitation so severe that little or no development takes place; that the prevailing trend today may even be towards deepening underdevelopment. Nairn's model merely has the advanced countries exercising a political domination over the poor ones, a domination which somehow inhibits development but does not amount to a politico-military superstructure installed specifically for the purpose of maximising the possibilities for exploitation by companies based in the dominant countries – the classical Marxist model of the process.

The difference between the two models is quite fundamental, not least for Nairn's theory of nationalism. If exploitation is the basis of the process, we will look for, and find, a class of people in the dominated country who are exploited, and we would expect to find national liberation movements emerging with their roots in the exploited classes and with a very definite class struggle function: that of fighting against foreign rule not because foreigners 'dominate' but because they exploit. For Nairn, however, political domination seems to have no basis in exploitation. It seems to consist in nothing worse than a denial to the elite classes in the dominated society of the opportunities for greater wealth: for progress. In this model, the victims of uneven development are the elites of peripheral countries. These groups feel that their ambitions are being thwarted by external domination. But external domination is not even required by Nairn's model. In some peripheral countries there is merely envy of the more highly developed countries, and an impulse on the part of the elite to cut short the normal development process in an effort to catch up. In both cases, the elites feel a characteristic sense of frustration, and experience a characteristic reaction. This is nationalism.

Nationalism, then, emerges as a psychological frustration reaction on the part of the elites of backward countries to the trauma of uneven development. The reaction, according to Nairn, is 'emotional', 'instinctive', and 'irrational' (all references in this chapter are to *The Break-Up of Britain* unless otherwise indicated). Nationalism is

> the pathology of modern development history, as inescapable as 'neurosis' in the individual, with . . . a similar built-in capacity for descent into dementia, rooted in the dilemmas of helplessness thrust upon most of the world (the equivalent of infantilism . . .) (p. 359)

These psychological symptoms appear among the elite, who, in Nairn's theory, are the victims of uneven development. But irrationality, subjectivism, and the like, reappear at another point in the theory, and here they affect the masses. The elite cannot build an effective national movement, to win freedom from domination, without the participation of the masses. Nairn's 'masses' do not, however, play a leading, much less an intelligent, role in the nationalist process. They are 'mobilized' by the elite for the purpose of assembling the forces needed to win the struggle. Hence the movement is called by Nairn a 'populist' one: led by the elite, for its own purposes, but drawing in the masses as well. However, says Nairn, the masses can only be mobilized by resort to the subjective and the irrational.

> Such mobilization can only proceed, in practice, via a popular mass still located culturally upon a far anterior level of development, upon the level of feudal or prefeudal peasant or 'folk' life. That is, upon a level of (almost literally) 'pre-historic' diversity in language, ethnic characteristics, social habits, and so on. This ancient and (in a more acceptable sense of the term) 'natural' force imposes its own constraints upon the whole process, lending it from the outset precisely that archaic and yet necessary colour, that primeval-seeming or instinctive aspect which marks it so unmistakeably. (p, 101)

And again:

> [Nationalism] had to function through highly rhetorical forms, through a sentimental culture sufficiently accessible to the lower strata [*The lower strata!*] now being called to battle. This is why a romantic culture quite remote from Enlightenment rationalism always went hand in hand with the spread of nationalism. The new middle-class intelligentsia had to invite the masses into history; and the invitation had to be written in a language they understood . . . It is unnecessary here to explore the process in detail. Everyone is familiar with its outline, and with much of its content. We all know how it spread from its West-European source, in concentric circles of upheaval and reaction: through

Central and Eastern Europe, Latin America, and then across the other continents. Uniformed imperialism of the 1880–1945 variety was one episode in this larger history, as were its derivatives, anti-colonial wars and 'decolonization'. We have all studied the phenomena so consistently accompanying it: the 'rediscovery' or invention of national history, urban intellectuals invoking peasant virtues which they have experienced only through train windows on their summer holidays, schoolmasters painfully acquiring 'national' tongues spoken only in remote valleys, the infinity of forms assumed by the battle between scathing cosmopolitan modernists and emotional defenders of the Folk . . . and so on. (p. 340).

I have quoted Nairn at some length here because this passage tells us a great deal about his theory. The concrete postulate about the diffusion of nationalism ('concentric circles', etc.) will claim our attention later. The strange, even, for a Marxist, bizarre, descriptions (ordinary people are 'prehistoric', 'natural', 'primeval', colonialists are 'scathing cosmopolitan modernists' while those who fight against colonialism are 'emotional defenders of the Folk', etc.) will be passed over without comment. Here I want to call attention to Nairn's thesis that the masses do not enter history on their own, and for their own material – that is to say class – ends. They are led (or 'invited') into battle by the elite, spinning nationalist fairy-tales (the 'invention of national history', etc.). Therefore nationalism is not class struggle of the ordinary sort, pitting exploiters against exploited. Is it, then, the special sort of class struggle which takes place between competing bourgeois class communities, one peripheral and the other metropolitan? No, says Nairn, the peripheral elites are not, as the traditional Marxist argument would have it, being ground under by metropolitan capitalism, and fighting to preserve their class position and hopefully to rise. They are just suffering a sense of frustration. Their nationalism is basically the envy of someone looking over the wall into his neighbour's larger, more colourful, garden.

Naturally enough, Nairn's nationalism was invented in Europe. His model of origins has a literal centrepiece, a 'West-European source', an 'Anglo-French centre' (p. 98). At the end of the Napoleonic wars there emerged two modern nation states, Britain and France. Coincident with what Nairn calls 'the tidal wave of modernization' (pp. 96, 98, 338), 'transmitted outwards and onwards' (p. 99) in 'concentric circles' (pp. 98, 340), there spread also the idea of imitating the Western European nation state, an idea which, translated into practice, became national movements and nationalism. The first true nationalism arose in Germany and Italy, countries which Nairn, following Wallerstein (another diffusionist in our midst), calls 'semi-peripheral'. Then the tidal wave advanced 'through Central and Eastern Europe, Latin America, and across the other continents' (p. 340). Elsewhere in his book Nairn inserts Japan after eastern Europe and before 'the rest of the globe' (p. 98), but on the whole the geometry of the model remains internally consistent. This is helpful to a critic, because the model can be tested fairly easily by reference to particular dates and places: did the diffusing trait, nationalism, arrive at the expected time and in the expected manner? This is by no means the only basis for a criticism of Nairn's theory of nationalism, but it quickly reveals just how defective the theory is.

Germans and Italians were probably the inventors of the more important conservative theories of nationalism, but Germany and Italy were by no means the first countries to generate a national movement and enter the process of nationalism: that is, to struggle for state sovereignty through unification (as in these two cases) or through secession (as in most others). The German national movement had no palpable reality before the 1820s; the Italian, later still. By then national movements had arisen and triumphed in the United States (1783), Haiti (1804), and most of the Latin American mainland (c. 1820). And by the time unification had been achieved by Germany and Italy, a number of other countries, among them Greece and Belgium, had won their independence. Nairn's space–time model simply does not fit.

If we next trace the spread of national movements within Europe down through the 19th Century and into the 20th, there does, indeed, seem to be a broadly west-to-east spread, as required by Nairn's diffusion model, although exceptions like Greece, Belgium, and Norway, must be noted. But this space–time movement was not really associated with the process that Nairn puts forward as explanation. The bourgeois states which emerged in central and eastern Europe gained their independence not through a diffusion eastward of nationalism, along a slope of 'uneven development', but through a conjunction of two processes external to Nairn's theory. One was the defeat of Germany, Austria–Hungary, and Turkey in the First World War (something which had precious little to do with the frustration of the Bohemian and Croatian elites). The second was the Bolshevik revolution.

It would be idle to speculate about what the post-war map of Europe would have looked like had there been no Bolshevik revolution, with its echoes in Hungary and Germany. Certainly the danger of spreading revolution compelled the victorious powers to form, at Versailles and later, a band of bourgeois states in the buffer zone between Soviet Russia and capitalist France, states which were rather scientifically carved out so as to maximize their potential viability – in this case meaning safety from revolution – by minimizing ethnic complexity as much as possible without creating weak mini-states. Having said this, I have to concede that one sort of diffusion process was, indeed, involved in this overall process. This was the perfectly well-known spread of capitalism, and the brute necessity on the part of young bourgeois class-communities in oppressed areas of eastern Europe to strive for the establishment of a state in which no other class community would be able to prevent them from accumulating capital. But, as Lenin, Luxemburg, and Bauer could all agree, this necessity did not have to result in secession, and therefore the diffusion of capitalism was not at all the same thing as the diffusion of the nation state.

Let us now recall Nairn's 'tidal wave of modernization', which is supposed to have carried nationalism 'in concentric circles' out across the extra-European world. The word 'modernization' is, to begin with, very slippery. When Marxists apply this word to the colonial countries and the colonial period they ordinarily mean simply 'capitalism' (for, in the logic of historical materialism, capitalism is more 'modern' than feudalism). 'Modernization' does not at all imply, to Marxists, economic development, an industrial revolution, or a significant improvement in the lives of working people. Industry did not spread to colonies. The conditions of life in most colonies grew markedly worse during the colonial period: we think, for instance, of the increase in the frequency and severity of famines in India during the British occupation, the evident decline in life expectancy during that period, and so on.[9] For Marxists, then, the word 'modernization', like the word 'development', describes a process that is now, in newly independent countries, just barely getting underway. So, to put it bluntly: there has been no 'tidal wave of modernization', no 'great shock-wave' (p. 338) or 'expanding wave' (p. 102) or 'march of Western Progress over the globe' (p. 337). Such things are cognitive models in an ideological universe which has no empirical reference, and are, moreover, much more than wrongheaded ideas: they are constructed myths, designed to persuade people of something that Marxists know to be false: that capitalism can bring progress and prosperity to the poor countries of the world.

Yet the idea of a 'tidal wave of modernization' is necessary to Nairn's theory. Nationalism for him is the mechanism which allowed countries to enter upon what he calls 'the forced march out of backwardness and dependency' (p. 343), hence to overcome uneven development and grow modern. No such 'forced march out of backwardness' has taken place in the world of former colonies, the world of peripheral nationalism, except in the case of socialist countries, a case which Nairn seems to disallow (he applies the word 'socialist' to no country other than Yugoslavia). Thus no tidal wave, and no Nairnian nationalism.

Diffusionist models cannot explain the space–time pattern of decolonization, much less peripheral-country nationalism in general. Among successfully decolonizing national liberation movements, the main sequence runs from Haiti to other parts of Latin America, to Ireland, to India, to Indonesia, and thereafter in a seemingly random space–time pattern across the rest of Asia, Africa, and the West Indies (excepting only a few not-yet-liberated colonies, like Puerto Rico and Namibia). As to the process behind this pattern, it is of course much too complex to epitomize in a sentence or two of description, but it reflects neither diffusion nor modernization. It reflects, in brief, the rise of classes which, suffering exploitation or marginalization under colonial rule, adopted nationalism as the central strategy to relieve themselves of these burdens, a strategy which, if not sufficient – witness the neocolonies of this world – was at the very least necessary. Ignoring this process entirely, Nairn gives us instead a model of the diffusion of an 'irrational' ideology and political movement, as though resistance to exploitation were itself irrational.

## Nationalism and Fascism

The next problem for Nairn is to explain how nationalism, this irrational ideology borne outward from Europe on the 'tidal wave of modernization', came, somehow, to infect the core countries: Germany and Italy during the first part of the present century, and then other countries, most especially that bastion of world capitalism and beneficiary (not victim) of uneven development, the United Kingdom. (Let us recall, it is the nationalism of Scotland, Wales, and Northern Ireland that Nairn is mainly concerned to explain and defend.) Nairn harks back to the time when Germany and Italy were somewhat backward countries, in comparison to Britain and France, were countries in which, according to Nairn's theory, uneven development engendered nationalist movements. Then Nairn skips half a century or more, not pausing to explain how it was that nationalism persisted in these countries after unification had been accomplished and down through a long era of massive industrial development and rising prosperity, an era which saw Germany surpass France and nearly catch up with Britain in most economic spheres. Finally, says Nairn, the old nationalism of Germany and Italy effloresced into fascism. The transformation was, for him, quite natural. Fascism is nothing more than hypertrophied nationalism. It is the 'archetype' of nationalism, or nationalism 'carried to its "logical conclusion", as an autonomous mode of socio-political organization' (p. 347). It is nationalism writ large.

The exact mechanism by which quantity becomes quality, nationalism becomes fascism, is given meagre attention. Germany, Italy, and Japan (whose 'militarism' Nairn brackets with fascism) were late-developing countries of the semi-periphery, hence they had become nationalist in the usual Nairnian way. But, since they were semi-peripheral rather than peripheral, late-developing rather than underdeveloped, they managed to become strong states. Thus they acquired 'modern socio-economic institutions enabling them to mobilize and indoctrinate their masses effectively'. And thus 'these societies were able to realize the ideology of "nationalism" with unprecedented force' (p. 346). But something else seems to have been involved: a 'fear of "underdevelopment"', a sense that their 'position remained precarious'.

> In the first half of this century [Germany, Italy, and Japan] were confronted with the fact, or the immediate likelihood, of breakdown. For all of them this implied relegation: permanent confinement to the secondary, semi-peripheric status, exclusion from the core-area's 'place in the sun'. Physical or moral defeat, the menace of internal collapse, or (as they saw it) continued or renewed aggression by the central imperial powers – these were the motives that impelled them into a still more intensive form of nationalist mobilization. (p. 347)

that is, fascism. In commenting on this exposition, I will not dwell on the almost Hegelian way Nairn has of ascribing psychological properties to whole nations. Nor will I stress that this passage is full of factual errors. (For instance, that prior to the fascist era, there had been no 'defeat' for Italy and Japan, and no 'breakdown' for Japan.) There are, rather, two points to be made. First: while all scholars find some relationship between post-First World War traumas and the rise of fascism, Nairn's attempt to present the latter as, on the one hand, a psychological reaction and, on the other hand, a nationalist reaction, is far-fetched, and certainly not established as valid in the few sentences quoted above, the only argument provided. And second, if we add these sentences about the rise of fascism to Nairn's direct and simple equation of nationalism with fascism, we have an entire theory of fascism, albeit a theory presented with neither argument nor evidence. To explain fascism is not at all my intent in the present essay. But to show that fascism is something absolutely unrelated to national liberation struggles in oppressed countries, and only symptomatically related to nationalism in general, is a necessary part of the argument.

There is much disagreement about the relationship between fascism and nationalism. The problem is a muddle of conceptual difficulties, scholarly disagreements, and political differences. One reason why we shall not easily solve it is the fact that we have no very good theory of fascism itself. If we did, there would not be heated debates on the Left as to whether there is or is not a danger of fascism emerging in the liberal capitalist states, nor confusion as to whether contemporary gorilla regimes in countries like Chile, Guatemala, South Korea, Thailand, and so on, should be described as fascist. Another reason is the fact that nationalism is usually, but not always, a significant feature of fascist countries. To be specific, most but not all of these countries have tended to engage in expansionist national struggle and to evolve the corresponding ideological formulae which rationalize the conquest and subjugation of other territories and peoples. (Loyalty to the state is always, of course, emphasized, but to describe this ideological element, in isolation, as nationalist, or to find nationalism wherever ideology of this sort is displayed, is to employ a concept of nationalism so broad as to be useless, and at the same time much too narrow since it excludes all social and political processes implied in the concept of 'national struggle', the characteristic Marxist synonym for 'nationalism'.) Franco's Spain and Salazar's Portugal did not engage in expansionist adventures, apart from the usual campaigns to pacify portions of colonial territories. Italian fascism certainly had the classic features of expansionist nationalism, replete with the rhetoric of rebuilding the Roman Empire. But Mussolini's colonial expansion in Ethiopia and even Albania was not much more than a belated form of classical colonial imperialism, and the rhetoric may have been no more outrageous than the ideology of 'manifest destiny' in the United States and comparable ideologies of imperialism in Britain and France. Fascist Italy indeed displayed a racist and anti-semitic ideology (though perhaps not much more so than the United States at that time), but its main hatred was reserved, in a perversely logical way, for socialists. And, in any case, the assumption (made by Nairn among others) that racism and anti-semitism are somehow identifiable with nationalism is quite false. In national liberation struggles the belief-systems deal not with who is superior and who is inferior, but with who is free and who is not. In imperialist expansionism the belief-systems may indeed be nakedly racist but they may also be (superficially) egalitarian and democratic, as when the British public is assured by its leaders that the Empire is being enlarged in order to civilize the savages, or when the American public is assured that the Korean and Vietnam wars are aimed at preserving freedom and democracy in those lands. Nationalist movements may be progressive or reactionary; likewise their ideologies.

The really complex case is Nazism. It is quite true that one of the ideologies of nationalism, one of many, takes the form of a belief-system which justifies foreign conquest on grounds that the people to be conquered are inferior to the conqueror. Nazism certainly employed this formula, and used it to cover truly inhuman acts. But certain points need to be made, not to ameliorate but to assist in generalization. For one thing, the reference group was typically not the national category, 'Germans', but the pseudo-racial category, 'Aryans'. For another thing, a similar racist ideology and its attendant behaviour were far from uncommon during the course of colonial expansion. (Recall Aimé Césaire's comparison of colonialism and Nazism in *Discourse on Colonialism*.) Under colonialism in general, non-Europeans tended to be considered inferior or even subhuman, and whether they were genocidally massacred, enslaved, or merely subjected to colonial exploitation as wage labourers depended most of all on the interests and power of the colonizing country, not on differences of ideology.

Four things seem to me to be crucial here about the Nazi case. First, the 'inferior' people, hence the victims, were white and European. Second, genocidal massacre reached technological heights: the gas chambers at Auschwitz were incomparably more efficient than the US Cavalry at Wounded Knee. Third, race hate and genocide were being preached and practised in modern times, not in the bad old days of history. (But comparable ideas and acts, on a smaller scale, were still to be found in the colonial world, including Puerto Rico, in the Nazi period. And race hate was by no means absent in the democratic countries in this period: it is no accident that the American Nazis today make common cause with the Ku Klux Klan.) And fourth was the special holocaust visited upon the Jews.

There is one model in which all four of these features are at least schematically explained, and it does not derive them from nationalism. (Says Nairn: racism and anti-semitism are 'derivatives' of nationalism. Racism and anti-semitism are very, very old, as Nairn well knows, and nationalism in his theory goes back only to the last century. Another error and another contradiction.) In this alternative model, the central and crucial basis for Nazi ideology is the imperative of functionality in one historical context and towards one goal: defeating the ideologies of the communists and social democrats, this at a time when capitalism was in a state of collapse in Germany and revolution threatened. The ideological arguments and models had to convince the workers and petty bourgeoisie that the enemy was not the ruling class, in its public or private guise; the enemy was external to the society, and this enemy was the cause of all of Germany's ills. Translated into the subjective, emotive language needed to re-direct the passionate feelings of an already inflamed people away from hatred for capitalism and established authority, the message became one of blame and hatred for all those groups who could be identified as 'enemy', including the internal 'enemy', the Jews, and external 'enemies' comprising foreign governments, plotting to hold Germany in a permanent condition of poverty, and foreign peoples, enjoying prosperity on lands and resources stolen from their rightful owners, the Germans. I will not try to explain why German workers permitted themselves, for a time, to be persuaded by this ideology. I merely wish to emphasize the fact that Nazi ideology is much more plausibly explained in this model than in Nairn's theory, according to which everything is explained by invoking the prime cause and autonomous force of nationalism. It seems to me that Nazi expansionist nationalism should, itself, be explained by something more fundamental: the defensive class struggles of capitalism.

Much of the horror that was the Nazi epoch in Germany can be explained by invoking the Marxist theory of colonialism. The place to begin is with Lenin's theory about the causes of the First World War, a theory which asserted that the basic cause of this war was colonialism. To be more specific: (1) the new era of imperialism was one in which colonialism had become more crucial for capitalism than ever before; but (2) it was an era in which the whole world had already been claimed (partitioned) as colony or sphere of influence by one or another of the great capitalist powers; and therefore (3) it was an era which would be characterized by cannibalistic fighting among the powers for what Lenin described as the 'repartition of the world'. (See Chapter 5). Germany was thus fighting mainly to retain and to enlarge her colonial empire, and of course she failed.

But the ideology of colonialism cannot have disappeared after Versailles. It is likely, rather, to have grown still more intense during the post-war economic crisis. The boundaries of colonialist ideology are both broad and ill-defined. They comprise nearly all racism and much ethnocentrism, ideological elements which, as we well know, were marshalled in the service of colonialism over several centuries, although their origin is generally older. These elements do not clearly differentiate between the notions of 'colony' and 'annexed territory', so that expansive German nationalism within Europe would be seen as having the same basic justification and purpose as expansive nationalism in Africa or the Pacific. Deployed in post-war Germany, this ideology becomes the argument that prosperity can indeed be regained, under capitalism, if Germany can succeed in annexing adjoining territories, surrogate colonies which, like colonies everywhere, will provide raw materials, markets, and, more generally, value, a part of which can filter down to the German working class and ameliorate their suffering. And of course the (non-German) people of these territories, like colonials elsewhere, are defined as inferior and in need of German 'tutelage' (the single most favoured noun in the colonialists' vocabulary). Thus the ideology of classical, capitalist colonialism is twisted and transformed into the Nazi ideology of expansive nationalism.

Following this line of thought a single step farther, we come upon an argument which may help to explain the Jewish holocaust. The Jews of Germany had many of the attributes of a colonial people. To begin with, they possessed resources which could be expropriated. This could be and was justified in quite typical colonialist terms, and the results of expropriation, like colonial spoliation elsewhere, would be seen as an increase in the wealth of other (non-Jewish) Germans. Second, the Jews were culturally just different enough from other Germans to permit racist ideology – already widely diffused in a country which had only recently owned colonies, and in which anti-semitism was chronic – to be directed forcefully at Jews. This would not only provide the rationalization for the expropriation of Jewish property, but it would, more significantly, permit the Jews to serve as the surrogate target for the German workers' hatred of capitalism (not capitalists but *Jewish* capitalists were to blame), for German hatred of the foreigners who, at Versailles, stole their wealth and caused their misery (the Jews were just sufficiently 'foreign' in culture to serve this surrogate role), and, finally, the Germans' need to have colonies and colonial subjects: 'natives'. Perhaps I should not say 'the Germans' need' and 'the Germans' hatred', because we are, after all, discussing a carefully manufactured ideology, that of Nazism. All of these roles created for the Jews in Nazi ideology were designed to fashion a substitute enemy in the class war.

Is fascism, then, the 'archetype' of nationalism? A 'central sector of the phenomenon' of nationalism? Nationalism carried to its 'logical conclusion'? (pp. 345–347.) Set aside the questions of theory for a moment and consider the real implications of this position. It requires us to believe that all national movements, including national liberation movements against colonialism, are intrinsically fascist. It requires us to believe that their source is ideology, not class exploitation and the oppression that is imposed, and resisted, in connection with exploitation. None of this is true, but it is all required by Nairn's theory. As to the theory itself, I have shown that it has no substance. National movements can have feudalist, bourgeois democratic, fascist, socialist, and other sorts of ideologies. Likewise the forces that oppose such movements. Fascist movements can make use of the politics of national aggrandizement, and even the politics of secessionism. But nationalism has no direct and close connection to fascism, and the problem of fascism cannot be solved within the theory of nationalism.

## Neo-Nationalism and Counter-Diffusion

Nairn's theory-building efforts, like most serious contributions to the Marxist theory of nationalism, are anchored in a particular, concrete manifestation of the national question. Nairn is concerned with what he calls the 'neo-nationalist' movements of Scotland, Wales, and (Protestant) Northern Ireland, movements which in his view will bring about the 'break-up of Britain'. Nairn has a certain amount to say about the evolution of these movements and their present-day characteristics, but he knows that something more is needed if he is to persuade the Left to accept his two principal contentions: that these movements are, indeed, important and that they are progressive. He thinks the problem lies with the Marxist theory of nationalism, with its obsession with class struggle and its unrealistic contention that nationalism is a fading anachronism, a relic of the era of early capitalism and thus a force no longer powerful and no longer progressive. Departing from this position – an incorrect one, as I will show in the final section of the present chapter – he rebuilds the theory, not on the basis of class struggle but on the basis of a supposed frustration-reaction to 'uneven development'. As we have seen, this theory has no real evidential support, but it does at least construct a barely plausible model for the countries of the periphery and the 'semi-periphery' (Germany, etc.). Such countries are supposed to have acquired nationalism as a response to the 'tidal wave of modernization', the outward diffusion of progress. All very well. But how can Nairn then explain the return, the counter-diffusion, of nationalism from the periphery back to the centre, back to Britain, there to emerge as the new ('neo-') nationalist movements within its borders? One would now be swimming upstream against the current of diffusion. But how is this to be done?

This question is perhaps the most important one we can ask about Nairn's theory. It is the put-up-or-shut-up question: here you have a theory and there you have a set of facts, facts about neo-nationalism, which the theory is supposed to explain, is designed to explain. Well, then, explain. But Nairn disappoints us. He has a separate explanation for each of the component parts of this problem: the return of nationalism to the nation states of Western Europe; the rise of neo-nationalism in Scotland; the rise of neo-nationalism in Wales; the (by Nairn) hopefully anticipated rise of neo-nationalism in the Protestant community of Ulster. These explanations have nothing much to do with one another and nothing at all to do with Nairn's central theory of nationalism. Scotland, we are told, is a 'unique' case (p. 110), 'a historical oddity' (p. 134), and Scottish neo-nationalism is '*sui generis*'. (p. 128). Nairn's explanation for the rise of neo-nationalism in

Scotland is thoughtful and interesting, but it has nothing to do with Nairn's 'tidal wave' and the rest of his general theory. For Wales, we are told that Welsh 'cultural nationalism', itself unexplained, somehow turned into political nationalism, and matters are basically left at that. The discussion of Northern Ireland is so peculiar, and so full of danger signals for Marxist theory and practice, that I will treat it separately, though briefly, later in this chapter, but this case, too, is given its own private explanation. Even the general, underlying fact, the return (as Nairn has it) of nationalism to the core countries and thus to Britain, is explained in a way that has no connection to the general theory – if, indeed, we can call this particular construction an explanation. The closest we come to an explanation is in this passage:

> 'Uneven development' is not just the hard luck tale of poor countries. It dragged the wealthy ones in as well. Once the national state had been ideologized into 'nationalism' and turned into the new climate of world politics – the new received truth of political humanity – the core-areas themselves were bound to become nationalist. As the march-lands caught up in the later nineteenth century, as Germany, Italy, and Japan emerged into . . . extra-rapid industrialization . . . was it surprising that England and France developed their own forms of 'nationalism'? There resulted a struggle between founder-members and *parvenus*, where great-power nationalism was forged from the new notions and sentiments. In other words, 'uneven development' is a dialectic. The two sides involved continuously modify each other. Nationalism may have originated as a kind of 'antithesis' to the 'thesis' of metropolitan domination. But it was rapidly, and inevitably, transmitted to the whole process. (p. 344)

In all this there is only one really empirical argument about the counter-diffusion of nationalism. It is the reasonable-sounding assertion that, if Germany, Italy, and Japan are compelled by virtue of their nationalism to go to war with Britain and France, then naturally ('was it surprising . . . ?') their antagonists would also become nationalist, and nationalism would thus diffuse across the battlelines from semi-periphery to core. But this is chop-logic. Wars have been with us a long time. and they have had no necessary relationship to nationalism. Bellicose attitudes may, indeed must, be transmitted from one warring side to the other unless they are there already, but not much else diffuses. Nazism did not diffuse at Stalingrad or fascism at Salerno. And so on. But there are other sorts of objections. For one thing, 'uneven development' does not enter the picture. For another thing, Nairn is here slipping into the argument an extraordinary new theory about 'great power nationalism'. It seems to have diffused from Germany, Italy, and Japan to the other great European states during the present century. Therefore, according to Nairn, there was no great power nationalism in Britain and France, not to mention Russia and Austria–Hungary, in earlier times, and the trait, moreover, came to these states by diffusion. And where, in all of this, is great power imperialism?

As for the rest of this passage, it adds no further explanation as to how nationalism seeped back into the core, offering instead a few rhetorical flourishes of the sort which, I regret to say, Marxists very often use to fill out incomplete arguments: invoking the word 'dialectic' to paper over gaps in reasoning and unresolved contradictions; lacing the text with argument-pushers like 'bound to' and 'inevitably' and 'was it surprising that . . . ?' (and elsewhere in Nairn's book a barrage of 'truly's' and 'of course's' and 'naturally's', along with the occasional 'any fool knows that' and 'it is the simplest matter of historical fact . . . that'); and, more generally, reinforcing a simple and thin argument by expressing it in the most elegant and convoluted language, replete with obscure allusions, foreign words, and resounding though empty phrases like 'the new received truth of political humanity'. I lean on this point for two reasons. First: Nairn's theory as a whole is just this sort of thin argument fattened out by rhetoric. And second: the absence of a real, empirical explanation as to how peripheral nationalism, semi-peripheral nationalism, core-area nationalism, and inner-periphery 'neo-nationalism' all connect up together is both a glaring, perhaps fatal, weakness in the theory and also an invalidation of Nairn's most pretentious claim for the theory: that it brings all the forms of nationalism into a single explanation about a single, whole (though Janus-faced) phenomenon. We are left with the nationalism supposedly generated by uneven development and an altogether different sort of nationalism in the core countries. And these two categories are, themselves, taxonomically dubious. The first includes national liberation struggles but it also includes fascism. The second does not include imperialism.

I must dwell a bit more on this matter of counter-diffusion. Although Nairn says very little about the mechanisms by which nationalism returns from its home in the periphery to enter the core countries, he does, nonetheless, create a kind of mood in which this counter-diffusion seems almost natural. This mood-setting, which pervades the whole of Nairn's book, seems again to be derived (perhaps unwittingly) from classical Eurocentric diffusionism. Central to that perspective is what we may call 'the principle of ideological contagion', that is, the spread of ideas for no particular reason other than their innate infectiousness. The contagion occurs in both directions: centrifugally and centripetally, outwards and inwards. In the outward direction, it is the bestowal of modernizing, enlightening traits. Inwards, it tends to be identified with things savage and irrational. The schematic logic of this model, in its classical form, is as follows: since cultural evolution tends to occur at the (European) centre and spread centrifugally, the outer regions must always be more backward than the inner, because their culture must reflect an earlier stage in the evolutionary process. Therefore any counter-diffusion will be a passage of older and thus less civilized traits into the core. At any given time, there is a duality between core and periphery – each seen as a single region – which maps into space such familiar (and today mainly neo-Kantian) oppositions as reason and unreason (instinct, emotion), abstract and concrete, mind and body, science and sorcery, discipline and spontaneity, adult and child, sane and insane, progressive and stagnant ('traditional'), and of course civilized and primitive. Ideological contagion, then, is a passage of the one sort of trait from core to periphery and of the other sort from periphery to core.

Nairn employs a version of this model in his descriptions of the core and the periphery (plus 'semi-periphery') and the currents passing between them. The core, western Europe, is repeatedly described as 'rational', or with epithets denoting its intellectual stature: 'the rationalism of our Enlightenment heritage', 'the Enlightenment' (repeatedly used as an epithet for Western culture, as on p. 338:

'The Enlightenment was borne into wider reality' to the 'less-developed lands'), 'Western rationality' (p. 337), 'western-founded "progress"' (p. 361), the 'west-wind of progress' (p. 360), and so on. It is important that we keep in mind the fact that, for Nairn, 'the West', or the core, comprises only western Europe – perhaps only Britain and France. So Nairn's position, however ethnocentric and elitist it may be, seems not to be racist.

Nairn does not simply characterize the periphery as irrational, unenlightened. His description of peripheral culture is developed in three steps. First, we read about the peripheral regions before 'the spread of civilized progress' (p. 99) began to change them. Before the 1790s they were 'buried in feudal and absolutist slumber' (p. 96), in 'barbarism' (p. 108), their masses 'still located culturally upon a far anterior level . . . feudal or pre-feudal . . . archaic . . . primeval-seeming', etc. Notice, by the way, that Nairn is describing here the semi-peripheral Germany of Bach and the Italy of Vivaldi, along with Moghul India, Ming China, and the rest. Then the 'tidal wave' arrives (mainly, I infer, in the form of colonialism), along with the somewhat indefinite effects of uneven development. And finally, all of this produces an explosive reaction. One dimension of the reaction is nationalism, seen as a doctrine and policy, but the overall process is much deeper and wider. In one context Nairn identifies it with 'romanticism', which he describes as 'the search for inwardness, the trust in feeling or instinct, the attitude to "nature", the cult of the particular and mistrust of the "abstract", etc' (p. 104). In another context he employs a psychoanalytic analogy (or homology), likening the reaction to the forces of the unconscious which are unleashed in childhood; invoking concepts like 'regression', 'instinct', 'inwardness', 'dementia', and 'infantilism'; and describing the whole process as 'the pathology of modern developmental history', and as a manifestation of 'the collective unconscious' (pp. 348–350). In all this Nairn is not simply attaching descriptors to the concept of nationalism; he is describing some underlying cultural force in these peripheral societies: he is characterizing the societies themselves, as in this passage:

> The powers of the Id are far greater than was realized before Freud exposed them to theoretical view. In the same way, the energies contained in customary social structures were far greater than was understood, before the advent of nationalist mobilization stirred them up and released them from the old mould. (p. 349)

Having been thus stirred up and released, these savage forces then spread back and forth across the globe, and brought neo-nationalism to Great Britain.

The nationalism which came in this way to Britain is considered by Nairn to have lost most of its virulence. English nationalism is not described with terms like 'instinct' and 'irrationality'. It is civilized, mild, and rational. It is 'dignified' and 'politically inert'. It is nothing worse than a 'reverence for the overall nature' of British society, 'a faith in the . . . system', an acceptance of 'a "way of life" basically worth defending' (pp. 42–44). Thus no dementia or infantilism. Nairn explains the peculiarities of English nationalism in terms of the gradual development over three centuries and more of a rather stable and well integrated society, one in which the class war has never grown to such proportions as to tear apart the social fabric. In fact, according to Nairn, there has never really been much class struggle in Britain. He describes this country with phrases like 'social cohesion' (p. 69) and writes of 'the English class-compromise' (p. 32), the 'deep class alliance' (p. 59) and, for present-day Britain, 'the frozen ice of the class struggle' (p. 59). I will not comment on this curious (for a Marxist) view of British society and history.[10] I need merely note Nairn's argument that the effects of steady economic decline in this cohesive society will be a kind of internal decomposition which, assisted by the external pressures of neo-nationalism in the British periphery, will bring about the 'break-up of Britain'. This will also, he hopes, lead to a break-up of the 'frozen ice' of class struggle, and thus, via nationalism, regenerate social progress in this part of the world. I need hardly add that this construction bears little resemblance to common-or-garden Marxism.

The relative stability of British society is not in dispute. Nairn attributes it, as do most Marxists and quite a few others (including most notably Hobson), to the extraordinary wealth which flowed to Britain from the Empire, wealth sufficient to ease the burden of exploitation just enough to keep social conflict from erupting into revolution. Hence the British working class permitted itself to be led into the occasional European war on behalf of the bourgeoisie, and in this sense succumbed to nationalism (as it also did in the faith-in-the-system sense discussed above, and as it will do, Nairn hopes, in still a third sense: a kind of resurrection of national will or purpose which may come, somehow, after the 'break-up'). But Nairn carries this argument about the effects of Empire too far in one direction and not far enough in another. Too far in that he thinks, wrongly, that it has led to a 'class alliance', a freezing of the class struggle. Not far enough in that Nairn quite fails to see that Empire – that is, British colonialism – was itself inseparable from nationalism.

Empire, for Nairn, is simply a given fact, something that produces certain effects on British society but does not call for analysis within his theory. It is, he says, 'uneven development' which 'generates these "given facts" of imperialism and nationalism' (p. 21n) (thereby giving further magical powers to 'uneven development'). But the growth of the British Empire was surely one of the really dramatic and significant cases of great power nationalism. It was, among many other things, genuine national struggle, in that it involved territorial expansion and the establishment of British colonial government over previously sovereign states and self-governing societies. Its ideology was, among other things, an ideology of nationalism. If in certain periods it was less strident than some other nationalist ideologies, this mainly reflected the fact that colonial expansion brought self-evident rewards to many members of British society, who therefore needed less ideological prodding than would otherwise have been the case. Nairn, however, fails altogether to assimilate classical imperialism to the concept of nationalism. We recall that he attributes great power nationalism to the Germans and their allies in the two World Wars and imagines it to have infected a still-innocent Britain in that era. He does not consider as nationalism the continental and later overseas expansion of the United States, a process which was typically imperialist and was provided with a typical nationalist ideology, known as 'manifest destiny'. If all such cases of imperialism can be seen as expansive national struggle, or expansionist nationalism, then we have to see the resistance to such expansion, at least in the case of organized states, as defensive nationalism; and if this formulation is accepted, in its turn, then the nationalism of peripheral areas began much earlier than Nairn's theory requires and reflected the stark fact of invasion, not the crypto-psychology of frustration with uneven development. And, by the same token, the nationalism of countries like Britain proves to be older than and far removed from uneven development. British nationalism seems dignified and civilized to Nairn only because its more brutal and, yes, 'demented' aspects are completely ignored.

Nairn claims two prime virtues for his theory: that it explains all the many manifestations of nationalism in terms of a single, underlying process, uneven development; and that it places each case and country in a world perspective, avoiding what Nairn calls the 'country-by-country attitude' according to which each national movement is explained in terms of the internal and idiosyncratic history of that particular country. All of this is forgotten when Nairn turns to Northern Ireland. Now the analysis is exclusively, resolutely, idiosyncratic, as though Nairn were trying to will out of existence the larger forces, such as British imperial interests and those of multinational capitalism. And there is no recourse to uneven development. Indeed, Nairn readily concedes that Ulster has not suffered from uneven development. He does not try to explain how nationalist movements might (or might not) arise in the absence of this primal force, but rather presents, instead of an explanation, a taxonomy.

To begin with, there are what Nairn calls the 'mainstream of "backward" or "underdeveloped" societies anxious to catch up':

> However, it has never been the case that this main current exhausts the meaning of nationalism. There have also been a number of what could be termed 'counter-currents' – examples of societies which have claimed national self-determination from a different, more advanced point in the development spectrum. These somewhat more developed social formations have struggled for independence against the 'backward' nationalities around them . . . Impelled by the same underlying historical force . . . they represent none the less eddies in a contrary direction. (pp. 248–249)

That national movements have arisen in economically advanced areas is no secret: witness the cases of Belgium and Bohemia in the last century and Catalonia and Vizcaya today. But to place all such cases in a single category is to call for an explanation, not simply an allusion to 'counter-currents' and 'eddies'. No such explanation is offered, however, and we are left to infer that Northern Ireland has evolved into a nation, and deserves the right of self-determination, just because it belongs to the same category of phenomena as Belgium, Czechoslovakia, Catalonia, and so on.

> The Ulster Protestant territories clearly belong to this group. And one must put the same question about them as about the other members of this rather marginal and select 'rich men's club'. Does it follow that they have no right to self-determination because they are (relatively) economically developed? (p. 249)

The question is of course rhetorical, since no one seems to have made such an accusation, but notice the strategic 'does it follow . . . ?' by which the assertion of membership in the class (or 'club') somehow automatically confers the right of self-determination.

Nairn next carves out a sub-category within the 'rich men's club' consisting of settler colonies. In this group he places Northern Ireland, 'White South Africa', Singapore, and Israel, and asserts that Israel and Northern Ireland have particularly much in common. Again we are left to infer that statements made about the class, or other attributes of its members, are, somehow, descriptive of Northern Ireland. For example, the settler colonies – including, mind you, 'White South Africa' – are described as

> genuine, self-sustaining, middle-class societies . . : more or less complete social formations, capable of independence and self-defence, and with their own variety of nationalism . . . islands of relative over-development in relation to backward areas around them. (p. 188) . . . These settler-based bridgeheads of development defend an existing state against the 'backward hordes' surrounding them. They see themselves as custodians of a civilization which would 'go under' if they were politically assimilated to native society. (p. 189)

Then the comparison is made with Israel, which, says Nairn, 'for a quarter of a century . . . fought for independence against the less-developed Arab lands on all sides of it' (a distortion of history) and which, along with Protestant Ulster, 'can be accused by the more *echt*-looking [puristic] nationalists around them of being on somebody else's land' (p. 249). Thus, all-told, a series of judgments – some quite strange – about other countries and an inference that Northern Ireland acquires the same attributes by class membership. Not, one would think, a typical example of Marxist theory building.

The argument is not entirely limited to metaphor. Nairn ventures a few generalizations about the history of Northern Ireland in order to sketch in the picture of a genuine nation in the process of being formed.[11] The society, he says, stems from alien settlement; that is, the Protestant community today is directly descended from settlers and thus forms a settler colony. The fact that Irish folk were there beforehand is neglected (reminding one of the way White South Africans try to erase from history the knowledge that the land they occupy had prior owners), and also neglected are the later histories of these indigenous Irish folk along with the fact that some, at least, of today's Protestants are descendants of converts (a common pattern in colonies everywhere).

Next Nairn alludes to the 'uneven development' visited upon southern Ireland during the 19th Century but not upon the north; and without trying to explain this fact he asserts that the north–south differential created at that time somehow established the inexorable logic of a boundary between northern and southern Ireland. No mention is made of the way British industrial capitalism extended itself to Belfast during the industrial revolution while the rest of Ireland was systematically de-industrialized, depopulated (to mobilize labour in England), and impoverished by an archetypically colonialist form of superexploitation, a process described by Marx and Engels and today well understood. Failing to deal with these processes, Nairn leaves the impression that Northern Ireland's economic development was self-generated, rather than an integral part of British industrialization. He is trying to refute the claim, so often heard from Ulster Protestants, that they are truly British, and the parallel claim, heard among Ulster Catholics (and many others), that all Ireland is one nation.

Meanwhile, in a 'standard tale of under-development, peasant [southern] Ireland was . . . dragged into modern existence by English industrialism and then forced to a nationalist self-mobilization against these same forces' (p. 228). It seems, then, that Irish nationalism was anti-industrial, not anti-British. The Irish resisted, according to Nairn, 'in the same way as and at the same time as the rest of under-developed Central and Eastern Europe' (p. 229), and obtained its independence in the same set of post-First-World-War boundary-making ceremonies. Nothing is said, therefore, about the explicitly colonial oppression and exploitation visited upon Ireland and not upon most of the other non-self-governing countries of Europe. And nothing about the powerful, mass based, and ultimately victorious nationalist movement. We are left to infer that independence was, instead, a casual decision by the British: the Republic of Ireland was just 'one in the interminable list making up this post-war settlement' (p. 229). Hence the boundary between north and south was quite natural. 'It corresponded . . . to the "development gap"' (p. 229). So Northern Ireland and the Republic are natural and distinct spatial entities, with a natural (or at least sensible) boundary. The boundary does not, then, reflect the bitter rearguard efforts of retreating British imperialism to hold on to that one corner of Ireland from which it gained the most surplus value and in which it retained the most influence.

Nairn does not seem to believe that the British had any interest in, or anything much to do with, events in Ireland, until 'the escalating violence forced . . . London to break with the long British tradition of reluctant, last-minute intervention in Irish affairs' (p. 251). It was, he says, Protestant violence 'which brought the British army to Ulster' (p. 238). (But why, then, are there so many Catholic prisoners in Long Kesh?) Next a tear is shed for the Catholic minority in Ulster: 'Stranded on the wrong side of the boundary, the Catholic-nationalist minority joined the huge number of Europe's displaced persons and communities [which] . . . dotted the landscape from Fermanagh to the Black Sea' (p. 229).

Thus the picture of Northern Ireland in the 20th Century: the settler community now formed into the 'Protestant nationality' and into a 'Protestant nation' (p. 245), within a state possessing a historically natural boundary and yet plagued with a minority people who, far from being part of the nation, are merely 'displaced persons' whose misfortune it was to be 'stranded on the wrong side of the boundary'.

In the 1960s, says Nairn, the Catholic minority became 'restless' (p. 229). In earlier times there had been no nationalist movement among the Catholics because the two states in Ireland were seen to be 'equally odious'. When nationalism finally arose it did not have a material basis in national oppression or in the superexploitation of Catholic workers (something Nairn fails altogether to mention). Rather, this newly arising nationalism is a product of prosperity: of improving conditions. At this point Nairn introduces a different theory:

Ethnic conflicts do not arise naturally from the coexistence of different groups in one society . . . It is when conditions improve and horizons enlarge that they become intolerable. For it is only then that the disadvantaged group feels the full constraints placed on it. (pp. 227–228)

Is it to be supposed, then, that hunger is only noticed when the pangs lessen? Now it is true, of course, that national movements emerge at times under conditions of rising prosperity, rising expectations, and so on. This was perhaps the typical background of bourgeois national movements in 19th Century Europe. But in our time, in the great majority of cases, national movements and national struggles are generated by exploitation and suffering: they constitute a class-based process in which – putting the matter summarily – exploitation by a foreign ruling class is resisted in the strategically logical way, by a struggle for independence, that is, a struggle for state power. This latter sort of process is not, however, acknowledged by Nairn, for whom national struggles are at root frustration reactions by the elite, and are therefore just a part of that mythical scenario, the 'revolution of rising expectations'. To assimilate typical national struggles to this scenario is to believe one of the most basic and dangerous components of conservative ideology: that exploitation and oppression are easing, not worsening, under capitalism.

Little more remains to be said about this curious cognitive map of Northern Ireland. Perhaps we need merely add that the Protestant community as a whole – not to mention its progressive sector – seems far less enthusiastic about secession than Nairn does. Nairn concedes this to be true, as he must, but edges around the contradiction with two arguments. He claims that the tendency of Ulster folk to identify with the British was somehow a voluntaristic choice made quite long ago, and for not very fundamental reasons; hence, by implication, a choice that can be easily revoked. And he tries in every possible way to minimize the closeness and importance of the relationship between Northern Ireland and England, past and present. He states that the British today, as in the past, have no interests at stake in Ulster. 'Partition was not a mere conspiracy of empire'. 'There is no "anti-imperialist" struggle going on' (p. 232). 'Great-power interests' are not involved. 'As a separate entity Northern Ireland has become quite useless' to Britain (p. 236). And, beyond that, capitalism as a whole 'has its interest in removing the mythic "frontiers" of racist dominance and inter-ethnic feuds, not in erecting them into actual map-boundaries and customs-posts' (p. 236). If these assertions are not transparently false, the reader may turn to the articles by Perrons and Anderson, cited previously, for a refutation. Only one comment is called for here.

The belief that capitalism is dissolving national frontiers and eliminating national (and racial) oppression is held by many Marxists besides Tom Nairn. And it is wrong. The empirical evidence against it is self-evident. Have any frontiers been removed from the map of late? But what we are really dealing with, here as in all other manifestations of the national question and nationalism, is the state. National struggle is struggle for state power. And state power is as important to capitalism today as ever it was in the past. It is equally important to the working class. Therefore national struggles are not likely to lose their intensity for some time to come.

## Neo-Marxism and the National Question

We are now, I think, in a position to assess Nairn's theory of nationalism as a whole. It is presented as an effort to correct the errors and transcend the limitations of the traditional Marxist theory, but the traditional theory itself is misunderstood.

Nairn's first error, which appears to stem mainly from an unfamiliarity with or misreading of post-1914 Marxist literature on nationalism, is to believe that the Marxist theory of nationalism associates national struggle with, and only with, the rise of the bourgeoisie, and that this theory therefore asserts that nationalism is important only during the period of young, rising capitalism, growing less important as capitalism matures. To be sure, this equation of nationalism with early or rising capitalism is to be found in most of the pre-1914 literature, and mainly because it is enshrined in Stalin's influential (!) essay of 1913, 'Marxism and the National Question', it is still believed by a few dogmatists today (See Chapter 5). But Marx and Engels themselves did not strictly equate nationalism with the bourgeoisie and the period of its rise. And Marxists at the time of the First World War became aware rather abruptly that nationalism was growing stronger and more politically important than ever. And Lenin, at that time and for that reason, provided a thorough and adequate explanation for the fact that nationalism does not decline but rather intensifies as capitalism matures into its monopoly or imperialist phase. And, finally, Marxists since that time have viewed the increasingly important national struggles, such as colonial liberation movements, as phenomena fully predicted by Marxist theory. (See Chapter 5). Therefore Nairn is quite wrong in asserting that Marxist theory consigns nationalism to the era of rising capitalism.

And being wrong in this matter, he is wrong in another: a proposition which is in a sense the enabling legislation for his own theory of nationalism. According to Nairn, the traditional Marxist theory, precisely because it predicted the decline of nationalism, has been discredited as a theory, and moreover cannot explain the newer forms of nationalism, such as the modern national movements in parts of Western Europe. Hence the need for a new and radically different theory, one which sees nationalism as a force autonomous from class struggle. But the premises are false, and thus also the conclusions.

Nairn's second basic criticism of the traditional theory is embodied in his denial that the processes of nationalism can be derived from the processes of class struggle. In part this reflects the error discussed above. But this error aside, Nairn does not present any analytic critique of the traditional argument that nationalism emerges from class processes and is a form of class struggle. (See Chapter 2 above.) Instead he unquestioningly accepts the basic assumption common to most conservative theories that something which we label 'nationalism' is a primitive existent, a given, to be accepted at the outset of any argument. This given, for Nairn, seems to be an ideological (or psychological) force. Although he finds its antecedents in something called 'uneven development' (not to be confused with the uneven development of ordinary Marxist discourse) he does not really try to explain the nature and characteristics of the force itself: it remains a given. In the traditional Marxist theory, all phenomena of nationalism, including the strictly ideological phenomena – and most certainly including the passionate and sometimes irrational attitudes associated so often with national struggle – all these are considered to be manifestations of class processes. (For, let us recall, there is passion and irrationality in all of class struggle, not least in the Paris commune, the storming of the Winter Palace, the conquest of Dien Bien Phu.) But Nairn does not even examine the arguments for a class basis to nationalist phenomena: he ignores them, and then merely assumes that nationalism is an autonomous force.

Still another dimension of the traditional theory is ignored by Nairn, although this must be accounted an error of commission, not omission. I refer to the fact that the traditional theory, and most of its variants, have carefully and systematically related the national question to exploitation. Indeed, Marxists have generally supported those national movements which seemed to have a basis in resistance to class exploitation and impoverishment and withheld support from, or supported only tactically, those movements whose political struggle did not have this concrete economic and class basis. Nairn builds a quaint model grounded in what he calls 'uneven development', one in which the process of exploitation – the extraction of surplus labour and surplus value – plays no part whatever. Instead, 'uneven development', or more properly the failure of an area to develop, is supposed to engender feelings of frustration, of envy, among the local elites, the local exploiters, who then somehow 'mobilize' the masses ('the lower strata') into a nationalist campaign. So Nairn's theory resembles conservative theories in what is perhaps their most important feature: it discusses nationalism without relating it to economic exploitation, and it deals with national oppression as in essence a psychological and cultural process and one which affects the elite and not in any important way the masses: oppression without exploitation.

But the indictment goes somewhat farther. Nairn asserts that his view of nationalism is basically the same as Lenin's, meaning that he, like Lenin, appreciates the power and historical importance of this force, hence supports some national movements instead of dismissing, ignoring, or attacking all such movements out-of-hand, as so many Marxists did in Lenin's time and some still do today. Nairn thinks, however, that Lenin's correct positions were not grounded in theory: they were merely, he says, 'pragmatic'. But Lenin's view of nationalism, as we will see in Chapter 4, was not at all what Nairn makes it out to have been. It was not pragmatic: on the contrary, Lenin brought the Marxist theory of nationalism to a new and higher level by associating national struggle with monopoly capitalism or imperialism. Nairn says nothing whatever about imperialism, except in the vague sense of 'domination', 'subjugation', and unspecific 'oppression' – the sense used routinely by non-Marxists – and it is impossible to tell whether Nairn rejects Lenin's theory of imperialism or merely does not understand it. I do not refer here to the details of this theory, such as the hypothesis concerning capital export, but to the family of present-day models which are grounded in Lenin's basic proposition that imperialism is a process necessary to capitalism and one which engenders underdevelopment, superexploitation, and national oppression. (See Chapters 4 and 5). Nairn ignores all of this, and he fails to see (or remark) any connection between national struggles and imperialism, in terms of cause, character, or effect. Instead he deploys the quite antithetical theories of conservative social science, those which depict the impact of developed capitalism on peripheral countries as a 'modernizing' process, one which embodies an essentially psychological and, in a sense, moral process of maturation – reaching civilization and thus adulthood – and one which leads, if 'unevenly', to economic progress. It is no sin for a Marxist to make use of conservative theories, but to substitute them for the Marxist theories of class struggle and imperialism is something else altogether. Whether or not the outcome will be a 'Marxist' theory is quite beside the point. It will be a bad theory, and Nairn's is a case in point.

Nairn's theory fits firmly into a general tendency within modern Marxist thought. By 'tendency' I do not mean a political movement, although at times it seems as though the Marxists who make up this tendency are engaged in forming an international, neo-Marxist party whose members will be exclusively professional scholars and whose theoretical journals will somehow serve as so many revolutionary sparks. One of the identifying positions taken by this group of scholars is to view Marxism itself as a simple extension of the European Enlightenment. As a parallel, class struggle is viewed as merely one component in the steady upward stream of progressive social evolution, a process which emanated from some ancient or medieval source in European culture and ever since has grown and effloresced in Europe (or among Europeans), at the same time diffusing its fruits around the world.

On a more concrete level, this perspective tends to reject several specific tenets of Marxist theory (not to say Marxist practice). Most basic, perhaps, is its denial of the argument of *The German Ideology* to the effect that ideas, including the Enlightenment along with the entire realm of ideology, are not the prime movers of history. Next it denies, or forgets, that the masses are the makers of history. (For Tom Nairn, the intelligentsia and the elite are the main actors in nationalism. For Perry Anderson, Nairn's intellectual soulmate and former colleague at *New Left Review*, kings and statesmen were the main actors in European historical development.[12]) Finally, in this school of thought, exploitation tends to be a very abstract component of events – it cannot be ignored entirely thanks to *Capital* – and it is rarely seen, as Marx and Engels saw it, as a matter of suffering and oppression, and the prime source of resistance and thereafter social change.

On the level of practice, or the inspection of practice, these scholars tend to look down on most efforts in the real world to defeat capitalism. Some of them just do not accept the idea that there have been successful socialist revolutions anywhere in the world. Others are less extreme in their views. All, however, in consonance with the notion that socialism is merely the evolutionary extension of capitalism, and socialist thought merely the extension of Enlightenment thought, tend to undervalue the revolutionary accomplishments of the exploited classes in the Third World, at the same time underplaying the efficacy and even occasionally denying the existence of class struggle at the centre of the system.

Nairn, as I have said, belongs to this tradition. Class struggle at the centre is, in his view, 'frozen' into immobility. In the periphery there seem not to be socialist countries, and instead of the class struggle which presents itself as a national liberation struggle there is only a form of elitist, bourgeois nationalism, generated by envy and led – how could it be otherwise? – by the intelligentsia. Nairn's theory of nationalism thus falls within a larger and, on the whole, internally consistent body of neo-Marxist thought. The signature of this entire stream of scholars and scholarship is the denial that class struggle is the motor of history.

One final thought. The national liberation struggles of colonial and neocolonial nations are a form of nationalism which, I assume, every Marxist deems progressive. Let us then ask what relevance Nairn's theory of nationalism would have for such struggles – in Puerto Rico, Namibia, El Salvador, or anywhere else. This theory would, to begin with, bracket any such struggle with fascism. Second, it would deny or ignore the fact that such a struggle has a basis in exploitation and, more generally, imperialism. Third, it would find the interested sectors to be the bourgeoisie and the intellectuals, not the working classes, these latter, in Nairn's theory, being merely 'mobilized' in a process he describes as 'populist'. And finally, Nairn's theory would flatly reject the ideological and political claim, which, I have no doubt, is made by every Marxist who participates in a national liberation struggle, that the quite realizable goal of that struggle is not to eliminate foreign-controlled capitalism and substitute it with a native equivalent, but to make a socialist revolution. For all these reasons, but mainly for the last one, Nairn's theory must be judged irrelevant.

# Notes

1. T. Nairn, 'The Modern Janus', *New Left Review* 94 (1975).
2. See Chapter 1, note 9.
3. 'The Modern Janus' p. 5.
4. Ibid., p. 3.
5. Ibid., p. 21.
6. Ibid., p. 17.
7. Ibid., p. 16.
8. T. Nairn, *The Break-Up of Britain* (1977).
9. See B. N. Bhatia, *Famines in India* (1967).
10. See E. P. Thompson's essay, 'The Peculiarities of the English', in his *The Poverty of Theory and Other Essays* (1978), for a fine, caustic critique of this view as it had been put forward in earlier writings by Nairn and Perry Anderson.
11. For a more true-to-life geography, see essays by two of my colleagues: Diane Perrons, 'Ireland and the Break-up of Britain', *Antipode* 11, 1 (1980), and James Anderson, 'Regions and Religions in Ireland: A Short Critique of the "Two Nations" Theory', ibid. I am discussing Nairn's factual assertions about Northern Ireland only as part of my critique of his theory of nationalism, not as an intervention in the debate about Northern Ireland, a subject that is beyond the scope of this book.
12. Perry Anderson, *Lineages of the Absolute State* (1974).

# 4. Hobsbawm on the Nation State

'Nationalism', says Eric Hobsbawm, is 'devoid of any discernible rational theory'.[1] He means by this that (1) national movements today are irrational, and (2) no rational theory exists to explain nationalism, which is something that 'has been a great puzzle to (non-nationalist) politicians and theorists ever since its invention'.[2] Hobsbawm is a respected Marxist scholar, but here he dismisses a great deal of quite rational Marxist theorizing about the national question and a great many quite rational struggles against colonialism and neocolonialism – national liberation movements, some of them guided by the same Marxist theory which he dismisses. He inserts just one real qualification: nationalism did have a sensible, rational purpose in 19th Century Europe, because 'nation states were the main building blocks of world capitalism' in those times.[3] But the times have changed. Nationalism today, in Hobsbawm's view, is the rather aimless tendency to split up existing states into smaller ones in a process which he describes as 'the fissiparous nationalisms of our time', a process which he takes to include all forms of the struggle for independent sovereign statehood.[4] It is this process which has no 'discernible rational theory', and Marxists therefore have to deal with it pragmatically, as a given, a 'fact':

> Marxists . . . have to come to terms with the political fact of nationalism and to define their attitudes toward its specific manifestations. Ever since Marx, this has for the most part, and necessarily, been a matter not of theoretical principle . . . but of pragmatic judgment in changing circumstances. In principle, Marxists are neither for nor against independent statehood for any nation . . . even assuming that there can be other than pragmatic agreement on what constitutes 'the nation' in any particular case.[5]

But can it be true that 'Marxists are neither for nor against independent statehood for any nation'? Do not Marxists give unqualified support to the independence of Puerto Rico? Namibia? All colonies? And is this not a matter of 'principle', that is, something fully and, yes, rationally comprehended within Marxist theory? And is it quite fair to describe the immense corpus of Marxist writings on the national question as 'pragmatic judgment in changing circumstances'? It seems to me that Eric Hobsbawm, fine scholar though he is, on these matters is very wrong. He is wrong, moreover, in ways that are particularly unhelpful for the national liberation struggles – hardly 'fissiparous nationalisms' – which are still being waged in many countries, some colonial, some neocolonial, and some free but embattled.

In this chapter I will try to refute the view that it is no longer rational to struggle for national liberation or for the defence of national states. Hobsbawm is the most persuasive modern advocate of this essential position. For this reason, and because the position is unhelpful for national liberation struggles (though this is an unintended effect), I will focus on Hobsbawm's writings. But Hobsbawm will serve as a stand-in for many other Marxist theorists who hold the position that nationalism today is basically irrational: that national movements are more or less pointless (whether or not they are progressive) and national states are more or less obsolete.

This view is held in common by two important, and very different, currents of Marxist thought. One sector rejects the class struggle theory of history or refuses to apply it to national struggle. For these Marxists, nationalism (in various senses of that word) is a force autonomous from class struggle. Either it is primordially an ideological phenomenon (the 'idea of self-determination', etc.), or it emerges in some mystical way from the 'nation' (or the 'principle of nationalities') and immediately assumes this ideological form. It is irrational because it is ideology disengaged from external social reality, and it may be irrational in a second sense, the sense implying an emotional, infra-intellectual level of the human psyche. (For Tom Nairn, we recall, it is the Id.) Enough was said earlier about this current of thought, and we can turn to the other one, which is epitomized by Hobsbawm.

If it is agreed that national struggle is class struggle, then one asks rather quickly: which classes are involved, in what sorts of class struggle? There is a distinctive tradition within Marxism – distinctive in the intellectual sense but not clearly so in the political sense – which identifies national struggle mainly, or only, or 'rationally', with one class: the bourgeoisie. The narrow, or fundamentalist, form of this position comes down to us from pre-First World War Marxism and particularly from Rosa Luxemburg. It is the view that the bourgeoisie is the only class with a material interest in the national movement and its ideology, and in the national state, and only so during the period of youthful or rising capitalism; not only does the working class reject everything 'merely national' but so does the mature, fully-risen bourgeoisie. Within this frame of reference, national movements are irrational for essentially all class sectors other than the 'rising bourgeoisie'. So, too, is the national state. It follows that classes and class groupings which are more 'advanced' in historical terms than the youthful bourgeoisies participate in national struggles only, or mainly, as a result of ideological contagion, adopting 'the ideology of bourgeois nationalism' as 'false consciousness'. Therefore, all nationalism is a manifestation of 'bourgeois-nationalist ideology'. I will call this doctrine in its pure form the 'all-nationalism-is-bourgeois' theory, although the theory asserts that non-bourgeois classes can be infected with bourgeois-nationalist ideology and act against their own class interests – act, therefore, irrationally.

During the period when national liberation movements were gaining victories all over the Third World, the all-nationalism-is-bourgeois theory was not very popular within Marxism, except among a few Trotskyists.[6] Some national movements, of course, were bourgeois, but some others were struggles against the bourgeoisie, local and foreign, and the ideological basis of some of these anti-bourgeois struggles was Marxism. During the 1970s, however, the all-nationalism-is-bourgeois theory regained some of its popularity as part of the critique of 'Third-Worldism'. It is of course true that Marxists everywhere had tended to idealize national liberation struggles, to ignore or explain away their failings (which were sometimes well-hidden behind orthodox Marxist rhetoric). But a more influential factor was the retreat from Leninist theory concerning imperialism, colonialism, and the role of anti-colonial struggles in the struggle against capitalism on a world scale. And perhaps most influential was the return by some Leninists and most social democrats to the apologetics of diffusionism, with colonialism seen as a 'modernizing' (formerly a 'civilizing') process, and anti-colonialism as a simple continuation of that process. In any event, after the early 1970s it became increasingly popular to argue that Third World liberation movements were essentially a continuation of the bourgeois revolution – the rise of capitalism – and that their ideologies, strategies, and leading class elements were bourgeois. National liberation, in a word, was bourgeois nationalism.

Something like this view has been argued during the past few years by many Marxist theorists who consider themselves to be following the main line of Marxist analysis that goes back (via Lenin) to Marx. National struggle, for them, is indeed a form of class struggle, but it is a form that is essentially bourgeois, or part of an essentially bourgeois revolution (whatever may be the class composition of a given movement). By the same token, an ideology of national liberation is, or incorporates, some variety of bourgeois nationalism, usually the variety called 'the principle of nationalities' ('each nation its state; each state its nation'). All of the phenomena associated with national struggle were important and valid during the period when capitalism was rising in Europe, the 19th Century. But today capitalism is fully risen. Bourgeois revolutions are essentially things of the past. Even the capitalist state, typically a nation state, is a thing of the past: capitalism today is international or multinational, not national. The most distinguished, and most nearly persuasive, exponent of this basic viewpoint is Eric Hobsbawm.

## Hobsbawm's Theses

Hobsbawm's position is set forth in several of his writings, but most fully in an essay in *New Left Review* entitled 'Some Reflections on "The Break-up of Britain" '.[7] This essay was written as a critique of Tom Nairn's view, put forth in *The Break-Up of Britain*, that the nationalist movements on the British periphery (Scotland, Wales, and 'Protestant Northern Ireland') are politically significant – that they can indeed 'break up Britain' – and that they are progressive and deserve the support of Marxists. Hobsbawm's critique of Nairn is primarily an answer to these arguments about peripheral British nationalism: they are not progressive, he argues, and, significant or not, they are irrational.

But Hobsbawm is not content to mobilize only the arguments which are specific to the British case. He introduces as well his own larger view of the national question, the history of its treatment in Marxist thought and practice, and, most crucially, the present and presumptive future status of national questions of all types on a world scale – nothing less. His cardinal proposition is that nationalism has made little sense in the present century, will make no more sense in the future, and cannot, therefore, claim the support of Marxists. All of this discussion is of course directed at the target of peripheral British nationalism, but Hobsbawm fires a massive broadside at substantially all present-day national movements, bringing even the anti-colonial liberation movements into his sights, and declaring modern nationalism in general to be the rather pointless, irrational, 'fissiparous nationalisms of our time'. This argument consumes most of Hobsbawm's essay, and thus the essay as a whole is less a response to Nairn than it is a presentation of Hobsbawm's own theory of nationalism. (He would object to the use of the word 'theory' in this context, since he considers nationalism to be 'devoid of any discernible rational theory'. Later in this chapter I will show that Hobsbawm's non-theory is a theory.) Hobsbawm had dealt with the national question in others of his writings, but the *New Left Review* article is, to the best of my knowledge, the major vehicle for his views.[8] My criticism of these views will focus mainly, though not entirely, on this article.

I will not venture a systematic critique of the article as a whole. For one thing, much of what Hobsbawm has to say about the national question, in Britain and in general, is valuable and important. For another thing, I confront Hobsbawm's theory in order to refute or turn aside those arguments which, in my view, are likely to lead to false judgements concerning national liberation struggles not yet won, struggles mainly in small countries like Puerto Rico. (The matter of spatial scale is rather critical in Hobsbawm's thinking, as we will see.) Another purpose of my essay, naturally, is to advance our general understanding of nationalism.

Given these purposes, it seems important to criticize four primary theses which Hobsbawm advances and quite strongly defends. Three of these are reasons put forward by him for opposing, or at least neglecting, national struggles in the modern world. The fourth pertains to the history of the Marxist theory of nationalism, and also relates directly to present-day national struggles because Hobsbawm's thesis is in essence a denial that there exists such a theory in any comprehensive sense ('. . . a matter not of theoretical principle . . . but of pragmatic judgement'). Hobsbawm's four theses can be stated in summary form as follows:

(1) The nature and goals of national movements have changed profoundly since the First World War. Some of the older forms were rational, and all could be judged from the standpoint of a rational theory. This is not true of newer forms.
(2) The development of capitalism has tended to diminish the importance of sovereignty, of nation states, which are losing their significance in proportion as capitalism becomes more fully international.
(3) 'The virtual disappearance of formal empires ("colonialism") has snapped the main link between anti-imperialism and the slogan of national self-determination.[9] Struggles against neocolonialism are not national struggles. Therefore, nationalism today is mainly confined to 'the fission of "developed" capitalist states'.
(4) Marxists have tended to relate to national movements as a matter of pragmatism, not theoretical principle: when national movements are progressive, they are given essentially tactical support. In particular, there is no Leninist theory of nationalism; there is, instead, a set of pragmatic positions, such as support for the

right of self-determination, positions which tended to be correct, although (mainly Luxemburgian) criticisms of these positions are not entirely unfounded. I will discuss each of these four theses in turn, but first a brief but necessary comment on matters of terminology with regard to the national question is required. This chapter will conclude with a brief analysis of Hobsbawm's fundamental theory of nationalism as a social process, and will relate this theory to the larger Marxist theory of nationalism.

## A Note on Terminology

Discussions about nationalism, the national question, the nation, and so on, are apt to lose themselves in a fog of terminological confusion, so it is important to straighten out pertinent matters of terminology at the outset of the discussion.[10] Pride of place must of course go to the word 'nationalism'.

Hobsbawm uses the word 'nationalism' in all of the senses indicated in Chapter 1 – applied to national struggle in general, to one or both sides in a national struggle, to 'narrow' and 'bourgeois' nationalism – but he does not make the required distinctions of meaning. This assertion will be brought down to specifics as we proceed. He uses the word 'nation' broadly in the way it was used by Marx, Engels, Lenin, and Luxemburg, but not in the way it was used by Bauer and Stalin. Both Bauer and Stalin supposed that the nation is a definite, discrete, whole phenomenon, with invariant properties (what A. N. Whitehead would have called a 'natural entity').[11] Stalin in particular applied his definition of 'nation' as a yardstick to determine which groups of people and national movements deserved the right of self-determination, on grounds that they were, indeed, genuine nations, because only genuine nations had the capacity to become independent states. This definition is discussed in Chapter 5.

No attempt to provide a rigorous definition of 'nation' was made by Marx, Engels, Lenin, or Luxemburg, and Hobsbawm follows their practice in noting that there are many different sorts of communities deserving the appellation 'nation', and that their internal characteristics do not always warrant a judgement of their potential to form a sovereign state. Thus, of the two approaches to the concept of the nation, Hobsbawm rejects the aprioristic one and adopts the realistic one. Since most Marxists, including those who have nothing friendly to say about Stalin, accept the Stalinesque form of definition, Hobsbawm's approach is refreshingly undogmatic. He uses the word 'nation' either to describe a community which, realistically or not, is striving for independence, and thus has spawned a national movement, or to describe an existing political community which may be a sovereign nation-state or a non-sovereign entity like a colony. These meanings are very clearly specified in context, and thus one of the usual sources of confusion in discussions about the national question is nicely avoided.

There is, however, one problem with regard to Hobsbawm's usage of 'nation'. Recall his doubt whether 'there can be other than pragmatic agreement on what constitutes "the nation" in any particular case'. Here he moves towards the position of Luxemburg and away from the position of Marx, Engels, and Lenin. Luxemburg considered nations to be, in essence, fictions: either they were the product of bourgeois ideology beamed at the working class or they were some sort of slapped-together economic entity created by capitalists for their convenience and cast aside when capitalism had reached its mature, international, stature.[12] Marx, Engels, and Lenin, on the other hand, were very respectful of human cultural processes and cleavage planes, and, however unwilling they were to try to define precisely and universally what a nation is, they certainly recognized its reality in the sense that they perceived the significance of cultural qualities and groupings in political life. Hobsbawm does not retreat all the way to Luxemburg's position (although he shares with her the tendency to put the word 'nation' in quotes, as though nations were truly unreal). But he clearly prefers to work with the much more concrete historical concept of 'nation-state'.

Hobsbawm's use of the concept of nation-state is also refreshingly undogmatic, although it is not without problems. He notes that a nation-state may start out as a state, then become homogenized, or at least simplified, in cultural terms to the point where the inhabitants of the state see themselves as a nation. Hobsbawm also notes that culturally and territorially defined national communities have no inevitable destiny or cosmic right to become sovereign states (according to the mystical 'principle of nationalities' which was widely accepted in the 19th Century, and which Hobsbawm rightly criticizes). He notes also that multicultural states, whether capitalist or socialist, are as viable in the modern world as are culturally uncomplex states of the sort which is usually called a nation-state. Thus Hobsbawm's essential concept of the nation-state is a political concept, not a cultural one. He does not try to define the term in any formal sense, but the meaning is nonetheless clear in context. He is concerned about the substantial, persistent, consequential states of the modern world, some of them large, others small (but not *very* small), some of them multicultural, others culturally uncomplex; these he calls 'nation-states'. His focus is thus on the politics of states and state formation – a perspective on the national question which is all too uncommon in modern Marxist writings on this subject. This focus does not lead him to neglect matters of culture, of ideology, and the like, in favour of matters more coldly 'political'. He is merely arguing, in essence, that the Marxist theory of nationalism is at heart a theory of politics. And I fully agree.

Hobsbawm's errors on the matter of nation-states relate not to terminology but to what can be thought of as their natural history. He puts forward a theory about the origin, dispersal, and imminent extinction of the capitalist nation-state, a theory which I will criticize at some length. And he projects the view that very small states are not nation-states and are not viable. This, too, I will criticize.

## Are National Movements Irrational?

### Nation-States of Yesteryear

Hobsbawm maintains that national movements had a proper function in the days when the formation of nation states was appropriate to the politics of youthful or rising capitalism, but national movements no longer have that function or indeed any other. He argues that the principal form of nationalism in the 19th Century, and down through the period of the First World War, was

> not nationalist in the current sense, inasmuch as it did not envision a world of nation-states irrespective of size and resources, but only one of 'viable' states of

medium to large size . . . The evidence is overwhelming that at this stage the crux of nationalist movements was not so much state independence as such, but rather the construction of 'viable' states, in short 'unification' rather than 'separatism' – though this was concealed by the fact that most national movements also tended to break up one or more of the surviving obsolete empires of Austria, Turkey, and Russia.[13]

Hobsbawm then lists among the 19th Century national movements which sought '"unification" rather than "separatism"', not only the German and Italian movements (the well-known cases) but also the Poles, the Romanians, the Yugoslavs, the Bulgarians (with Macedonia), the Greeks, and the Czechs and Slovaks. He also notes that the ideal of medium to large states was shared by Mazzini, Marx and Engels, and the Wilsonian boundary-makers. Overall, this was a form of nationalism that was aimed at creating 'a world of . . . "viable" states of medium to large size', and not a world of mini-states and other such peculiar entities.

Today, however, the situation is altogether different in Hobsbawm's view. There has been a 'Balkanization of the world of states', and

> any speck in the Pacific can look forward to independence and a good time for its president, if it happens to possess a location for a naval base for which more solvent states will compete, a lucky gift of nature such as manganese, or merely enough beaches and pretty girls to become a tourist paradise.[14]

Hobsbawm envisions all of this as both a modern state-of-being and an ongoing tendency: not only is the world already filled with mini-states, but fission, separatism, attempts to break up existing nation states of the proper old-fashioned form, are 'the characteristic nationalist movement of our time'.[15]

There are several objections to this model of contrasting forms of nationalism, old and new, and objections also to Hobsbawm's political geography of both the 19th and 20th Centuries. Let us begin with his characterization of 19th Century national movements as aiming at '"unification" rather than "separatism".' In every case mentioned by Hobsbawm, separatism was explicitly involved, however strong may have been the desire also for unification, and thus for the creation of larger states. These were independence movements. The fact that the Poles, for instance, had to seek independence from three separate empires, each of which held a portion of Polish territory, does not alter this fact. Separation, that is, independence, had to come before unification. Indeed, in the case of Poland I doubt whether the national movement could have concerned itself as much with the goal of viable size as it did with the goal of freeing, and then uniting in one state, all lands considered 'Polish' (granting the mini-imperialism which, as Luxemburg pointed out, went with the idea of a fully restored Polish state, since many regions of historic Poland were non-Polish in culture).

I am not splitting hairs in arguing that the essential character of these national movements was their struggle for independence, exactly as is the case with modern movements, and the matter of the size and shape of the sought-after sovereign state was a somewhat different and subordinate question. Czechs and Slovaks, for instance, might agree to go it in tandem, rather than separately, but they would not agree to remain under foreign rule. The case of Czechoslovakia leads us into another objection. Did the post-World War boundary-makers have in mind an abstract 'viable' state in such a case, or did they intend, rather, a state strong enough to (viably) resist Bolshevism, within and without? And, more generally, did these boundary-makers – as distinct from the Marxist theoreticians and the small-nation national leaders – give a fig about viability for any of the new eastern European states for any reason other than that of buffering and bolstering themselves against Bolshevism? The same query applies, incidentally, to the Wilsonian efforts to adjust state boundaries as much as possible to cultures and culture regions, 'nationalities'. Was this much more than an attempt to minimize the danger of ethnic conflicts and, behind them, revolutions? I do not mean to suggest that small-nation nationalists were unconcerned with the issue of economic and political power, and therefore the size of the state, but I wonder whether any of them would have refused a chance to form a mini-state if sovereignty could be achieved in no other way.

I will go a step farther now and question whether the 19th Century ideal which Hobsbawm describes as 'a world . . . of "viable" states of medium to large size' was really much more than that: an ideal. Before proceeding to this point, however, I must register a small doubt about the ideal itself. Marx and Engels certainly considered it such.[16] However, at the beginning of the present century Marxists in both the Russian and Austro-Hungarian empires had as their immediate objective the establishment of bourgeois democracy within the existing empires, not the break-up of the empires into medium-to-large-sized states. The Austrian party, for example, explicitly rejected the right of secession for nations within the empire, and Otto Bauer developed an elaborate argument in favour of very large states in general (with his eye of course cocked to that one very large state, Austria–Hungary).[17] Even Lenin hoped that the nations held captive by the Tsar would voluntarily agree to remain within (or return to) the single state after it had become democratized.[18] The operative word was 'concentration' (read: size); large states were thought to offer the advantages of economic 'concentration'. Thus the specific ideal of Britain-or-France-sized states, and indeed of nation states in general, was by no means universally supported. One can assume also that conservative politicians and theorists of the Russian, Turkish, and Austro-Hungarian empires did not exactly favour the decomposition of their own imperial states into medium-to-large-sized nation states, viable or not.

But the ideal of a medium-to-large bourgeois nation state was perhaps not realized anywhere. Great Britain and France are of course the classic examples, the countries considered to be realizations of this ideal. But both countries were states with huge overseas empires, and their internal characteristics cannot really be understood without taking into account this external bonding.[19] For one thing, it is very likely that the wealth and power derived from colonial, and other external, enterprise had much to do with creating something like a 'melting pot' situation of the type later found in the United States, such that France and Great Britain (save for colonial Ireland) had become partly melted down from multinational to national status by the beginning of the 19th Century. For another thing, it can be argued that the relatively stable boundaries of both Britain and France during the 19th Century (after the Napoleonic period), and down to the First World War, reflected in part the fact that their territorial expansion was taking place outside of Europe. Pursuing this argument to its logical conclusion, one might assert that the ideal of a medium-to-large bourgeois nation-state is only realistic, for this period, if one adds 'with appended colonial empire'. And of course this argument applies also to the other colonizing powers, notably the Netherlands, Spain, and Portugal. Russia, Austria–Hungary and of course Turkey represented another type of state: the large territorial or continental empire. Then there were, Hobsbawm's generalization notwithstanding, a fair number of 'mini-states': Greece, Serbia, Belgium (prior to the Congo adventures), Denmark, and a few others of lesser significance, to mention only the European cases. This leaves, by my reckoning, imperial Germany and Italy. But unification in both these cases was rather quickly followed by colonial expansion, relatively unsuccessful because most of the choice plums had already been plucked.

My general conclusion on this matter of the 19th Century ideal of the medium-to-large nation state is as follows: to the extent that there was an accepted nation state ideal for 19th Century nationalism in Europe, it was utterly discordant with a complex reality embracing everything from empires to mini-states, and with real-world examples of the classical bourgeois nation-state which were impossible to copy (except by one or two exceptional late-comers) because they came equipped with – could not exist without – world-wide empires, empires which could not be emulated in a world of finite size. To all of this I would add an observation that the boundary-making which took place after the First World War, including the Versailles process and events soon thereafter, did, in fact, create or legitimize an impressive number of very small states, 'mini-states' in Hobsbawm's vocabulary, from Estonia to Albania, suggesting that the ideal of creating medium-to-large-sized states was honoured mostly in the breach. States of this size would surely threaten troublesome competition in the world economy; perhaps only the threat of Bolshevism could persuade the boundary-makers to accept, to a degree, such competition, and create medium-to-large-size states like Poland, Czechoslovakia, Yugoslavia, and the rest.

The real question here is not what nationalism looked like, what forms it took, in 19th Century Europe. The question is how you leap across time and space from the 19th Century to the 20th Century, and from Europe to the Third World.

**'Separatist Nationalisms of the Present'**
The other side of Hobsbawm's contradistinction between rational national movements then and irrational ones now is something which he considers to be a new form of nationalism, characteristic of the world since perhaps the end of the Second World War (he is not precise as to its date of birth). This new form, labelled the 'separatist nationalisms of the present', has led to a 'Balkanization of the world of states', a 'transformation of the United Nations into something like the later stages of the Holy Roman Empire' (that is, the mass of petty principalities of Central Europe in early modern times).

The United Nations seems in fact to be, for Hobsbawm, an important yardstick of the new nationalism: 'The majority of the members of the United Nations is soon likely to consist of the late-twentieth-century (Republican) equivalents to Saxe-

Coburg-Gotha and Schwarzburg-Sondershausen'.[20] 'If the Seychelles can have a vote in the UN as good as Japan's . . . then surely only the sky is the limit for the Isle of Man or the Channel Islands'.[21]

This matter of the UN as yardstick deserves a comment in its own right before we proceed along the main thread of the argument. Hobsbawm's basic contrast between large, viable states yesterday and mini-states today really requires a standard for measuring what is, and what is not, a sovereign state. Membership in the UN provides something like this standard in our own time. But the UN did not exist in those former times which Hobsbawm associates with rational nationalism. The question is: how does one determine what was, and what was not, a sovereign state in those days, by way of setting up some sort of comparison with the present? What about those Balkan entities which had merely nominal allegiance to the disintegrating Turkish empire? What about those many 'protectorates' on the fringes of the British empire, some of which (like the Malay States) were legally, and in their own eyes, sovereign states with merely treaty ties to Britain? And what about those very same German principalities in the days before there was a German customs union and thus the beginnings of a unified German state? (You can't have it both ways.) Hobsbawm notes correctly that the sovereignty of the small German states was limited, but he sees no special significance in this fact of dependency while – as we will discuss below – he considers highly significant the limited sovereignty of small (UN-member) states today, a phenomenon which he labels 'sovereignty as dependence'.[22] Was there not 'dependent sovereignty' in former times? And if so, what basic difference is there between Schwarzburg-Sondershausen then and the Seychelles now? And between the two types and eras of nationalism?

A valid distinction can certainly be made between two forms of nationalism characteristic, respectively, of Europe in the 19th Century and the colonial world in the 20th. Allowing for exceptions – Ireland, for instance, was a colony within Europe – the former type can be described as a dimension of the rise of capitalism in areas (mainly) of eastern and central Europe which were suffering some degree of national oppression, oppression which was visited on exploited classes but also, and more consequentially, on the young bourgeoisie, at the very least inhibiting its efforts to 'rise'. The latter type cannot be understood apart from the central economic function of colonialism, which was (and is) the superexploitation of colonial workers and peasants and, usually, rather thorough suppression of the independent sectors of the colonial bourgeoisie. Under these colonial conditions, nationalist movements were (and are) a response to the distinctive form and degree of national oppression which has as its material basis the political enforcement of superexploitation, and no Marxist has any hesitation in using the term 'national liberation movement' in describing this form of nationalism. But Hobsbawm's contradistinction is somewhat different.

What I have described above as the 19th Century rising capitalism form of nationalism is one of Hobsbawm's two categories. But the second, the modern form, embraces, for him, both the national liberation struggles in colonies and the 'fission of "developed" capitalist states'. Hobsbawm sees a common process underlying both of the modern forms. Although he would certainly not deny the importance of a distinction between national liberation struggles of the anti-colonial type and the other sorts of modern nationalism, he lays considerable stress on what he sees as a common underlying process and a common result: the 'Balkanization of the world of states', the world-wide proliferation of 'mini-states', the 'separatism', the 'fissiparous nationalisms of our time'. Moreover, he declares the anti-colonial form to be no longer significant today because of the 'virtual disappearance of formal empires'. (This announcement will seem premature to Puerto Ricans, Namibians, and the rest of the 30 million or so people still living in colonies.) And Hobsbawm most pointedly excludes from consideration the struggles of neocolonies, states which are nominally independent but actually dependent and not really sovereign, claiming that their struggles for real independence are not really national struggles (a thesis that I will examine in detail later). Therefore, for Hobsbawm the modern 'fissiparous nationalism' is mainly characterized today by the national movements in developed capitalist states like Britain, France, and Spain.

What accounts for this new sort of fissiparous nationalism, characteristic both of colonial areas and developed capitalist states? The immediate cause, says Hobsbawm, is 'a complete transformation of the concept of state viability'.[23] But how is this to be explained? Hobsbawm lists three reasons. The first is 'the process of decolonization, which left a half-globe full of small territories (or large territories with small populations) which could not or would not be combined into larger units or federations'.[24] ('Would not' sticks in my craw. Does Hobsbawm believe that the West Indies Federation, the Mali Federation, and so on, would have survived but for a lack of will?) Decolonization itself is not explained, presumably because Hobsbawm expects his readers to share with him an understanding of and opposition to colonialism. Yet there is ambiguity, as when he criticizes 'the assumption that state independence, or what amounts to it, is the normal mode of satisfying the demands of any group with some claim to a territorial base (a "country")',[25] and when he second-guesses the Irish Marxists and asserts that 'the Connolly Marxist-nationalist policy must be regarded as a failure', stopping just short of the suggestion that independence for Ireland was not progressive.[26]

Hobsbawm's second reason for the presumed change in the notion of viability and the tendency toward fissiparous nationalism is relatively uncontroversial, and he rightly gives it little emphasis. It is the international situation in our time which to some degree protects small states from conquest by large states because of the general fear that small wars may escalate into nuclear conflagration. (Yet in the 19th Century too there were many small states which retained their independence for no other reason than the world balance of power.) Hobsbawm's third reason is his crucial one. This is nothing less than a 'change in world capitalism . . . the relative decline of the medium-to-large nation-state and "national economy" as the main building block of the world economy'.[27] Hobsbawm's argument is that small states can now proliferate and fissiparous national movements can flourish because the main historic check upon these processes no longer operates. No longer is there an economic rationale (the 'national economy') for the old-fashioned nation state, and for the rejection of unviable national projects: capitalism is no longer national in scale, hence national movements are no longer rational. Hobsbawm's argument here is terribly significant, not least for the understanding of past colonial liberation movements and for the pursuit of independence by those which have not yet won their struggles. The fact that arguments quite similar to Hobsbawm's were advanced by Rosa Luxemburg seventy or eighty years ago, and were answered then by Lenin, is of some interest, but it does not obviate the need to display Hobsbawm's arguments and respond to them. This will be our next task.

## International Capitalism and the National State

### Are States Dissolving?

Hobsbawm notes that capitalism is no longer national in scale but is now quite thoroughly international. This, he says, has produced 'a new phase in the international economy',[28] one in which 'the relation between national states and global capitalist development, internally and internationally, is no longer what it was'.[29] Down through the First World War there was, according to Hobsbawm, a congruence between the national economy and the medium-to-large-size state, such that this form of state (in Europe) was the basic building block of capitalism. But now, he argues, the scale of capitalism has outgrown the state and the latter is thus left without its functional relationship to a 'national economy'. Therefore the (national) state in general is of much less significance today than it was in earlier times. And by implication, any effort to create such a state today is likely to be irrational. There is much more than this to Hobsbawm's argument concerning this putative decline (dissolution, disintegration) of states and related matters. I had best quote two long passages which convey the pith of this argument.

> The Balkanization of the world of states . . . [in part] reflects a change in world capitalism, which Marxists have not hitherto brought seriously into the discussion of nationalism: namely, the relative decline of the medium-to-large nation-state and 'national economy' as the main building block of the world economy. Quite apart from the fact that in the era of nuclear superpower even a fairly high potential of production, men, and resources is no longer sufficient for the military status which was formerly the criterion of a 'great power', the rise of the transnational corporation and international economic management have transformed both the international division of labour and its mechanism, and changed the criterion of a state's 'economic viability'. This is no longer believed to be an economy sufficiently large to provide an adequate 'national market' and sufficiently varied to produce most of the range of goods from foodstuffs to capital equipment, but a strategic position somewhere along the complex circuits of an integrated world economy, which can be exploited to secure an adequate national income. While size was essential to the old criterion, it appears largely irrelevant to the new . . . Of course, in military terms most mini-states are negligible; but so are most large states today. The difference between Britain and Barbados in this respect is no longer one of kind, but only one of degree.[30]

> The multiplication of independent sovereign states substantially changed the sense of the term 'independence' for most of them into a synonym for 'dependence' . . . We may leave aside the obvious fact that many of them exist as independent states only on sufferance or under protection . . . They are

economically dependent in two ways: generally, on an international economy they cannot normally hope to influence as individuals; and specifically – in inverse proportion to their size – on the greater powers and transnational corporations. The fact that they today prefer – or find indispensable – a neocolonial relationship rather than something like a formalized dependence, should not mislead us. On the contrary. The optimal strategy for a neocolonial transnational economy is precisely one in which the number of officially sovereign states is maximized and their average size and strength – i.e., their power to effectively impose conditions under which foreign powers and foreign capital will have to operate – is minimized.[31]

This argument, needless to say, is complex, and each of its subordinate positions calls for a definite response. First I will try to respond to the central thread of the entire argument, the thesis that the internationalization of the capitalist economy diminishes the significance of sovereign states – states called 'national' by Hobsbawm to signify scale, not culture – be they neocolonies like Barbados or great powers like Britain.

We have to begin with basics. In Marxist theory the capitalist state is considered to have as its primary function – there are disagreements about the degree of primacy, but they need not detain us – the maintenance of a political environment which permits the capitalist system (in all its dimensions) to continue operating, the capitalist class to hold on to its property and privileges, and capital itself to keep on accumulating. Stating the same thing negatively: capitalism cannot survive without political power, and without a state which it controls. Furthermore, the greater the weight of contradictions in the system, and the closer it is to collapse, the more important the state must surely become. Here I use the word state to mean government and all that goes with it, including most particularly the well-known 'monopoly of legitimate force'. Now I ask: how does any of this change as the scale of capitalist activity becomes more and more international, comes more and more to transcend the scale of the state-as-sovereign-country? The function of governance does not decline in importance. And no super-state emerges, to expand in congruence with the expanding supra-national economy.

Rather, what occurs is an effort by capitalism to change the specific activities of the state in order to adapt it to the new economic landscape. Thus for instance the advanced capitalist countries develop rapid deployment forces (a form of reserve military power, to be applied where and when needed, be it Suez or Santo Domingo), secret mercenary armies, foreign military bases or detachments billeted on foreign soil at the request of client states or with their acquiescence, covert military action or covert economic and material support for military action, police and military training programmes euphemized as foreign aid, and so on *ad nauseam*. Let us not forget that the so-called multinational or transnational corporations are still rooted in, and generate most of their capital for, the advanced capitalist country which is the 'home office'. The state which surrounds that home office will tend to provide, either alone or in some formal or informal alliance, either overtly or covertly, the international political and military support needed by its own multinational corporations, as the US did in Brazil and Chile for ITT, as Britain did in British Guiana for Bookers, as various states did in Katanga for

Union Minière, and the like.[32] The state-as-government in these advanced capitalist countries must remain as strong as ever, to deal with the external problems associated with transnational capitalism and, of course, to keep the workers in their place at home. Otherwise the system collapses like a house of cards. The great states do not crumble into mini-states.

But this is still only half the global map. It is not a coincidence that brutal gorilla regimes have come to power in so many neocolonial states, and that democracy is at best shallow-rooted in all neocolonies. The deeper the penetration into these countries by multinational corporations and more broadly by foreign corporations (many of which have been there since long before anyone used the word multinational), the greater will be the intensity of exploitation. The greater, then, will be the associated oppression, aimed specifically at maintaining low wages and generally at supporting the regime; the greater, we may assume, will be the resistance; and, finally, the greater will be the need for a powerful state as agent both of repression and of indoctrination. A somewhat parallel scenario can be described for the role of the neocolonial state in relation to domestic capitalism, much of which is directly tied to and dependent on the foreign corporations. Indeed, multinational corporations under certain circumstances prefer to leave production relations in the hands of domestic companies or even in the hands of the neocolonial state, precisely because the state's power to keep down labour costs is sometimes greater when the multinationals have no direct presence in domestic production and merely buy the product at very low prices and market it elsewhere at a satisfying profit.

It would probably be wrong to argue that neocolonial governments are very much more dictatorial and repressive than were the colonial governments which they replaced, because colonial governance is, without exception, the antithesis of democracy. But it is probably true as a historical tendency that regimes tend to grow more repressive as the threat of revolution grows stronger. Be that as it may, the basic fact is this: neither in advanced capitalist countries nor in neocolonies nor in paleocolonies (like Puerto Rico) has the state grown weaker or less significant in modern times. Hobsbawm is simply wrong. The internationalization of the capitalist economy has not weakened the state in the existing sovereign countries. Nowhere has it erased the boundaries of existing nation-states and changed the political map of the world.

Hobsbawm is concerned with the strength of states mainly as it is reflected in their ability to resist what he sees as the forces tending to decompose them, forces which he essentially identifies with nationalism. In the 19th Century, he argues, the 'national economy' was a cementing force for the medium-to-large states which he considers to have been the building blocks of capitalism, and the lack of that cement today is the primary reason for what he calls the 'Balkanization of the world of states', the 'fissiparous nationalisms of our time'. This is an interesting proposition, but I fail to see any evidence to support it.

To be precise, I see no evidence on the world political map that any 'Balkanization' has taken place, and no evidence that any sort of 'fissiparous nationalism' is tending truly to break up the advanced capitalist countries. Apart from the Basque and Quebec cases, the centrifugal tendencies discernible today in advanced capitalist countries seem either to be relatively weak or to aim at some degree of regional autonomy short of independence. It goes without saying that I am not talking about the ex-colonies of advanced capitalist countries. In the Third World, the danger of fission is much greater, because the process of national integration in former colonies is often slow and painful, and often hindered by the machinations of foreign economic and political forces. But, perhaps surprisingly, there has been only one significant secession thus far in the formerly colonial world – the splitting off of East Pakistan, now Bangladesh, from thousand-mile-distant West Pakistan – and there have been enough contrary cases, where secession movements were defeated, or never arose, to suggest that no general trend toward state fragmentation exists in the Third World today.[33]

### Is Decolonization a 'Balkanizing' Tendency?

Tom Nairn, in his book *The Break-Up of Britain*, maintained that there is indeed a general tendency, in the world as a whole, towards state fragmentation, and that this tendency is progressive. Hobsbawm disputes the latter proposition but accepts the former, calling this tendency the 'fissiparous nationalisms of our time', the 'Balkanization of the world of states', and so on. He puts forward reasons for this tendency (for example, 'a change in world capitalism') but does not really support these causal propositions with arguments. He relies mainly on one empirical fact: in recent decades there has indeed been a great increase in the number of sovereign states, thanks to the process of decolonization. Hobsbawm exhibits decolonization as the initial phase, and the exemplar, of the new tendency toward 'Balkanization'. But his description of the decolonization process is not entirely accurate, and it can be shown that the process bears no relation at all to the 'fissiparous', 'Balkanizing' tendencies discussed by Hobsbawm.

There are important errors in Hobsbawm's account of decolonization. First, the process cannot be explained in terms of some abstract internationalization of the world economy combined with, or perhaps signalized by, a change in the preferences or needs of capitalism such that colonies are more or less deliberately transformed into neocolonies. (The greater powers and transnational corporations 'prefer – or find indispensable – a neocolonial relationship rather than something like formalized dependence'.) If this were all there was to decolonization, it might be plausible to argue that an internationalization of the world economy has led to a proliferation of independent states and that these states are themselves subject to further fission because they are dependent and weak. And there might in fact be what Hobsbawm calls an 'optimal strategy for a neocolonial transnational economy . . . one in which the number of officially sovereign states is maximized and their average size and strength . . . is minimized'. This is another interesting hypothesis for which there is no real supporting evidence, however plausible the hypothesis may sound.

But if we look at decolonization as a single process in history and geography, it is clear that the main dynamic in that process was, and is – let us not forget Puerto Rico and all the other remaining colonies – the resistance of the colonized peoples. The advanced capitalist countries gave up their colonies, in general, because they had no choice. This was patently true in the first major instances of 20th Century decolonization: Ireland, the Philippines, Korea, greater India, and the Dutch East Indies (now Indonesia). Some colonizing powers, notably Great Britain, learned eventually to accommodate to the situation, and sometimes to yield, gracefully, peacefully, having found from experience in such areas as Latin America, China, and parts of the Middle East that it should be possible to maintain the same exploitative economy without direct political control, that is, through neo-colonialism instead of old-fashioned colonialism. In a very few cases (among them some French African colonies) independence was given as a direct decision by the colonizing power, but always, I am convinced, this was a tactical manoeuvre in the face of some degree of resistance to maximize the probability of a smooth conversion to neocolonialism, and, conversely, to minimize the probability of a socialist or anti-foreign revolution. And then in other cases (Algeria, Kenya, Vietnam, Angola, etc.) the colonizing powers exhausted themselves in futile attempts to hold on to colonies at all cost. In sum: decolonization was some combination of popular resistance and imperialist strategy, but mainly the former.

The pattern of new states which resulted from decolonization did not reflect processes of 'fissioning' (unless we define the empire itself as a state, as Lord Acton did but as Hobsbawm cannot do without undercutting his theory of the medium-to-large-size building-block states of the 19th Century).[34] What had been discrete colonies in one epoch became in most cases discrete independent states in the succeeding epoch. For many valid reasons the national liberation struggles tended to take place at the level of the existing economic–political–administrative–military unit, the colony, and typically the colonial boundaries were retained as those of the independent state. There are exceptions, but in general it can be said that the pattern and number of discrete colonial territories which we find on the world political map for, say, 1939, has become the pattern and number of independent states (and surviving colonies) which we find on the world political map of today. Figuratively speaking, Hobsbawm's 'speck in the Pacific' was a colonial speck before it became an independent speck. There was no fission. And we should really talk about the 'mini-colonies' of former times if we propose to talk about the 'mini-states' of today.

It may conceivably be true that a world of neocolonies generates greater aggregate surplus value for the (corporations of the) advanced capitalist countries than does a world of classical colonies, because formerly monopolized colonial economic spaces are now thrown open to competition among the multinational corporations and the states behind them. But this remains to be demonstrated. There is, for instance, the stubborn fact that US corporations find the classical colony of Puerto Rico much more profitable than they do the neocolonies of Latin America. One third of all US investment in Latin America goes to Puerto Rico, and profit ratios are much higher there than elsewhere.[35] In any case, a comparison of profits and other economic categories across epochs would be very difficult to make. Thus Hobsbawm's proposition that the great powers and multinationals 'prefer – or find indispensable – a neocolonial relationship' is certainly invalid as an explanation of the decolonization process. One very telling argument against this thesis is the evident fact that there was always the danger that independence would lead not to neocolonialism but to socialism, as happened in a number of instances, some quite early in the decolonization epoch. Furthermore, neocolonies have their own ambitious bourgeoisies which provide at least the threat, if not usually the reality, of economically costly competition. Certainly capitalism has learned, since decolonization, to extract much greater surplus value from (most) former colonies than ever it did during the colonial epoch, but this has no bearing on Hobsbawm's argument.

## Lessons From History and Geography

It would be silly to dispute Hobsbawm's thesis that we have entered 'a new phase in the international economy', a phase in which 'the relation between national states and global capitalist development . . . is no longer what it was'. But it would be equally silly to exaggerate the differences between past and present. First of all, capitalism has always been international. Pre-industrial capitalism drew much, perhaps most, of its sustenance from Mexican and Peruvian mines, Brazilian and West Indian plantations, Indian pepper gardens and cotton fields, and so on. Industrial capitalism, as Hobsbawm himself has brilliantly shown, had manifold relations of supply and marketing with the non-industrial parts of the world, while industrial nations traded intensively with one another. Moreover, classical industrial capitalism grew within giant empires upon which the sun never set, and one may wonder whether the boundaries of each industrial nation state were more significant, economically, than the bounds of the larger empire. Formal and informal empires expanded until, at the end of the 19th Century, the array of imperial states, dominions, colonies, semi-colonial spheres of influence, and a few other odds and ends like mini-states, covered the entire world. At that moment capitalism became thoroughly, indisputably, international: it covered the globe.

Just a few years later, before and during the First World War, Marxist theorists began to debate the effects of this internationalization on the national state. The high point of the debate (which we will discuss later in this chapter) came in 1916 when a number of Marxists contended that the economic internationalization of capitalism, which they viewed as a fundamental attribute of the new era of capitalist development, the 'era of imperialism', had rendered the national state essentially obsolete. Said Radek and a group of Polish Marxists associated with Rosa Luxemburg: 'Imperialism represents the tendency of finance capital to *outgrow the bounds of a national state*'.[36] Said Pyatakov: 'This form, the national state, fetters the development of the productive forces'.[37] Similar positions were enunciated by Bukharin and Trotsky.[38] Thus it was widely believed that new sovereign states would not emerge – even that colonies would never, under capitalism, attain independence – in this new era of fully international, imperialist capitalism. Lenin was the outstanding opponent of these views, which he labelled 'imperialist economism' because (in essence) they noticed only the economic attributes of the new era of imperialism, losing sight of its political attributes and exigencies. (Said Lenin in reply to Bukharin: 'The same old fundamental mistake of the same old Economism: inability to pose *political* questions'.[39]) Lenin also pointed out that the tendency towards concentration or centralization was an economic tendency, not a political one, and that internationalized capitalism is fully compatible with the nation-state.[40]

I do not suggest that Hobsbawm is making these same errors. But he is not the first Marxist to draw incorrect political conclusions from novel economic tendencies, and more particularly to believe that the internationalization (or multinationalization) of capitalism somehow corrodes the national state. Certainly the multinational capitalism of our own time is a far cry from the early-imperialist era with its colonial empires and inter-imperialist warfare. Certainly the multinational corporation of today is not the same as the great colonial and international corporations of a half-century ago and before. (Let us not, on the other hand, forget those ancestral multinationals: the East India Companies, the colonial production giants like United Fruit, Lever Brothers, and the rest.) The transformation is qualitative as well as quantitative. But it has not redrawn the political map of the world or eliminated nation-states.

Before leaving this matter of the relation between the internationalization of capitalism and the fate (if it is that) of the nation state, I want to dispute Hobsbawm's thesis about the 'optimal strategy for a neocolonial transnational economy . . . one in which the number of officially sovereign states is maximized and their average size and strength . . . is minimized'. Another interesting but unsupported proposition. I am not privy to capitalist strategy decisions, but I can even so show that the present pattern of sovereign states is not a reflection of any 'optimal strategy'. Most of the argument has been made already. The size and shape of states can largely be explained as a relic of colonial times. The strength of those states which are neocolonial is also in part a function of the colonial legacy and the difficulty of acquiring power or strength (not to say wealth) in a world in which independent capital accumulation tends to occur mainly in the core countries. Moreover, we have seen that a vital – not merely optimal – strategy of multinational capitalism is to maintain the strength of neocolonial governments in order to hold down labour costs and prevent revolutions. Theoretically, then, it is not at all a sensible strategy to maximize the number of neocolonies and minimize their size and strength.

But empirical evidence is even more persuasive. Neocolonial profits have been more abundant in large countries like Brazil, Nigeria, India, and Indonesia than in tiny ones like Sierra Leone and the Seychelles, and the politico–military power of states in the former category has from time to time proved distinctly useful to multinational capitalism. And when we examine the pattern of socialist revolutions in former colonies and semi-colonies, we find that they cover the spectrum from very large states (China, Vietnam, etc.) down to very small ones (Guinea-Bissau, Nicaragua, etc.). Thus neither theory nor fact seems to support the thesis that neocolonialism favours the proliferation of mini-states.

## Neocolonialism and the National Question

It must be borne in mind that Hobsbawm's *New Left Review* article is intended mainly to be an attack on Tom Nairn's 'break-up of Britain' thesis, and not an essay on the national liberation of colonies or an effort to put forward a comprehensive theory of nationalism. But Hobsbawm sweeps with a broad broom, proffering generalizations about 'nationalists' and 'nationalism' without qualification or limitation as to context, and without paying attention to the Marxist's caution signal to take heed of the difference between the nationalism of the oppressed and that of the oppressor, a procedure grounded in the valid argument that general theorems supposed to govern both of these categories are always suspect and usually wrong. But nearly every theorem put forward by Hobsbawm with regard to the really reactionary nationalisms of this world can be read as applying also to progressive national movements, such as those movements which did, and those which still do, struggle for national liberation from colonial oppression. Indeed, there is a general theory of nationalism underlying Hobsbawm's position which establishes a fundamental distinction, not between oppressor and oppressed, but between the supposedly rational national movements of the 19th Century and the supposedly irrational movements of our own century, the latter including both reactionary nationalism and, as well, the progressive struggles against colonialism.

This brings us to the last specific criticism of Hobsbawm's argument. He posts just one warning that his discussion should not be applied to the world of former colonies. That is an assertion – it is indeed a major thesis – that struggles in neocolonies are not national struggles:

> The virtual disappearance of formal empires ('colonialism') has snapped the main link between anti-imperialism and the slogan of national self-determination. However real the dependence of neocolonialism, the struggle against it simply cannot any longer be crystallized around the slogan of establishing independent political statehood, because most territories concerned already have it.[41]

Not only is this argument invalid, but Hobsbawm proves it so himself. Consider the following:

> The multiplication of independent sovereign states substantially changed the sense of the term 'independence' for most of them into a synonym for 'dependence' . . . We may leave aside the obvious fact that many of them exist as independent states only on sufferance or under protection . . . They are economically dependent . . . on an international economy and . . . on the greater powers and transnational corporations which today prefer – or find indispensable – a neocolonial relationship rather than something like formalized dependence.[42]

One or two very peculiar theories are embedded in this passage, among them the notion that dependence is somehow a result of 'the multiplication of independent sovereign states' and the notion, already remarked upon, that decolonization was somehow a result of imperialist strategy, not of colonial liberation movements. We may also defer until later a comment upon the resemblance between Hobsbawm's argument that independence is generally not real, is 'a synonym for "dependence",' and Rosa Luxemburg's argument of long ago that self-determination is an illusion because sovereign states under capitalism are really dependent, not independent. What I wish to call attention to now is the contradiction between the two passages of Hobsbawm's quoted above. In the first he asserts that 'the virtual disappearance of formal empires ("colonialism")' has meant that struggles against neocolonialism are not really national struggles, struggles for sovereignty, 'because most territories . . . already have it'. In other words, once a state has gained formal sovereignty its international struggles are no longer matters of national liberation. But in the second passage, Hobsbawm asserts that these newly independent states are 'dependent', not 'independent' (they exist 'on sufferance or under protection', etc.). If they do not enjoy real sovereignty, if they are 'dependent' – which of course is a political as well as an economic condition – then it must follow that they are still engaged in national struggle for real independence and real sovereignty.

We do not have to remind Hobsbawm that there are degrees of sovereignty, and that these gradations are found in the array of newly independent states, former colonies, just as they were found in the supposedly sovereign 'nation-states' of 19th Century Europe (Portugal, Denmark, etc.), in the supposedly non-sovereign dependencies of that time and place (Saxe-Coburg-Gotha, several Balkan entities, etc.), and in the vast number and forms of classical colonies – forms ranging from nominal sovereignty (as in some 'native states') through various intermediate conditions (for example, 'indirect rule') to absolute lack of self-governing institutions. What logic, then, would justify an assertion that neocolonies are not engaged in national struggle when they fight for real political independence? This is not just a matter of juggling terms.

The progressive sectors in what I think must be every neocolony on the planet insist that they are, indeed, fighting a national struggle, a struggle for independence from dominant foreign powers and multinational corporations, as well as, of course, a domestic struggle against exploiting classes. (This is often articulated, I think wrongly, as a dual struggle, a national struggle externally and a class struggle internally. But, as we saw in Chapter 2, national struggle *is* class struggle. In these neocolonial cases it is struggle against exploiting classes based in other countries and using local subalterns for the local struggle.) The matter is even more stark in the case of all but the largest socialist states. Each of these perceives itself to be – and is – threatened with invasion and subversion by capitalist powers, and each defines its own posture as one of engagement in a national struggle for self-determination, a struggle to defend and preserve its sovereignty. We might recall, also, that socialism was won in many of these states, among them Vietnam, Cuba, and Nicaragua, in struggles against a domestic enemy (regardless of whom that enemy fronted for, and how); would Hobsbawm deny that these, too, were national struggles?

Hobsbawm thus deletes from the national question the generally progressive struggles against neocolonialism. This leaves him free to declare that the only important form of national struggle, the essential content of the 'fissiparous nationalisms of our time', is the irrational sort of national movement which springs up in a developed capitalist country and the supposedly frivolous independence movement of some 'speck in the Pacific'. It leaves him free, moreover, to dismiss nationalism in general as irrational.

To all of this the response must be that Hobsbawm's perfectly justified critique of reactionary national movements can stand by itself. It can be justified by the empirical facts of class forces and class struggles. Insofar as it needs theoretical backing for its empirical assertions, this can be the unpretentious generalization that all national struggle is a struggle for state power, that struggle for state power is a form of the class struggle, and that we can in principle determine whether a given case is progressive or not, rational or not, in much the same way that we make that determination with other forms of class struggle. But if instead we use a convoluted theory which declares modern national movements in general to be atavistic and irrational, then very dangerous consequences ensue. Legitimate and progressive struggles, like the Puerto Rican struggle to win independence and the Nicaraguan struggle to defend independence, will be misunderstood and thus hampered.

## Hobsbawm and the Marxist Theory of Nationalism

### Hobsbawm's Theory

Hobsbawm's essential theory, as I read it, describes the interplay between two distinct sorts of historical process. One is nationalism, which he conceives to be a very complex phenomenon made up of ideology, political programme, political movement, and rather deep-lying cultural processes. Two forms of this phenomenon seem to be important. One is the form of the conventional national movement, a 'nation-building' process which has as its aim the establishment of a state congruent with the community in which the movement arises, typically a language community or a culture. Hobsbawm traces the origin of this process and movement back to the convulsions and dislocations associated with the great transformation from feudalism to capitalism. The other form of nationalism, also called 'nation-building', is generated within an existing state, and constitutes what he calls (as do others) a 'civic religion' by means of which the inhabitants of the state are cemented into a socio-cultural whole, a mass of patriotic and law-abiding citizens.

Both forms of nationalism interact with a set of basically different processes which are characteristic of the rise of capitalism, processes associated with the establishment of the capitalist state and the definition of its internal characteristics. On this matter, Hobsbawm's view is the conventional one among Marxists and many others. Capitalism, in its rise, has the need for an adequate-sized 'national' economy, and the need to maintain state power over this territorial whole. ('Need' is of course not to be read anthropomorphically.) Hence the emergence of a finite number of capitalist states. Where no state yet exists, nationalism or nation-building creates national consciousness, a national movement, and so on. Where capitalism seizes (so to speak) an already existing state, nationalism or nation-building tends to transform the state into a nation. Thus both cases tend towards the formation of nation states.

We see, then, that nationalism in Hobsbawm's theory is distinct from capitalist state-formation but gains its historical significance in association with the latter. Hobsbawm suggests rather offhandedly that nationalism as a process may have a prehistory antedating the rise of the capitalist state, but he asserts firmly, in several of his writings, that effectuated nationalism is a product of the 19th Century, of Europe, and thus of the politics of rising capitalism.[43] (For the non-European world there seems not to have been any proper nationalism during most of that century, according to Hobsbawm.[44]) On the other hand, Hobsbawm pointedly discusses cases of nationalism in 19th Century Europe which were quite unrelated to the normal rise-of-capitalism state-forming process. These were the 'Ruritanian' nationalisms, the national movements of (usually) small areas or small societies which sought to form states but were, so to speak, destined to be absorbed within larger states and come to nothing. They were thus, according to Hobsbawm, irrational.

This brings us to the crucial objections to Hobsbawm's theory. It is a theory about nation-building processes, and it speaks of two forms, a rational form which is associated with the rise of capitalism and the formation of capitalist nation states, and an irrational form which seems – there is some ambiguity – to cover all other sorts of nation-building efforts. This formulation leads to a number of serious problems, among them the following:

1) Hobsbawm's theory postulates a single sort of phenomenon to which the label 'nationalism' is to be attached. But there are other sorts of phenomena which do not fit into Hobsbawm's theory yet are, so to speak, begging to be described as 'nationalism'. One of these, to my mind the most important, is the expansionist nationalism of imperial states, including most pointedly Britain and her fellow colonizing powers, but also including Nazi Germany, imperial Japan, and the rest. Is this not nationalism? And when an imperial state resists a national movement in some part of its territory or in its colonial empire, is this resistance to nation-building (etc.) not also nationalism? Stated differently: if there is an ideology, political programme, and political movement – a national movement – fighting to create a state, must there not be an ideology, programme, political force, etc., fighting to prevent the state from emerging? Must there not be (at least) two sides in every national struggle? And do we not need a comprehensive theory which will deal with such struggle in all its dimensions? This is not only true in theory; it is true in Marxist practice on the national question. Since the time of Marx and Engels, and more concretely since Lenin, Marxists have concerned themselves at least as much with 'great nation nationalism', and with 'the nationalism of the oppressor nations', as they have with the nationalism of nation-building and state formation.[45]

2) Hobsbawm's theory describes as rational only the sort of state forming process which is associated with the rise of capitalism. Before the First World War this would have been considered basically correct. But Lenin (and others) argued theoretically that colonies and semi-colonies might, for various reasons, win out to socialism without enduring a capitalist purgatory. And national liberation movements have not only established this in practice, but they have shown that fully capitalist colonies and neocolonies can win through to socialism. Hence we now must have a theory of socialist state formation. Hobsbawm's does not suffice.[46] Stating the matter differently: a Marxist theory of nationalism must be able to explain national struggles, like those of Vietnam, Angola, Cuba, Nicaragua, which are not part of the 'bourgeois democratic revolution', which are not themselves associated with 'the rise of the bourgeoisie', but which are in fact led by socialists and result in the formation of a socialist, not a capitalist (nation) state. This also applies to struggles not yet won. For example, Marxists struggle for the independence of Puerto Rico not to create a 'bourgeois democratic state' but to liberate the country from capitalism.

3) Some of the difficulties with Hobsbawm's basic concept of nationalism as a phenomenon or process derive from the very fact that he views nationalism, ontologically, in that way: as a definite phenomenon, a distinct process. He supposes that all forms of nationalism have a common nature, from which it must

follow that modern national liberation struggles are somehow of a piece with 19th Century rising-capitalist national movements and even with the reactionary separatist national movements within some present-day socialist states (like Yugoslavia). All are seen as sharing a common ideological, political, and social character and (at least implicitly) a common relation to capitalism.[47] I think I have dwelt enough on the blind alleys into which this approach leads us to obviate the need for further comment on that matter.

What needs to be said is that there is a distinctly different way of conceptualizing nationalism which avoids these problems, and which is closer to the main line of Marxist thinking about the national question. It starts with the proposition that creation and control of a state is the crux of political struggle in all recent and contemporary forms of society. One form of this political struggle is national struggle. It broadly describes all cases of forming states, enlarging states, seceding from states and thus forming other states, unifying states into larger states, absorbing states into other states, and so on. There are thus many forms and combinations of national struggle. Each must display a certain pattern of class participation (on both sides of the struggle, needless to say), and hence is subject to class analysis like any other moment of the class struggle – of which national struggle is one type. Thus we would fully expect to find every major class grouping and type of social formation to be involved somehow in national struggle, and we would thus speak of the struggles of the rising bourgeois (and retreating aristocracy), the monopoly bourgeoisie, the fascists, the proletariat (alone and in combinations), and so on.

By the same token, we would expect to find all types of modern states engaged in national struggles. For instance, most Marxists well understand the problematic of socialist states having to engage in forms of national struggle to defend their revolutions within a world geographical environment which is still predominantly capitalist. There is nothing 'bourgeois' about doing so. And, as we noted earlier, most Marxists are aware that the way to build socialism in the world of today is to do it piece by piece, that is, state by state; hence the working classes must engage in national struggle to seize or form their particular local state, not wait for socialism to, magically, descend upon the whole earth all at once. My point in saying all this is relatively simple. We can analyse all forms of the national question without assuming any particular class character of the participating actors, or any 'stage' of history. The integrating principle, on which our theory of nationalism as a whole is based, is simply that the national question is one form or category of the struggle to seize state power.

## Lenin's 'Pragmatism'

Let us recall again Hobsbawm's comment that nationalism is 'devoid of any discernible rational theory'. There was rationality, he argues, in the process of nation state formation during the 19th Century, and there seems to have been rationality in at least some instances of state formation in our own time, instances which represent, he says, 'something like the "bourgeois-democratic phase" in the development of backward countries'.[48] (We will take a second look at this revealing remark in a moment.) The rationality in this state forming process was the logic of rising capitalism and its – or, to avoid anthropomorphism, the bourgeoisie's – need to have state power over, preferably, largish and culturally uncomplex territories, thus national economies, and therefore nation states. Hobsbawm's argument here is faithful to Marx and Engels, and the theory is in large part derivative from the Marxist theory of capitalism itself.

But this is not nationalism. Nationalism, says Hobsbawm, is an ideology and social and political movement, often a blindly irrational 'civic religion', a demand and struggle to obtain independent statehood for one's own cultural community (or 'nation') regardless of the size and political viability of this community and regardless of all other circumstances, internal and external. According to Hobsbawm this political ideology and movement sometimes coincides with the normal capitalist state forming process and thus acquires, as it were by induction, a kind of rationality, sensibleness, logic, from the latter process. But other instances of nationalism in the 19th Century (the 'Ruritanias', etc.) and essentially all nationalism today do not coincide in this way with a historically normal process of capitalist state formation. These nationalisms are irrational. Their aims are irrational, and they cannot be brought under any sort of explanatory theory. Hence they are 'devoid of . . . rational theory'.[49]

Hobsbawm wants to associate Marxism, and particularly Lenin, with this view. He argues that Lenin's approach to nationalism was a matter not of theory but of 'pragmatism'. This was so, Hobsbawm maintains, because nationalism then, as today, was a powerful mass phenomenon, and was in many cases progressive in the sense that it furthered the aims of the proletariat, although in an indirect way because the directionality of national movements and that of Marxists' political struggles had different causal bases and thus could coincide only under special circumstances. Some of the ways Hobsbawm expresses this matter of Lenin's pragmatism on the national question, and of the pragmatism that Hobsbawm thinks has predominantly characterized Marxist positions on this question, are to be seen in the following quotations:

> Marxists . . . have to come to terms with the political fact of nationalism and to define their attitudes towards its specific manifestations. Ever since Marx, this has for the most part, and necessarily, been a matter not of theoretical principle (except for the Luxemburgian minority which tends to suspect nations *en bloc*) but of pragmatic judgment in changing circumstances. In principle, Marxists are neither for nor against independent statehood for any nation . . . even assuming that there can be other than pragmatic judgment on what constitutes 'the nation' in any particular case.[50]

> The Marxist attitude toward nationalism as a programme is similar in many respects to Marx's attitude towards other *a priori* abstractions of what in his day was petty-bourgeois radicalism, e.g., the 'democratic republic'. It is not unsympathetic, but contingent and not absolute. The fundamental criterion of Marxist pragmatic judgment has always been whether nationalism as such, or any specific case of it, advances the cause of socialism or conversely, how to prevent it from inhibiting its progress; or alternatively, how to mobilize it as a force to assist its progress.[51]

Lenin, in fact, did not recommend socialists in the countries concerned to *favour* secession except in specific, and pragmatically identifiable, circumstances.[52]

The real danger for Marxists is the temptation to welcome nationalism as ideology and programme rather than realistically to accept it as a fact, a condition of their struggle as socialists ... Quite apart from implying the abandonment of the values of the Enlightenment, of reason and science, such a conversion also implies a withdrawal from realistic analysis of the world situation, Marxist or otherwise.[53]

[The] practical attitude of Marxists to the concrete political problems raised by 'the national question' hardly requires serious modification. They will, no doubt, continue to be as conscious of nationality and nationalism as they have been for most of the twentieth century: they can hardly not be.[54]

Finally, a quotation which reveals Hobsbawm's belief that national struggle and class struggle, the programme for achieving state independence and the programme for achieving socialism, are radically disjunctive – from which it would have to follow that Marxists can relate only 'pragmatically' to nationalists:

There is no way of turning the formation of 'national' communities (i.e., the multiplication of nation-states *as such*) into a historic engine for generating socialism either to replace or to supplement the Marxian historic mechanism.[55]

The 'Marxian historic mechanism' I suppose is class struggle. Hobsbawm is asserting that national struggles can neither replace nor even 'supplement' class struggle.[56] Nationalism is a wild card. Whence comes the 'pragmatism' of most Marxists and in particular of Lenin. (But did not the Vietnamese, to take an example not quite at random, consider national liberation to be an essential component of the 'historic engine for generating socialism' in their country, as indeed not a supplement to but a part of the 'Marxian historic mechanism' for them?)

Hobsbawm does not credit Lenin with a proper theory of nationalism. 'Ever since Marx', says Hobsbawm, the attitude of Marxists towards nationalism has been a matter of 'pragmatic judgment in changing circumstances', thus not a theory, except in the specific case of the theory of 'rational' nation state formation in the period of rising capitalism. Lenin, according to Hobsbawm, revolutionized Marxist practice on the national question, but there was, in effect, nothing to theorize about: the issue was now in the arena of 'pragmatic judgment'.

I believe that Hobsbawm is completely wrong on this issue. Lenin developed a comprehensive theory of nationalism, and it is this theory, not pragmatism (and implicitly opportunism), which has guided Marxist practice on the national question since Lenin's time. Furthermore, Lenin's mature theory of nationalism is not reconcilable with the theory which Hobsbawm himself puts forward on these matters. In particular, Lenin's theory provides a reasoned, logical basis for Marxists' judgement as to which sorts of national movements Marxists should support – and sometimes fight and die in – as a matter of principle, and it likewise provides such a basis for Marxists' implacable opposition to national movements which are discovered to be reactionary. Hobsbawm's theory entails, rather, a vision of national movements in which all of them are one or another shade of grey: some should be supported, though with suspicion; others should be opposed, though with 'pragmatic' willingness to 'mobilize' them 'as a force'.

From the point of view of the present chapter, the most crucial difference is that Hobsbawm's position would force us to view with at least some degree of suspicion all liberation struggles of colonies. Lenin's, on the other hand, plainly and simply requires such a struggle for liberation in colonial-type oppressed countries, and requires, moreover, that Marxists in these countries fight for real independence as a matter of principle (and theory) while it censures those Marxists in other countries, particularly those in the oppressor country, who fail to support these colonial struggles for independence. It is flatly untrue that Lenin 'did not recommend socialists in the countries concerned to *favour* secession except in specific, and pragmatically identifiable, circumstances' – in the case of colonies.[57] It is pertinent to recall here that Lenin argued against the admission of a group of British socialists into the Third International because they were not fighting hard enough for the independence of British colonies.[58]

I will try now to summarize Lenin's theory of nationalism or national struggle, mainly to show that Hobsbawm's assessment of it is wrong. Let it be said that a great many modern Marxists, orthodox and heterodox alike, are as wrong about this theory as Hobsbawm is. He is in good company.

### Lenin's Theory

In a sense there are two Leninist theories of nationalism or the national question. Hobsbawm's essential error lies in his neglect of the second and later theory. This second theory is not associated with some intellectual 'break', some biographical phenomenon of intellectual maturation of the sort which certain Marxists claim to find in the life and ideas of Karl Marx. In Lenin's case it was the World War which forced this great thinker to try to come up with an explanation for a historical crisis which was catastrophic, unexpected (at least in its effects on the workers' movement), and not comprehensible within the corpus of Marxist theory as it existed at that time. (I will call this corpus of pre-war ideas 'post-classical Marxism' to distinguish it from the 'classical' Marxism of the Marx–Engels period.) Post-classical Marxism contained a body of accepted ideas about the national question, national movements, and the emergence of nation states during the period of 'rising capitalism'. There were indeed differences of theory and practice, but most of the central ideas were held in common. Lenin broke with this post-classical corpus of ideas on national struggle (and on other matters of theory, notably imperialism) in his writings of the period 1915–1920. By 1920 he held a radically different view of national struggle.

The emergence of this distinctively Leninist theory of nationalism or national struggle has tended to be neglected for a number of reasons, one being the high visibility of Lenin's earlier debates with Luxemburg, another being the prominence of Stalin's 1913 essay on national struggle, 'Marxism and the National Question', in most respects a typical example of post-classical Marxist thought which nonetheless continued to be accepted as biblical dogma all through the Stalin period and beyond. (See Chapter 5 below.) In 1913 and thereabouts it was agreed by all the major theorists on the national question, including Lenin, Stalin, Luxemburg, Bauer, and Kautsky, that the set of phenomena embracing national movements and the emergence of nation states was characteristic only of the period of early or rising capitalism. As Marx and Engels had said before them, nationalism would tend to quieten down or disappear as capitalism matured, because mature capitalism was fully international: because the modern bourgeoisie had become or were becoming a world-wide class with common, world-wide interests, and with no interest in maintaining the 'fetters' (as they were called) of national barriers. In a nutshell: national struggle was part of the struggle of the rising bourgeoisie, was thus innately 'bourgeois', and would have no function after capitalism had matured and the bourgeoisie had 'risen'.[59] Some Marxists then extended this argument to the point where it became transformed into an argument against all national struggles, and against any participation by socialists or workers in such struggles. This view we associate mainly with Luxemburg, although others agreed with her. She maintained that the era of nationalism was definitively ended; that new nation states were very unlikely to emerge anywhere; that national movements were thus rather idle and utopian, and they should not be supported for that reason and also because they were now, in the period of mature capitalism, reactionary.[60]

Lenin replied to Luxemburg by attacking this extended or elaborated argument, but holding to the basic position they both shared with post-classical Marxism in general. He said in effect: of course national movements and national struggles are characteristic of the period of rising capitalism, and of course they will tend to die out, along with the national question in general, as capitalism matures. But, he said, the maturation of capitalism is very uneven over the face of the earth. In eastern Europe capitalism is still rising, and national movements may still, in certain circumstances, have a chance of success, of forming new nation states. Furthermore, the peculiarly barbarous character of the Russian Empire leads to intense national oppression, hence to intense and popular resistance which may take the form of national movements. And finally, the peculiar characteristics of the Tsarist empire tend to unite the national movements in oppressed nations with the struggle for bourgeois political democracy – another feature of the period of rising capitalism – and hence to bring the national question close to the centre of the socialists' struggles for democratic rights.[61] There is of course much more than this to Lenin's pre-war position (and to Luxemburg's), but what I have said will suffice for our purposes. And what I have said would probably not be challenged by Hobsbawm.

We have to note two additional elements for a theory of nationalism which were enunciated by Lenin before the start of the World War. The first of these was the proposition that discussions about nationalism could not be limited to the nationalism of small and oppressed nations and aspiring national movements. What he called 'great nation nationalism' tended to be ignored by Marxists – notably, he pointed out, by Luxemburg – but it was something that had to be taken account of as seriously as, and indeed more seriously than, the nationalism of those who aspired to state independence.[62] In essence, great nation nationalism was the dialectical opposing force to national movements. It was also, in its ideological form, easily disguised behind arguments that great states are more progressive, more suitable for modern capitalism, etc., than small ones. In later years Lenin elaborated this idea of great nation nationalism into a major theoretical proposition about the intensification of great nation nationalism in the era of imperialism. In the pre-war period he was far ahead of his contemporaries in understanding the nature and significance of great nation nationalism.

The second theoretical element was an extension of the argument that national movements in eastern Europe were still viable, important, and in some cases progressive. Lenin began to argue this clear and simple proposition: national movements in the advanced capitalist countries of western Europe are a thing of the past; those of eastern European imperial states, a thing of the present; those of the colonial world, a thing of the future.[63] In other words, anti-colonial national movements and those of semi-colonies (like China) were progressive and viable, and deserved support. Hobsbawm agrees on this matter: the Leninist position, he notes correctly, 'widened the category of "national movements" regarded as essentially "progressive" in their impact much beyond Marx's and Engels' own'.[64] On the other hand, Hobsbawm badly neglects the other Leninist proposition, that great nation nationalism needs to be looked at through the same theoretical lens as the nationalism of small and oppressed nations and national movements aspiring to independence. I suppose he accepts the proposition in principle, but there is scarcely any mention of great nation nationalism in his discussions of nationalism and when he uses the word 'nationalism' it seems to refer almost always to movements for autonomy or independence.

Lenin developed his theory of imperialism mainly in 1915 and 1916. It was inherently a political theory, designed to explain the political realities of a war which was destroying the European workers movements, and necessary to reveal the basic features of the era in which the war was taking place. The overt problem was flag-waving nationalism, but Lenin did not make the mistake of imagining this to be some merely ideological epidemic. It was clear that a profound change in both the economics and politics of capitalism was taking place. Capitalism had always sought to export its crises by spatial expansion, mainly colonial and semi-colonial. With the rise of finance capital and monopoly capitalism the need for expansion (including the export of capital) increased very greatly, but, the earth being finite in extent, fields for new territorial expansion had disappeared. Therefore, according to Lenin, two basically novel and very powerful political forces had come into play: first, struggles among great powers to 'repartition' (Lenin's word) the already 'partitioned' world, which necessarily implied political struggles among the powers and thus eventually world war, and second, the growth of national liberation movements in colonies and semi-colonies, roughly in proportion to the intensifying economic exploitation and deepening national oppression which the new era brought forth.[65] This analysis led Lenin to a series of fundamental theorems about nationalism.

(1) Nationalism is not merely characteristic of the era of early or 'rising' capitalism, dying down as capitalism matures, and associated only with the early capitalist process of state formation. In the era of imperialism, the 20th Century, nationalism becomes more intense than ever, and acquires new functions. Great nation nationalism becomes more important and powerful than ever because of the

need to repartition economic space, and this leads to world war. This newly intensified great power nationalism is not precisely a new phenomenon, since great power nationalism already had its own inglorious history prior to the 20th Century; it is new in that it is immensely increased in intensity and in significance, leading to the Great War and all its consequences.[66]

(2) The nationalism of colonies and semi-colonies is called into being by the intensification of exploitation and oppression. In an important way, this is a new phenomenon, or, to be more precise (since anti-colonial resistance also had its history), it cannot be assimilated to the theory of national movements which emerge during the rise of capitalism and have as their (as it were) purpose or goal the simple creation of a bourgeois state. The nature of colonialism is such that producing classes suffer along with whatever young or incipient bourgeoisie may exist. Therefore the national liberation movements in colonies and semi-colonies are profoundly different from the national movements of earlier oppressed nations such as those in non-colonial portions of the Tsarist empire. It is not innately a bourgeois struggle against feudal forces for the creation of a classical bourgeois state. It is a multi-class struggle directed primarily against imperialism.[67]

(3) The old-fashioned nationalism of rising capitalism continues to be found in various parts of the world, but it is distinct from, and now less important than, the two new forms: the intensified bourgeois nationalism of the great capitalist states and the national liberation struggles in colonies and semi-colonies. What all three forms have in common is struggle over the sovereignty of states. And indeed for Lenin this is the essence of the national question, and the subject matter for the theory of nationalism.

Lenin's ideas on colonial liberation struggles had evolved in his later years. By 1920 Lenin was convinced that workers and other exploited classes, with the proletariat in the van, could take the leading role in such struggles sooner or later. Even when these movements had bourgeois leadership they were struggles against monopoly capitalism and could be turned onto a socialist trajectory or a non-capitalist trajectory which would result in socialism.[68] On the basis (mainly) of this reasoning Lenin quite categorically argued that national independence movements *must* be supported.[69] (Hobsbawm notes only Lenin's pre-war position, which did not call for categorical or unconditional support of national movements in oppressed nations.)[70] And it was clear to Lenin that colonial liberation movements were a new form of national movement in the sense that they could not be assimilated to the old model of the rise of capitalism. New states and new nations were emerging under conditions of monopoly capitalism, not early capitalism. Some of them were part of the rise of socialism.[71]

All of this adds up to a new Marxist theory of nationalism, new in the precise sense that it implies the negation of some important theorems of the earlier theory, the view characteristic of post-classical Marxism. Nationalism is not simply a part of the state-forming process of the young, rising bourgeoisie; of early capitalism. It is also characteristic of monopoly capitalism. And it is also characteristic of the struggle for socialism during the period when monopoly capitalism still dominates most of the earth, a period during which the rise of socialism must take the form (from a geographical perspective) of a multiplicity of struggles to create socialist states. Nationalism is not an innately bourgeois phenomenon: in the colonial and semi-colonial countries the national struggle is engaged in by workers and peasants as well as the conventional 'rising bourgeoisie', and workers and peasants can, under the right circumstances and with the right politics and tactics, take the lead. In the case of these struggles, though not necessarily in other sorts of national struggles, the proper posture for socialists is to provide full and unqualified support.

The difference between Hobsbawm's approach to the theory of nationalism and Lenin's should now be fairly clear. Hobsbawm builds his theory on the basis of post-classical Marxist thought, which includes Lenin's pre-World War writings. Hobsbawm appears to maintain that all nationalism, if it is indeed rational, is part of the state forming process associated with the rise of capitalism. He certainly believes that national liberation movements in colonies are likely to be progressive but he seems to assimilate these, in their turn, to the rise of capitalism in a straightforward diffusion model: capitalism arose in Europe in the 19th Century and then spread outwards across the world, bringing nationalism with it.[72] Lenin, on the other hand, postulates that national movements in colonial countries are essentially different, and may either be struggles for socialism, not capitalism, or will at least be struggles against monopoly capitalism. And they are struggles which deserve pretty much unconditional support, unlike earlier national movements involved in the rise of capitalism, movements to which socialists were expected to concede the unconditional right of self-determination, of independent statehood, but movements which socialists were not enjoined to support.

Hobsbawm's second definite category of national processes consists of the 'irrational' nationalism of our time (and that of the 'Ruritanias' of yesterday), a category which appears to include all sorts of cases of 20th Century national movements including those of colonies and those of ethnically distinct regions within advanced capitalist countries. Nationalisms of this type are 'devoid of any discernible rational theory': they have no theory and they succumb to no theory. Lenin, on the other hand, provides a theory that broadly explains these movements. Perhaps the matter should be put negatively: the old Marxist theory could not explain major tendencies towards state formation, with their national movements, in the era of mature or modern capitalism. It was Lenin, then, who added certain crucial propositions to the Marxist theory of nationalism and deleted others which were inapplicable to the modern period. Lenin may not have prevised the special sorts of nationalism which one now finds in some developed capitalist countries (for example, Scottish or Basque nationalism). But the fact that nationalism would be intense and important in the era of imperialism is very explicit in Lenin's theory.

Lenin's theory also provides an explanation for a phenomenon which clearly puzzles Hobsbawm to the point where he must make fun of it: the process leading to the creation of small peripheral states, some of them 'mini-states'. ('Any speck in the Pacific' with 'enough beaches and pretty girls to become a tourist paradise . . .'; 'Kuwaitis . . . treated like the English milord of old'[73]; a 'vast Saharan republic resting on 60,000 nomads'[74]). It is a fairly direct deduction from Lenin's theory of nationalism to argue as follows: the overall force of superexploitation in colonies and semi-colonies, and its attendant political force, national oppression, is the basic, underlying cause of the rise of national movements in these sorts of areas. Hence the cause has nothing intrinsically to do with the size of the eventual independent state. Presumably there are forces of nationalism in every town and village over great portions of the colonial world. What turns some of the resulting movements into struggles which eventually create mini-states is a completely different set of circumstances. Usually it is nothing more than the conversion of a 'mini-colony' into a 'mini-independent-state'.

The national liberation process would be at work almost regardless of the size and shape of the territory to be liberated. It is in essence the same force in India as in the Seychelles, in Nigeria as in Grenada. I think it most unlikely that any leader of any genuine national liberation movement anywhere fails to see the desirability of a large and powerful state. But for an oppressed, exploited, colonized people, a mini-state is likely to appear better than no state at all. And the conditions which lead national movements to create small states, occasionally mini-states, conditions which include the colonizer's cartography and also matters of ethnic complexity, political ambitions of local despots, intrigues of the CIA and multinational corporations, etc., all such forces are fundamentally distinct from the basic and prior force, the national struggle against colonial exploitation and oppression. Here, I believe, is Hobsbawm's most serious error. A large share of the political problems of the world of modern states he attributes to one or another sort of irrational nationalism. But the national struggle of colonial areas is perfectly rational: it is a struggle for freedom.

### 'Imperialist Economism' – A Renascent Trend?

Reading Hobsbawm and certain other modern Marxists on the national question I have the eerie feeling of being transported back into the midst of the debate which was raging on this question in 1915 and 1916, the debate in which (as I mentioned previously) Lenin characterized the position of his opponents as 'imperialist economism'. This was part of the larger debate in and around the Zimmerwald Left concerning the wartime crisis and the issues of theory and practice which it raised. The issue of wartime annexations by belligerents (e.g., Germany's occupation of Belgium) became fused with the issue of the liberation of colonies (including Ireland), and with the issue of whether or not to retain the demand for self-determination in the Bolshevik programme and whether or not to assert this principle on a wider scale than the Russian. All such questions merged into a great debate on the national question, probably the most important one in the history of Marxism. On one side of the debate were Lenin along with what must have been a majority of the Bolshevik participants, and doubtless other socialists. On the other side were Bukharin, Pyatakov, Radek, Luxemburg (who was in jail in Germany and participated indirectly, through her 'Junius' pamphlet), Polish socialists close to Luxemburg, and others.

One central issue was the right of self-determination of nations as a general principle, and the question whether and how socialists should fight for the liberation of oppressed nations. Among many arguments put forward by Lenin's opponents (as I will describe them for brevity's sake) were the following:

(1) Big states are more progressive than small states, and it is therefore

reactionary to advocate the secession, or even the right of secession, of portions of these big states. The Luxemburgians and others extended this argument to the matter of the secession of colonies, which was judged by them to be something to advocate publicly but with no confidence in the possibility, perhaps even the desirability, of realization under capitalism, since colonies were parts of big states.[75]

(2) 'Imperialism', said Radek and two Polish associates, 'represents the tendency of finance capital to *outgrow the bounds of a national state*'.[76] This is the argument that capitalism is now a single international system, and thus the national state (or any state) is rendered obsolete, while under socialism ultimately there will be, of course, no states at all.

(3) To advocate the right of self-determination and, beyond that, to advocate secession (or liberation) for any country is to throw the workers of that country into the arms of the bourgeoisie, and at the same time to cut off this community of workers from their brother workers of the larger (or oppressing) state. In sum: socialists are interested only in self-determination for the working class, not for the nation (which in any case no longer exists except as an abstraction, thanks to the differentiation of its population into warring classes). Bukharin advanced this argument even after the October revolution; it seemed to him to be an important reason for refusing the right of self-determination, of secession, to the nations within post-Tsarist Russia.[77]

(4) National liberation movements, whether or not they are progressive, are inherently bourgeois, because nation state formation is a dimension of the rise of the bourgeoisie, of capitalism, and not part of the rise of socialism.

Lenin forcefully and successfully answered the opponents of self-determination and national liberation, responding to the first two of the four arguments in the 1915–1916 debates and dealing with the latter two arguments somewhat later. Lenin also found a phrase which seemed to provide an accurate label for his opponents. He described them as 'imperialist economists' in a series of articles written in 1916, the first of which (directed mainly against Bukharin) was called 'The Nascent Trend of Imperialist Economism'.[78] As we noted earlier, Lenin considered an 'imperialist economist' to be someone who advocated a new form of the old disease called 'economism' (i.e., stressing economic forces and neglecting the political ones), a form suited to the new era of imperialism. Why were the arguments of Lenin's opponents 'economistic'? Because, he said, they were asserting that the new era of imperialism is one which renders obsolete all partial and local struggles for political democracy, including most pointedly struggles for national independence. Why obsolete? Because, they claim, capitalism in its imperialist stage is now fully international, and this means that the principle of scale or concentration renders small states irrelevant and struggles to create small states reactionary, while the internationalization of this economic system, capitalism, makes all individual states, large or small, obsolete. Thus the arguments (1) and (2).

Lenin's answer deserves to be read, not summarized. His most telling points were perhaps the following.

(1) The Marxist principle of concentration is an economic principle, not a political one:

The law of economic concentration, of the victory of large-scale production over small, is recognized in our own and the Erfurt programmes . . . Nowhere is the law of political or state concentration recognized . . . Everyone would laugh at this amusing imperialist Economism if it were expressed openly and if, parallel with the law that small-scale production is ousted by large-scale production, there were presented another '*law*' . . . of small states being ousted by big ones![79]

(2) In the era of imperialism, political struggles are no less important than they were in capitalism's preceding era, because capitalism is inherently a political system as well as an economic system; or, stated differently, the capitalist economic system cannot function without a political environment which it controls, and that political environment is mainly supplied by states and state power, in the present era as in others. In Lenin's words:

A vast distance separates the era of the establishment of capitalism and the national state from the era of the collapse of the national state and the eve of the collapse of capitalism itself.[80]

The question is the relation of economics to politics: the relation of economic conditions and the economic content of imperialism to a certain political form.[81]

(3) In the same text there is the kernel of an argument that national movements need not be inherently bourgeois – as there is the kernel of such an argument in Marx's and Engels' writings about Ireland many years earlier – but this argument in its full form, as an assertion that working masses and socialists can and should lead national movements in colonial countries, was developed in Lenin's later works.[82]

(4) The argument that national liberation struggles 'divide the class' or 'unite workers with bourgeoisie' was answered by Lenin in a number of subtle arguments. In 1918 he responded to Bukharin by pointing out that in no modern country, including even capitalist Germany and revolutionary Russia, had the 'differentiation of the classes' approached anything like completion; hence, the nation was still a reality, not an abstraction.[83] (Elsewhere in later writings he went further, discussing, for instance, the distinctiveness and cohesiveness of national cultures, which would persist after the withering away of states.)[84]

It would take us too far afield to discuss in full Lenin's response to those whom he called 'imperialist economists'. In the course of this debate Lenin asserted, I think for the first time, the general principle that liberation struggles in colonies should be supported categorically, providing only that they were genuine and serious, of the type of a 'national uprising or a serious popular struggle against oppression'.[85] In later writings he stated the principle more fully.[86] It clearly followed from his analysis of the politics of imperialism.

The direction of my own argument should by now be apparent. The four generalizations advanced by Lenin's opponents are very similar to the arguments of those Marxists today who assert that (1) the creation of mini-states and even nation-states in general is irrational or reactionary, (2) capitalism is now fully international and its characteristic institutions, multinationals and other giant corporations, are able to transcend the bounds of national states at will, thus rendering all states more or less obsolete, (3) to advocate the secession or independence of any state, colonial or otherwise, is to 'throw the workers into the arms of the bourgeoisie', 'conciliate the nationalists', 'divide the working class', or 'undermine proletarian internationalism', and (4) national struggles are essentially bourgeois struggles, because they are inherently part of the rise of capitalism, and thus all nationalism is 'bourgeois nationalism'.

Hobsbawm, as I think I have shown in the present essay, subscribes to generalizations (1) and (2).[87] As to (3), Hobsbawm is frustratingly ambiguous. He asserts that nationalism – meaning in context any national movement whatever – 'by definition subordinates all other interests to those of its specific "nation"',[88] while nationalists – meaning in context any fighters for state independence, anywhere – 'are by definition unconcerned with anything except their private collective'.[89] It is unthinkable that Hobsbawm would mean such statements to apply to the past struggles in Vietnam, Angola, Cuba, and other socialist countries which gained victory in a national liberation struggle, or to struggles such as those in Puerto Rico and Namibia where the same goal is being sought today.[90] These statements are of course devastatingly correct when applied to reactionary and unrealistic national movements. Yet Hobsbawm proffers no qualifications. Hence the ambiguity.

Hobsbawm is again ambiguous about generalization (4). He speaks of 'the category of movements directed against imperialist exploitation and representing something like the "bourgeois-democratic phase" in the development of backward countries', a 'category' which seems in context to include all anti-colonial national movements. Thus he seems almost to argue the diffusionist thesis that nationalism equals rising capitalism, and to deny that Lenin was right to categorize anti-colonial national movements as 'national revolutionary' and not 'bourgeois democratic' (a question of theory, not simply terminology).[91] Hobsbawm has explicitly called it an error to equate nationalism only with capitalism and thus to dismiss contemporary nationalisms as 'troublesome "bourgeois" . . . survivals'.[92] But the statement, in context, seems directed at the reactionary nationalisms within socialist countries, and perhaps also the nationalisms within advanced capitalist countries. Thus we cannot tell whether Hobsbawm truly enlarges the national process to include struggles, not for capitalism, but against it. Yet Hobsbawm is not one to denounce any socialist revolution, including those in colonies. Hence, again, the ambiguity.

Hobsbawm is not an 'imperialist economist', although some other modern Marxists richly deserve that title. Yet Hobsbawm's position on the national question is an extremist one. He is just about as strongly opposed to national movements and national struggles as one can be without departing entirely from the mainstream tradition on the national question, the tradition which both he and I consider to be Leninist.

There is, in all of this, a very important question about the long-term development of Marxist thought, a question which has immense political implications for the struggles of the 1980s and beyond. I would express the matter as follows. It appears that there has always been a differentiation among Marxists, sometimes even an oscillation in the thinking of a given Marxist at different periods, on the subject of national movements and the national question. In each period there is a 'Luxemburgist' position which tends to limit its vision to cosmopolitan or international horizons and be suspicious of, or hostile to, the merely national forces. And there have been the 'Leninists', taking more or less opposing positions, and not for merely pragmatic reasons. The first great cycle of 'Leninist versus Luxemburgian' quarrels occurred before and during the First World War. Leninism officially won, and the Third International became a powerful force for national liberation in the colonial world. Within national communist parties of advanced countries, I suspect that the Luxemburgian view was rather powerful, and must have had something to do with the far from proud record of some of these parties in the matter of the liberation of 'their own' colonies. Nevertheless, the Leninist position on the national question was the dominant one, and this explains a great deal about the relative ease with which Marxism became the philosophical underpinning of very many national liberation movements.[93] And in the period from 1945 to the present the Leninist position has been far more prominent than the Luxemburgian. This has been the era of national liberation movements, and the theory and practice of 'imperialist economism' has had precious little to offer this kind of movement.

Today, however, a change seems to be taking place, at least in the universe of discourse embracing Marxist journals and books in advanced capitalist countries. It may well be the trend of 'imperialist economism' renascent. Certainly it projects the view that national struggles today are of secondary importance, emphasizes their limitations and failings rather than their successes, and so on. And certainly this is done with the use of theoretical arguments which would have sounded familiar to Lenin in his day. (Capitalism is no longer national. Nations, states, and nation states are no longer important, are indeed dissolving. Multinational corporations are not fettered by national boundaries.) The world of the 1980s is of course different from that of Luxemburg's and Lenin's time. But not *entirely* different. Old arguments may seem still to make sense, and likewise the answers to these arguments. 'Imperialist economism' may be as relevant today as it was in 1915–1916. Or as irrelevant.

The bottom line is political struggle. Perhaps thirty million people still live in old-fashioned colonies and are still fighting for their freedom. A billion people live and struggle in neocolonies. Arguments like Hobsbawm's and those of the 'imperialist economists' can have a progressive effect with regard to silly and reactionary national movements, of which there are many. But they can have a damaging effect on anticolonial liberation movements, like that of Puerto Rico. And they can be just as damaging for countries like El Salvador in which there is a national struggle for genuine state sovereignty and against neocolonialism, and likewise for countries like Nicaragua which have won a precarious national liberation and are struggling to hold on to what they have won. Arguments like Hobsbawm's do not help these struggles at all.

# Notes

1. E. Hobsbawm, 'Some Reflections on the "The Break-Up of Britain"', *New Left Review* 105 (1977).

2. Ibid., p. 3.

3. Ibid., p. 4.

4. Ibid., p. 7.

5. Ibid., p. 9.

6. See for instance Nigel Harris, *Beliefs in Society* (1968) esp. pp. 28, 167–203, 214.

7. See note 1.

8. See also the following writings by Hobsbawm: *The Age of Revolution: 1789–1848* (1962), Chap. 7 ('Nationalism'); 'The Attitudes of Popular Classes towards National Movements for Independence', in *Mouvements Nationaux d'Independance et Classes Populaires* 1 (1971); 'Some Reflections on Nationalism', in *Imagination in the Social Sciences* (1972); *The Age of Capital: 1848–1875* (1975), Chap. 5 ('Building Nations'), Chap. 7 ('Losers'), and Chap. 8 ('Winners'); in Hobsbawm, (ed.), *The History of Marxism* 1 (1982), his 'Preface', pp. vii–xxiv, and Chap. 8 ('Marx, Engels and Politics'); in Hobsbawm and T. Ranger (eds.), *The Invention of Tradition* (1983), Hobsbawm's Chap. 1, 'Introduction: Inventing Traditions', pp. 1–14, and Chap. 7 ('Mass-Producing Traditions: Europe, 1870–1914'; *Workers* (1984), Chap. 2 ('Notes on Class Consciousness'), pp. 15–32, and Chap. 4 ('What Is the Workers' Country?'), pp. 49–65.

9. Some reflections on "The Break-up . . ."', p. 11.

10. Also see Chap. 1 of this volume.

11. O. Bauer, *Die Nationalitätenfrage und die Sozialdemokratie* (1907); J. Stalin, 'Marxism and the National Question', in his *Works* 3.

12. R. Luxemburg, *The National Question: Selected Writings of Rosa Luxemburg*, esp. pp. 135–75.

13. 'Some Reflections on "The Break-up . . ."', pp. 4–5.

14. Ibid., pp. 6–7.

15. Ibid., p. 5.

16. See for example Engels' 'Po and Rhine', in MEW 16, pp. 211–255, esp. p. 254.

17. Bauer gives the text of the (Brünn) programme of the Austrian party on pp. 527–8.

18. See for example Lenin's 1913 letter to Shahumyan, in *Works* 19, pp. 499–502.

19. Luxemburg made this general argument as part of her critique of the idea of the nation state. The nation state is the 'historical form in which the bourgeoisie passes over from the national defensive to an offensive position, from protection and concentration of its own nationality to political conquest and domination over other nationalities. Without exception, all of today's "nation-states" fit this description, annexing neighbours or colonies and completely oppressing the conquered nationalities'. Luxemburg, *The National Question*, pp. 162–3.

20. 'Some Reflections on "The Break-up . . ."', pp. 5–6.

21. Ibid., p. 7.

22. Ibid., p. 7.

23. Ibid., p. 6.

24. Ibid.

25. Ibid., p. 8.

26. Ibid., p. 11. See also Hobsbawm's *Workers*, pp. 62–3.

27. 'Some Reflections on "The Break-up"', p. 6.

28. Ibid., p. 7.

29. Ibid., p. 11.

30. Ibid., pp. 6–7.

31. Ibid., pp. 7–8.

32. See in this connection J. Villamil (ed.), *Transnational Capitalism and National Development* (1979).

33. I must emphasize that this discussion deals with general trends at the world scale. I do not seek to minimize the very serious national questions which exist in many Third World states, including socialist states. It would be beyond the scope of the present book, which deals with the theory of national struggle and directly applies to only one real case, the struggle for Puerto Rico's independence, to analyse cases of the national question within existing Third World states. Used scientifically in combination with empirical facts and socialist morality, the theory has profound importance for these struggles.

34. J. E. E. Dalberg-Acton, *The History of Freedom and Other Essays* (1922). Also see note 19.

35. R. Campos and F. Bonilla, 'Bootstraps and Enterprise Zones: The Underside of Late Capitalism in Puerto Rico and the United States', *Review* 5, 4 (1982); L. Bergman and others, *Puerto Rico: The Flame of Resistance* (1977); Economic Research Group, Puerto Rican Socialist Party, 'The Economic Importance of Puerto Rico for the United States', *Latin American Perspectives* 3, 3 (1976). As Campos and Bonilla note, about 40 per cent of all profits generated for US companies in Latin America come from Puerto Rico (p. 560).

36. Quoted in Luxemburg, *The National Question*, p. 303. A comment by Radek alone: 'It cannot be to the interests of the proletariat to turn back the wheel of history, and thus to limit the economy which has outgrown these national borders'. Quoted in: W. Lerner, *Karl Radek: The Last Internationalist* (1970), p. 45.

37. Quoted in Lenin's article, 'A Caricature of Marxism and Imperialist Economism', *Works*, 23, p. 37.

38. Bukharin: 'We do not defend national boundaries', quoted in Lenin's article, 'The Nascent Trend of Imperialist Economism', *Works*, 23, p.18n. Trotsky (Oct. 1914): 'The war of 1914 represents first of all the collapse of the *nation-state* as a self-sufficient economic area. Nationalism can continue as a cultural, ideological, psychological factor – the economic basis has been cut from under its feet . . . The war heralds the breakup of the nation-state.' Quoted in H. B. Davis, *Toward a Marxist Theory of Nationalism* (1978), p. 84. Trotsky again (1916): 'The national state has outgrown itself – as the frame for the development of the productive forces, as the basis for the class struggle, and especially as the state form of the dictatorship of the proletariat.' Quoted in R. Daniels, *The Conscience of the Revolution* (1960), p. 33.

39. 'The Nascent Trend of Imperialist Economism', p. 18.

40. Lenin's position on this issue is not very widely known. See his 'A Caricature of Marxism and Imperialist Economism', pp. 28–76, esp. pp. 37–51. See also in Lenin's *Works* 21, pp. 407–14; 22, pp. 143–56, esp. pp. 146, 150; 24, pp. 299–300; 26, pp. 175–6; 29, pp. 170–5 and 193–6; 39 pp. 736, 739; and 41, p. 389.

41. 'Some Reflections on "The Break-up"', p. 11.

42. Ibid., p. 7.

43. See 'Some Reflections on Nationalism' and the chapter 'Nationalism' in *The Age of Capital*. My own view is quite different: see Chapter 7 below.

44. In his *The Age of Revolution: 1789–1848*: 'Outside of Europe it is difficult to speak of nationalism at all' (for the period) (p. 174); 'Nationalism in the East was . . . the eventual product of Western influence and Western conquest' (p. 177). Also see his 'Preface' to *The History of Marxism* 1, pp. xiv–xv, and other writings. Of course, 'nationalism' can be so narrowly defined that any appearance of it in the colonial and semicolonial world of the 19th Century would have to be a product of diffusion from Europe. But Hobsbawm uses the word in narrow and broad senses, and seems to ignore Latin America, China, etc.

45. See Chapter 5.

46. Hobsbawm unaccountably asserts (in 'Some Reflections on "The Break-up"') (pp. 10–11) that 'there is no denying the fact that only in a few cases have Marxists succeeded in establishing themselves as the leading force in their national movements', this undeniable fact suggesting, then, that the 'Leninist national policy should not go uncriticized'. Hobsbawm is wrong for (at least) two reasons. First, his arithmetic is faulty. Twenty or more former colonies and semi-colonies are now socialist states, and a dozen or more present-day colonial liberation movements and insurgencies are Marxist in orientation. Secondly, in movements which were not Marxist and eventuated in some sort of neocolony, there was usually a prior pattern of intense repression, sometimes disguised (e.g., as the infamous 'emergency regulations' promulgated in British colonies when the authorities felt it necessary to jail people without charge or justification – sometimes for having a volume of Marx in the bookshelf – and to suspend all civil rights indefinitely). Adding repression to other factors at work in colonies, we can reject Hobsbawm's thesis that the 'Leninist policy' was to blame. No other policy would have done better.

47. Hobsbawm's conflation of very different concepts of national struggle can be seen, for instance, in 'Marx, Engels and Politics': Marx and Engels did not believe in 'what was then called "the principle of nationality" and today "nationalism"'. The principle of nationality asserted that each ethnic or linguistic group deserved its own independent state; this is not the most typical form of nationalism (as ideology) today and it has been a secondary element, sometimes lacking entirely, in anticolonial liberation movements.

48. 'Some Reflections on "The Break-up . . ."', p. 10.

49. Ibid., p. 3.

50. Ibid., p. 9.

51. Ibid., p. 10.

52. Ibid.

53. Ibid., p. 14.

54. Ibid., p. 21.

55. Ibid., p. 12.

56. The trailing 'as such' has me baffled. Perhaps it means 'alone' or 'purely'.

57. Lenin's position on the need to support anti-colonial struggles without exception or qualification developed (or hardened) over time. For an early view, (1907) see his 'The International Socialist Congress in Stuttgart', *Works* 13, pp. 86–87. Thereafter (a selection): 22, pp. 145, 151–2, 337; 29, pp. 505–506; 31, p. 209 ('Terms of Admission into the Communist International', No. 8: 'Parties in countries whose bourgeoisie possess colonies . . . must support – in deed, not merely in word – every colonial liberation movement, demand the expulsion of its compatriot imperialists from the colonies . . . and conduct systematic agitation among the armed forces against all oppression of the colonial peoples'). An evolution of Lenin's views regarding the independence of Ireland (from tentative disapproval in 1913 to very strong support in 1916 and thereafter) is worthy of

special note: see his *Works* 19, pp. 332–6 and 22, pp. 353–8.

58. *Works* 31, p. 261.

59. Lenin's best-known statement of this position is in his (1913) essay, 'Critical Remarks on the National Question', *Works* 20. The following passage from that essay is still very frequently quoted by Marxists of all tendencies, in spite of the fact that Lenin specifically rejected this theoretical position in later years: 'Developing capitalism knows two historical tendencies in the national question. The first is the awakening of national life and national movements, the struggle against all national oppression, and the creation of national states. The second is the development and growing frequency of international intercourse in every form, the break-down of national barriers, the creation of the international unity of capital, of economic life in general, of politics, science, etc. Both tendencies are a universal law of capitalism. The former predominates in the beginning of its development, the latter characterizes a mature capitalism that is moving toward its transformation into socialist society' (p. 27).

There is no problem with regard to the first of the two tendencies, nor with the concept of growing internationalization of capital, science, etc. But the idea of 'break-down of national barriers' as 'mature capitalism' transforms itself into socialist society was completely superseded. Lenin's later position, as I show in the present chapter, substituted a theory of intensified and profoundly altered national processes under imperialism for the concept of 'mature capitalism . . . moving toward its transformation . . .' More precisely, the period of the 'break-down of national barriers', etc., was later seen by Lenin as having ended in 1914.

60. See Luxemburg, *The National Question*, particularly the essay entitled 'The Nation-State and the Proletariat' and other essays in the 1908–1909 series 'The National Question and Autonomy'.

61. The basic statement is Lenin's essay of 1914 'The Right of Nations to Self-Determination', *Works* 20.

62. See for example Lenin's 'The National Programme of the RSDLP', *Works* 19, and 'The Right of Nations to Self-Determination'.

63. The division is almost explicit in 'The Right of Nations to Self-Determination' and completely so in 'The Socialist Revolution and the Right of Nations to Self-Determination: Theses' (early 1916), *Works* 22.

64. 'Some Reflections on "The Break-up . . ."', p. 10.

65. Lenin's *Imperialism: The Highest Stage of Capitalism* is of course the basic source on the economics of imperialism (*Works* 22, pp. 185–304). But, as Lenin warned in the preface to the book (which was not published until April 1917), he had been forced to avoid political analysis in this work, and concentrate only on economics, in the hope of passing the censor. This caution is cavalierly ignored by very many modern Marxist and non-Marxist scholars, who for that reason hopelessly misunderstand Lenin's theory of imperialism. Because of the widespread misunderstanding, I give the following partial list of the works by Lenin which present the *political* dimension of this theory and which in particular discuss matters relevant to the present essay: 'The Question of Peace', 21, pp. 290–4; notes for a lecture in Geneva, Oct. 1915, 39, pp. 735–42; 'The Revolutionary Proletariat and the Right of Nations to Self-Determination', 21, pp. 407–14; 'The Discussion of Self-Determination Summed Up', 22, pp. 320–60; 'A Caricature of Marxism and Imperialist Economism', 'Imperialism and the Split in Socialism', 23, pp. 105–20; 'War and Revolution', 24, pp. 400–21; 'Revision of the Party Program', 26, pp. 149–78; 'Report on the International Situation' (2nd Congress of the Communist International), 31, pp. 215–34; and 'Report of the Commission on the National and

the Colonial Questions' (2nd Congress C. I.), 31, pp. 240–45.

66. 'Imperialism is the era of the oppression of nations on a *new* historical basis', *Works* 39, p. 739. See also 21, p. 293; 31, pp. 215–18.

67. See, e.g., 'A Caricature of Marxism and Imperialist Economism'. See also later discussions, e.g., 31, pp. 240–45; 332, pp. 481–2.

68. See *Works*, 31, pp. 240–45; 33, pp. 350, 500. See also, on non-capitalist development: V. Solodovnikov and V. Bogoslovsky, *Non-Capitalist Development: An Historical Outline* (1975). On the specificity of the national liberation struggle and its differences from the classical bourgeois nationalist struggle see: K. N. Brutents, *National Liberation Revolutions Today* (1977).

69. See note 57.

70. 'Lenin, in fact, did not recommend socialists in the countries concerned to *favour* secession except in specific, and pragmatically identifiable, circumstances'. 'Some Reflections on "The Break-up of Britain"', p. 10.

71. *Works* 29, pp. 172–3.

72. '"progressive" nationalism was therefore not confined only to the category of movements directed against imperialist exploitation and representing something like the "bourgeois-democratic phase" in the development of backward countries', 'Some Reflections on "The Break-up . . ."' p. 10.

73. Ibid., p. 7.

74. Ibid.

75. Pyatakov: 'we limit ourselves, in respect to the colonies, to a negative slogan . . . "get out of the colonies!" Unachievable within the framework of capitalism, this demand serves to intensify the struggle against imperialism, but does not contradict the trend of development'. Quoted in Lenin's 'A Caricature of Marxism and Imperialist Economism', pp. 64–5. For Luxemburg, see *The National Question*, esp. pp. 131, 290.

76. From 'Theses' of the editors of Gazeta Robotnicza (Radek, Stein-Krajewski, and Bronski), English text given in Luxemburg, *The National Question*, p. 303. Lenin's 'The Discussion of Self-Determination Summed Up', is in part a reply to these 'Theses'.

77. See Lenin's *Works* 29, pp. 170–75 (a response to Bukharin).

78. 'The Nascent Trend of Imperialist Economism', 'Reply to P. Kievsky (Y. Pyatakov)' 'A Caricature of Marxism and Imperialist Economism' Lenin's *Works* 23.

79. 'A Caricature', pp. 49–50.

80. Ibid., p. 37.

81. Ibid., p. 45.

82. See Chapter 5.

83. See note 77.

84. See, e.g., '"Left-Wing" Communism – An Infantile Disorder', *Works* 31, p. 92.

85. 'A Caricature . . .', p. 61.

86. See note 25.

87. There is ambiguity in Hobsbawm's position on the growing obsolescence of states, or perhaps he has changed his mind: see his *Workers* (1984) p. 22.

88. 'Some Reflections on "The Break-up . . ."', p. 9.

89. Ibid., p. 7.

90. In one of his characteristically sweeping and unqualified generalizations about the national question, Hobsbawm asserts: 'It is or ought to be obvious that

the specific character of regions or groups does not point invariably in one direction . . . *Political independence is one option out of several'*. ('Some Reflections on "The Break-up"'', p. 20, italics added.) Does Hobsbawm mean to apply this statement to colonies like Puerto Rico and Namibia which are struggling for independence today? Is political independence just 'one option out of several' for classical colonies? (Note also Hobsbawm's criticism of 'the assumption that state independence, or what amounts to it, is the normal mode of satisfying the demands of any group with some claims to a territorial base . . . a "country",' ibid., p. 8.)

91. See 'Report of the Commission on the National and Colonial Questions', p. 241.

92. 'Some Reflections on Nationalism', p. 405.

93. See, in this regard, Ho Chi Minh's essay, 'The Path Which Led Me to Leninism', *Ho Chi Minh: Selected Articles and Speeches: 1920–1967* (1970).

# 5. The Theory of National Minorities

This chapter and the following one deal with one important form of the national question: the struggles of oppressed minorities for self-determination. There are many kinds of minorities and many kinds of struggle, and it would be impossible to examine all of the issues in a few pages, much less try to work out solutions to the many complex national problems of minorities around the world. I will be concerned mainly with two quite important aspects of the problem. One is the matter of correcting mistakes in the Marxist theory of minorities, which I view as a part of the larger Marxist theory of national struggle, and particularly to show that the history of our theory of minorities has been seriously misinterpreted, thanks in part to the intellectual legacy of Stalin (and for many other reasons). My other concern is to criticize the idea that there is some natural and inevitable drift, in capitalist countries, towards the assimilation of minorities and towards their political decomposition. Minorities created by colonialism tend not to decompose: their special oppression continues in one or another form, and so does their struggle for self-determination. The present chapter, therefore, deals with general theory and the history of theory; the following chapter, with the empirical problem of assimilation (and non-assimilation), under conditions of advanced capitalism.

Chapters 5 and 6 have a political as well as scientific purpose: they argue against those who believe that the two million Puerto Ricans in the US are losing their Puerto Rican nationality and their identification with and commitment to the struggle for the national liberation of Puerto Rico.[1] This belief has harmed the liberation struggle, hindered the minority community's efforts at self defence, and in no way furthered the cause of internationalism. And the belief is illfounded in theory and fact. The two chapters are meant to apply to general questions of theory and to many minority struggles, as well as paying special attention to Puerto Rico.

The present chapter has much to say about the Marxist theory of nations, as well as the theory of minorities, because the two categories are dealt with together in Marxist theory, as we will see. I am not going to attempt to discuss every aspect of the theory of nations, a very complex matter in its own right, and not reducible to definitions. I hope, nonetheless, to contribute something to this theory, by way of clearing away many tangles of confusion.

Some sectors of the North American Left are convinced that Puerto Ricans in the US do not belong to the Puerto Rican nation; that this community is merely a 'national minority' – an ethnic subdivision of a different nation, the United States. This national minority theory bears some resemblance to the old idea of the 'melting pot', or at least to its liberal variant ('Puerto Rican-Americans', 'ethnic heritage', 'minority rights', etc.), but there is one crucial difference. The national-minority theory is said to be grounded in Marxism, and specifically in a doctrine derived from a 1913 essay by Stalin, 'Marxism and the National Question'.[2]

In essence, the argument is simple. Stalin listed the attributes which, in his opinion, a group must possess to qualify as a nation. This was Stalin's famous 'definition of the nation', which became the orthodox Marxist concept of the nation, accepted by most Marxists, Stalinists and non-Stalinists alike, down to recent times. Complementing the concept of 'nation' was the concept of 'national minority', a term which designated ethnic communities that failed to qualify as nations. The distinction was terribly important. Real nations had the potential to become independent states, and deserved the right of self-determination. National minorities had no such potential, and were fated to dissolve, in political terms, through assimilation. Moreover, national forms of political struggle were justifiable for nations, but not for national minorities. One of Stalin's crucial criteria for nationhood was the possession of undivided national territory. Ethnic communities which were divided, fragmented, or dispersed, were not real nations: they were national minorities.

Puerto Ricans living in the United States would be, by this criterion, a national minority. They could not be viewed as part of a single Puerto Rican nation. The same judgment would apply to many other minority communities around the world, including, for instance, West Indians, Africans, and Asians in Europe and Koreans in Japan. All such groups would be seen as national minorities, doomed to dissolution and enjoined from engaging in national forms of struggle, including, most crucially, the struggle to liberate their homelands.

But there are *two* Marxist theories dealing with minorities. And there are two very different kinds of minorities, each needing its own distinctive analysis. Puerto Ricans do not fall within the purview of Stalin's theory, but within another theory which was prefigured in Marx's and Engels' analysis of the Irish community in England and was then developed into a general theory by Lenin in the period 1915–1923. The fundamental difference between the two theories is defined by the facts of colonialism and imperialism. Lenin provided the first comprehensive analysis of imperialism, and of modern colonialism.[3] In the process, he developed a theory of nations which applies to colonial nations like Puerto Rico and the Puerto Ricans. Stalin, in 'Marxism and the National Question', barely mentions colonial nations, and his theory of nations and minorities does not in any case work for colonies. Even for the non-colonial nations of Europe, in fact, the theory is only applicable to an early period in their history, the 'epoch of rising capitalism', an epoch which ended almost everywhere with the outbreak of the First World War. All of this notwithstanding, Stalin's 1913 article was significant as a contribution to Marxist theory and to the Russian revolutionary struggle – a judgment concurred with by many non-Marxist scholars as well as Marxists (even by Trotsky!).[4] But the theory does not apply to Puerto Ricans. Lenin's theory, by contrast, does apply. And Lenin's theory compels the conclusion that most Puerto Ricans in the US are still part of the colonial nation of Puerto Rico.

In the discussion which follows, I will not be arguing in defence of any sort of narrow nationalism. To say that a community created by forced emigration from a colony may retain its original nationality, as in the case of Puerto Ricans in the United States, is not to argue that this community will, or should, separate itself from workers' struggles in the country in which it resides. Puerto Rican workers in the United States are completely within the US working class, as well as the Puerto Rican working class, and their commitment to the struggle for social justice in the US is as great as that of any other group of workers. But they remain Puerto Rican. This is not paradoxical: it is explained by the logic of Marxist theory, as I will now try to demonstrate.

## The Theory of Minorities in Classical Marxism

We can begin, I think, with a small incident involving Friedrich Engels a century ago. The setting is a General Council meeting of the International Working Men's Association (the First International) in 1872. As recorded in the minutes, Mr. Hales, the Council's Secretary, proposed the following motion: 'That in the opinion of the Council the formation of *Irish* national branches in England is opposed to the General Rules and Principles of the Association.' Mr. Hales then explained his motion:

> He said . . . the fundamental principle of the Association was to destroy all semblance of the nationalist doctrine, and remove all barriers that separated man from man . . . The formation of *Irish* branches in England could only keep alive that national antagonism which had unfortunately so long existed between the people of the two countries . . . No one knew what the Irish branches were doing, and in their rules they stated that they were republican, and their first objective was to liberate Ireland from a foreign domination, [but] the International had nothing to do with liberating Ireland.[5]

The motion was debated, and Engels rose to speak.

> Citizen *Engels* said the real purpose of the motion, stripped of all hypocrisy, was to bring the Irish sections into subjection to the British Federal Council [of the International], a thing to which the Irish sections would never consent, and which the Council had neither the right nor the power to impose upon them . . . The Irish formed a distinct nationality of their own, and the fact that [they] used the English language could not deprive them of their rights . . . Citizen Hales had spoken of the relations of England and Ireland being of the most idyllic nature . . . but the case was quite different. There was the fact of seven centuries of English conquest and oppression of Ireland, and so long as that oppression existed, it would be an insult to Irish working men to ask them to submit to a British Federal Council. [The motion] was asking the conquered people to forget their nationality and submit to their conquerors. It was not Internationalism, but simply prating submission. If the promoters of the motion were so brimful of the truly international spirit, let them prove it by removing the seat of the British Federal Council to Dublin and submit to a Council of Irishmen. In a case like that of the Irish, true Internationalism must necessarily be based upon a distinct national organization, and they were under the

necessity to state in ... their rules that their first and most pressing duty as Irishmen was to establish their own national independence.[6]

Thus we have Engels' opinion concerning the nationalism of two million Irish men and women who had been forced to emigrate to England (as two million Puerto Ricans have, to the US).

But consider now another opinion which Engels expressed at about the same time, concerning the 'right to independent national existence of those numerous small relics of peoples which, after having figured for a longer or shorter period on the stage of history, were finally absorbed as integral portions' of powerful European nations. Here he is talking about a different type of minority, a small European nation somehow lying within the borders of a larger European nation and, in Engels' view, undeserving of independence. Equally undeserving is the 'detached fraction of any nationality' which might wish 'to be allowed to annex itself to its great mother-country', a situation very common then, particularly in eastern Europe where the recurring tides of invasions during a thousand turbulent years had 'left on the shore ... heaps of intermingled ruins of nations ... and where the Turk, the Finnic Magyar, the Rouman, the Jew, and about a dozen Slavonic tribes, live intermixed in interminable confusion'.[7] In such cases Engels would withhold support from any separatist movement. But how can all this be reconciled with Engels' fierce defence of nationalism, and of separate political organization, among the minority Irishmen in England?

Engels' reference to 'small relics of peoples', 'ruins of nations', and the like, was in the context of an article in which he was passionately defending the right of Poland to independence, and defending a proclamation in support of that right by the First International. His disparaging remarks about minority nations were part of an analysis aimed at distinguishing between the case of viable nations, like Poland, and non-viable, fragmentary, minority nations, thereby refuting the charge that support for Polish independence implied support for all manifestations of nationalism. Engels made the distinction, in characteristic Marxist fashion, by referring to history. The 'ruins of nations' became that way through a thousand years of tangled mixing of nations; the 'detached fraction' was once attached; and so on. But compare the history of these minorities with that of Ireland. The latter exists as a definite, viable, but (for 700 years) oppressed nation. The organization of its socialist movement must take place in the midst not only of colonial oppression but also of massive, forced emigration to England – a matter to which Marx and Engels referred repeatedly in their writings.[8]

Now the lot of Ireland in the mid-19th Century was extraordinarily like that of Puerto Rico in the mid-20th Century; both enduring destruction of their rural economies and forced emigration to a nearby industrial nation, the effect being the establishment of ghettos in the oppressor nation's cities; and in both cases persistent back-and-forth movement of the population between colony and oppressor nation because of the proximity of one to the other.[9] (Today we have the 'air bridge' between New York and San Juan.) Everyone now agrees that Marx and Engels did not have a comprehensive, general theory of imperialism and colonialism; that was Lenin's later contribution. But they did have an excellent special theory for Ireland, this one example of imperialism and colonialism which lay on Europe's doorstep. And they related to the Irish movement in their revolutionary practice. So they could not fail to support Irish independence, conceptualize the Irish minority in England as an integral part of the Irish nation, and defend the right of the Irish forced emigrants to organize politically in England. At the same time, Marx and Engels refused to take this same stand in the case of the non-colonial minorities of eastern Europe, which had not suffered national oppression of the Irish variety, including, most notably, forced emigration. The moral is this: Stalin, in 'Marxism and the National Question', was talking mainly about the eastern European case, and his analysis was (for 1913) largely correct. But his conclusions did not apply to colonial peoples, like the Irish then and the Puerto Ricans now. The two kinds of minority, and the two corresponding theories, and forms of practice, had already been distinguished by Marxism, long before 1913.

## Stalin's Theory

'Marxism and the National Question' was written only to deal with a particular situation at a particular historical conjuncture. This will be clear if we look closely at the context in which it was written, long ago and far away.

In 1912 the Bolsheviks were in the midst of what proved to be the most serious crisis in the history of their party.[10] Nationalism of a certain sort was the major symptom of the crisis, though not the major cause. The cause, as described by both Lenin and Stalin, was counter-revolutionary repression by the Tsarist authorities following the abortive revolution of 1905. The effect was a dangerous weakening of the revolutionary movement. The Bolsheviks were convinced that their pre-1905 programme and their long-term strategy continued to be correct, and that victory would come very soon (as it did). But many socialist groups and factions had become demoralized; succumbing to repression, they chose to abandon the hard-line Bolshevik position which sought the overthrow of the Tsarist government and to adopt instead a gradualist, reformist programme and to retreat to aboveground (legal) political action. This set the stage for an immense ideological struggle, one which took place on two levels: basic programme, or theory, and party organization.

The major issue on both levels was nationalism. Whereas the Bolsheviks were determined to overthrow the Tsar, the reformists were willing to settle for a different, more democratic form of the Russian Empire; an improved version of the Austrian Empire, which seemed at the time to be more democratic than the Russian, mainly because it granted basic civil rights to minority nations. One precedent for a socialist–reformist position of this sort was to be found in the Austrian Social Democratic Party's platform, but the clearest precedent lay in a proposal by the Austrian Marxist Otto Bauer for a scheme which he termed 'cultural–national autonomy'.[11] Applied to Russia, this scheme would call for civil equality and a form of federalism among the nations within the empire – but still within the single empire, and therefore far short of the Bolshevik goal of destroying the empire. Thus, at the level of programme, or theory, the reformists wanted national autonomy within the Russian state, while the Bolsheviks rejected this form of limited nationalism in favour of the overthrow of the state. In the long run the

Bolshevik position implied much more intense national struggle, since it called for the destruction of the integral empire and the right of all nations within it to secede. But in the short run the reformists seemed to be nationalists, and nationalism seemed to be reformism.

Nationalism was also the main issue at the organizational level. An underground, Bolshevik-style revolutionary party had to be a centralized party. A non-revolutionary, legal party could perhaps afford to be a loose federation of sub-parties, each with a great deal of autonomy. Since the reformists' programme was nationalistic, the proposed federal structure would naturally involve a cleavage along national lines. To the Bolsheviks, however, a federation of national parties was simply not a revolutionary party.

Lenin called a party conference in January, 1912, to force these issues. The reformists countered with a conference of their own in August. Then Lenin opened his full-scale offensive. One battlefront was of course nationalism, and 'all serious-minded Social-Democrats' were urged by him to 'raise and discuss the "national question"'.[12] Stalin prepared the first major polemic, 'Marxism and the National Question', which was followed in train by two major articles by Lenin himself.[13] The Bolsheviks regained their strength and party unity without sacrifice of programme or structure, and Stalin's article played an important role. It was an attack against manifestations of nationalism which were objectively counter-revolutionary in the Russia of 1912–1913. It was a strong and consciously one-sided critique on those forms of nationalism which posed an immediate threat to the Bolsheviks. It was, in short, a polemic. Thus it was not an academic essay, still less a Marxist textbook on nationalism in general. Its argument should not be taken out of context.

Stalin himself made this point very clearly. In 'Marxism and the National Question' he castigated those 'pedants who "solve" the national problem without reference to space and time'. Solving the problem, he said, will always depend on 'the concrete historical conditions in which the given nation finds itself', and 'conditions, like everything else, change'.[14] Writing five years later, he commented in retrospect that the October Revolution, and related events of the period, had 'widened the scope of the national question and converted it from the particular question of combating national oppression in Europe into the general question of emancipating the oppressed peoples, colonies and semi-colonies, from imperialism'.[15] And he returned to this theme again in 1924: Lenin 'linked the national problem with the problem of the colonies', transforming it 'from a particular and internal state problem . . . into a world problem of emancipating the oppressed peoples in the dependent countries and colonies'.[16] I quote all these remarks to emphasize two points which, to us, are fundamental. Stalin became aware that his 1913 argument had concerned only one part of the world, one type of nation, and one historical epoch. He also came to realize that Lenin had transformed the national question, in fact had evolved a new theory – which we will discuss in a moment – to deal with the non-European world, the colonial nations, and the epoch of imperialism; in effect, the conditions surrounding Puerto Rico and the Puerto Ricans. Realizing this, we can proceed to develop a fair and correct analysis of Stalin's argument itself.

'What is a nation?' Stalin asks, and then proceeds to give a rather formal definition. A nation is a human group which possesses certain definite characteristics. It is a historically stable community of people. It has a common vernacular language. It occupies a single piece of territory. It has an integrated, coherent economy. It possesses a 'community of psychological make-up' (a folk-psychology, or national character). And it is 'a historical category belonging to a definite epoch, the epoch of rising capitalism'.[17]

Stalin's definition of 'nation' had, like the article as a whole, a polemical purpose. It served to underpin his attack on reformist nationalism. There were, broadly speaking, two reformist tendencies, and each was vulnerable to an attack from the vantage point of Stalin's definition. First, there were those who advocated a combination of 'cultural–national autonomy' and organizational autonomy within the socialist movement. The essence of Bauer's 'cultural–national autonomy' scheme was the thesis that members of a nation, regardless of where they lived within the state, would share the autonomy of that nation. Thus, for instance, Georgians everywhere in Russia would come under Georgian governance. But if a nation must occupy a single, common piece of territory, then Georgians outside of Georgia would simply be a *national minority* in some other nation's territory, and it would be absurd, Stalin argued, to place them under Georgian governance. It would be even more absurd in the case of the Jews, who had no territory of their own, and were therefore not a nation anywhere. In the case of the Jews, the demand for cultural–national autonomy was paralleled by an even stronger demand for organizational autonomy. For more than a decade, the Jewish socialist organization, the Bund, had been demanding recognition as the sole spokesman for Jewish proletarians, and insisting on a federative relationship to the Russian Social Democratic Party. In 1913 this demand had become part of the reformist-nationalist reaction. Stalin's emphasis on territory as an attribute of nationhood was a particularly effective answer to the Bund: Jews have no territory, hence Jews are not a nation, hence the Bund can have no standing as a national organization within the all-Russian movement.

The second form of nationalism was a more diffuse tendency within what Stalin considered to be genuine nations to substitute national aims for revolutionary aims. The way to deal with this was to show that nationalism is strictly, and necessarily, a bourgeois (capitalist) sentiment by incorporating capitalism into the very definition of the nation. Thus we have the historical criterion: a nation is characteristic of the epoch of rising capitalism.[18] This would be a very telling argument among Marxists because an essential tenet of Marxism was (and is) the thesis that capitalism is indeed progressive during its rising stage of development, before it succumbs to internal contradictions and generates more and more misery. If nationalism is a feature of capitalism during its progressive stage, then nationalism will no longer be progressive when capitalism no longer is so. Thus a Russian Marxist in 1913 might become convinced that nationalism is simply out of date, and might refuse to defend a nationalist programme.

Stalin's definition had a third function as well. Attacking nationalism within the framework of the Bolshevik programme was a rather delicate task because the Bolsheviks, unlike some extremely anti-nationalist groups, like Rosa Luxemburg and her associates, insisted on the inalienable right of nations within Russia to self-determination, that is, to full independence. How does one attack nationalism and at the same time defend the right of self-determination? Stalin's way was to, first of all, give a precise definition of 'nation' to make it clear that certain ethnic groups, being genuine nations, did have this right, while others did not. The Jews did not. Nor did those 'detached fractions' of nations like the German settlements scattered across Russia. Then, by tying the idea of the nation to the epoch of rising capitalism, Stalin was able to defend the right of genuine nations to self-determination and at the same time hint that nations really should not exercise that right, on grounds that it would be reactionary to do so.

Colonies did not qualify as nations under Stalin's definition. This can be shown both by example and by reference to Stalin's theory of nations. In few colonies (or semi-colonies) was a single vernacular language spoken in 1913. (In India, for example, there were dozens.) Common territory was often missing. Colonies did not really possess an integrated economy, given their dependent economic status. And equally inapplicable was the concept of 'rising capitalism' ('semi-feudalism' and 'underdeveloped capitalism' are more appropriate terms).

In Stalin's theory, nations came into existence in two ways. Western European nations formed themselves as nation states from the moment of their birth at the beginning of the capitalist era. Hence they had no national problem, to speak of, within their borders. In eastern Europe, however, the great territorial empires (Russia, Austria–Hungary, Turkey) emerged before the ethnic groups within their boundaries had formed into nations; hence these states were multi-national almost from the start; and hence the gravity of their national problem. Ireland, according to Stalin, was an anomaly: it followed the eastern European route, forming itself as a nation after its absorption into the British Empire. But Stalin was wrong about Ireland; it was a classic colonized nation; and this significant error shows that he really had no theoretical model (in 1913) for colonial nations in general. He did not, as a matter of fact, discuss them in 'Marxism and the National Question'. Had he done so, or had he at least taken account of Marx's and Engels' analysis of Ireland in relation to England, Stalin would have seen that his model for Western European nation states was also imperfect. Countries like Britain, France and Holland emerged as integral nation states not by chance, but because they were colonizing nations. They exported their national problem, as it were, to their colonial empires. Thus to understand England one must understand Ireland, Jamaica, India, and so on. One must understand imperialism. But in 1913 Marxism had not yet analysed imperialism.

Stalin's theory of nations was not therefore wrong, but it was not world-wide in scope. It was adequate for the multi-national states of eastern Europe, partly so for the nation states of western Europe, and wholly inadequate for the world of colonies and semi-colonies of Asia, Africa, and Latin America.

This brings us at last to Stalin's theory of national minorities. It is merely the obverse of his theory of nations: an ethnic group is a national minority if it does not possess the defining attributes of a nation. Four sorts of national minority communities are discussed in Stalin's paper, and it will be a straightforward matter to show that none of them resembles the Puerto Rican community in the United

States today.

Two of the cases barely deserve mention. The first is what Engels would have called the 'detached fraction' of a nation. The argument here is weak, since many such 'fractions' are quite sizeable, and many possess all the attributes which Stalin required of a nation. (Stalin in fact cited the example of the United States to show that new nations can form as a result only of territorial separation.) But the argument would only be relevant if one were claiming that the North American *barrios* are part of the national territory of Puerto Rico, and no one, to my knowledge, is doing so.

Stalin's second case concerns what he described as undeveloped nationalities, with primitive culture. His argument here is best forgotten, although at times it is resurrected by chauvinists who deny the right of self-determination to certain nations by demoting them to the status of 'tribes': the argument is, in any event, irrelevant.

The third type of national minority is an ethnic group which has no territory of its own, anywhere. The Jews of Russia provided Stalin's one example of this type, but he devoted more attention to it than to all the others combined, because his primary purpose in discussing national minorities was to prove that Jews were not a nation, in order to polemicize against Bundist organizational separatism. Not only did the Jews lack territory, they lacked a common language as well, according to Stalin who thought that they spoke the various vernaculars of their many areas of settlement and could not communicate with one another readily. And finally, they lacked an integrated economy: most crucially, they were entirely non-agricultural (though not by choice), and thus were deprived of that association 'with the land, which would naturally rivet a nation'.[19] Stalin's argument that the Russian Jews were not a nation is unassailable. But, curiously, it is his analysis of this thoroughly unique Jewish minority which is most often used by those who wish to prove that Puerto Ricans in the United States are, too, a national minority. The analogy is false. Unlike the Puerto Ricans, the Jews had no territory – anywhere. The Jews of Russia *did* speak a common language, and so do the Puerto Ricans. (As far as Stalin's theory is concerned, it would make no difference whether the common language were Spanish or English, or whether bilingualism prevailed, as it does in about 30 modern nation states, so long as Puerto Ricans were able to communicate with one another.) It is of course true that the Puerto Rican community in the US is detached from the land. But not from the land of Puerto Rico.

The fourth type of national minority is the only one which bears even a superficial resemblance to Puerto Ricans in the United States. In this case, Stalin's argument focuses on a causal process, not the resulting community. The process he described was one of migration under capitalism. 'In the early stages of capitalism nations became welded together', but later 'a process of dispersion of nations sets in' and 'groups separate off from the nations, going off in search of a livelihood and subsequently settling permanently in other regions of the state'.[20] In the Russia of 1913, the migration was to new (border) areas of agricultural settlement and to newly expanding cities. The resulting situation was one of mixed populations, the inhabitants of these new areas of settlement bearing various ethnic heritages and forming various national minorities. The apparent resemblance to the Puerto Rican condition is obvious.

What Stalin is describing here is the familiar 'melting pot', which worked in 1913 Russia as it worked in 1913 North America. I say 'worked' because melting did take place: the migrants lost their original nationalities and became ethnic minorities. Why did it work? There were at least two reasons. First, this was still the epoch of rising capitalism, after all: living conditions were improving, employment was expanding, and the destination areas, rural and urban, were able to absorb the immigrating populations both economically and culturally. Second, the whole process was taking place within what we now call metropolitan capitalism. It did not, in general, involve the colonial and semi-colonial periphery in this pre-First World War era, and non-Europeans were not invited to participate in the process. In the US, Blacks did not participate. Nor did Puerto Ricans. (How else can we explain the fact that millions of Europeans came thousands of miles, in that period, to settle in the US, while Puerto Ricans remained in nearby Puerto Rico?) In Russia, Central Asians did not participate. And so on. Thus there can be no comparison between this form of migration and the process which filled up Spanish Harlem in later years. Stalin was discussing a process that bears no relation to the ghettos of today. The process that takes place today is forced migration from colony to metropolis. The resulting community is not a national minority but an exiled portion of a colonial nation. Stalin had nothing to say about this new and different type of minority. His theory just does not apply.

## Minorities in the Era of Imperialism

The development of a theory of minorities which does apply to today's Puerto Ricans was begun only two years after the publication of Stalin's article, by Lenin. But those were crucial years for socialism, and for socialist theory. The outbreak of the World War, in 1914, demonstrated that the older Marxist theory of nations, and nationalism, was very inadequate: nations were *not* merely a vestige of the epoch of rising capitalism, and nationalism was *not* a thing of the past. In 1913 Lenin could write that 'the awakening of national life and national movements, the struggle against all national oppression, and the creation of national states' is a tendency which 'predominates in the beginning of [capitalism's] development', while 'the break-down of national barriers, the creation of the international unity of capital . . . characterizes a mature capitalism that is moving toward its transformation into socialist society'.[21] But in August, 1914, the 'national barriers' were re-erected and turned into battlefields. And European workers, instead of joining their fellow proletarians of all nations in a revolution against the bourgeoisie, were following the bourgeoisie into a war against the proletarians of other nations. To deal with this shocking situation, Lenin had first to analyse it. The result was Lenin's new theory of imperialism, and one of its principal components was a new theory of national struggle and nations.

'Imperialism', Lenin wrote in 1915, 'is the era of the oppression of nations on a new historical basis'.[22] In fact, 'the division of nations into oppressor and oppressed . . . forms the *essence* of imperialism'.[23] Why so? Because, to begin with, capitalism does not really 'mature', first becoming 'international' and then commencing its 'transformation into socialist society'. Instead, it becomes parasitic: imperialistic. Each advanced-capitalist country strives to resolve its deepening internal contradictions – declining profits and rising workers' resistance – by expanding its empire of colonies and semi-colonies, thus amassing what Lenin aptly called the 'superprofits' from imperialism. But there must come a time when no more places remain to be colonized. At this point, two new processes supervene. One is the intensification of economic exploitation, and political oppression, in the existing colonies and semi-colonies. The other is described by Lenin as the 'repartition of the whole world'[24]: the advanced-capitalist countries now try to steal one another's colonies and spheres of influence. This latter process must inevitably lead to general war among the colonial powers. Thus we arrive at Lenin's essential model. At the root of the whole process is the dialectic of oppression: advanced capitalist nations transform themselves into oppressor nations in order to acquire the sustaining superprofits; other nations suffer deepening oppression in order to yield these superprofits. And derived from this are two distinct political processes in each of the two types of nation: among the oppressors, a cannibalistic form of warfare; among the oppressed, a struggle for national liberation.

The era of imperialism is therefore an era of *increasing* nationalism. In the oppressor nations it is bourgeois nationalism, though of a new and more reactionary sort. The bourgeoisie distributes a large enough share of the superprofits to bribe the 'labour aristocracy' and make life slightly easier for the majority of the workers, a share just large enough to gain the workers' (temporary) loyalty to the capitalist state and their willingness to fight its wars.[25] But in the oppressed nations, imperialism generates a very different form of nationalism, a form that resembles neither the old bourgeois nationalism of rising capitalism in Europe nor the new bourgeois nationalism of the imperialist countries. This different form of nationalism is the struggle for national liberation. And corresponding to it is a different kind of nation.

'Colonial peoples *too* are nations' – a fact, said Lenin, that Marxists often forget.[26] Lenin was aware that colonies did not originate in the same way as those European nations which emerged, with the rise of indigenous capitalism, out of medieval territorial–linguistic units. Often enough he wrote that colonialism leads to a forcible carving-up, a partitioning, of pre-existing cultural regions, and that a colony's economy is not internally integrated but externally dependent. But the main distinguishing feature of colonial nations, for Lenin, was the special way in which their classes, and class struggles, evolved.

In colonial nations, there was no epoch of rising capitalism, that is, no epoch dominated by a rising domestic bourgeoisie. Domination was exercised by foreign monopolies; part of the local bourgeoisie rose to the extent of becoming a class of managers and agents, or occasionally very junior partners, but the remainder were rapidly disenfranchised by colonialism. At the same time, the workers, peasants, and impoverished petit bourgeoisie were also forced into rapid class evolution and struggle by colonial oppression. Under these circumstances, the nation was not the outcome of a struggle waged primarily by a rising capitalist class against the fetters of feudalism – the classic model for Europe. It was the outcome mainly of an anti-imperialist struggle waged by all the oppressed classes, and primarily the working masses. This, for Lenin, made it likely that colonial nationalism, the national liberation struggle, would lead *not* to a form of 'mature' capitalism (and thus to the classical capitalist nation, the type described by Stalin), but to socialism. So the nature and dynamics of colonial nations in the era of imperialism were inherently different from that of the old European nations, and the old theory of nations had to be supplanted.

From 1915 until the end of his active life in 1923, Lenin discussed the national liberation of colonies and other oppressed nations in one hundred or more articles and speeches. In none of these did he refer to or make use of Stalin's definition of 'the nation'. Nor did he use Stalin's nomenclature: 'nation', 'nationality', and 'people' were applied almost interchangeably, and 'national minority' was used to describe differing kinds of communities, including a small nation within a larger state.[27] In 1915 he commented that the issue of self-determination in the era of imperialism is 'not the "national question"' and thereafter he used this phrase very sparingly in relation to oppressed nations (outside of Russia), eventually coming to distinguish fairly sharply between the 'national question' and the 'colonial question'.[28] Even to dwell, as I am doing here, on matters of definition and nomenclature is foreign to Lenin's method, which was to reject what he called 'abstract' and 'formal' approaches to questions of national liberation. 'In this age of imperialism', he said, 'it is particularly important . . . to proceed from concrete realities, not from abstract postulates, in all colonial and national problems'.[29] Lenin, after all, was a dialectician, not a catechist.

Imperialism has evolved and changed since Lenin's time, and one of its newer modes of appropriation, exploitation, and oppression is the forced migration of tens of millions of workers to the imperialist heartlands. This process may have been limited mainly to Ireland in the 19th Century (as we discussed before), and to peripheral parts of Europe in the first years of the present century, because of the cost of long distance transportation and the immaturity of this new phenomenon of imperialism. Lenin was certainly aware of the phenomenon and its growing importance, and he did not confuse it with the older forms of labour migration which had characterized the period of developing capitalism. In his earlier writings Lenin had indeed provided a thorough analysis of labour migration under pre-imperialist conditions, and had concluded, correctly, that its effects were generally progressive. This was capitalism's era of rapid growth; migration to areas of expanding employment and higher wages was characteristic of the period; and the advanced areas, among them the United States, were able to absorb the immigrants fully into a burgeoning labour force. The result in general was national assimilation. It was part of a 'break-down of all national barriers by capitalism', and was therefore 'inevitable and progressive'.[30] But all this changed when capitalism entered the era of imperialism, the era of 'the oppression of nations on a new historical basis'.

It is clear that Lenin came to view the new era as one in which the conditions for national assimilation were disappearing, to be replaced by increased national oppression 'both in the colonies and at home'.[31] One comment which he made just a few days before the October Revolution, during a discussion of the new Bolshevik party programme, is particularly revealing:

[Comrade Sokolnikov] proposes to add the phrase '. . . the labour of unskilled foreign workers imported from backward countries'. This addition is valuable and necessary. The exploitation of *worse paid* labour from backward countries is particularly characteristic of imperialism. On this exploitation rests, to a certain degree, the *parasitism* of rich imperialist countries which bribe a part of their workers with higher wages while shamelessly and unrestrainedly exploiting the labour of 'cheap' foreign workers. The words 'worse paid' should be added and also the words 'and frequently deprived of rights'; for the exploiters in 'civilized' countries always take advantage of the fact that the imported foreign workers have no rights.[32]

It is significant that Lenin speaks here of 'foreign workers', not 'immigrants' or members of 'national minorities', that he relates the whole process to the imperialist stage of capitalism, and that he identifies a sector of foreign workers – legally alien, and therefore unassimilable – as being 'particularly characteristic' of this stage. Equally significant is his description of the imperialist country itself. Its capitalism now depends, parasitically, on superexploitation (and national oppression: deprivation of rights) within its borders, hence imperialism has been internalized into its own class structure. Lenin also alluded to the rise of an oppressed Afro-American nation in connection with the transition to imperialism, referred to the national oppression of the Irish in England, and gave various other examples of unassimilated communities in the imperialist heartlands. Most crucially, he showed that the conditions which lead to assimilation are disappearing: imperialism is an era of deepening national oppression, of capitalism which is now reactionary and moribund, not progressive and growing. It is not surprising, therefore, that Lenin said nothing after 1914 about the dissolution of nations or the formation of national minorities.

Stalin's theory of national minorities is incompatible with Lenin's theory of imperialism. To be more precise, the former is inseparable from a theory of nations which was descriptively accurate for an earlier stage of European social evolution (the stage of 'rising capitalism') but which has now been displaced by a theory of *all* nations under *modern* capitalism – that is, monopoly capitalism or imperialism. National minorities were only created where, and when, capitalism was expanding. In those times and places, job opportunities were growing, proletarian living conditions were objectively improving in the centres of expansion, and immigrants were assimilated, quickly or slowly, into the host proletariat and the host nationality. During the period of transition, the immigrants formed national minorities, communities which, for a time, remained ethnically distinct but were nevertheless becoming assimilated. I do not deny that the transition was painful: capitalism made full use of the transients for slave-wage labour and union-busting; and the immigrants did, indeed, live in ghettos. But they *escaped* from the ghettos.

Even in those days, however, there existed another kind of labour migration, signalized by the African slave trade and the forced migration of Irishmen to England, East Indians to the Caribbean, Chinese to Southeast Asia, native Americans to reservations – all colonies and semi-colonies. These forced migrations were another, nastier face of evolving capitalism; and none of the communities which they created have anywhere (under capitalism) become fully assimilated:

they are demographic minorities of another type, a type that does not satisfy Stalin's definition of a 'national minority'.

Under modern imperialism, almost *all* migration is forced migration. The era of imperialism is not one of developing, expanding capitalism, but of decaying capitalism which is using every device it knows merely to survive. A most effective device is colonialism: the superexploitation of colonial, semi-colonial, and (we now must add) neocolonial workers, with the necessary aid of political domination and national oppression. Today the device of colonialism has become, as it were, technologically perfected, and thereby immensely versatile. It can extract its colonial superprofits *within* the metropolis – in ghettos, migrant labour camps, and foreign worker barracks – as well as abroad. The forced migration of colonial peoples is simply one of the options of colonialism, an option which is utilized under those conditions where greater surplus value can be obtained by translocating the colonial workers from colony to metropolis than can be obtained by superexploiting them at home. Forced migration of this type is merely colonialism internalized – or internal colonialism (although we cannot speak of each ghetto as an 'internal colony' in the strict geographic sense). But internal colonialism is inseparable from external colonialism. The greatest surplus value is realized if the reproduction costs of labour and the maintenance costs of sick, old, and unemployed workers can be exported. (This explains, in part, the 'air bridge' between New York and San Juan, the constant, massive, back-and-forth movement between colony and metropolis.) When these social costs are borne within the metropolis, they are costs of maintaining a *colonial* workforce – not costs of assimilating immigrants.

It follows that colonial forced migrants do not leave behind the special forms of political and national oppression which prevail in the colony. Nor do they find, when they arrive, a set of circumstances markedly more favourable than those prevailing in the homeland. All they find, in essence, is a replica of the same colonial conditions. In the colony, the imperialists impose the fiercest forms of cultural aggression, the purpose of which is not to assimilate the colonial people to the colonizer's nationality, but to pacify them by wresting from their culture all possible sources of resistance – including, if possible, their language. The same aggression descends on them in the metropolis. And so they do not lose their nationality.

I am tempted to suggest the term 'colonial minorities' to designate those communities of forced migrants which have been created by imperialism, and to distinguish them from the 'national minorities' described by Stalin. Certainly the term 'colonial minority' would perfectly fit that portion of the Puerto Rican nation which lives in the US. But Marxist theory is not much farther along in its analysis of forced migration, internal colonialism, and related phenomena than it was in the days of Lenin, and we are perhaps not ready for new terminology. Our legacy from Lenin is simply the recognition that there exists a general type of minority which originated in imperialism, and which differs fundamentally from the national minority of the pre-imperialist epoch, the epoch of the melting pot. But the newer type is almost infinitely variable in form. It includes workers who are legally defined (by the imperialists) as 'foreign', some of whom are even considered aliens in their own age-old homelands. It includes workers translocated from classical colonies, like Puerto Rico (and in earlier times Ireland), as well as workers translocated from internal and external neocolonies. Lenin himself would not have called for any further exercise in definition. He would probably have asked just one more question: are these workers engaged in a struggle to liberate their nation? Do they share with their compatriots a 'will towards national existence'?[33] For Puerto Ricans, the answer is yes.

# Notes

1. Chapter 5 is based on my essay: 'Are Puerto Ricans a National Minority?', *Monthly Review* (1977); in Spanish (retitled as 'Marxismo y la cuestión nacional: el caso de Puerto Rico') in *Pensamiento Crítico* (1978) and elsewhere. Chapter 6 is based on my 'El mito de la asimilación', *Claridad (En Rojo)* (1982); in English (retitled and expanded as 'Assimilation versus Ghettoization') in *Antipode* (1983).
2. J. Stalin, 'Marxism and the National Question', in Stalin's *Works* 3, pp. 300–381. Originally published as 'The National Question and Social-Democracy', in 1913.
3. Lenin's major contributions on this subject, in my opinion, are: 'The Socialist Revolution and the Right of Nations to Self-Determination', Lenin's *Works* 22, pp. 143–56; 'Imperialism: The Highest Stage of Capitalism', ibid., pp. 185–304; 'A Caricature of Marxism and Imperialist Economism', 23 pp. 28–76; 'Preliminary Draft Theses on the National and the Colonial Questions', 31, pp. 144–51; 'Report of the Commission on the National and the Colonial Questions', ibid., pp. 240–45; 'The Question of Nationalities or "Autonomization" ', 36, pp. 605–11. The structure of Lenin's theory of imperialism and the attendant theories of colonialism and national struggle is very clearly shown, probably for the first time, in Lenin's notes for a lecture delivered on October 28, 1915: *Works* 39, pp. 735–42.
4. Among non-Marxist scholars who concur in this view are E. H. Carr and B. C. Shafer. (See note 32 to Chapter 1.) Trotsky, no friend of Stalin, calls 'Marxism and the National Question' Stalin's 'one and only . . . theoretical work' on the basis of which, Trotsky grudgingly concedes, 'its author is entitled to recognition as an outstanding theoretician'. But Trotsky hastens to add his opinion (not widely accepted) that the essay was 'wholly inspired by Lenin, written under his unremitting supervision and edited by him line for line' – in effect, ghost-written. Lenin indeed 'inspired' the work and gave Stalin some guidance. See L. Trotsky, *Stalin* (1967), pp. 156–7.
5. International Workingmen's Association, *The General Council of the First International, 1871–1872: Minutes* (1968), pp. 194–5.
6. Ibid., pp. 197–8. Engels expressed similar views with regard mainly to Poland in an 1882 letter. So long as Poland remained unfree, he maintained, her socialist movement would be centred among Poles 'living abroad as emigrants'. Independence was essential to the struggle for socialism: 'To be able to fight one must have firm ground to stand on, air, light and room. Otherwise it is all idle talk . . . I adhere to the view that two nations in Europe are not only entitled, but obliged to be national before they become international: they are the Irish and the Poles. They are most of all international when they are truly national'. *Marx and*

*Engels on Proletarian Internationalism*, anthology (1972), p. 62.

7. Quotations are from Engels' article, 'What have the Working Classes to Do with Poland?', in: D. Fernbach, (ed.), *Karl Marx: Political Writings*, vol. 3, *The First International and After* (1974), pp. 388–92.

8. See Marx and Engels, *Ireland and the Irish Question*, anthology (1971), pp. 54–8, 162, and elsewhere.

9. The rural portion of Puerto Rico is rapidly becoming depopulated; some very fertile regions are now almost empty of people and unused for agriculture. The overall population of the colony has remained about the same for two decades, with in-migration by Dominicans, Cuban exiles, and North Americans roughly compensating for the net out-migration of Puerto Ricans.

10. See in particular: Lenin's *Works* 17, and 18, esp. 'The "Vexed Questions" of our Party: The "Liquidationist" and "National" Questions'; Stalin, 'Marxism and the National Question', pp. 300–3.

11. See H. B. Davis, *Nationalism and Socialism: Marxist and Labor Theories of Nationalism to 1917* (1967).

12. Lenin, *Works* 18, p. 412.

13. Lenin, 'Critical Remarks on the National Question', *Works* 20, pp. 17–51; 'The Right of Nations to Self-Determination,' Ibid. pp. 393–454.

14. Stalin, 'Marxism and the National Question', pp. 324 and 331.

15. Stalin, 'The October Revolution and the National Question', *Works* 4, p. 170.

16. Stalin, *Foundations of Leninism* (1939), pp. 76–7.

17. Stalin, 'Marxism and the National Question', pp. 303–14.

18. The definition reads: 'A nation is a historically constituted, stable community of people, formed on the basis of a common language, territory, economic life, and psychological make-up manifested in a common culture' (ibid., p. 307). 'Historically constituted' is elaborated (on p. 313 ff): 'A nation is not merely a historical category but a historical category belonging to a definite epoch, the epoch of rising capitalism'.

19. Ibid., p. 345.

20. Ibid., p. 339.

21. Lenin, 'Critical Remarks on the National Question', p. 27. I comment on this famous passage in Chapter 4, note 59.

22. Lenin, notes for a lecture on 'Imperialism and the Right of Nations to Self-Determination', [October, 1915], *Works* 39, p. 739. Also see 21, p. 293.

23. Lenin, 'The Revolutionary Proletariat and the Right of Nations to Self-Determination', *Works* 21, p. 409.

24. Lenin, 'Imperialism and the Split in Socialism', *Works* 23, p. 106. Also see 21, p. 226; 22, pp. 189–91, 254, 341–2; 26, pp. 163–7; 31, pp.215–18.

25. Lenin's view on this matter is with great frequency misunderstood. See his *Works*, 22, pp. 193–4 and 283–4; 23, pp. 55–6, 114; 31, pp. 193, 230, 248; 32, p. 454; 33, pp. 498–9; 39, pp. 588, 615.

26. Lenin, 'A Caricature of Marxism and Imperialist Economism', p. 63. For Lenin's view of colonial nations, their character, their struggles, and their significance, see Lenin, *Works*, 21, p. 291; 22, pp. 151–2, 312–13, 355–6; 23, pp. 33–4, 59–68, 196–7; 26, pp. 168–9; 29, pp. 505–6; 30, p. 208; 31, pp. 144–51, 209, 240–46, 328, 490; 32, pp. 480–82; 33, pp. 143–8, 349–52, 372, 476–9, 500–501; 39, pp. 736–42. On this matter, too, there is frequent misunderstanding of Lenin's view – his theory of colonialism – and it is helpful to consult the appropriate writings.

27. Ibid., 36, pp. 608–9.

28. Ibid., 39, p. 736. Note, for instance, the report of the 'Commission on

the National and the Colonial Questions', at the 2nd Congress of the International, ibid. 31, pp. 240–46; see also 31, pp. 144–51.

29. Ibid. 31, p. 240; also see 31, p. 145; 33, p. 149, and 36, pp. 607–609.
30. Ibid., 19, p. 457.
31. Ibid., 22, p. 151.
32. Lenin, 'Revision of the Party Programme', *Works* 26, p. 168.
33. Ibid., 24, p. 434.

# 6. The Myth of Assimilation

One false assumption has seriously interfered with an understanding of Third World immigrant communities in the United States, Britain, and most other advanced capitalist countries. It leads to false judgements about these ghettoized, essentially working-class communities, about the ghettos in which they live, about their national and cultural characteristics, and about appropriate strategies for social action. This false assumption concerns the phenomenon of assimilation. It can be expressed in the form of two false statements. One is that people who live in these Third World ghettos are undergoing a process of directional social change, the terminus of which is assimilation into the host culture and nationality. The other is that the ghettos themselves, as culturally distinct and economically depressed regions within the cities of advanced capitalist countries, either will dissolve in time or will persist as the home space for successive communities of immigrants, each group arriving, dwelling for a time in this space, becoming assimilated, moving out, and having its place taken in turn by another immigrant community, the process then being repeated over and over in an eternal cycle of replacement. The assumption, then, is that the single force at work in ghettos is assimilation, and that assimilation will dissolve the cultural alienation of ghetto-dwellers and eventually lift them out of the ghettos, dissolving the physical ghettos themselves or leaving these in place to serve as receptacles for the next arriving group.

This assumption is false, as I will try to show in the present essay. But the assumption is peculiarly tenacious. This can be explained in part by the fact that the process of assimilation did indeed prevail in 19th Century cities in advanced capitalist countries, although there were important exceptions, such as the Irish ghettos in England. And in part it can be explained by the fact that the assimilation assumption is believed in, axiomatically, by mainstream social scientists and by very many Marxists as well. The assumption is conformist for the former group: to believe that the social problems of ghetto communities can and will be solved under capitalism is a crucial tenet of establishment ideology. Among Marxists, however, the belief in assimilation is mainly a vestige of earlier Marxist thought, and specifically the pre-First World War theory, which we discussed in the previous chapter, that capitalism dissolves national differences and does so with great rapidity in the case of long-distance labour migration to the urban centres of development. It did do so in prior times, but it does so no longer.

In this chapter I will show why the assimilation assumption is false, not by reviewing the Marxist and non-Marxist errors which have been built on this assumption, but by discussing the reality of the present period, the era of imperialism, the era in which millions of Third World workers are transported to the metropolis and there remain, in ghettos. Only one word will be said about Marxists themselves (ourselves) by way of introducing the topic of this chapter. The struggle for social justice would be in better shape than it is today if progressive workers (and parties) had not been confused for so long by the myth of assimilation. We accepted that myth because it seemed to conform to the old theory that immigrant workers form 'national minorities' and 'national minorities' dissolve. We accepted it, more importantly, because it predicted what we all wanted: the 'break-down of national barriers', the unification of the working class in terms of unified consciousness and unified forms of struggle, and the somehow natural disappearance of that peculiarly intense oppression and exploitation of immigrant workers which was, temporarily we thought, dividing the class. We thus reached the final paradox: by ignoring or denying the reality of national barriers, we failed to work out strategies to remove these barriers, and so, in the name of 'proletarian internationalism', we strengthened them. Internationalist unity is vital, but the myth of assimilation stands in the way of achieving it.

## Assimilation

Assimilation is a process of absorbing an immigrant group into the host culture (hence the word 'acculturation' means about the same thing when applied to this kind of situation). Assimilation occurs only under certain conditions, and these conditions are very rare in advanced capitalist countries during the present century. For assimilation to take place, even in part, there must not only be a loss of the culture of origin but also a gain of the host culture. Culture cannot be divorced from class, which is one of its components and one of its determinants; therefore, to gain the host culture means, among other things, to fit into the host class structure. This, however, can only occur when there is 'room' for fitting the immigrants in. And this, in turn, implies that there is demand for a great deal more labour; that the labour force is expanding rapidly.

These conditions only occur, in general, when capitalism itself is expanding, as was indeed the case in the United States throughout the 19th Century, with its insatiable need for new workers both as proletariat and to settle new lands and thus generate surplus value, directly and indirectly, from those who worked these lands. For European immigrants to the US during this period of expanding capitalism, assimilation was indeed occurring. I emphasize 'European' because, as we well know, native Americans, Afro-Americans, Asians, Mexicans, and (after 1898) Puerto Ricans did not participate in the process. They were hardly encouraged to settle land on the (so-called) frontier, and they did not move in substantial numbers to the expanding urban centres. Thus even in the period when assimilation was an important and powerful force, it was selective in its choice of subjects.

After the First World War two changes occurred. The growth rate of capitalism in the US slowed down, and the working class really began to organize itself, protecting the modest benefits it had already won and fighting for more. Since capital no longer needed a rapidly expanding work-force, and since the majority of the workers did not have a high enough level of class consciousness to appreciate the strategic implications of the situation, the owning class, assisted by pliant labour leaders, succeeded in getting legislation passed to severely restrict immigration. After the mid-1920s, very few immigrants were admitted to the US. And native Americans, Afro-Americans, Asians, Mexicans, and Puerto Ricans were not invited into the industrial cities in their stead, although a few migrants from these groups trickled into the cities even so. Conditions had changed.

During the prior period, new European immigrants had been absorbed into the class structure in (roughly) three stages.

(1) Upon arrival, most of them – excluding the many who came to the United States with some capital – joined a floating work-force which served both as a source of recruitment into the employed sector of the working class and as a major part of the reserve army of the unemployed.

(2) Sooner or later, however, the great majority of these immigrant workers, or their offspring, rose into the steadily employed sector itself and became totally absorbed into the proletariat, enjoying the modest benefits which the proletariat had won for itself, including the right to occupy dwellings in 'decent' neighbourhoods, to move to different parts of the US where opportunities for higher wages existed, to gain some education, and so on. The subjective factor here was very important. The act of 'rising' into the no-better-than-average proletariat convinced the majority of immigrant workers to remain in the country, and actively to become 'Americanized' – that is, assimilated. Objectively, they had become absorbed into the proletariat; subjectively, they were welcoming assimilation into the culture.

(3) In the third phase of absorption, a phase in which only a minority of the former immigrants participated, there occurred a process of selective recruitment into the petty bourgeoisie, even occasionally into the big bourgeoisie. Even if we exclude those immigrants who arrived in the US with some capital and, like many Cuban immigrants of more recent times, left the petty bourgeoisie of one country to join the petty bourgeoisie of another, it is nevertheless quite true that, as capitalism expanded, it did need to recruit new members of the petty bourgeoisie from the proletariat: it needed grocers, shoemakers, and the like, and it very particularly needed petty entrepreneurs in areas too risky, or simply too petty, for ordinary capital to enter.

And so, in these three principal ways, the earlier European immigrants were fully absorbed into the host country's class structure and fully assimilated into its culture. That many of them retained certain European ethnic traits is quite beside the point.

Between 1924 and the beginning of the Second World War there was no numerically significant immigration from Europe and no compensating internal migration, nor migration from US colonies like Puerto Rico. The migration of Afro-Americans from the rural south was quite modest, Mexicans were periodically deported, and there is even some evidence that segregation in cities increased, indicating that a new type of ghetto was being created.[1] But this was a complex period, punctuated by the Great Depression, and the full development of cultural and class patterns appropriate to the mature stage of monopoly capitalism had not yet occurred. This really happened during the Second World War in the United States and after the war in Europe.

By the early 1950s, the new patterns were entrenched in all advanced capitalist countries. The post-1945 expansion of capitalism in these countries was not spectacular, but it was indeed taking place. The demand for labour was growing at a moderate rate. The problem was that capitalism now was operating on a thin (and falling) profit margin, so it was vital to have the greatest possible control over the quantity, location, and above all wages, of labour. The existing proletariat was pretty strong; increasing relative surplus value was therefore very difficult. A number of mechanisms were of course used by capitalism to cope with this situation, among them a form of controlled inflation (responding to higher wages by jacking up prices), and a partial substitution of fixed capital and imported energy for labour.

One principal mechanism was what we may call the controlled introduction of new labour. This was done in two ways. Labour-intensive manufacturing processes were exported, first to Puerto Rico (in the case of US capitalism) and later to many other low-wage countries. (Typically a semi-finished product left a country like the US and the final commodity returned to it, so this expansion of the labour field for just one segment in a long chain of production processes was in no sense a diffusion of industrialization, much less of advanced capitalism, to peripheral countries, as some scholars, even some Marxist scholars, have asserted.)

The other mechanism for the controlled introduction of new labour began somewhat earlier and has proved to be at least equally important; perhaps in the long run it will be more important. This is the controlled import of labour from poor countries and regions to the industrial centres of the advanced capitalist countries. This mechanism was not in itself new: it had been used in a primitive way by British capital with Irish forced migrant labour, in the 19th Century, and by US capital in both world wars with (mainly) southern Afro-American workers. But this controlled import of labour really became a structural feature of capitalism in more recent times. Its essential feature is *control*. This means control of the rate and source of migration, control of the conditions of life and opportunity of the immigrant work force, and even, where possible (as in colonial Puerto Rico), control of the conditions determining emigration from the homeland. All this can be described as a deliberate policy, because by now capitalism had become modernized to the point where the state could be directed to enforce these forms of control, to the benefit of most and perhaps all sectors of the bourgeoisie, by means of overt legislation and covert regulation. One aspect of this policy was *to prevent the assimilation of the immigrants*.

Let us look around the world at the forms of control used on migrant – no longer can we call them 'immigrant' – workers. Wherever feasible, they are legally defined as 'foreigners'. This means that they are denied certain explicit rights, but, more important still, they can be deported if they should presume to demand higher wages, join a union, go out on strike, or even leave one employer for another. The most important example of this sort of controlled labour import is the 'guest workers' (*Gastarbeiter*) phenomenon which has brought at least 20,000,000 foreign workers into Germany, France, and other industrialized European countries. The closest parallel in the US is the body of documented ('legal') workers from Mexico and other New World countries. A further parallel is found in the South African racists' new policy – it did not exist in real force a couple of generations ago – to, first, force Africans by law to live in 'townships', and second, re-define them, again by law, as foreigners, by declaring them to have national 'homelands', Bantustans, far from the point of production, to which they can be 'deported'.

Not altogether different is the new immigration policy of Britain (with parallels in Canada) by which migrants from poor, non-white Commonwealth countries, formerly considered 'British subjects' and 'bearers of British passports' and automatically admissible, are now defined as foreigners and allowed to enter the country only as needed by British capital. A partial parallel is to be found in Japan, where long-time migrants from Korea were denied the right of citizenship until recently and are still for the most part non-citizens. Again in the US, there is still another parallel (or caricature) in the massive in and out flow of undocumented, so-called 'illegal', migrants, from Mexico, the Dominican Republic, and other countries. It is clear that this 'illegal' migration is deliberately encouraged by US capital, or certain of its sections, behind a smokescreen of condemnation (rather like Shell exhorting people to save gasoline), because undocumented workers are under even tighter control than other 'foreign' workers. In all of these cases it would be silly to employ the word 'assimilation'.

Capital in the US is frustrated by its inability to apply the same sorts of controls to Puerto Rican workers, Afro-American workers from the southern United States, and Mexican workers from the Southwest. Unfortunately for capital, it must cope with the legal relic of pre-monopoly capital which conferred citizenship on these workers.[2] So other control mechanisms have to be used, though for the same ultimate purpose.

## Ghettoization

The main control mechanism is *ghettoization*. This has at least three dimensions. One is spatial segregation in the community – at the point of reproduction – a segregation enforced, not primarily by law, but by the way the law is applied and enforced. School segregation is unlawful, but persists nonetheless. Housing discrimination, in residential purchase, rental, and insurance, is unprosecutable. Police deal savagely with any sign of resistance, lawful or unlawful. And so on. Ghetto space is different from South African 'townships' mainly because the measures used to segregate the ghetto are precisely these matters of selective law enforcement and tacit encouragement of housing discrimination, not overt legal statutes, but the ghetto is not *much* less clearly defined than the 'township'. I think it is vital to add that few ghetto-dwellers have the opportunity to move out of the ghetto (except to other ghettos, or back to Mississippi or Texas or Puerto Rico) regardless of the number of generations they have lived there. Evidence for this is to be seen in the oldest Afro-American ghettos, such as New York's Harlem and Chicago's South Side. (Puerto Rican and Mexican urban ghettos are generally too young to supply this category of evidence.) Except for the small percentage of people who rose into the petty bourgeoisie or other 'middle-class' levels (in consumption terms), and except for those who have moved to other ghettos or back to the South, almost every family that lived in these old ghettos in the 1920s is living there still. Everyone will agree that real assimilation does not occur without the social interaction provided by residential mobility. Culture change takes place in the ghetto, but it is not assimilation.

The second dimension of ghettoization is segregation at the point of production and, more generally, segregation within the work-force, including the reserve army of the unemployed. I do not want to get into the sticky argument about a 'sub-proletariat' or an 'under-class', but all of us will surely agree on certain obvious and well-known facts. For one thing, Puerto Ricans, Mexicans, Afro-Americans, etc., make up the majority of the reserve army, although they make up less than one quarter of the work-force. The official unemployment rate for minorities in the US is at present nearly three times the rate for whites. Secondly, minority workers are systematically excluded from many crafts and craft unions and, beyond that, are unable to get almost any sort of well-paid and secure job in most areas. (There are exceptions, explainable in historical terms, such as the Afro-American, Mexican, and Puerto Rican workers in the steel mills of Gary, Indiana, and the Afro-American and Mexican workers in Michigan auto plants.) Thirdly, these groups are concentrated, much more so than is typically the case with majority workers, in unorganized industries and relatively weak unions. When many other such indices are added to the list, it becomes clear that capitalism is seeking, as a policy, to divide the working class into a no more than ordinarily exploited and oppressed sector and a sector which is superexploited and super-oppressed. (The class is divided on other cleavage lines as well.)

This policy is merely a mechanism, an attempt, which the more conscious workers resist. But it is indeed policy, because it is needed for capital accumulation. It has been successful enough thus far to allow us to speak here of a superexploited sector, so long as 'sector' is understood to be a fuzzy category, since some minority workers are outside it and many majority workers are inside it.[3] And it goes without saying that a sector of the labour-force which works under the constraints imposed upon Latino and Afro-American workers in the US is not being assimilated, or absorbed, in class terms. Rather the opposite is the tendency. A small percentage is, indeed, being admitted into the petty bourgeoisie. ('Admitted' is not precisely the right word. The reality is a dynamic tension between the struggles of minority workers to 'rise' into security and sometimes into the petty bourgeoisie, and the selective resistance to that 'rise', greatest in spheres implying competition in the accumulation process, least in spheres which established capital cannot penetrate and in spheres which participate in control of the minority community.) An additional small number enjoy middle-class consumption patterns because they work for the state or hold low-level managerial jobs. And a large number in absolute terms but a small number in percentage terms do manage to get well-paying and secure jobs. It may be correct to speak of class assimilation for these groups. But they add up only to a small fraction of the minority work-force. And it is not an increasing fraction.

The third dimension of ghettoization is something that can be called 'cultural colonialism'. When I introduce the word 'colonialism' I must at the outset indicate precisely what it means in the context of discourse. The ghetto is not a true colony in the geographical sense: a bounded political region under the explicit rule of a foreign state. (Puerto Rico, for comparison, is a true colony. 'Commonwealth' status carries with it no more political autonomy than was possessed by the most typical of the old British, French, and Dutch colonies.) The ghetto is not, in addition, a true neocolony, given the technical meaning which that term has acquired during the past decade: an officially sovereign state which is nonetheless under the economic domination of foreign corporations, usually those of a former colonial power, and typically under the political domination of that power. The ghetto is best called a 'semi-colony', because it possesses most of the defining attributes of colonies, to some extent at least, but lacks others. But this is still a matter of homology, not analogy (or 'model').[4]

The essential attribute of colonies is the use of political oppression to enforce and sustain a pattern in which labour suffers superexploitation – exploitation to the point where reproduction of labour is barely possible, and even in some cases beyond that point – and not merely exploitation. Ghetto workers are superexploited in this sense (often outside the ghetto's boundaries), and in political terms they and their families do not possess very much real, as opposed to merely formal, enfranchisement and power in any respect from participation in law-making to control over the police. Conditions are perhaps not as stark as they are in most classical colonies (and in South African 'townships'), but the basic colonial traits of superexploitation enforced by oppression nonetheless are possessed by US ghettos. The homology is most apparent when we look at industrialized colonies, like Puerto Rico. The class structures and modes of superexploitation in Puerto Rico are strikingly like those in the Puerto Rican ghettos of the United States.

In terms of the traits of ordinary political geography, such as the presence of political boundaries and the constraining of inhabitants within this space, ghettos of the urban American sort are not true colonies, or rather they are so only to the extent that segregation is enforced: and let us not underestimate this extent. But ghettos do not possess the single most essential political–geographic trait: the realistic ability to strive for state independence. The demand for self-determination which is constantly voiced in ghettos is a demand for enfranchisement and people's power, not for independence.

What, then, is this cultural colonialism? In classical colonies this is a mechanism designed to pacify: to suppress resistance. It includes such devices as forcing the colonized to speak the colonizer's language, and teaching the colonized in schools that the only true history is the history of the colonizer's country. (Therefore, said Amilcar Cabral ironically, when we win our independence we re-enter history.[5]) Clearly, cultural colonialism as it occurs in classical colonies is in no sense a process of assimilation. Nor is it such in the ghettos.

The meaning which establishment social scientists give to the words 'assimilation' and 'acculturation' is usually neither spatial nor political nor economic: it is social and psychological. (It is 'cultural' only in the sense of that term which excludes many aspects of culture, most particularly matters of political and economic power.) Cultural colonialism as a dimension of ghettoization is neither socially nor psychologically an effort to assimilate. It is the process, enforced in many ways, of forming migrants into a mould which is qualitatively different from that of the host culture. Here we have to distinguish means and ends. The ends are to pacify the migrants, prevent them from protesting their living conditions, fighting for equal rights in the community and on the job; prevent them from demanding, or even expecting, the privileges enjoyed by the host proletariat – the privilege of moving to 'decent' neighbourhoods outside the ghetto, the privilege of gaining reasonably secure and well-paid employment, and the like. The end, in short, is not assimilation but ghettoization. But the means towards this end are sometimes mistaken for the mechanisms used in the old days to assimilate immigrants.

This is most strikingly the case in the matter of forcing 'Latino and other non-English-speaking migrants to the US to learn English. Most mainstream social scientists simply equate the transition to English with assimilation to the host culture. It is not that. Language is only one part of culture. Many colonized peoples have endured the partial or total destruction of their language, yet have retained their culture, sometimes using the colonizer's language after independence has been attained (as in Jamaica), sometimes relearning the old language (as in Ireland). Migrants to US ghetto communities are forced to learn English (elsewhere it may be Afrikaans, German, French, etc.) in order to function as workers and consumers; it is a matter of survival in a place to which they were involuntarily translocated, and which they cannot leave.[6] Beyond that, the pressure placed on migrants (and most of all on their school-going children) to learn and speak English, and forget the language of origin, is an important aspect of the effort to pacify, in part because ideology is transmitted through language and in part because the establishment itself believes that language equals culture, hence that loss of the old language means abandonment of the old culture. This is why something called 'bilingual education' is accepted and even favoured by at least part of the US educational establishment, because it is thought to serve as a mechanism for 'transitioning' the migrant children to English-language instruction, while something else called 'bilingual–bicultural education' – education in the language and the culture of origin as well as the host culture – is furiously resisted by the establishment and just as fiercely demanded by the community.

This aspect of cultural colonialism is particularly transparent in the Puerto Rican ghettos. Since 1898 the United States has been attempting to impose English in the schools of Puerto Rico. (For a time the colonial government attempted to displace Spanish entirely as a language of instruction, but this was successfully resisted.) Exactly the same sort of pressure is now experienced in the Puerto Rican *barrios* in the US. It is resisted in both sectors. Indeed, resistance to cultural colonialism in every arena from education to art is, at the present time, in the island as in the *barrio*, one of the strongest manifestations of popular resistance in general. In Puerto Rico it is widely realized that cultural colonialism is ghettoization.

Ghettoization involves certain profound cultural changes at the level of the individual, and it is easy to misinterpret the nature of these changes and take them as signs of assimilation. Some of the changes are components of a process of adaptation to big-city life for people who come, for the most part, from rural areas and small towns, and forced changes of this sort have been the lot of rural–urban migrants since the English peasants were forced into the 18th Century mill towns. (I refer here to changes in the type and size of family, in the rhythm of daily activities, in the scale of home space, in the strategies of keeping warm and well-fed, and the like.) Acquiring the host language is traumatic in itself, particularly when the acquisition has to be accomplished without much help, and when any accent – even that of a different dialect of English – is an economic handicap. Apart from these sorts of adaptive changes, there are values and behaviour patterns which the dominant culture (or rather its elite sector) tries to impose on the migrants and their children, patterns designed to pacify, to encourage appropriate consumption habits, and so on.

One very important dimension of change is the partial growing-together of the cultures of ghettoized communities. This, too, is often mistaken for assimilation (as when Latino youth in some areas speak English in the streets in preference to Spanish, but it is the English of the Afro-American ghetto community). It seems probable to me that this growing-together is ultimately a reflection of capitalism's need for one homogeneous type of ghetto society but the process – a very slow one in any case – has a positive consequence: the healthy interfertilization of cultures, the efflorescence of new creative forms of painting, poetry, music, and the like, and the linking-up of struggles.

Concerning the entire process of cultural change of the type I have called 'cultural colonialism' (because it is homologous to the forced cultural change that takes place in true colonies, and has the same essential political and economic function), three additional observations must be made. First, there is fierce and continuous resistance to those changes which are unwanted. Second, it is characteristic of most ghetto communities in the industrial countries, including the US, that members of these communities frequently travel back to the home area, remain there for a while (working or looking for work, taking care of elderly or sick relatives, and so on), and then return, repeating the process a number of times in the space of a lifetime. In the case of Puerto Ricans, the relative (not absolute) rise and fall of employment opportunities in the island as compared to the mainland leads to strong surges, first in one direction, then in the other. Thus we speak of an 'air bridge' between San Juan and New York, a constant stream of people moving in both directions. And comparable processes are to be seen in other ghetto communities in the US and Europe, along with the 'guest workers' in Europe and other instances of the process we are discussing. The result of all this movement back and forth is a constant reinforcement of the native culture in the ghetto, hence a strong braking action on ghettoizing cultural changes. And the third critical observation, in part an implication of the prior two, can best be expressed as follows: ghettoization is *slow*. Before the process has gone very much farther, I suspect, it will have been stopped by socialism.

A certain number of people in the ghetto do, indeed, become assimilated. The number is quite large, although the percentage is quite small. The essential prerequisite for assimilation is absorption into the ordinary class structure, with its modest benefits to workers (job security, above-subsistence wages, and the like) and its much more modest opportunities for 'rising' into the petty bourgeoisie. Some minority workers succeed in fighting their way into this structure, although success is always some combination of skill and luck. (The skills are held by many. Only a few get the chance to capitalize on them.) When a worker has gained the class position giving him access to the modest privileges of the average proletarian, and in particular the chance to leave the ghetto or buy a house at its more affluent margin, he (or more rarely she) then, for the first time, has a genuine choice in the matter of assimilation, or at least a choice within the wider constraints of racism. Empirically it is true that many such workers and their families in the US opt for assimilation, for 'Americanization'. Many, on the other hand, make the opposite choice: for instance, they may return to the homeland to stay, now having the wherewithal to do so. The point is that either choice entails a rejection of ghettoization.

A second route towards the same goal is education. Again it is a combination of skill and luck that allows a Puerto Rican or Mexican or Afro-American youngster in the US to get into college and stay there. There is little if any correlation between these skills and the determinants of admission-test or aptitude-test scores, as evidence the fact that nationally-used tests predict literally nothing about the academic potential of minority people.[7] In the ghettos the great majority of young people have the ability to get in, stay in, and graduate from college, but the ability can only be put to use under those very unusual combinations of circumstances which I have designated rather crudely as 'luck'. Luck here includes such things as: a family income high enough so that a teenager does not have to leave high school and go to work; teachers who will instill the knowledge and test-taking skills needed to pass the admissions and (so-called) aptitude tests and thus to gain admittance to college; an environment permitting successful resistance to drugs and gang culture; and so on. A college or university is an assimilation factory. Without invoking the mysticism of a Hegelian 'will', we can nonetheless postulate that the number of ghetto youth whom the system willingly admits into and graduates from college is roughly the number that capitalism needs for recruitment into various roles requiring some degree of assimilation, along with specialized technical and academic skills. (Of course, an additional number of ghetto youths manage to go to college thanks to the community's struggles.) A certain number are recruited into interface jobs, like foreign-language radio and TV announcing, interpreting, advertising, and the like. Others are required for jobs that help to control and manage the ghetto community itself. Still others are required for the economic interface: minority-fronted businesses, ghetto stores of certain specialized types, low-level supervisory and managerial work involving supervision of minority labour, and the like. Hence there must be a measured – and a *controlled* – flow of ghetto youth through college and towards the roles which either require or permit assimilation.

Again, however, there is a degree of choice. Ghetto teenagers do not ordinarily discard the cultural and class attitudes of their families and community. Almost all who graduate from college have been shaped to some degree by this assimilation factory. But the force is not irresistible. And many of them will have encountered the ideas which help to reinforce their sense of cultural and class identity. Overall, the changes which the college experience engenders are assimilative in their directionality, but the individual can choose to take a different path. I must add that one of the most important reasons why thoughtful people in the majority culture believe that assimilation is truly taking place is their tendency to interact only, or primarily, with individuals from the ghettos who are college-educated. Most are not.

## Resistance

Ghettoization is a necessary component of modern capitalism. It is the principal mechanism for maintaining a superexploited sector of the labour-force within the advanced capitalist countries. It follows that the only way to put a permanent stop to the ghettoizing process is to eliminate capitalism itself. However, there are manifold ways to resist the process: at the aggregate scale of entire communities, to slow the process down; at the scale of the individual ghetto-dweller and his or her family, to fight it off successfully. Since superexploitation is the economic engine which drives the process, a crucial form of resistance is at the workplace. A second form is the political fight for legislation to protect the rights of labour in general and superexploited labour in particular, along with the fight for legislation to protect migrant workers, especially undocumented ('illegal') workers, and legislation to defend the ghetto community. Still another form of resistance involves the community's own struggle on many fronts – against arson, police brutality, Nazis, forced sterilization, drugs, substandard education, community destruction euphemized as 'urban renewal', and so on. These and many other forms of collective resistance are too well-known to require discussion in the present context. I need only add that resistance at this level, in the US at least, has apparently slowed the ghettoization process to the point where most ghetto communities in recent years have almost been able to hold their own, even under Reagan. Things have not improved but they have not grown rapidly worse. They may well do so during the depression years which lie ahead.

Resistance to ghettoization at the level of individuals and families is in part a matter of participation in the collective forms of struggle which were mentioned above. But there are, in addition, strategies which can work for some people in a community while they cannot work for the community as a whole. I will call attention to two such strategies. One is the process, mentioned in the preceding section, of fighting free of ghettoizing forces to the point where a partially free choice of life-trajectory is possible. One such trajectory, paradoxical though this may seem, is assimilation. A migrant worker and his or her family can take this trajectory without giving up all of the valued components of their native culture. They can take advantage of the much vaunted 'cultural pluralism', and become 'hyphenated Americans', providing only – but here is the rub – that they have previously won the basically economic struggle to fight free of ghettoization and its constant companion, superexploitation. In other words, assimilation is a fruit of resistance. It is not a gift from the system, much less an inevitable fate for all migrants. What the system forces, or tries to force, upon the individual is not assimilation, but ghettoization. On the other hand, some individuals and families choose another trajectory: retention of the culture of origin. For Puerto Ricans in the US, and for some other migrant communities, this choice would normally (but not necessarily) involve a return to the native land. There are, of course, two sorts of return. One is the desperate strategy of returning to seek a livelihood when such cannot be obtained in the US. The other sort presupposes successful resistance to ghettoizing forces and in particular the acquisition of savings or attainment of a skilled trade or profession, such that the return will perhaps bring a life free from further superexploitation. Let me once again emphasize that these relatively free choices are only accessible to a small minority within any ghetto community.

One other strategy of resistance remains to be discussed. Whether it is available to all ghetto communities or not I do not know. I will outline it first for the Puerto Rican community, and later venture some tentative generalizations. Puerto Ricans in the US, or almost all of them, have retained their Puerto Rican nationality. Just why this is so, and why we can speak of Puerto Rico as a 'nation divided', with two-fifths of its five million nationals living as forced migrants in the US, I have tried to explain in Chapter 5. In this chapter I have noted two crucial reasons: the 'air bridge', and the fact that the vector of imposed cultural change in the US ghettos is not assimilative but ghettoizing, a process that does not destroy the native nationality and replace it by the host nationality. In any event, Puerto Ricans in the US consider themselves to be Puerto Ricans. And this leads them to participate, sometimes very actively, in the struggle to free their country. True independence for Puerto Rico must entail not merely 'flag sovereignty' but also socialism, as most *independentistas* agree, because, among other things, the Puerto Rican economy is almost entirely (90 per cent) US-owned, and colonialism in Puerto Rico is itself mainly a reflection of the profitability of this island for US corporations.

One of the real, and often quickly attained, fruits of socialism for poor countries has proved to be a transformation from a labour-surplus condition to one of labour shortage. Thus we may argue that not very long after the liberation of Puerto Rico there will begin to be opportunities for Puerto Ricans who now live in the US to return under circumstances in which they will be able to find work and enjoy a perhaps modest but certainly supportable standard of living. (Today the circumstances of return are unemployment and food stamps.) Not all, and perhaps not even the majority, will choose to return. But it is clear that one side-benefit of the liberation of Puerto Rico will be an opportunity for Puerto Ricans in the US to fight free of the ghetto by returning to a socialist Puerto Rico. This strategy is not at all a withdrawal from struggle in the US. In general, immigrant and foreign workers tend to be among the most militant participants in labour's struggles in the host country while they also fight for the liberation of their native land. Militancy is not, after all, a substance to be decanted out of one struggle into another. It is a well-spring.

## Notes

1. See G. Davis and F. Donaldson, *Blacks in the United States: A Geographic Perspective* (1975), Chap 6.

2. Citizenship was conferred on Puerto Ricans in 1917, but it entailed no civil or political rights other than the privilege of free entry into the US. That privilege did not become significant until 30 years later: the Puerto Rican population in mainland US today is about ten times what it was at the beginning of the Second World War. Note that the free entry privilege was also accorded British colonial subjects for immigration to Great Britain in former times. They were technically 'British subjects', but they gained no political or civil rights from this status.

3. The sectors identified here are congruent with the sectors distinguished, and by now established empirically, by dual (or split) labour market theorists. See M. M. Piore, *Birds of Passage: Migrant Labor and Industrial Societies* (1979), and R. S. Bryce-Laporte (ed.), *Sourcebook on the New Immigration* (1980). Duality, and its relationship to migrant labour, is given a Marxist theoretical interpretation by M. Castells in his essay, 'Immigrant Workers and Class Struggles in Advanced Capitalism: The West European Experience', in R. Cohen and others (eds.), *Peasants and Proletarians: The Struggles of Third World Workers* (1979). Although Castells does not discuss ghettos or assimilation, he demonstrates, for Western Europe, that the maintenance of a 'permanent fraction of immigrant workers' is a 'unified interest of the dominant classes' (p. 370), and that 'the status of foreigner' is crucial to the functionality of these workers.

4. J. M. Blaut, 'The Ghetto as an Internal Neocolony', *Antipode* 6, 1 (1974). (I would now use 'semi-colony' instead of 'neocolony' but would not otherwise change the argument of this paper.)

5. A. Cabral, 'National Liberation and Culture', in Africa Information Service (ed.), *Return to the Source: Selected Speeches by Amilcar Cabral* (1973).

6. 'Translocation' seems a better term than 'migration' in cases such as those we are discussing in which movement is essentially involuntary, or forced; in which 'the decision to migrate' is a forced decision.

7. It proved to be true for Latino applicants to my university (the University of Illinois at Chicago) that test scores on the 'American College Test', or 'ACT', a college admission test used in many universities throughout the United States, were absolutely uncorrelated with academic success. Many other studies have yielded comparable findings with minority students for this and similar tests. These tests have become a key device for denying a university education to Third World people in the US.

# 7. Class Struggles across a Boundary

## The Problem of Eurocentrism in the Marxist Theory of Colonialism and Nationalism

The purpose of this chapter is to generalize the Marxist theory of national struggle; to infix it firmly in the broader framework of historical materialism. This is more than a matter of fitting the part into the whole. Some rather serious problems are involved, and something will have to be said about these problems before we turn to the main task at hand.

There is one underlying problem: Eurocentrism, with its constant companion, diffusionism. There is Eurocentric diffusionism within each of the two aberrant views of the Marxist theory of nationalism or national struggle against which I have argued in this book. One of these is the view that nationalism is at root an idea, a European idea, which diffused outwards from northwestern Europe to the colonial world, and that national liberation movements do not, therefore, reflect the colonial peoples' response to oppression and superexploitation, but simply reflect the spread to and through the colonies of a supposedly enlightening European idea, the 'idea of the nation-state', or the 'idea of freedom'. (See chapters 2 and 3 above.) The second aberrant view – it was, as we have seen, the dominant Marxist view in the years before the First World War but was then challenged by Lenin and later discredited by the reality of national liberation – is the thesis that national struggles are inherently bourgeois; that they arose with the rise of the European bourgeoisie and later appeared elsewhere as some form of belated bourgeois revolution (or emergence of capitalism); that they must somehow decline in importance, or become irrational, as capitalism itself becomes fully international, no longer having need for the national state; and that national struggles have no integral place in working-class struggles against the bourgeoisie. (See Chapter 1, Chapter 4, and Chapter 5.) I have tried to show that the central Marxist position, sketched in by Marx and Engels and then developed by Lenin, holds that national struggle is specifically a form of the class struggle for state power, that it can be employed by any of several classes, including the working class, and that it became a central arena of struggle in the Third World precisely because externally imposed oppression and colonial superexploitation required this response: a struggle to seize state power. This conception of the national question is not Eurocentric.

But historical materialism as a whole is still not free of Eurocentrism. If we are to understand national struggle as a form of class struggle, we have to understand the manifold forms which are taken by class struggle itself wherever and whenever it takes place: that is, throughout the space–time region that embraces the class phase of social evolution. Much present-day thinking about class processes in the Third World is too narrow for this purpose. Some writers, for instance, misconstrue production relations as 'relations of exchange', leaving us with the false idea that production is somehow governed by pre-class or non-class social relations, or is, at most, pre-capitalist. Other writers misconstrue Third World class struggle as some sort of boundary transaction ('articulation') between different modes of production, not as a relation, and struggle, between definable classes and class-combinations. These positions (which I have oversimplified), and others like them, seem to me to be grounded in a conception of class, of exploitation, and of class struggle which uses as its templates the industrial working class of 19th and early-20th Century Europe, the rising bourgeoisie of that place and time, and a supra-national bourgeoisie of the present day. Within this conceptual framework, an adequate understanding of national liberation movements, and of national struggle in general, is very difficult.

But the problem of Eurocentrism is much larger than this. It extends to our view of history as well as geography. In fact, the weakest part of Marxist theory as a whole is that portion of it which seeks to explain social evolution at the very largest scale, that of human history since the dawn of class society. We understand the dynamics of the capitalist mode of production quite well. Likewise the socialist mode, or socialist transition. We know relatively little about pre-capitalist modes of production (anywhere) and about pre-capitalist forms of the class struggle. This is not simply a lack of empirical, factual knowledge. We suffer from historical tunnel vision about pre-capitalist modes of production. We see the sequence of modes in the historical space–time column which embraces Europe and the Near East, but, failing to have adequate understanding of the modes of production in other parts of the world at given historical times, and failing even to have an adequate methodology for comparison across areas and cultures, we cannot successfully establish some of the most crucial causal generalizations.

For example: we note that fact $B$ appears in Europe after fact $A$. But we do not know whether $B$ follows $A$ in other areas at comparable epochs, hence gives evidence of a general causal process. We do not even know whether $B$ and $A$ are related: $B$ may have diffused into Europe from somewhere else. We do not know enough about historical non-Europe, or consider ourselves obliged to seek to obtain such knowledge as part of our methodology for studying these facts I label $A$ and $B$. This is historical tunnel vision, or tunnel history.

Marx and Engels made errors because of this same tunnel history, but they could not have avoided these errors, since crucial knowledge about the non-European world either did not exist in their lifetimes, or had not yet diffused into Europe, or was actually suppressed for political reasons. An example of the last is quite relevant. The importance of private property in land in India was a body of fact which the British government and the East India Company deliberately suppressed, because, in essence, non-private land could be aggregated to the Crown and thereafter sold or otherwise used to produce revenue.[1] (Much the same legal trickery was performed in other colonies, British, Dutch, French, etc.) Marx and

Engels had no access to the truth about private landed property in India. If they had had such access, a major part of the theory concerning the causal forces leading to capitalism would have been modified. In particular, the idea of Asiatic 'stagnation' would have been rejected, and the causal model for the transition from feudalism to capitalism would have had to be modified very drastically, because the historical facts thought to be causally efficacious occurred outside Europe as well as inside, yet the transformation to capitalism completed itself only in Europe. (More on this problem below.) But errors of this sort, which could not have been avoided by Marx and Engels, are still being made today. And they cannot now be excused in the same way. Some of them give evidence of a dogmatic parroting of, so to speak, the master's words. Some reflect the kind of Eurocentrism which permeates conservative social thought but is incompatible with Marxism.

Not all of the failings of the Marxist theory of social evolution result from Eurocentric tunnel history. Another methodological hobble is geographical diffusionism, a very close relative of tunnel history. The former leads us to make false causal generalizations because we only look down, so to speak, the European tunnel of time, and fail to consider extra-European historical events both as data for historical or evolutionary generalization and as possible causes of events known to have occurred in Europe. The latter, diffusionism – as we have seen in prior discussions, particularly those in Chapter 3 – assumes that the only historically efficacious events, those which are innovative and have evolutionary consequences, occur within Europe (and, for pre-Christian times, the Near East, the Bible Lands) and then diffuse outwards to the rest of the world. Both habits of mind find evolutionary causes only in the European sector. They fail to notice the processes occurring outside this sector. Therefore they fail to see the larger processes comprehending social evolution on a world scale.

But there is still a third habit of mind to be added to the list of reasons for our failure to develop a truly adequate body of evolutionary theory, comprehending all class society and all of the world. This third element is a kind of time-boundedness which leads into one of the crucial contradictions in contemporary Marxist theory: on the one hand, our theory of social evolution based on class struggle and modes of production has as its universe of discourse the entire history and geography of human society since the emergence of the first class-based mode of production (and even earlier). On the other hand, we scrutinize the capitalist mode in such a myopic way that we assume its major attributes to be peculiar to this mode alone, or only to the phase of industrial capitalism. It should be evident that many of the fundamental features of the capitalist mode must be features also of earlier class-based modes, and sometimes features of class society in general. Yet Marxists airily discuss, for instance, exploitation as though there were no pre-capitalist forms of exploitation; class struggle in the same way; likewise the state. Yet there can be no general historical–materialist theory which does not consider these three categories (and others) as facts of class society *in general*.

These limitations of Marxist theory as a whole are, unsurprisingly, found also in the theory of nationalism or national struggle. For various reasons that we have explored in this volume, all the processes associated with national struggle are usually placed within the period of industrial capitalism. And the origins of these processes are generally assumed either to be European or to reflect a reaction to some impact, some diffusion, from Europe. This is not a matter of describing the spread, diffusion if you will, of exploitation, oppression, and misery as capitalism enlarges its domain. It is, rather, a matter of seeing all of the essential traits associated with national struggle as being, themselves, European, and products of Europe's 'modernity'. Nations are placed within this framework. So, too, are national movements. So, too, are states. This last is crucial.

I have argued in this book for a conception of national struggle which sees all of it as a form or type of the class struggle to seize state power. National struggle is the form of political class struggle which is associated, in general, with states which are externally governed (that is, by 'foreigners'). But consider again our concept of the state. There were states within pre-capitalist class-based societies in Europe and indeed everywhere else. Lenin argued that every class society has its form of the state, and I find no cogent arguments against this view.[2] Are there not struggles for state power in all of these sorts of societies? And do they have no underlying common features with the national struggles associated with capitalist states? This is not a matter of discovering, as conservative social scientists are wont to do, some interesting forerunner of nationalism, or some precocious early national movement. It is a matter of determining whether we are dealing with phenomena appropriate to *one* class mode of production, capitalism, or to *many* modes, or to *all*. On the other hand, it is not a matter of succumbing to that other tendency of mainstream social science: to imagine that contemporary social processes in capitalist society are somehow rooted in man's essential human or animal nature, and thus have been with us since the dawn of time. National struggle per se is a relatively modern emergent. The question is: does it emerge from a general phenomenon of class society which has been around for a very long time?

The central argument of this chapter is the thesis that there is indeed a general feature of all class modes of production, in all parts of the world though not in every individual class society, which is the essential underlying process that in our own times becomes nationalism or national struggle. This feature is a form of the class struggle for state power, something, I need hardly add, which is very old and very widespread over the earth. I am not – this needs re-emphasis – denying the specificity of the nationalism which is characteristic of the capitalist era. And I am certainly not arguing that nationalism transcends class society itself, is 'transhistorical' (Poulantzas), or is an attribute of man's biological nature as is argued by the right-wing theorists of 'territoriality', 'aggression', and the like.[3] My argument is simply an attempt to generalize the theory of nationalism within the Marxist theory of social evolution and nothing more.

I will develop the argument of this chapter in a series of steps. First, I will discuss the phenomena which I call 'external class struggle' and 'external exploitation', and show how these have been features of class society in general; eventually, in our epoch, becoming national struggle and related phenomena. Secondly, I will show why external class struggle and external exploitation are, indeed, important forms of class struggle and class exploitation in all modes of production though not all individual societies. Emerging from all this will be a generalized theory of national struggle.

A word must be said now about this writer's theoretical presuppositions concerning social evolution. I maintain, and have argued elsewhere, that social evolution was proceeding in about the same way, and at the same rate of progress, in Africa, Asia, and Europe down to the end of the 15th Century. Europe's rapid rise thereafter I attribute only to its location – or rather the location of its mercantile–maritime centres, centres of incipient capitalism or proto-capitalism – many thousands of miles closer to the New World than was the case with the nearest competing mercantile–maritime centres (East African and Asian port cities).[4] The sudden rise of Europe, then, I conceive to have been a process fuelled by European-dominated production in the New World. (It was production, not merely exchange, and it related European pre-industrial capitalists, and their allies, to several exploited class sectors, slave and non-slave, in modes of exploitation as close to capitalism as one can find anywhere in the world at that precise period.) This allowed the process whereby European proto-capitalists were able to overcome feudal class power and to defeat competition from other proto-capitalist centres, eventually destroying them as a prelude to direct colonialism. As to social evolution after the time of the bourgeois revolution in England, I attribute much greater causal efficacy to colonialism, and specifically to the super-profitable production in colonial and semi-colonial areas, than do many Marxist and most non-Marxist writers. Thus, without denying the importance of autonomous developments within Europe prior to the 19th Century, I argue that the non-European world, throughout history, has been much more significant than is usually conceded to be the case. ('Europe' is of course an abstraction standing, for example, for Northwestern Europe in one period, all of Europe plus Anglo-America and minus colonial areas like Ireland, in another. This is not an argument about culture but about the differentiation of what became, on the one hand, the advanced capitalist world, including Japan, and, on the other hand, the underdeveloped capitalist world, including a bit of Europe and most of the tricontinent: Asia, Africa, and Latin America.)

I emphasize the foregoing for the following reason. As I discuss internal and external class struggle in history and geography, I will be bringing to bear my own theoretical position. The arguments concerning external class struggle and external exploitation are not contingent upon this historical position, although they are strengthened by it. The argument would remain valid even if a moderately Eurocentric historical model were accepted as reality. But the kind of Eurocentrism which is encapsulated within a space that includes only a European causal efficacy, and within a time that includes only the period since the rise of industrial capitalism, is a more difficult matter. Scholars in this tradition, some of them Marxists, are like the people chained in Plato's cave: they see nothing beyond the confines of their (Eurocentric) cave except flickering and meaningless shadows.

## Internal and External Class Struggle

The place to begin our analysis is with the most basic postulate of historical materialism. The history of all class-stratified societies is the history of class struggle. More concretely, the most important motor force of social change since ancient times has been the dynamic tension between ruling classes, which control the means of production and demand an ever-increasing share of production, and the producing classes, which in resisting this demand in some ways, acceding to it in others, engage in unceasing economic, cultural, and political struggle not only to retain the fruits of their labour but also to gain control of the means of production.

But now we ask: *who*, in reality, are the contenders in this struggle? It is not sufficient to answer 'ruling class' and 'producing class' if these categories are left hanging in the air of abstraction. A geographer will want to know: *where* is each of these classes to be found on the face of the earth? An anthropologist will want to know whether the two or more class groups belong to the same society and share the same culture, are connected perhaps by a common language, participate in a common web of social relationships, and engage in constant face-to-face interaction, or whether the rulers belong to one society, over here, and the producers to another, over there.

When the question is posed in this concrete way, our attention is drawn to a fact so obvious that its importance tends to go unnoticed. The ruling class of a given society may exploit two groups of producers, one 'native', the other 'foreign'. I will refer to them as, respectively, an *internal* producing class and an *external* one. Likewise, from the point of view of the producers, there will be an *internal* ruling class and there may also be an *external* one. Many combinations are possible: class conflict may be entirely a relationship between a ruling class and its internal producing class. It may involve both internal and external producers in varying weights and kinds of exploitation. It may involve, from the standpoint of a class of producers, a combination, often quite complex, of internal and external ruling classes; sometimes, more than one of each. It can never be purely an exploitation of external producers, since this would imply no exploitation at home.[5]

It goes without saying that not all ruling classes have had the political power to exploit external workers. But in some societies, in all class modes of production, in all portions of the world, we find the situation in which a ruling class is powerful enough to gain from an external producing class a significant portion of the surplus (or surplus product) upon which it subsists. Let us briefly review this matter historically and geographically, then draw implications from it for the theory of national struggle.

### External Exploitation: Its History and Geography

Class society emerged sometime during the fourth millennium B.C. or perhaps earlier. Why it arose is of course a matter of speculation, but Marxists would argue that the transformation must have been an evolutionary advance: the ruling classes in the first epoch of their existence would have performed a function for the societies out of which they emerged, a function such as food distribution in times of shortage, defence, ritual, or the like. It is very probable, therefore, that the earliest ruling classes did not, strictly speaking, exploit the producers.[6] They obtained surplus production from the producers but they performed a social function in return. Quite possibly the first people to be truly exploited – using 'exploitation' in the Marxist sense as implying a substantial one-way transfer of the value created in production, and measuring value in terms appropriate to the particular mode of production – were slaves: thus external producers. By the beginning of the first millennium B.C., slaves were used by ruling classes in various parts of all three Old World continents, slaves who had been obtained in conquest, or through trade, or perhaps as tribute, and then put to work within these ancient class societies in the direct service of the ruling classes.[7]

In ancient society there also appeared other forms of external exploitation. One of these was tribute, a relationship in which, typically, a local ruling class was forced to deliver part of the surplus obtained from local producers to an external ruling class.[8] This should not be conceptualized as a relationship of exchange rather than production, since the external ruling class maintained the same relationship with the producers as did the internal ruling class, who merely forwarded surplus from producers to external rulers. Perhaps at this point I should call attention to the fact, not necessarily an obvious one, that exploitation can take place even when producers and rulers reside in different localities. The spatial movement of surplus does not become a process of exchange unless the product is transferred from hand to hand, and at a price.[9]

Still another important form of external exploitation was the settlement of internal producers on lands obtained in conquest, sometimes with the genocide or forced displacement of the original population. This form remains important in all subsequent class-based modes of production including capitalism (for example, settler colonialism). Admittedly, the domain of the term 'external' can become somewhat blurred here, since internal producers now deliver surplus on external lands. However, in some of these cases the original producers remain as an exploited or superexploited class. And in all cases of this type the labour productivity of internal producers now settled on external lands must become much higher, and therefore also the potential rate of surplus obtainable from each producer, because a given population of producers is now exploiting more land.[10] Many other cases can be found in which it is difficult to tell whether a form of exploitation should or should not be called 'external', but such blurring of distinctions in some situations does not alter the fact that external exploitation can by and large be distinguished from internal without much difficulty.

When we come down to the period of the Roman Empire and its contemporary civilizations in Africa, India, China, and elsewhere, it is evident that both forms of class exploitation had by now become intense. The ruling class was now fully a class for itself, thus whatever functions it served for the generating society were relatively inconsequential in comparison to the amount of surplus it demanded from the producers in that society. During this period, in some class societies across the Old World, there was exploitation and class struggle in both the internal and external dimensions. The internal dimension was perhaps typified by the form of landlordism, incipient feudalism, found on Roman estates in Italy and France and on similar estates in contemporaneous India and China.[11] The external dimension now made quite heavy use of pillage and a level of exploitation of conquered societies that was no doubt so intense that it could only last for brief historical periods, since it could not have allowed these societies to retain enough of their production and labour to permit social reproduction.

But now the use of slaves was even more intense, and in the urban centres of the Mediterranean area, India, China, and elsewhere, as well as in the rural estates which supplied these centres with food and raw materials, slave labour was the most important source of surplus and also the most intense focus of class struggle. (Witness Spartacus.) In this precise sense, some though by no means all of these societies were grounded in the slave mode of production: that is slave labour was the major source of surplus for the ruling classes, although not usually the society's main form of productive labour, which would still be that of free peasants and artisans. Still, in some areas, including much of China, while the use of slaves was ubiquitous, the basal mode of production in this period was not slave-based. Since exploitation was primarily visited on the (internal) peasants, the mode of production was feudal.[12]

The relative importance of internal and external exploitation and class struggle is more difficult to ferret out in the feudal period, partly for lack of clarity of concepts, beginning with the concept of feudalism itself. I will take it as agreed that the feudal mode of production has as its essential features a landlord class (titled or not) and a dependent peasantry forced, even when not legally in serfdom, to deliver surplus to the landlord in kind, in money, or in labour, with the means of production, principally land, owned by the ruling class and not by the peasant producers. The social and political attributes of northwestern European feudalism were epiphenomena, most of them not found even in southern European feudalism much less in non-European areas, and in no sense serving as defining attributes of the feudal mode of production. This agreed, it is clear that the feudal mode dominated broad areas of Asia and Africa as well as Europe for a very long time, sometimes under centralized kingdoms, sometimes under fragmented polities.[13]

In Europe, India, and perhaps other areas, classical civilization collapsed into a 'dark age'.[14] Associated with this collapse was a decline in the surplus produced by slave labour and probably also tribute from conquered peoples – the unstable basis of the ancient, urbanized, ruling classes. In the centuries thereafter the dominant mode of production was feudal, and the principal producing class in most of these societies was the internal peasantry. But matters were not quite that simple. As a feudal ruling class inevitably attempted to enlarge its power and surplus, it did so both by intensifying exploitation of the local producers and by expanding its rule in space. A significant part of the increased surplus came from the local producers, and here, doubtless, was the main seat of class exploitation and struggle for most feudal societies at most times. The producers responded to the intensified demands, as they had to if the needs of social reproduction were to be met, by increasing labour productivity, doing so in part by inventing or borrowing technology intended to intensify production on existing acreage, and in part by expanding cultivated acreage in a given region. But this did not suffice.

Externalization on a very large scale took place through major expansions of the regions dominated by the feudal mode. In Europe this involved, for instance, the spread of deep ploughing into northern Europe (a development that resulted from the exigencies of feudalism, not, as some conservative historians maintain, from a supposed miraculous technological revolution in European agriculture, none having occurred), colonization by feudal societies of the Marchlands of eastern Europe, and other spatial expansions.[15] Parallel processes occurred in northeastern (Gangetic) India, southern and southwestern China, and elsewhere.[16] But the feudal ruling classes were insatiable (again following the logic of the mode of production, which is always in disequilibrium), and everywhere we see major moves of conquest. Some of the colonization just mentioned was facilitated by conquest of external societies and their lands. In addition, kingdoms and principalities expanded, bringing external peasants within the given feudal ruler's sphere of power and sometimes, over time, internalizing them. To this must be added the almost purely external exploitation associated with the large-scale conquests of the Mongols and other comparable expansions. This process displays a further complexity in the system, as the conquerors usually superimposed their own demands for surplus upon the existing demands made by the local feudal ruling classes.

Finally, during this period, a relatively new form of urbanization was emerging, with its economic base in long-distance trade and medieval industry. Although there was direct exploitation of an internal producing class in these new mercantile–maritime–industrial centres of Europe, Africa, and Asia, external exploitation was also centrally involved: for instance, use was often made of slaves (as in Venetian galleys, plantations, and manufactories), and also of an external class of peasant producers tied to urban merchants, as in the case of pepper cultivators in South India, cotton farmers in Fukien, sugar-cane farmers in the Venetian colonies and in Egypt, and the like.[17] Overall, when we examine the entire array of class-stratified societies in medieval times, it is clear that external class exploitation and struggle still remain important, although the substantial increase in agricultural productivity (mainly reflecting areal expansion of cultivation and adoption of more intensive cropping systems) which characterized this period everywhere suggests that internal exploitation and class struggle had greater significance than before the feudal period, greater also than external exploitation and struggle during that period.

This brings us to the period of the emergence of capitalism and the rise of Europe. All would agree that external exploitation was immensely important during this period (the 16th, 17th and 18th Centuries).[18] I argue that, for Europe, it was more important than the internal exploitation of Europe's producing classes; and I argue further that external exploitation by Europeans accounts for the fact that capitalism triumphed first in Europe, and accounts for related facts, such as the later suppression of emerging capitalism in Asia and Africa and, thereafter, the expansion of European colonialism. Call this the 'strong' argument for the importance of external exploitation (and colonialism). But if only the 'weak' argument is accepted, the importance of external exploitation and struggle during this period will still be admitted.

Iberian Europe's late-medieval expansion in the Atlantic was in no important way different from the maritime expansions radiating outwards from mercantile–maritime centres in other regions, stretching from East Africa to East Asia, at the same time. Europe's single advantage was a position closer by some 5,000 miles to the New World.[19] Conquest of the New World gave European merchants, among other things, an amount of gold and silver possibly equal to one-fourth of the total stock of these metals in the Old World as a whole. The significance of this fact has nothing to do with monetarism. In an already monetized urban and rural economy stretching unbroken from Europe to China, one group of merchant capitalists suddenly acquires the cash resources sufficient both to out-compete every other such group in every major market across the hemisphere, hence in this way to accumulate, and the resources sufficient to allow them to offer better prices for land, labour, and commodities within Europe itself, hence to accumulate in this way as well and at the same time to buy out the European feudal class opposition (or some of it). And this goes on unabated for a century and more, at a rate of precious metal supply and capital accumulation that always remains ahead of the (inevitable) inflation.[20]

But this process is seen more revealingly when we look at the forms and extent of external exploitation which it entailed. One form, in the 16th Century, was pillage and the forced labour of millions of Americans in mines and other European-owned enterprises. Another was slave labour and much free labour on plantations to an extent not often appreciated for this early period. (For instance, it appears that, in the year 1600, the value in £ sterling of sugar exported from Brazil alone was double the value of all exports of all types to all of the world from England in that year.)[21] There is also the beginning of the process of externalizing European producers through emigration to the New World, to the trading factories of Asia and Africa, to eastern Europe and Siberia, and so on.

In the 17th Century external exploitation became much more intense, both in terms of the number of producers involved in the process and the amount of surplus transferred into the hands of European capitalists.[22] The focal process now was slave-plantation production in the New World and associated with it a large amount of non-slave labour in the plantation colonies, ships, slave-trading enterprises, and the like. In 1689, capitalism's formal moment of triumph in England's Glorious Revolution, the slave labour force in British colonies may have been one third as numerous as the proletariat in Britain itself, and more than one third as significant if we consider the respective rates of surplus extraction for slave and free labour, while the thousands of non-slave labourers associated in one way or another with British plantations and colonies added further external exploitation.[23] By this time, also, there was substantial exploitation of Asian peasants and artisans by Europeans and their allied merchants and landlords, and a somewhat parallel process associated with the slave trade in Africa. And there was further externalization of European producers by emigration to less densely populated and fertile lands in the New World, a process which (as we discussed above) increased the surplus obtainable from each producer.

In sum, the 16th and 17th Century was a period of rapidly expanding exploitation of an external working class, paralleled by an expansion, but far less rapid, of internal exploitation within Europe. By 1689 the external producing class (classes) consisted of millions of native American farmers and miners, millions of African slaves, a relatively smaller number of Africans exploited in their own continent, a large though uncounted number of Asians working directly or indirectly for Europeans, and another large though uncounted number of externalized European producers working as farmers, overseers, artisans, fishermen, sailors, soldiers, etc., in most of the extra-European world. And already there were notable slave uprisings, wars of resistance, and more subtle forms of external class struggle.

Not all readers will agree with the assessment that external class exploitation and struggle was more important than internal, during this period of early capitalism, and that it was crucial and central to the rise and triumph of capitalism in Europe. But everyone will agree that external exploitation was, in absolute terms, of great significance.

We need not try to assess the relative contributions of external exploitation, mainly colonial, and internal exploitation in the development of capitalism in western Europe in the 18th and 19th Centuries. Suffice it to say that it is difficult for any Marxist scholar who is a student of colonialism to accept the conventional, vulgar, teleological, tunnel-historical belief, not properly attributable to Marx himself, that the evolution of industrial capitalism down to the late 19th Century was an unfolding, sui generis, of processes internal to Europe (and European settlement elsewhere). During the 18th and 19th Centuries the now enlarged power of capitalism permitted the rapid proletarianization of European workers, and after the industrial revolution gained momentum a tremendous increase occurred in the productivity of each industrial worker. These and other factors make it certain that internal exploitation was increasing at a much greater rate than external exploitation during the period, say, from 1789 down to the late 19th Century, and was, on balance, of much greater economic significance (for capitalism) than external exploitation. The same held true for internal class struggle, which during this time was forcefully pushing capitalism along its road to ruin.

But external exploitation was nonetheless of great importance, from the early role played by Indian craftsmen and peasants and US and West Indian slaves in the rise of the British cotton textile industry, the leading sector in the industrial revolution, to the eventual proletarianization and semi-proletarianization of uncounted millions of workers in the colonies and semi-colonies, and to the externalization of millions of European workers on lands newly emptied by genocide. And there was class resistance in all of this, starting with resistance to enslavement and colonial conquest; continuing through the many wars of resistance and liberation in the 18th and 19th Centuries, including the 'Sepoy Rebellion' or First Indian War of Independence, the Taiping Revolt, the immensely important Haitian war of liberation – as close to a proletarian revolution as you will find in its time – and many other such struggles; then continuing with both economic and political class resistance throughout the history of all colonies and settler colonies.[24] All of these struggles were, in one form or another, class struggles, and their opposing class was the bourgeoisie, with or without feudal allies.

Colonialism assumed greater proportional and absolute significance in the late 19th Century, the beginning of what most Marxists call the period of monopoly capitalism or the era of imperialism.[25] The extent to which class exploitation in colonies, semi-colonies, and neocolonies has propped up capitalism in the present century is a subject for serious debate. I would argue, with Lenin, that it has been the single most important prop, partly because it has permitted capital to sustain the incremental growth of accumulation when this is obstructed or stopped, mainly by working class struggle, in the metropolitan countries, and partly because higher productivity of workers in metropolitan countries seems to be offset by the much greater number of workers, overall, in the colonial and neocolonial sector, the sector which is now conventionally called 'the Third World'. Differing opinions on this issue are matters of emphasis. Everyone would agree, I think, that there is indeed a distinction to be made between sectors of the capitalist world which today deserve to be called 'internal' and 'external', crudely, the advanced capitalist countries and the Third World respectively.[26] Allowing for exceptions and intermediate cases, we can generalize that producers in the external sector encounter qualitatively different conditions, economic and political, and are subject to greater exploitation in the sense of that term which indicates the amount and share of produced value which is retained by the worker, and thus indicates the worker's standard of life. The external worker, in this precise sense if not in others, is superexploited. The conditions surrounding this situation reflect colonialism and its various offspring. For instance, it is no accident that rates of profit in the colony of Puerto Rico are more than twice as high as they are in the US, and that real wages are 25 per cent of the US rate.[27]

To be precise, these conditions reflect the political environment of colonialism in its many guises, and the political struggles appropriate to this environment, in the external sector or Third World. As we noted in Chapter 1, the two world sectors do not differ merely as a matter of geographical distance from the foci of advanced capitalism (and accumulation), in a sort of continuous cline outwards to the ends of the earth, a cline which is supposed to be a momentary snapshot picture of continuous outward diffusion of economic development, industrialization, and wealth from centre to periphery, such that each peripheral (or Third World) country will eventually become an advanced capitalist country in its turn. Built into the structure of world capitalism, for reasons emerging from the colonial experience, is the quite necessary strategy of maintaining a repressive political environment in the colonial and neocolonial part of the world in order to permit superexploitation of workers in this sector. This, I would argue, is the present-day form of the dichotomy of internal and external exploitation. I should emphasize that we must not underestimate either the intensity of exploitation and oppression nor the power of resistance by the working classes in metropolitan capitalist countries. I am in essence summarizing the argument, almost a conventional one among Marxist scholars, which delineates the systematic increase in exploitation and oppression of external workers since the onset of the imperialist or monopoly-capitalist era. Class contradictions in advanced capitalist countries intensified, after the end of the 19th Century, to the point where increments of accumulation had to be drawn to an ever-increasing extent from the exploitation of external workers: further burdens placed upon the internal working classes would have produced revolution, and other ways of increasing accumulation, such as technological change and population growth, were incapable of providing the increments of accumulation without which capitalism would collapse.

Hence, in the modern world, and down to the present, external class exploitation has continued to gain in importance. So has external class struggle.

The new increase in the importance of external exploitation has taken two rather different forms: on the one hand, much more intensive exploitation of workers in colonial and neocolonial areas, accompanied by a great increase of proletarianization in such areas; and on the other hand, a truly massive importation of workers from these areas into the advanced capitalist countries themselves. Unlike earlier migrations under capitalism, when immigrating working-class populations were internalized – that is assimilated – relatively rapidly, because of the rapid and continuous expansion of the labour force during that period of rising capitalism, today the external workers who are forced to migrate to the metropolitan countries are, by and large, neither internalized economically nor assimilated culturally. Usually, as I explained in earlier chapters, they remain external workers. They serve, within the metropolitan countries, essentially the same function (super-exploited workers and components of the industrial reserve army) that other external workers do in the colonies and neocolonies themselves. It is not crucial for the present discussion to weigh the question whether most of the increment of accumulation now comes from the exploitation of these two types of external workers or from internal workers. The process has not lifted the burden of exploitation from the backs of the internal workers, and both groups are engaged in the same struggle with the same ruling class.

Thus, in a rapid survey of four or five millennia of class exploitation and struggle, we find that during all stages of class society, the role of external, more or less foreign, workers or producers has been unmistakably important.

We can generalize as follows: the history of class society has been grounded in class struggle, but a significant portion of this struggle has crossed cultural and political boundaries, involving the struggle of workers in, or from, one society against two class groups of exploiters, some from their own society, some from an external society. Also, at times there has been class struggle between the two ruling-class sectors, internal and external. Until we insert this socio–spatial element into our theories of historical materialism, we shall not fully understand the past evolution of class society and its present condition. And, for modern times, we shall not understand the mechanisms and functions of national struggle, which, as I will try to show in the following discussion, is a direct manifestation of external class struggle.

### External Exploitation: Its Specificity

There is nothing particularly surprising in the fact that class societies with powerful ruling classes are able to expand in space and thus enlarge the number of producers from which the ruling class gains surplus. Nor is it remarkable that this has occurred in all class modes of production down through the capitalist mode, so that internal and external exploitation have coexisted, though not everywhere, since the earliest class societies. Much less obvious is the fact that external exploitation tends to be significantly more intense than the internal kind, that the forms of class struggle which it engenders are in some ways, and to some degree, different from the internal forms, and that all of this leads to certain political differences in the struggle for state power and in the nature of the state, differences which in modern times explain the specificity of national struggle.

In the discussion which follows, I will take care not to overemphasize the differences between internal and external exploitation, oppression, class struggle, and politics, for to do so is to retreat into a non-Marxist kind of argument which maintains, falsely, that the working class in advanced capitalist countries is not exploited, not oppressed, and not engaged in serious class struggle, including the struggle for state power. But there is a danger also in the opposite direction: that of failing to notice that there are, indeed, differences: that external exploitation tends truly to be more severe, to be superexploitation; and that political struggle in externally ruled societies is something more consequential than 'bourgeois nationalism'.

When Marxists argue that class conflict is the motor of history, they are referring to all stages in the evolution of class-stratified society, not merely the capitalist stage or form. Each ruling class must engage in a process of ever-expanding accumulation; if it were ever satisfied with a particular volume of surplus product, and a particular rate of exploitation, we might have a condition of equilibrium, in which the equation of forces between a ruling class which demands no more than a specific amount of surplus and a producing class which accedes to these demands so long as they do not reach a point threatening its biological and cultural reproduction, would lead to a kind of class armistice. But we know that history works (so to speak) in a different way. The ruling class is never satisfied, and each social formation thus eventually reaches its final crisis. Therefore, although the conflict of classes is, overall, the motor of history, it is the intensification of that conflict which really pushes history forward.

This reasoning provides us with the first and most important proposition needed to explain the coexistence of, and differences between, internal and external exploitation. The amount of surplus which any ruling class, in any social formation (or society), can obtain from its own, internal, working or producing class is finite and limited. Processes such as technological advance and population growth can indeed increase the surplus, but only at certain times and necessarily at a rather slow rate. (If the rate of increase is faster under capitalism, the rate of increase in ruling class demands is proportionally faster still.) It follows that a ruling class will attempt, wherever possible, to gain an increment of surplus outside its own society. That is, it will attempt to exploit external workers as well as internal ones. For reasons that I will address in a moment, the mechanisms used in exploiting an external workforce are necessarily to some degree different. They must involve forms of oppression that are not, and cannot be, visited upon the internal workforce, and they will typically generate a per capita level of exploitation much higher than the internal one if suitable power is at hand. In fact, external exploitation would seem to be a close correlate of power. Internally this is not the case. There are compelling reasons why a ruling class should, in its own long-term interests, restrict the internal level of exploitation.

Buried within the conventional wisdom of Marxist thought is the idea that every ruling class attempts to extract the absolutely maximum amount of surplus from the workers. This theoretical maximum level (and rate) of exploitation is the limit beyond which the workers will not be able to retain enough of the means of subsistence to survive and reproduce themselves as a class. If, however, surplus extraction were adjusted to this biological maximum, a given mode of production would have a very short lifetime. It would in short order kill the goose that lays its golden eggs. Let us briefly examine some of the reasons why the average long-term level of exploitation has tended to be well below the biological maximum during those long periods when a mode of production is functioning with relative smoothness and class contradictions have not yet begun to pull apart the fabric of a social formation. We will then see that these limitations do not apply in the same degree to the exploitation of external workers.

In pre-capitalist agricultural modes of production – there is a partial parallel for the capitalist mode – one very important factor which operated to limit the level of exploitation was the extreme fluctuation in annual per capita production, a fluctuation that moved in deep and long cycles (often climatic cycles). Thus there were great variations from year to year in the amount of production and labour which was surplus to the biological needs of the producing population. In principle, a ruling class can vary its demands for surplus from year to year. But it can only do so within a fairly narrow range, because the social processes within the ruling class itself are fuelled by this surplus. During periods of low production, and hardship in the producing class, there is no surplus after the subsistence needs of the producers have been met; if, even so, the ruling class enforces its demands, the working class will at the very least lose some of its population and therefore its long-term productive capacity, through disease, famine, emigration, and so on, and if the period of low production is long enough the system as a whole will be threatened. It follows that the long-term typical level of exploitation would adjust itself to the production level of high production years, so that some surplus labour or production would always be available without threatening the reproduction of the producing class. Really disastrous crop failures probably occurred only once in several generations, so the actual exploitation level would have maintained itself well below the biological capacity of the working population to produce in nearly all years.

On the other hand, the producing class could not be allowed to accumulate surplus: this also would destroy the social fabric, since the ruled would begin to become the rulers. Thus we can define in principle a very rough level of exploitation in pre-capitalist agricultural societies, falling somewhere between these two limits, a level which must have been the typical one during the very long periods when a social formation was enjoying reasonable stability. The level of exploitation is always a resultant of the two opposing forces of ruling-class exaction and working-class resistance, so the generalization just stated must be slightly reformulated: even when a ruling class has the power to demand surplus up to the biological maximum, it will tend not to do so, in the light of its own long-term interests.

This, then, is the first limitation on exploitation of an internal producing class. It remains only to note that this dynamic applies to peasant farming communities in the essentially capitalist environment of most rural Third World areas today, and to note as well that the boom-and-bust cycle of industrialized capitalist societies seems to obey a very similar dynamic, with some of the surplus value being shunted off to public sector functions which ensure the survival of the working class during times of recession or depression.

Productive behaviour takes place within a total cultural framework, and in stable social formations the maintenance of production, and hence the supply of surplus, requires that cultural mechanisms function relatively smoothly, mechanisms which embrace all aspects of the life of a community of producers, and include such elements as religion, art, and all types of formal and informal social interaction. If surplus demands were so high that the producers lacked the time and physical resources needed to maintain these cultural processes, the mode of production itself would tend rather quickly to collapse. This holds true for the capitalist mode as for others. Those situations in which the working class in this mode has become immiserated to the point where social life and culture in general are sacrificed to the elemental need to earn a living, are situations of severe disequilibrium. One possible outcome is inadequate social reproduction of the working class, which must be compensated for by the proletarianization of new workers (such as occurred in early 19th Century Britain). Another outcome is revolution.

We see, then, that the exploitation of an internal working or producing class is governed not only by the productive capacity of the workers, in situations where the ruling class possesses the relative power, in the face of resistance, needed to force production up to this limit. It is governed also by the need to constrain exploitation in ways which will ensure the biological and cultural reproduction of the producing class, and thus ensure the long-term stability of the system. We will see in a moment that these constraints do not apply, broadly speaking, to the exploitation of an external producing class. To understand the specificity of the latter we must consider briefly the mechanisms which govern the internal constraints.

The constraints on exploitation of an internal producing class in any mode of production are expressed in *rules* which regulate, and in a sense govern, internal class relations, using the word 'rule' to indicate both the customary patterns of behaviour and the ideological imperatives which persuade people, rulers and producers alike, to continue to conform.[28] These rules should be seen as rules of the game, or, somewhat imprecisely, as rules of class struggle. They are patterns of social behaviour and patterns of belief and value to which both classes, rulers and ruled, conform out of necessity. For the rulers, they ensure stability and continuous delivery of surplus. For the producers, they permit the retention of enough production and productive labour time so that biological and cultural reproduction, and social life, can continue unimpaired. Obviously, the rules change during the lifetime of a social formation, and conformity to them – never complete – is out of the question in the disruptive or revolutionary situation preceding the collapse of the formation. Less obviously, these rules do not govern external class relations: they do not apply to 'foreigners'.

To say that rulers and producers are constrained by a set of social and ideological rules is to say that the two classes participate in a common culture. (Participation in a common culture does not imply commonality of interests.) During those periods when a social formation is providing the producing class (or classes: I use the singular form as a generalization) with at least minimal subsistence, social life, and culture, and when the achievement of an alternative social formation grounded in a higher mode of production is not realizable, it would not usually be in the interest of the producers to destroy the social formation (though it is always in their interests to struggle for better conditions). Even when, in the declining years of a social formation, oppression is intensifying and contradictions are sharpening, and it is in the producers' interest to destroy the class structure, it is still not in their interest to destroy most facets of the common culture, including art, science, technology, religion, language (obviously), and so on. For all such matters, we can argue that the interests of the producing class in defending their culture tend to run parallel to those of the ruling class. I stress all of this to avoid the serious error, to which Marxists are rather prone, of believing that a working class does not have its own self-interest in the culture which it shares with the ruling class, a culture which, to a large degree, the working class itself created.

Commonality of culture between rulers and ruled within – internal to – a society seems to manifest itself in two principal ways. The first is a matter of social interaction. In all class societies there is some degree of interaction between the two polar classes. In the most ancient forms of class society, and particularly in the societies emerging from pre-class character, rulers and producers were joined in common kinship, and at least a fictive relic of this survived for a long time thereafter. In all class modes of production, inter-class interaction remains important. It consists primarily of participation by all members of the society in smaller social networks, each of which embraces class fractions not too distant from one another (for instance as serf and free-tenant, soldier and knight, worker and foreman, petty bourgeois and middle bourgeois), all such networks being interlinked in an overall network extending throughout the society, the point here being the continuity of a chain of interactions extending from the lowest producer to the highest ruler. In addition, in all class modes of production, from ancient society to monopoly capitalism, there is, in reasonably stable periods, at least some inter-class mobility, involving on the one hand a trickle of recruitment from the producing class into the ruling class (via small incremental movements from one class fraction to the adjoining higher fraction), and on the other hand demotion downwards in the class structure (the gentry family 'fallen on hard times' etc.).

The second set of commonalities resides at the level of ideology. Only when a social formation has reached the stage of intense, pre-revolutionary contradictions, can we say that the public ideological realm is largely dominated by those beliefs and values which are generated by the ruling class for the purpose purely of mystification and pacification, of generating false consciousness in the producers' minds so that they will misperceive their class interests and remain quiescent. At all other times, although mystification is always present, the ideological realm as a whole is vastly larger and more complex than that area embracing only ruling-class ideology and its projection as false consciousness, and it would be both untrue and terribly elitist to argue that the ideology of the working class is merely one that has been handed down from the rulers. Such would imply both a denial of working-class culture and values – for some societies, peasant class culture and values – and a denial that the ideology of the producers at all times incorporates attitudes of anti-ruling-class struggle. In general, then, it can be seen that the rules of behaviour and belief, which are incorporated in culture, and which constrain both rulers and producers, play an important role in conditioning, indeed tempering, the internal class struggle.

We come now to the crux of the argument. External exploitation is the principal means by which a ruling class can continue – if it has the power to do so – the incremental increase in accumulation after internal exploitation has reached such a level that a substantial increase in the delivery of surplus from the internal producing class is no longer possible or no longer prudent. Immediately our attention is drawn to the matter of social and ideological rules, rules of culture, and we notice two things: first, the limitations on exploitative behaviour which one observes in the case of internal class relations do *not* extend to external class relations, to the exploitation of 'foreigners', either in their own homelands or after their importation in statuses such as that of slave, 'guest worker', or the like. And second, the ideological rules governing and legitimizing internal class relations do *not* apply to external class relations. This last requires a bit of discussion.

Internal workers are conceptualized, both by themselves and by the ruling class, in a category which can rather loosely be described as 'citizen', or at least as 'member of the society'. In all class-stratified societies, from the most ancient to the most modern, this status has provided an internal worker with a bundle of rights, defined by ideology and sanctioned by law or by a binding moral code. Such rights may include, in one society, the right to inherit property (a right not accorded a slave); in another, the right to vote (a right not accorded colonial workers or 'guest workers' in modern times). All such rights are won in struggle, and they institutionalize the means by which a producing class defends itself from incremental increases in exploitation. Some of these rights are very general, but no less important for being so. For example, there is a definition of 'murder' in every class society, sharply constraining the conditions under which a producer can be put to death. But the killing of 'foreigners' is much less constrained, if at all. Foreigners can be killed, if it suits the interests of an expansive ruling class to do so, in battle, in the ordinary repression visited on a conquered people, and, beyond this, in plain genocide, as when the ruling class wishes to empty the conquered lands of their inhabitants and resettle internal workers on these lands.

In sum, the rules which restrain internal exploitation do not restrain external exploitation. Foreigners always have diminished rights; sometimes they have no rights at all; sometimes they are not even defined, and treated, as human beings. All of this is to be explained in simple historical–materialist terms by the fact that within a class-stratified society social and ideological rules are necessary to maintain stability and continuity in the mode of production. Exploitation outside that society, and exploitation of external workers forced to move into the space of that society, need not be so constrained by rules. Or, to be more precise, the rules are strikingly different: they allow for a much higher level of exploitation, a level that often throughout history has been so high as to prevent the biological and social reproduction of the external producing class.

It is true, of course, that, sooner or later, the ability of an expansive class society to shift the incremental burden of exploitation onto the backs of foreigners diminishes. At a certain moment in the life of a given social formation, one of two things is likely to happen: either the ruling class becomes dependent on external producers to just the same extent that it had been dependent upon internal ones, at which point the social and ideological rules constraining exploitation of the internal producers are extended to external producers, who may even become internalized, culturally redefined as 'citizen'; or the rules are not extended in this way, the outcome being continued superexploitation and oppression up to the point at which the external surplus ceases to flow, because of successful rebellion or destruction of the external producers as a class. In both cases, the option of gaining an increment of surplus from external producers is withdrawn, and class contradictions within the rulers' own society become much intensified, conceivably to the point of successful revolution. It is also possible that the resistance of the class of external producers will significantly help such an internal revolution. This has happened often enough in the past and may happen again today or tomorrow.

External exploitation involves more than an internal ruling class and an external producing class. We have to consider as well the role of the internal producers in this process, and also the role of the external ruling class, for most conquered societies are themselves class-stratified. It is true, to begin with, that members of the internal producing class participate directly in the conquest, subjugation, and exploitation of foreign workers, doing so, at the very least, as members of a military force. Such participation is, basically, one of the job-assignments forced on a producing class, one of the alternative ways in which members of that class are exploited. Never, I suspect, does the internal working class as a whole – as a class – gain absolute benefit from foreign exploitation: no part of the burden is lifted from its shoulders. At most, its members gain some respite from additional, incremental, exploitation: the burden does not increase, or increase quite as rapidly, when additional surplus can be extracted from foreign workers instead of themselves. This matter is very complex, of course, and deserves much more attention than I can give it here. For the purposes of the present argument, it is only necessary to emphasize the fact that internal and external exploitation co-exist: the latter does not replace the former.[29]

We come finally to the external or dominated ruling class, the fourth class-group in our highly simplified model of two class-stratified societies interacting as dominant and subordinate, each with one ruling class and one class of producers. Obviously, we would not usually find in reality just two clearly defined and neatly segregated classes in each of the two societies, but at the level of abstraction of the present discussion, which seeks in the space of a few pages to generalize for *all* class modes of production, no further elaboration is possible. I should just add that one additional case can be neglected in this discussion: that of a class society dominating a classless society. As I noted in Chapter 2, this case is far less common than theorists tend to realize. Most of the so-called 'tribal' societies are class-stratified. Many of them have (or had) a state. All, today at least, live within one or another sort of state and most experience external exploitation; and this held true in times prior to the rise of capitalism to a greater extent than is generally realized. 'Civilization', if you will, is and has been far more widespread than conservative and some Marxist theories would lead us to expect.

Just as there are cases in which an external producing class is wiped out or forced to emigrate, and internal producers then take their place, so there are cases in which an external ruling class is wiped out and the external producers thereafter maintain class relations of production only with the (from their perspective) foreign ruling class, with or without the participation of subaltern groups drawn from either of the two producing classes. This having been noted, we can turn to the far more widespread and significant case in which the external (subordinate-society) ruling class remains in place and continues to rule. This is significant mainly for two reasons. First, from the outset there is competition and a consequential form of class struggle between the two ruling classes. (I assume a situation in which the two societies are sufficiently distant in terms of culture and social interaction that the two ruling classes do not participate in a single web of customary interaction and kinship.) This competition between spatially and socially separated ruling groups, as it occurred during the period of rising capitalism in central and eastern Europe, was the paradigm for not a few general theories of nationalism, including the post-classical Marxist theories. It was argued that national movements in this region tended to reflect the efforts by local elites, petty bourgeoisie, bourgeoisie, perhaps also landowners, to fight off the competition of the larger bourgeoisie of the dominant, imperial society, by trying to secede and form a state in which they, the local elite, would hold power and a more or less exclusive licence to accumulate. Hence small nation nationalism and its adversary, great nation nationalism. The difficulty here is that this kind of case is paradigmatic only for one of many kinds of national struggle, a kind which is no longer in any sense typical.

The conflict between internal and external ruling classes can have a second type of outcome, somewhat different in character from the one just described although, I suspect, all real-world cases reflect some combination of the two types. This second form involves a relationship of tribute between the external (subordinate-society) ruling class and the internal (dominant) one: the former shares surplus with the latter. This must imply a great increase in the exploitative burden on the external producing class. Indeed, failure to impose this added pressure would force the external (subordinate-society) ruling class either to accept an erosion of its class position or to engage in the kind of inter-ruling-class struggle discussed in the preceding paragraph. The latter strategy is usually unavailable in a situation of real dominance. The most typical outcome seems to be intensified exploitation of the external (subordinate-society) producing class. This implies, among other things, a systematic violation of the customary rules governing exploitation, class relations, and the like, in that society. Thus incremental exploitation is accompanied by intensified social and cultural oppression. The results must be volatile.

**The Politics of External Class Struggle**
All class struggle is political, as anyone ever involved in a strike picket line knows very well. But the different forms of struggle lie at differing distances from the core of power, the state. The winning of state power does not always signal definitive victory – witness Chile and Grenada – but it is a safe generalization that the winning of real political power, the seizure of the state in the fullest sense, is normally the closest measurable point to victory in the struggle of subordinate classes to displace ruling classes, whether or not the victory is progressive and whether or not it produces a change in the underlying mode of production. This holds true for all class modes of production if we agree (with Lenin and many other theorists) that wherever there is a class society there is a state of one sort or another.[30]

External class struggle employs the same essential forms of struggle as does internal class struggle, but there are nonetheless important differences between the two. One such difference underlies, and in major part explains, all the others. This is the specificity of external exploitation. External exploitation is almost always more intense than internal exploitation, intensity here meaning the proportion of production which is appropriated by the ruling class, a proportion which cannot exceed a certain level without impeding the maintenance (reproduction) of the producing class and generating instability. For the reasons already abundantly discussed, internal producers are not pushed beyond this limit during most segments of the life-cycle of a social formation. This is not true of external producers. Exploitation, in all class modes of production, has tended to be much more intense for external producers than for internal ones.

There are a number of fundamental differences between the politics of class struggle in externally ruled societies and autonomous societies, differences which more or less directly reflect the specificity of external exploitation. Four such differences are particularly important for an understanding of the roots of national struggle.

The first of these differences is quite simply the fact that external class struggle is more nakedly political than internal class struggle. This follows from the fact that customary and stabilizing relations exist between ruling class and internal producers in a given society, such that exploitation will continue without the need for much resort to naked, that is, political, power. In the case of external producers, we are dealing with a situation in which greater exploitation occurs, and one which therefore incorporates overt political oppression from beginning to end: it begins with pressure for increased delivery of surplus, and it continues to apply pressure for further incremental increases, such pressure necessarily involving political oppression. In our own time the difference can be seen, for instance, if we compare the primarily, but not exclusively, economic struggle of the proletariat in 19th Century England with the intensely political and military struggles in Britain's old and new colonies in the same period. Not only was there a striking contrast but, as Marx, Engels, and Lenin all pointed out at one time or another, the two contrasting situations were dialectically related to each other.[31]

Secondly, the form of the state is likely to be very different in societies which are externally dominated. It goes without saying that this is true in the capitalist era: we need merely note the forms of the state found in colonies, in neocolonies, and, in the recent past, in the externally ruled societies within the great multinational continental empires which existed up to the end of the First World War. In earlier social formations the same basic difference would be found. These societies are *oppressive*. The producers are subjects of superexploitation and, to enable this, special oppression. The local ruling class, in these externally ruled societies, does not in general retain real power, its class position is likely to be under attack from the external (dominant) ruling class, and it cannot transmit all this pressure to the producers since they are already exploited more than is, so to speak, normal for a given mode of production. Moreover, the local ruling class has very little chance to increase its ability to accumulate, thus to 'rise', under conditions of domination.

One might say that these externally ruled state forms are undemocratic, although this begs a very complicated question. We would not, for instance, speak of democracy in feudal societies, yet it seems to be objectively true that the oppression of their producing classes, even including serfs, is restrained within limits governed by one or another form of the customary rules which we discussed previously.

Hence, it is legitimate to suggest that externally ruled societies in feudal and other pre-capitalist class modes of production were in a real sense less democratic than the autonomous societies. As to the capitalist epoch, it seems true that essentially all externally ruled societies, including colonies, semi-colonies, and neocolonies, are, and must be, less democratic than autonomous societies, that is, the metropolitan countries, again because of the imperatives of superexploitation and its constant companion, oppression. Nor is it certain that we must make an exception for advanced capitalist countries which are (or were until recently) fascist. There is no democracy under fascism, yet the most fearful characteristic of fascism is its ability to mobilize majority support for some, at least, of its inhuman policies. In externally ruled societies in which producers are superexploited, that is, in colonies, neocolonies, and the like, it seems likely that there is less consent, less constraint upon the rulers, than even there was in European fascist countries.

Consent is not the same as quiescence, that is, acceptance of externally imposed rule as a reality against which one may struggle but with the knowledge that liberation will take some time to organize. It is classically true that colonized peoples have seemed, to the colonizer and to literary travellers, to be consenting to their colonial condition, simply because life seems to be going on in a normal sort of way and signs of struggle are not apparent. One recalls in this regard the famous case of the French plebiscite in colonial Algeria, which seemed to show that 97 per cent of the people wanted to remain under French rule. Shortly thereafter the war of liberation broke out. After the French had been beaten, the Algerian government organized another plebiscite, asking the people whether they wanted to remain tied to France, and 97 per cent voted 'no'. So much for the appearance of consent.[32] In all colonies, with or without the evidence of an artificial plebiscite, the colonized people seem on the surface to be consenting to their condition until they are on the verge of winning their liberation, after which the idea that they had earlier consented to colonialism becomes ludicrous.[33] It is for this reason that I think we can support the proposition that there is no more real freedom in colonies than there is, or was, in the classical fascist societies. The proposition also holds true for some neocolonies. As I argued in Chapter 4, undemocratic states are essential for the maintenance of a political environment permitting superexploitation. One cannot really speak of consent in countries like Chile, El Salvador and Indonesia.[34]

The third of the salient differences in political process between externally ruled societies, with external exploitation of their working classes, and autonomous societies has to do with the fact that the struggle to seize the state is much more likely to be a viable short-run strategy for working classes in the former case than in the latter. In the latter, incremental victories are often to be won in the production process, in cultural struggles, in the winning of democratic reforms, and the like. In externally ruled societies, struggles are generally carried on in the midst of direct oppression and naked use of political power, and the direction of struggle tends, therefore, to turn towards the seizure of state power, or to do so more directly than is usually the case in autonomous societies. It is important to note here that the original imposition of external rule on a society is, itself, a nakedly political act. The state thereafter is intensely visible; its presence cannot be so easily mystified (as 'we the people', for example). And typically, though not in all cases of external rule, the state is more clearly, directly, and immediately the focus of class struggle than is true for autonomous class societies.

The fourth political difference concerns the relationship of classes in political struggle. The producers in externally dominated societies tend to be, as we have discussed, superexploited. This usually implies a superimposition of demands on those of the local (subordinate-society) ruling class. The posture of the local ruling class, as we saw, may vary from collaboration with the external rulers to opposition. Depending upon this posture, and of course upon a number of other variables – recall again that this discussion is supremely abstract, since its universe of discourse is the whole of class society – the producing class may find it advantageous to form an alliance with its own ruling class, or some fraction of that class, in a struggle to be rid of external dominance and superexploitation. Generally this seems to occur when, for whatever reason, the external (dominant) rulers truly undercut the class position and accumulation opportunities of the internal (subordinate) ruling class. But when this alliance occurs it tends to have major significance.

In pre-capitalist class societies wars were often waged without the masses of the producers becoming seriously involved: their participation was often limited to obligatory or mercenary military service, forced delivery of additional surplus, and the like. When rulers and producers were jointly involved in a struggle, this struggle tended to be qualitatively different. The whole society and indeed the whole of the culture shared by producers and rulers could now be directed towards the goal of struggle, and the struggle had a way of becoming much more intense, and much more successful. In many of the 19th Century European and Latin American national movements against external rule we find much the same process: most (not all) classes were mobilized towards a common political goal. Quite often the passions, irrationality (Hobsbawm), false glorification of national history (Nairn), appeal to folk heroes and symbols of national unity, invocation of the common religion, and the like, which tend to be traits of this kind of struggle, are denounced or satirized by theorists of nationalism, including as we have seen some Marxists. But there is passion, irrationality, etc., in all kinds of struggle including the struggle for socialism. And more concretely, the essential dynamic of unifying all patriotic classes and invoking all available symbols and attributes of unity may correctly reflect the logic of class struggle. Of course, it may not. There are countless cases of narrow nationalism in which the involvement of the producing classes reflects, not class interest, but simple false consciousness: mystification.

Probably the desideratum, in most cases though not all, is the presence or absence of superexploitation involving superimposed demands for surplus product. When producers are thus both externally and internally exploited, it tends to be to their advantage to fight against the external source of exploitation even if this involves some collaboration with internal exploiters, though only if the latter are truly engaged in struggle against external domination.

In anti-colonial struggles this logic of class struggle rather typically calls for some form of alliance between producing classes and those who are often described as 'patriotic local businessmen' – usually petty bourgeois figures, though middle-level bourgeoisie may occasionally join the ranks. It will be recalled that Lenin fought a major ideological struggle on this issue with those (like M. N. Roy) who considered it an abomination to make any sort of alliance, even a temporary one, with any bourgeois sectors in the anti-colonial struggle. Said Lenin, in effect, the national liberation movement must try to ally all anti-imperialist sectors.[35]

Now there is also a logic, under certain circumstances, to the forging of inter-class alliances in the advanced capitalist countries, as for instance in an effort to isolate monopoly capitalism from all other sectors and class fractions. But it tends to be a general, structural fact in externally dominated societies in which producers are superexploited and local elites are forced to fight to defend their class position from external attack, that some form of multiple-class alliance towards the seizing of state power is called for. In this sense, and noting many exceptions, there is a specificity to the politics of external class struggle, namely, the potential parallelism of class interests in opposition to external exploitation and rule.

We may conclude, then, that there is a degree of specificity to the politics of class struggle in externally ruled states, states in which the producing class has to cope with external exploitation. This specifically external form of class struggle is found in all class modes of production, though not in all social formations and geographical circumstances. In the modern world, dominated by capitalism, the politics of external class struggle becomes the national struggle.

## National Struggles and History

At the beginning of this chapter I undertook to broaden, or generalize, the theory of national struggle as class struggle, by taking up the question which had been posed in Chapter 1: is national struggle a feature of class struggle in general? I then proceeded to argue that there is a distinctive form of class struggle, and a form of the struggle for state power, which has been characteristic of certain societies and geographical circumstances in all class modes of production since ancient times. It is, briefly, the struggle for control of a state which is externally ruled, and in which external rule has the function of enabling what I have called external exploitation, that is, the peculiarly intense exploitation of the producing class or classes when part or all of the ruling class is from another society and another state. We concerned ourselves first with the various forms of external exploitation in differing epochs, then considered the inherent functions of external exploitation, or more properly its specific differences from internal exploitation, then examined the cultural nexus within which each form of exploitation is embedded, and finally considered the political implications of external exploitation and resistance to exploitation: external class struggle. We concluded with a summary of the specific political features of external class struggle in general, that is, in all class society.

Does it follow that national struggles go back to the dawn of class society? It does follow that a specifically external form of the struggle for state power is very old in class society. When we trace this form of struggle down to modern times it is clear that in all epochs, and in all class modes of production, this form has been both important and distinctively different from internal forms of struggles.

By concentrating nearly all their attention on the internal form, Marxists have not only built an incomplete model of class society, and of its history; they have also very seriously misinterpreted the nature of class struggles in externally dominated societies. Today these are, broadly speaking, the countries of the Third World, countries which share a common history of colonialism and in most cases a common experience of neocolonialism. Failing to perceive the specificity of their struggles, and the special oppression and superexploitation against which these struggles are fought, failing even to perceive these struggles *as* class struggles, many Marxists accept a model of the world in which the Third World sector is seen as relatively inconsequential for social change on a world scale, and social processes in this sector are reduced to the status of late-arriving diffusions from the metropolitan sector which have no historical potency. As I have tried to show in this book, many variants of the Marxist theory of nationalism or national struggle are flawed in precisely these ways. The 'idea of nationalism' is an artifact of diffusion. The 'bourgeois democratic revolution' is an artifact of diffusion. Like Sleeping Beauty, these societies have slumbered throughout history, waiting for the Prince to waken them. And the wakening, the national movement, is just that, an awakening; it is not a form of class struggle. There is no class enemy. And so on.

To avoid these illusions, modern struggles for national liberation should be seen against an historical backdrop of prior forms of struggles to seize state power from external ruling classes. The modern forms, like their predecessors, are class struggles, and class struggles of a relatively distinct type. But does it not follow that the entire social category should be labelled 'national struggle'?

The most important reason why we should reserve the term 'national struggle' for modern forms of external class struggle, those which take place during the lifetime (more or less) of capitalism, is precisely the importance of capitalism in this equation. National struggles of the capitalist era differ fundamentally from comparable pre-capitalist struggles for many reasons, reasons which boil down to the specific difference between capitalism and all prior forms of class society in the matter of external exploitation and class struggle. But these differences, as I argued at an earlier point in this chapter, are not absolute: there are many crucial processes which characterize class society in general, not merely capitalist society.

We have here two intersecting causal principles: the specific causality of external class struggles for state power, and the specific causality of political struggles within capitalism. National struggles can only be understood if both parts of the explanation are drawn together. In the case of national liberation struggles in Third World countries, we must take account of the fact that they are external class struggles, struggles fuelled by special oppression and by superexploitation, and struggles which are directed against external ruling classes and with their local allies. And we must take account of the fact that these societies are dominated by political forces unleashed by capitalism, with its special logic of accumulation and exploitation.

A second reason for reserving the concept 'national struggle' to external class struggles of the modern period is mainly a semantic matter but still an important one. This is the fact that it is sensible to bracket the term 'national struggle' with other important concepts labelled 'national', and notably the concept of the national state. Marx and Engels made a very sturdy argument about the importance to capitalism of forming moderately large states, and states which are relatively undifferentiated in cultural terms. This was classical bourgeois nationalism and the creation of bourgeois national states. The era during which these states emerged and grew powerful was indeed revolutionary in terms of the history of political forms, and all subsequent state forms, including socialist forms, have in some measure evolved from the primal capitalist national state.[36] (I prefer not to use the expression 'nation state' in this discussion because it tends to evoke the idea of a state with only one nationality or culture.) So it is appropriate to speak of national struggle as a matter which typically (but not always) involved forces struggling to create a national state and forces opposing this objective. (National struggle is *struggle*.) The objective may be a socialist state. It may be a multinational state. It may reflect some concept of federation without the loss of sovereignty, as in the political programmes of some native nations. It may take some other form. I would merely emphasize the semantic reasonableness of bracketing the notions of national struggle and national state. This is not to be confused with the Stalinesque dogma about 'the nation' with which we dealt in Chapter 5.

## National Struggles and Culture

The remaining task of this chapter is to examine some relationships between the theory of national struggle and two other bodies of ideas, one concerning the concept of the nation, the other the concept of culture. Both of these concepts have received some attention here already, but neither has been treated as really central, crucial, to the theory of nationalism. There is a widespread view among Marxists that the very heart of the theory is the exercise known as 'defining the nation'. The theory itself, in this view, is a theory of nations, and the principal application of the theory to instances of national struggle or the national question is a judgment whether a particular community engaged in some form of national struggle is, or is not, a genuine nation: if it is, its struggle may possibly deserve the support of progressives; if it is not, it does not. Period. Limited though this enterprise is, its very validity depends upon there being a definite and unvarying thing to be called a 'nation'. Stalin's 1913 essay, 'Marxism and the National Question', postulated such an invariant entity, and most Marxists who adopt this approach to the theory of national struggle also adopt Stalin's definition. In Chapter 5 I tried to show that Stalin's definition is not well-grounded and not very useful. But my basic argument is that we do not need a 'hard' (unvarying) concept of nation in order to construct a valid and useful theory of national struggle or nationalism.

From another quarter comes the thesis that 'culture' has much the same centrality for a theory of nationalism as Stalin accorded to 'nation'. This is mainly a conservative view, echoed by a few Marxists. Its traditional form is the once-famous 'principle of nationalities', the argument that each culture, or (synonymously) nationality, has some inherent urge to form its own separate state.[37] Today, pseudo-anthropological, pseudo-psychological, and even pseudo-biological arguments are added, to yield a theory which derives national movements, national aggrandizement, and indeed national frictions in general from a source deep in human culture or biology or both. The important point for the present discussion is that all versions of this theory deny that, first, national problems are rooted in exploitation; second, national struggle is a part of class society (it is, they say, as old as culture or older); and third, politics and the state are central to national struggle, not epiphenomenal.

Nations are important, not least to those who are trying to build nations and those who are trying to liberate nations. By the same token, culture is important, not least as an integrator of national states and as a dimension of liberation struggles. But to say this is not to reduce the theory of national struggle to a theory of nations or a theory of human culture. This point of view was implicit, at least, in the arguments of prior chapters and the first part of this chapter. In the following paragraphs I will try to make it entirely explicit.

## Nations

A distinction has to be made between two sorts of concepts of the nation, or two forms of definition for the word 'nation'. One is 'hard', the other 'soft'. The one asserts exactly what are the characteristics of all nations, and also asserts that the future political behaviour of nations can be predicted from these characteristics. The other, the soft concept or definition, merely gives a description of the sorts of things which are usefully labelled with the word 'nation'. In the Marxist literature, there are two very famous attempts to supply a hard concept, those of Bauer in 1907 and Stalin in 1913. Marx, Engels, Luxemburg, and Lenin never went beyond a soft concept; they did not try to give a technical definition to the word 'nation'.[38] For Bauer and Stalin, on the other hand, the idea that nations are definite, invariable, discoverable, highly predictable entities lay at the root of their theories of nationalism. As I explained in Chapter 5, Stalin defined the nation in terms of its invariable internal characteristics, all of which must be present in a community if it is truly a nation, and in terms of its invariable spacetime coordinates; ('. . . belonging to a definite epoch, the epoch of rising capitalism'); he then asserted that nations, and nations alone, enjoy the right of self-determination, that is, have a political biography, past, present, and future. Bauer, as I mentioned briefly in Chapter 2, used the same assertive form of argument, except that his definition was very different from Stalin's and conformed to his argument that nations do *not* have political biographies and do *not* have the right of self-determination.

Stalin's definition, and more consequentially his form of argument, became immensely influential in Marxist discussions about the national question. Few seemed to notice that Stalin really gave no theoretical grounding for the definition in his famous essay. Nowadays, as I showed in Chapter 5, the definition is only useful in describing one type of nation among several; most of the former colonies would not qualify as nations under this definition; nor would many other countries to which we would comfortably apply the word 'nation', such as Switzerland, Czechoslovakia, Denmark, and the German Democratic Republic (which emerged as a nation after the rise of socialism).

The specific definition is less important than the form of the argument. Can we look at the array of human communities and decide on the basis of fixed criteria which of them have the realistic potential to subsist, viably, as independent states? The answer is no. For one thing, viability relates to external as well as internal conditions. For instance, it takes nothing away from the revolutionary achievement of some of the younger and smaller socialist nations to say that their viability, their long-term ability to survive in a still largely capitalist world, has something to do with the fact that the world environment also includes larger, older, and more formidable socialist countries. For another thing, viability in one epoch may not be viability in another epoch, as witness the bisection of former Germany. But most crucially, the internal characteristics are predictors of viability only in a probabilistic sense: for instance, possession of a common language is a good integrative trait for a nation, but some multi-lingual states have achieved national integration, and have survived and flourished.

But notice, in addition, that the form of argument is like an equation: on one side are the necessary traits; on the other side is not simply the concept of nation, but the concept of politically independent state. In short: Stalin's definition of nations is really an effort, a good one for its time, to advise Marxists on the viability of states. He argued in essence: non-state communities occupying one space and possessing a single culture and an integrated economy can become viable states, though only in the period of rising capitalism ('since when have Social-Democrats begun to occupy themselves with "organizing" nations, "constituting" nations, "creating" nations?'[39]). The chief theoretical virtue of Stalin's definition and theory of nations was that it described the typical independent capitalist nation state of the 19th Century and showed (in part) why this kind of state was viable, cultural unity being a crucial factor.

We are no longer in the period when this model does us much good. We can get more use out of a soft concept of the nation. The one which I am comfortable with, and which I suspect (but cannot prove) was the concept in the minds of Marx, Engels, and Lenin, is roughly as follows. The term 'nation' is usefully applied to communities of two sorts. One is an independent state which is viable in the sense that it is unlikely to decompose or lose its independence. The other is a non-state community which clearly has the potential for becoming, and staying, politically independent. This potential is assessed in either of two ways; normally but not necessarily in both. One is the presence of fortifying, unifying characteristics, such as cultural and social integration, economic potential, size, and spatial coherence. The possession of a common piece of territory is crucial, in the sense that the community will have to have territorial expression when it has become an independent state: it will have to be the sole occupant of a space on the map. The second way of assessing the community's potential for becoming an independent state focuses on the national movement: is it a strong, popular, durable movement which, in the circumstances prevailing, is likely to win through to state independence in the future, near or distant? Guinea-Bissau, as Cabral pointed out, became a nation through its national movement and national struggle. 'Ten years ago we were Fula, Mandjak, Mandinka, Balante, Pepel, and others. Now we are a nation of Guineans.'[40]

There is a simpler and more direct way of expressing this soft and rather open concept of nation. We use the word 'nation' when we are talking about a political community. The word brings politics into any discussion about, for instance, a culture, a society, an economy. We may engage in any sort of discussion about Puerto Rico, for instance, but when we begin to talk about the Puerto Rican nation we are talking politics – serious politics: about the struggle for self-determination and independence. It is in precisely this sense that the concept of nation denotes something real, tangible, and important. There is a Puerto Rican nation because the people of Puerto Rico form a genuine, integrated culture and community and because they act together for a common political future. Something like this meaning emerges also in young independent countries which are struggling for integration and development: 'Our nation must have . . . must do . . .', and so on. Granted, this concept of the nation is not altogether precise; nor is it theoretically 'hard'. But no one has produced a concept which is so, and many have tried.

When we discard Stalin's definition, and the hard form of definition of the nation, we can produce a more meaningful theory of nations. We can, for one thing, look at communities empirically to decide their actual political potential, instead of depending upon a Stalinesque checklist. We can sensibly discuss socialist nations. And we can consider the possibility that some nations existed before the 'epoch of rising capitalism' without falling into the morass of mysticism which imagines that nations are as old as human culture, are, in Poulantzas' startlingly un-Marxist term, 'transhistorical'. This matter of pre-capitalist nations deserves a comment, by way of concluding our discussion about the nation.

Using a soft definition of the nation, we can certainly point to pre-capitalist nations, and not only to early modern, precocious nations and national movements. There seem to be two sticking points. One is our general theory of nationalism or national struggle. As we discussed previously, there can be no discussion of national struggle or nations in pre-capitalist eras if our theory simply asserts that national struggle itself is a product of modern capitalism. But, as I argue in this book, national struggle is class struggle, and the first class struggles in history occurred long before there was a bourgeoisie. The second sticking point is a little bit of Eurocentrism, expressed, typically, in the following proposition: before the rise of modern nations came the period of feudalism, which was one of extreme political fragmentation, hence of nothing that could be called a nation; and before that came the Roman Empire, again a polity that could not be called a nation; ergo, no pre-capitalist nations. But the political fragmentation which characterized medieval Europe (though not all of it, and not at all times) did not characterize some other regions in various pre-modern periods.

Suppose, for the sake of argument, that we were to apply the concept of nation as a description of historical societies which were politically independent states of some fair size and power and were reasonably well integrated communities in social and economic terms. We would allow for some degree of cultural differentiation, and for the fact that economic integration in pre-capitalist economies had to be somewhat limited (although the belief that pre-capitalist economies were completely unintegrated is another invalid generalization from feudal Europe). Given all of this, one could make a strong case that the following countries, among others, were nations during long historical periods: Vietnam, China, northern India (from the Mauryan period), Iran, Zimbabwe, Sudanic states (for instance Songhay), Egypt, France. My own preference, applying the reasoning used previously for the concept of national struggle, is to reserve the concept of nation for capitalist and socialist nations. But I cannot see that it makes much difference either way, so long as the concept of nation is congruent with the theory of national struggle; and so long as we accept the legitimacy of the claim by countries like Vietnam that their nations are very old; and so long as we avoid the dreary dogma that a country cannot be a nation until it is fully capitalist.[41]

## Cultures

The collective concept of culture, the idea of a community of people who hold a number of fundamental traits in common, language usually being one of these traits, has played a very important role in the theory of nationalism and in nationalism itself. As we discussed in Chapter 2, the first important European theory of nationalism, the mainly Hegelian Germanic theory, claimed that some cultures, the 'historic' ones, possess an innate need, right, and 'will' to become unified and sovereign states. The 'principle of nationalities' extended this to all cultures: 'Each nationality its state; each state its nationality.' (A 'nationality' in this sort of discourse is a culture.) 19th Century national movements in central and eastern Europe tended indeed to be grounded in particular cultures, and their struggles made important use of the culture's traditions. And, in general, there is no doubt that the pre-existing unity of a people, expressed in the facts which make it a single culture, is a powerful weapon in any struggle for independence. By no coincidence, the opponents of independence movements always try to destroy this unity and suppress the culture. In Puerto Rico, for instance, the United States has been trying without success since 1898 to suppress the Spanish language, and to destroy the consciousness of nationality. At the same time, the defence of Puerto Rican culture has been one of the most important arenas of struggle in the fight for independence.

All of this is fairly well understood in the Marxist theory of nationalism. Engels wrote about culture in relation to social evolution and to national struggle; in his 1866 essay, 'What Have the Working Classes to Do with Poland?' he developed what I think is the basal Marxist position on culture – he wrote of 'nationality' – and its relationship to the politics of national struggle, taking into account the importance of language, territory, external political context, and other factors, and he carefully distinguished the Marxist view from the 'principle of nationalities'.[42] Otto Bauer, in 1907, argued that a nation is simply a culture, from which he developed his argument that nations have nothing much to do with states; political implications aside, his treatise on nationality incorporated a profound analysis of (European) cultures and a very sensible set of ideas about defending minority civil rights.[43] For Stalin (1913), a nation is a culture with added attributes: definite territory, integrated economy, and historical emplacement in the period of rising capitalism; his discussion of cultural processes per se in the 1913 article is quite useful. In more recent times, Amilcar Cabral has written eloquently and profoundly on the role of culture, defence of culture, and culture unification, in the national liberation struggles of colonies; his analysis of this question is one of the most important new contributions to the Marxist theory of nationalism.[44] Other important new contributions have been made by Horace Davis, Roza Ismagilova, and many others.[45] This is not the most backward sector of the Marxist theory of nationalism, although serious problems remain to be solved.

But 'culture' is also the cloak for some very bad theories about the inherent nature of national struggle, its purpose, and its politics (or lack of politics). I will not go into detail on these matters now, but I will offer some generalizations about the views which place culture at the absolute centre of the national question and the theory of nationalism. Most importantly: there is a widespread view, found mainly in conservative thought but not unknown among Marxists, that a culture, sometimes called an ethnic group or nationality, is in some fundamental sense the source of national struggles, including the struggles for state independence and for territorial aggrandizement, and including also every sort of 'national friction' and 'ethnic conflict' among culturally different communities within states and between states.

All such views are variations of the thesis, criticized in Chapter 2, which describes nationalism or national struggle as an autonomous force: something unrelated to class struggle. The worst variant of this position turns up in fascist ideology and pseudo-science, in neo-racist doctrines like 'socio-biology', in the related right-wing animal fetishism of many 'ethologists' (I put this word in quotes because this school arose mainly as a political split from the science of animal ecology which, with its traditions going back to Kropotkin, was considered too socialistic by the early 'ethologists'), in more than a few college textbooks (including many in my own field of geography), and in many, many other places. It argues two juxtaposed theses: first, humanity is basically aggressive, acquisitive, competitive, bellicose (i.e., capitalistic). And second, people in groups, cultures, behave 'tribally', they naturally and inevitably engage in struggles with other groups, struggles for 'territory'. Such struggles emanate from a supposed instinct for 'territoriality', something bequeathed to us by our animal ancestors, and something which leads cultures to make war on one another, to fight for territory, for supremacy, and so on, *ad nauseam*.[46] This is often labelled 'social Darwinism', but, as Vladimir Novak has shown, it is not really Darwinian, but is rather a projection of the bellicose politics of some sectors of capitalist society today, who seek to persuade us that their point of view has the sanction of science – worse, is a reflection of true human nature.[47]

It would take me too far afield to discuss these unscientific doctrines in the present volume. Suffice it to say that even those versions of this view which seem mildest, least 'ideological', still postulate that human cultures, reflecting human nature, are innately given to struggling with one another, that is, to national struggle. There simply is no evidence to support this position. Or, to be more precise, the evidence that men and cultures are aggressive, territorial, and so on, is more than counterbalanced by the evidence that individuals and cultures are cooperative, social, sharing, and peace-loving. Yet this position is very nearly the conventional one in conservative social science. Even those social scientists (and others) who shrink from the suggestion that man is innately aggressive, territorial, and so on, allow the doctrine to slip in through various cracks in the wall: for instance, claiming that human territoriality is 'analogous' to animal territoriality, or falling back on the disguised Malthusianism (popular among some human ecologists) which argues that, food and other resources tending to be scarce, human groups naturally compete, and struggle with one another, instead of cooperating socially to distribute resources fairly and increase their aggregate availability – which tends to be what happens in the real world.

This doctrine of the innate antagonism of cultures offers a complete, packaged explanation for all problems of nationalism. Nationalism, supposedly, is natural. It has always been natural, and always will be. But if the illogicality, and ideology, of this body of doctrine be admitted, how shall we explain the importance of culture in national struggles? The answers to these and related questions are straightforward enough so that a skeletal argument should suffice for our purposes.

To begin with, we establish a historical base-line. There is no important evidence to suggest that cultures engaged in systematic struggle before the origin of class society. Conservative exponents of the doctrine of the innate territoriality of cultures are prone to point to examples of cultural struggles in putatively classless societies today as supposed evidence for the human past. But it is dangerously diffusionist to claim that attributes of classless societies today are a reflection of the pre-class past since these societies are always under intense pressure from class society, and ultimately imperialism: they are subject to forced requisitions, forced labour, forced compression of their lands or translocation from these lands, and the like. Even so, these few classless cultures are not notably bellicose. Furthermore, most struggles between so-called tribes are struggles within class society, as we noted in Chapter 2, and they too reflect the direct or indirect impact of imperialism. The pattern of exploitation and oppression in multi-cultural societies, colonies or former colonies, tends to be uneven, with some cultures holding privileged positions, either suffering less exploitation or participating marginally in the exploitation and oppression of other groups. Most of the inter-cultural frictions in supposedly classless (tribal) societies are frictions in and between class societies, and are incidents of class struggle.

Still, there remain the truly important inter-cultural struggles in class society, struggles mainly of two sorts: conflicts between state-organized cultures and conflicts between ethnic communities, cultures, within modern states. Some of these are genuine national conflicts. There is, I would suggest, a fairly straightforward argument which can show in principle that national struggles which incorporate whole cultures or whole ethnic communities are, like other national struggles, forms of the class struggle, and can be explained without invoking the idea of autonomous forces.

The essential principle is that class relations of production, and class struggles in general, are not something separate from culture: they occur within culture and make use of culture traits (like those of language), social networks, and the rest of culture as components of the exploitative process and the response to exploitation. This leads to various kinds of struggle which seem to be displacements of class struggle into non-class channels. For example, capitalism's need for a dual labour market, with a superexploited sector, in the urban centres of advanced capitalism, requires, as we saw in Chapter 6, the maintenance of ghettos, and this leads more or less directly to struggles over housing, which in turn seem to be conflicts between majority and minority communities, whereas in fact they are displaced conflicts between workers and capital. Other examples can be given in abundance of conflicts between culturally distinct groups on both the intra-national and international levels, in which the apparent basis for conflict is a matter of culture – it may, for instance, be religion, as in Northern Ireland today and in India at the time of partition – but the underlying forces are those of class exploitation, with its attendant oppression, and the resistance to both.

Much more needs to be said about this matter of national struggles which seem to be cultural conflicts but are, beneath the appearances, class conflicts. I will have to content myself here with a discussion of one of the least visible, yet most important, forms of the process which we describe as displacements of class struggle. I can best approach it by using a physical analogy. If external pressure is put upon an object, let us say, for instance, a piece of crystalline rock, and the object breaks apart, we have not one but two problems for analysis. One is the nature of the external force. The second is the way in which the object broke up: the shape and number and arrangement of pieces. In systems terms, a force acting on a system from the exterior will affect it, but in ways determined by the internal sub-systems. Thus, the cleavage planes, which determine the way in which an object breaks apart, must be analysed, along with the force acting on the object. This image of cleavage planes can be applied to cultures. Human beings live in groups of varying sorts and sizes, extending outwards from the family (of whatever type). Some of these groups are large, stable over time, and consequential in the sense that they strongly affect the behaviour of participant individuals. Any problem confronted by a population will tend to be passed on and responded to by the large, stable, consequential groups which structure it. I will call the boundaries between these groups cleavage planes. The two most important kinds of cleavage plane are whole-culture boundaries and state boundaries.

National struggle is class struggle, that is, it is fuelled by the exploitative behaviour of some classes towards other classes, understanding a class to be a group with some spatial definition (and not, e.g., all the workers of the world). Were it not for exploitation, there would be no serious and lasting oppression. The imposing of this exploitation and oppression on people of another community – what I have described in this book as external exploitation and external class struggle – is the nexus of national struggle. Now the way this struggle is carried out, and indeed the way external exploitation is carried out, will depend on the kinds of groupings in the societies which are involved. Some but not all of the units of social action will be whole cultures. Exploitation may, and in colonial situations usually does, attempt to make as much use as it can of the divisions between these groups: the cultural cleavage planes. Perhaps more typically, there is no deliberate plan to set groups against one another; there is, instead, one or another sort of exploitative or oppressive pressure on a large population such that the effect is, so to speak, a breaking up of the population along cultural cleavage planes, and conflicts between the differentiated groups, conflicts which represent a transmission of class struggle or a displacement of class struggle. The overall structure, described in the most general terms, would involve cleavage planes creating what Anselme Rémy has called 'ethno-class communities'. As the term suggests, there are two elements: first, exploitation, which produces class divisions, and second, the stable, large, consequential groupings of human beings, the cultures. Neither explains the other. Class struggle explains the *fact* of national struggle. Cultural and other cleavage planes explain many things about the *form* of the national struggle. The problem is much more complicated than this, of course, but further discussion will have to be left for another volume.

# Notes

1. On private property in land in medieval India, see, e.g., I. Habib, 'Structure of Agrarian Society in Mughal India', in B. N. Ganguli (ed.), *Readings in Indian Economic History* (1964); M. A. C. Liceria, 'Emergence of Brahmanas as Landed Intermediaries in Karnataka, c. A.D. 1000–1300, *Indian Historical Review* 1 (1974); R. S. Sharma, 'Indian Feudalism Retouched', *Indian Historical Review* 1 (1974). For a review of the evidence and its relevance to Marxist history, see, e.g., B. Chandra, 'Karl Marx, His Theories of Asian Societies, and Colonial Rule', in *Sociological Theories: Race and Colonialism* (1980).

2. V. I. Lenin, 'The State', *Works* 29.

3. On Poulantzas' description of nations as 'transhistorical', see Chapter 2 in this volume.

4. I pursue this argument in 'Where Was Capitalism Born?' *Antipode* 8, 2 (1976).

5. An exception would have to be made for egalitarian societies (the so-called 'nomads' and 'barbarians') which conquer other societies and impose themselves as a ruling class.

6. The classic statement of this proposition is in F. Engels, *Anti-Dühring* (1939 [1878]), pp. 198–199.

7. On slavery in China see, e.g., M. Elvin, *The Pattern of the Chinese Past* (1973), pp. 31–34. On India, see, e.g., R. S. Sharma, *Light on Early Indian Society and Economy* (1966), Chap. 5.

8. On tribute, see S. Amin, *Unequal Development* (1976), Chap. 1.

9. Among Marxists there is a strangely persistent, almost mystical belief that the facts of production are all aggregated at a single point in space; the movement of things somehow belongs to another sphere of reality, 'exchange' or 'circulation' (two terms meaning different things but placed together within this curious belief). Note that (1) there is a change of place in production as well as change of form, (2) physical enterprises engaged in moving raw materials, fuel, commodities – medieval sailing vessels, modern railroads, etc. – are productive enterprises (regardless of Wall Street's propensity to separate the 'industrial' and 'transportation' stock indices), with productive workers and production of value. The non-spatial idea of production, thing-fetishism, has led to some serious theoretical errors, many, and I think the most serious, of which relate to what I call here Eurocentric tunnel history, and to an underestimation of the importance of external exploitation and, in modern times, imperialism. For instance, dependency theorists are unfairly taxed with being 'circulationists', whereas the flows between the Third World or Tricontinent and Europe in the 16th–19th Centuries were *not* primarily involved in exchange, but were movements of commodities, or raw materials, typically within single international productive entities like the East India companies, the joint-stock plantation-cum-shipping companies, and agencies of the Spanish and Portuguese government. Ernesto Laclau subtly moves from this kind of argument (directed against A. G. Frank and others) to a conclusion that historical imperialism was somehow marginal to the development of capitalism. See Laclau's *Politics and Ideology in Marxist Theory* (1977). Not only is this tunnel-historical but it is also time-bound. When, for instance, Laclau maintains that (in essence) early imperialism was not capitalist because the production component (as against exchange) did not involve wages, he fails to notice that (1) wages and free labour were not dominant even in Europe at the same period while (2) wage labour was very important in colonial enterprises, shipping, military, etc. See Dale Johnson's

strong argument again Laclau *et al.*, in 'Economism and Determinism in Dependency Theory', *Latin American Perspectives* 8, 3–4 (1981).

10. In general, for a given agricultural technology, an increase in utilizable land per worker results in greater production per worker. I discuss this relationship for shifting agriculture in 'The Nature and Effects of Shifting Agriculture', in *Symposium on the Impact of Man on Humid-Tropics Vegetation* (1962). Thus when a given agricultural population is given expanded utilizable land, as in colonization, the total production and potential surplus will, in general, increase. Some highly intensive farming systems, like market-gardening, are, under some conditions, exceptions to this generalization.

11. For France, see C. T. Smith, *An Historical Geography of Western Europe before 1800* (1967), pp. 86–114. For China, see Elvin, *The Pattern of the Chinese Past*, Chapter 6. For India, see R. S. Sharma, *Indian Feudalism: c. 300–1200* (1965); L. Gopal, 'Quasi-Manorial Rights in Ancient India', *Journal of the Economic and Social History of the Orient* 6 (1963); B. N. S. Yadav, 'Immobility and Subjugation of Indian Peasantry in Early Medieval Complex', *Indian Historical Review* 1 (1974); for Sudanic Africa, see A. Smith, 'The Early States of the Central Sudan', in J. F. A. Ajayi and M. Crowder (eds.), *History of West Africa*, vol. 1 (1972).

12. A slave mode of production existed in most (all?) ancient class societies, but it was not usually the dominant mode, and its position in any evolutionary order is not entirely clear. For discussions of this problem, see M. Rodinson, *Islam and Capitalism* (1974), pp. 64–68, and I. Habib, 'Problems of Marxist Historical Analysis', *Enquiry* 3, 3 (1969). While we should avoid the old Marxist dogma that all societies pass through a slave 'stage', we must also avoid the Eurocentric tunnel-historical dogma that Europe alone, Greece and Rome, had a true 'slave mode of production', and that this somehow impelled Europe uniquely forward towards capitalism. (See the paradigm of this error, P. Anderson's *Passages from Antiquity to Feudalism* (1974).) Mostly, this erroneous argument is a chicken and egg matter: expansive, imperial societies, like some Greek states and Rome, acquire slaves in abundance, hence their exploited labour is crucial to the economy. Does slavery explain anything in these societies that is not more basically explained by imperial expansion? Which, then, is cause? Slavery was profoundly important in some advanced regions of Africa and Asia, just as it was in the advanced European Mediterranean. The problem is in part a matter of scale: comparing, e.g., Athens with all of China.

13. I pursue this question in 'Where Was Capitalism Born?' On feudalism in Asia and Africa see the works cited in note 11, above.

14. See Sharma, *Light on Early Indian Society and Economy*; and B. D. Chattopadhyaya, 'Trade and Urban Centers in Early Medieval North India', *Indian Historical Review* 1 (1974).

15. Some historians try to explain the rise of Europe in terms of European medieval inventiveness, supposedly not matched by contemporaneous societies elsewhere. The case is made most strongly by L. White, Jr., in his *Medieval Technology and Social Change* (1962). White simply ignores the fact that the critical innovations also occurred elsewhere, sometimes much earlier. His crucial argument, that the invention of a heavy plough explains settlement of the North European Plain and much else beside (for example, 'accumulation of surplus goods, specialization . . . urbanization', p. 44), cannot stand up to the fact that (1) heavy ploughs were used much earlier in North India (see D. D. Kosambi, *Ancient India* [1969]) and (2) the technological difference between northern heavy ploughs and

southern lighter ploughs is minimal, suggesting that feudal forces pushing cultivation into the heavy, wet, northern soils, explain the modification in technique, not vice versa. (For a critique of White from a conservative point of view, see J. Z. Titow, *English Rural Society, 1200–1350* [1969], pp. 37–42.) This issue is relevant to our discussion of externalization for two reasons: first, we attribute agricultural colonization of this sort to crises of accumulation, not to technology operating as an autonomous force; and second, the technological argument really dissolves into the Eurocentric ideological determinism which points, not to inventions, but to inventiveness, and maintains that only Europeans had, and have, this capacity. The classic position is Max Weber's truly bigoted claims for European 'rationality' (see his *The Protestant Ethic and the Spirit of Capitalism* [1958], pp. 13–31, and particularly p. 30, where he refers to 'differences of heredity'). Lynn White as much as admits, in another work, that his belief in the uniqueness of European inventiveness is grounded in his own religious faith: see his *Machina ex Deo: Essays in the Dynamism of Western Culture* (1968).

16. See, e.g., H. Wiens, *China's March into the Tropics* (1954).

17. See A. Das Gupta, *Malabar in Asian Trade: 1740–1800* (1967); esp. Chap. 4; S. Chaudhuri, 'Textile Trade and Industry in Bengal Suba, 1650–1720', *Indian Historical Review* 1 (1974); E. Rawski, *Agricultural Change and the Peasant Economy of South China* (1972); D. M. Nicholas, 'Town and Countryside: Social and Economic Tensions in 14th-Century Flanders', *Comparative Studies in Society and History* 10 (1967–68); F. C. Lane, *Venice: A Maritime Republic* (1973). On sugar in the Mediterranean (Egypt, Cyprus, Spain, etc.), see N. Deerr, *A History of Sugar* (1949–50). On Chinese pepper plantations in Southeast Asia, see J. L. L. Duyvendak, 'Chinese in the Dutch East Indies', *Chinese Social and Political Science Review* 11 (1927); V. Purcell, *The Chinese in Southeast Asia* (1951).

18. Marx and Engels called attention, for this period, to the importance of what I have called external exploitation, although they placed greater emphasis on intra-European processes. See Marx, *Capital*, vol. 1, Chapter 26–32; Marx and Engels, *The German Ideology* (1976), pp. 77–80.

19. As I argue in 'Where Was Capitalism Born', medieval mercantile–maritime centres of the Old World formed a single hemisphere-wide network or system, each node connected with all others in long-distance sea trade. This network connected ports of western Europe, the Mediterranean, the coasts of the Indian Ocean from Sofala to Malacca, insular Southeast Asia, and the China seas. In principle, any of the larger ports might have commissioned a voyage such as that of Columbus. However, centres with the requisite characteristics, technological and economic, were to be found in this period only in western Europe, East Africa (Sofala to Mogadishu), coastal southwest Asia, southern India, a few places in southeast Asia and southern China. All centres other than the European were very distant from the New World and subject to adverse climatic factors, notably the Westerlies off the Cape of Good Hope and the North Pacific storms. Early in the 15th Century the Chinese sent large expeditionary mercantile–naval fleets as far as East Africa, and it is known that Indian sailors explored into the South Atlantic; such voyages were easily as grand in scope as were the Portuguese voyages to Africa and Columbus's to the West Indies, and they took place many years earlier. I conclude that Europe's 'discovery' of the New World owes nothing to any attribute of level or rate of development not also found throughout the mercantile–maritime system of the Old World, and the single explanatory factor is distance: from the Canary Islands to Columbus's West Indian landfall was perhaps 2,500 miles; from Sofala or Calicut

the distance to South America is some 5,000 or so miles, or 7,000 to advanced West Indian civilizations like the Tainos. Across the Pacific the distances are greater still. No large mercantile–maritime centres are known for this period on Africa's western coast, probably because the great trade routes were continental, not maritime (as in much of eastern Europe and inner Asia), and the great cities were located inland. North African cities apparently were in a period of economic eclipse, prefigured by conditions described by Ibn Khaldun, and thereafter related to the Ottoman expansion. On the Chinese voyages (of Admiral Cheng Ho) see, e.g., Ma Huan, *The Overall Survey of the Ocean's Shores* ([1433] 1970); J. Needham, *Science and Civilization in China*, vol. 4 (1970). On Chinese long-distance trade in the period and replies to the myth of stagnation, see, e.g., J. Chan-Cheung, 'The Smuggling Trade between China and Southeast Asia during the Ming Dynasty', in F. S. Drake (ed.), *Symposium on Historical, Archeological, and Linguistic Studies on Southern China* (1967); Chang Teh-ch'ang, 'Maritime Trade at Canton During the Ming Dynasty', *Chinese Social and Political Science Review* 17 (1933–34); Purcell, *The Chinese in Southeast Asia*; So Kwan-wei, *Japanese Piracy in Ming China during the 16th Century* (1975); Ts'ao Yung Ho, 'Chinese Overseas Trade in the Late Ming Period', *Proceedings, 2nd Biennial Conference, International Association of Historians of Asia* (1962); Wang Gung-wu, 'Early Ming Relations with Southeast Asia', in *The Chinese World Order* (1967); Wiethoff, Bodo, *Die chinesische Seeverbotspolitik und der private Überseehandel von 1368 bis 1567* (1963); Wu Yu Kan, 'Chinese Overseas Intercourse and Trade in Ancient Times', *Eastern Horizon* 4, 2 (1965). On Indian Ocean trade and shipping in the period, see, e.g., R. R. Di Meglio, 'Arab Trade with Indonesia and the Malay Peninsula from the 8th to the 16th Century', in D. S. Richards (ed.), *Islam and the Trade of Asia* (1970); S. C. Jha, *Studies in the Development of Capitalism in India* (1963); A. Lewis, 'Maritime Skills in the Indian Ocean, 1368–1500', *Journal of the Economic and Social History of the Orient* 16 (1973); A. Chicherov, 'On the Multiplicity of Socio-Economic Structures in India in the 17th to the Early 19th Century', in *New Indian Studies by Soviet Scholars* (1976); P. Wheatley, *The Golden Khersonese* (1961); Frelimo, *História de Moçambique* (1971); Centro de Estudos Historicos Ultramarinos, Lisbon, *Documents on the Portuguese in Mozambique and Central Africa, 1497–1840*, vol. 1 (1962).

20. The inflationary pressure was transmitted on to Asia and, presumably, Africa. See A. Hasan, 'Silver Currency Output of the Mughal Empire and Prices in India During the 16th and 17th Centuries', *Indian Economic and Social History Review* 6 (1969). Also see K. N. Chaudhuri, 'Treasure and Trade Balances: The East India Company's Export Trade, 1660–1720', *Economic History Review*, 2nd ser. 21 (1968).

21. Simonsen estimates the value of Brazil's sugar export for the year 1600 at £2,258,300. Minchinton gives an estimate for total exports from England in 1601 of between £960,000 and £1,080,000. See R. C. Simonsen, *Historia Economica do Brasil, 1500–1820* (1944), p. 172; W. E. Minchinton, *The Growth of English Overseas Trade in the 17th and 18th Centuries* (1969), p. 9n.

22. I deal only with European capitalists here because our somewhat limited concern, for the period after 1492, is the internal and external economic sectors of European capitalism. Externality was to be found elsewhere, of course. For instance, Middle Eastern, Indian, and Chinese capital was important in this period in Southeast Asia. In this connection I should point out that my failure to deal with the New World in its own right, other than as an area of expanding European

forces, reflects the fact that complex economic and technological structures in the New World were largely destroyed in the Conquest. (The Conquest reflected two differential facts about the New World: its succumbing to epidemics of Old World diseases after contact, and its somewhat lower technology, particularly military technology, due to the fact that settlement of the New World occurred very late in human history, and was followed by technological evolution roughly paralleling Old World processes but taking place somewhat later.)

23. The ratio of slaves in British colonies to productive wage labour in England is estimated from Gregory King's data for England in 1688 (in P. Deane, *The First Industrial Revolution* [1969]) and Philip Curtin's data for slave populations in *The Atlantic Slave Trade* (1969).

24. On the Haitian Revolution, its character and significance, the classic work is C. L. R. James, *The Black Jacobins* (1963), 2nd edn.

25. On the expansion of colonial production in this period, see W. A. Lewis (ed.), *Tropical Development: 1880–1913* (1970).

26. 'Third World' is an ambiguous term, but it has entered ordinary discourse – particularly in the 'Third World' itself – and has a fairly (but not entirely) clear meaning in such discourse: it refers to that part of the world which was at one time under European colonial or semi-colonial domination. Many authorities object to the term because in its original meaning it postulated a 'third' world which was supposed to be neither capitalist (the 'First World') nor socialist (the 'Second World'). That original meaning, however, has been rather forgotten. The word 'Tricontinent' is probably a better term.

27. On the political economy of colonialism in Puerto Rico, see in particular *Puerto Rico: Class Struggle and National Liberation*, special issue of *Latin American Perspectives* 3, 3 (1976), esp. the article by J. Dietz, 'The Puerto Rican Political Economy', and the article by Economic Research Group, Puerto Rican Socialist Party, 'The Economic Importance of Puerto Rico for the United States'.

28. This concept of rule bears no relationship to structuralist metaphysics.

29. However, a small percentage of the internal (dominant-society) producing class, including some of those who participate directly in conquest, come to hold privileged positions in the productive enterprises in which foreign workers are exploited, gain higher material benefit in enterprises at home which are directly connected to and benefit from foreign exploitation, and the like. For this section, there may indeed be a significant improvement in level of living and class position: soldiers, for instance, often gain a share of pillage, and may be allowed the right to acquire some of the conquered land and even the right to exploit the foreign workers, thus in effect being recruited into a lower fraction of the internal (dominant-society) ruling class itself. To understand why broad masses of internal workers sometimes support the conquest and exploitation of foreign workers, as for instance English proletarians supported British colonialism in the 19th Century (see Engels' letter to K. Kautsky of September 12, 1882 in Marx and Engels, *Selected Correspondence* [1975], 3rd ed., pp. 330–31), we must, I think, return to the matter of rules. Ideological rules governing internal exploitation, and thus defining the status and rights of all participants in the process, evolve during a long period of time (and struggle) within a given society, but during all of this period their field of applicability remains the members of that society: they do not apply to foreigners. When the exploitation of foreign workers commences, the internal working class cannot be expected to demand automatically that these rules be extended to the foreign workers, even assuming that they have gained knowledge of the external

exploitation. This should not be considered 'false consciousness'. What we have in this type of situation, as it has repeated itself throughout history, is a particularly dramatic case of the power and partial autonomy of the ideological realm: the ideological rules themselves indeed have a material basis, but the fact that they do not apply to workers outside the society is a direct implication of the fact that they *do* apply to a particular, clearly defined set of human beings: those who are members of the society itself. It would take us too far afield to examine here the connection between these processes and modern racism.

30. See Lenin, 'The State', *Works* 29.

31. For Marx and Engels, see H. Davis, *Nationalism and Socialism* (1967). For Lenin, see Chap. 5 in the present volume.

32. On the Algerian plebiscites, see J. M. Abun-Nasr, *A History of the Maghrib*, (1975), pp. 336–40.

33. On the artificial plebiscites in Puerto Rico, which give the spurious impression that Puerto Ricans wish their country to remain a colony, see, e.g., L. L. Cripps, *Puerto Rico: The Case for Independence* Cambridge, Mass., (1974); L. L. Cripps, *Human Rights in a United States Colony* (1982).

34. In these exceptional cases like Malaysia and Venezuela there is at best formal, and partial, bourgeois democracy.

35. See Lenin's 'Report of the Commission on the National and Colonial Questions' of the 2nd Congress of the International, 1920, *Works* 31, pp. 240–45. For M. N. Roy's position (the so-called 'Supplementary Theses' submitted to the same Congress), see: G. Adhikari (ed.), *Documents of the History of the Communist Party of India* (1971).

36. But to say that all modern state forms evolved in some degree and in some ways from earlier capitalist state forms is not to argue – as Anthony D. Smith and countless other mainstream scholars argue – that the colonial state is somehow just a minor variation on the autonomous bourgeois–democratic state. Colonial states are absolutely unrepresentative and undemocratic, whatever local autonomy they may be allowed to exercise by the colonial rulers. See, e.g., A. D. Smith, *State and Nation in the Third World* (1983), pp. 25–36 and 87.

37. An exception is Otto Bauer's cultural theory of nations which identifies cultures with nations but explicitly denies the 'principle of nationalities'. See his *Die Nationalitätenfrage und der Sozialdemokratie* (1907), Chap. 15.

38. Although Lenin did not define the nation, it is clear from his writings that he would not accept the idea that a community which does not have a territorial base can be considered a nation. M. I. Isayev, in his informative work, *National Languages in the U.S.S.R.: Problems and Solutions* (1977), cites Lenin in support of his (Isayev's) view that a nation must have a common language. I believe this interpretation of Lenin's position is in error. Isayev cites Lenin as follows: '"The nation", he writes, "is not *Kultur-*, not *Schicksal-*, but *Sprachgemeinschaft* [language community]"'. But Lenin made this statement, in his reading notes, as a summary of Kautsky's views, not his own. See Lenin's *Works* 41, p. 316. Lenin never tried to define the nation, and this was not, I feel certain, an oversight.

39. Stalin's *Works* 3, p. 340.

40. A. Cabral, *Return to the Source: Selected Speeches of Amilcar Cabral* (1973), p. 78.

41. This dogmatism has emerged in Puerto Rican Marxist scholarship. A few scholars argue that Puerto Rico was not fully capitalist at the time it was invaded by the United States (1898), hence it was absorbed in the United States before it could

become a bona fide nation, with genuine national consciousness. The implication would be that Puerto Rico is not now a bona fide nation in political terms and that this fact, not the immense power and imperialist policies of the United States, accounts for the fact that the independence movement has not thus far been successful. These scholars, nonetheless, are strong *independentistas*. See, e.g., A. Quintero-Rivera, 'Notes on Puerto Rican National Development: Class and Nation in a Colonial Context', *Marxist Perspectives* 3 (1980). Intriguingly, Quintero-Rivera places at the masthead of his article this quotation from Lenin (1903): 'Class antagonism has now undoubtedly relegated national questions far into the background.' The whole weight of Lenin's work from 1914 forward was contrary to this position. Quintero-Rivera argues that Puerto Rico was a distinctly feudal society – he even uses the word 'seigneurial' – at the time it was invaded by the US (1898). But the remnants of feudalism in Puerto Rico at that time were no more salient than feudal remnants in most other colonies in the West Indies and around the world, and such remnants have not drastically impeded independence struggles in these other colonies. I profoundly respect Quintero-Rivera's efforts to analyse Puerto Rico's history as a basis for understanding her present and changing her future, but I think he fails to make a case that 19th Century Puerto Rico had attributes which would make it harder in this colony to win independence than it has been in other colonies. It seems to me that the differential factor is US power: the antagonist is stronger than others, though hardly omnipotent. Also see, for arguments similar to Quintero-Rivera's, History Task Force, Center for Puerto Rican Studies, *Labor Migration under Capitalism: The Puerto Rican Experience* (1979), which also argues that feudalism dominated before 1898, and that the US imposition of capitalism after 1898 created a single economic space embracing Puerto Rico, the US, and other regions and countries 'regardless . . . of political status', p. 104, thus obscuring the significance of colonialism in such matters as the migration to the US (which obtains a completely economistic explanation).

42. Engels, 'What Have the Working Classes to Do with Poland'? In: D. Fernbach (ed.), *Karl Marx: Political Writings* 3 (1974). Also see in the same volume Marx and Engels, 'For Poland'.

43. See note 37.

44. See in particular Cabral's 'National Liberation and Culture', in his *Return to the Source*. Also see other speeches and writings in this volume and in *Revolution in Guinea: Selected Texts by Amilcar Cabral* (1969); and see Cabral's speech, 'Declaration of Principles', in *Portuguese Colonies: Victory or Death* (1971) (condensed as 'The Weapon of Theory' in *Revolution in Guinea*).

45. H. Davis, *Toward a Marxist Theory of Nationalism* (1977); R. N. Ismagilova, *Ethnic Problems of Tropical Africa: Can They Be Solved?* (1978).

46. See, for instance, L. L. Snyder, 'Nationalism and the Territorial Imperative', *Canadian Review of Studies on Nationalism* 2, 1 (1975). Sober references to 'human territoriality', 'human aggression', and the like, are now routine in mainstream textbooks in Political Geography: see, e.g., Richard Muir, *Modern Political Geography* (1975).

47. See V. J. A. Novak, 'The Principle of Sociogenesis, Real Socialism, and the Problem of a Lasting Peace', *Antipode: A Radical Journal of Geography* 16, 1 (1984). Also see the volume by the same author, *The Principle of Sociogenesis* (1982).

# 8. In Place of a Conclusion

This book has argued that national struggle – 'nationalism' in the broadest sense of that word – is not an autonomous force or process: it is a form of class struggle. Nor is it only the class struggle of the bourgeoisie, 'bourgeois nationalism'. It is the contemporary form taken by a basic process within class society as a whole, going back to ancient times, namely, external class struggle, and more specifically the class struggle for state power when a ruling class is external or 'foreign'. Thus national struggle is engaged in by different class groups in different modes of production, both exploiting groups and exploited groups. Implied in this argument are a number of subordinate theoretical arguments, but three of them are given special attention here.

First, nationalism did not diffuse from Europe to the rest of the world and cannot be ascribed to the diffusion of 'modernization'. Second, nationalism bears no special, organic connection to fascism, or to any particular kind of social formation within capitalism. And third, the large-scale, long-distance labour migrations of the era of monopoly capitalism or imperialism do not, as a rule, lead to the creation of 'national minorities', communities which become assimilated and lose their national identity.

Most of these propositions are embedded within the traditional Marxist theory of nationalism or national struggle, originated by Marx and Engels and developed thereafter by Lenin and later Marxists, particularly those (like Amilcar Cabral and Fidel Castro) who write from the perspective of the national liberation struggle against colonialism. The theory has come under attack, but, as I think I have shown, the attacks are ineffectual.

Nonetheless, we do not yet have a complete, much less a perfect, theory of national struggle or nationalism. At least some of the profoundly difficult national problems of today's world would be more easily resolved in favour of human progress if our theory of nationalism were more satisfactory, more general, and more explicit. So this book has no conclusion.

In place of a conclusion, I will list several of the important issues of theory which have *not* been dealt with in this book, or have been dealt with only partially.

(1) Separatism in developed capitalist countries. We have seen that separatist national movements are forms of the class struggle for state power, but we have not examined the reasons why movements for state power may coincide spatially with cultures.

(2) Separatism in developed socialist countries. Marxists living in the capitalist world are likely to exaggerate the scope of this problem, although in some regions (for instance, southern Yugoslavia) it is very real. We do not yet have an adequate analysis of this phenomenon, but such an analysis will probably show that most cases reflect a form of class struggle which has little to do with the existence or non-existence of remnant classes. The typical case will probably resolve itself into some combination of three elements: direct intervention or ideological influence from capitalist countries, real problems in the construction of socialism (the persistence of some regional inequality, or of some great nation chauvinism, or of some old-fashioned bureaucratism), and the tendency of regional political movements, when they exist, to cleave along cultural lines.

(3) Native nations: what they are, and why their right to self-determination, to sovereignty, cannot be opposed by socialists. In Chapter 5 we saw that the old Stalinesque definition of 'nation' is not useful for colonial and neocolonial societies. This old definition (or theory), with its a priori judgement that nations arise only with the (internal) rise of capitalism, and that nations are fixed throughout history to a specific invariant territory, has been used by some Marxists to argue that native peoples, such as American Indians, do not possess or deserve 'the right of nations to self-determination'. When this inappropriate theory of nations is set aside, the Marxist view of this matter must change. Almost never have Marxists questioned the moral right of oppressed peoples to win equality with other peoples, including equal right to culture and to a self-chosen way of life. The problem for Marxists, almost always, has been a Stalinesque tendency to deny that native peoples can form viable sovereign (or co-sovereign) states, because they are 'national minorities' in process of dissolution. Setting this theory aside will simplify the problem. Under capitalism, native nations can viably, realistically, struggle for some control of land, for cultural survival, and for equality with other working people. In a socialist world, native nations will have the right to full self-determination, including state-independence or multinational co-sovereignty: viability will no longer be an issue. I think something that begins to approach this socialist solution may be emerging today. It cannot yet be put into effect in places where socialism is under siege, as in Nicaragua: here, as the Sandinistas have recognized, the immediate need is to guarantee the right of self-determination for native peoples as a principle and to provide regional autonomy for the troubled present. The problem of understanding native nations is terribly complex, but the starting point is basically the acceptance of the Leninist principle of self-determination and the rejection of old and inapplicable concepts of the nation.

(4) 'Nationalism' improperly invoked. Granting the fact that narrow nationalism may persist after socialists have won state power, it is nevertheless incorrect to declare every error of state policy, internal as well as external, to be due to 'nationalism'. Political errors are political errors, and they have to be analysed and understood, not consigned to a waste-basket category called 'nationalism'.

Much work remains to be done.

# Bibliography

Abdel-Malek, Anouar, *Nation and Revolution*, State University of New York Press, Albany, 1981

Abun-Nasr, Jamil, *A History of the Maghrib*, 2nd edn., Cambridge University Press, Cambridge, 1975

Acuña, Rodolfo, *Occupied America: The Chicano's Struggle Toward Liberation*, Canfield, San Francisco, 1972

Adhikari, G. (ed.), *Documents of the History of the Communist Party of India*, People's Publishing House, New Delhi, 1971

Amin, Samir, *Unequal Development*, Monthly Review Press, New York and London, 1976

—— *The Arab Nation*, Zed Books, London, 1978

—— *Class and Nation, Historically and in the Current Crisis*, Monthly Review Press, New York and London, 1980

Anderson, James, 'Regions and Religions in Ireland: A Short Critique of the "Two Nations" Theory', *Antipode: A Radical Journal of Geography*, vol. 12, no. 2, 1980, pp. 44–53

Anderson, Perry, *Lineages of the Absolute State*, New Left Books, London, 1974

—— *Passages from Antiquity to Feudalism*, New Left Books, London, 1974

Arrighi, Giovanni, *The Geometry of Imperialism*, New Left Books, London, 1978

Axen, Hermann, *Zur Entwicklung der sozialistischen Nation in der DRR*, Dietz, Berlin, 1973

Bauer, Otto, *Die Nationalitätenfrage und die Sozialdemokratie*, Ignaz Brand, Vienna, 1907

Bergman, L., Dolgin, G., Gabriner, R., McAdoo, M. and Raskin, J., *Puerto Rico: The Flame of Resistance*, People's Press, San Francisco, 1977

Berríos Martínez, Rubén, *La independencia de Puerto Rico: Razón y lucha*, Editorial Línea, México, D.F., 1983

Bettelheim, Charles, *Class Struggles in the USSR, First Period: 1917–1923*, Monthly Review Press, New York and London, 1976

Bhatia, B. N., *Famines in India: 1860–1965*, 2nd edn., Asia Publishing House, Bombay, 1967

Bishop, Maurice, 'Imperialism Is the Real Problem', in his *Selected Speeches, 1979–1981*, Centro de Estudios del Caribe, Casa de las Américas, La Habana, 1982

Blaut, J. M., 'The Nature and Effects of Shifting Agriculture', in *UNESCO Symposium on the Impact of Man on Humid-Tropics Vegetation*, Unesco and Government of Australia, Canberra, 1962

—— 'The Ghetto as an Internal Neo-Colony', *Antipode: A Radical Journal of Geography*, vol. 6, no. 1, 1974, pp. 37–42

—— 'Where Was Capitalism Born?', *Antipode: A Radical Journal of Geography*, vol. 8, no. 2, 1976, pp. 1–11. Reprinted in Peet (ed.), 1977

—— 'Are Puerto Ricans a National Minority?', *Monthly Review*, vol. 29, no. 1, 1977, pp. 35–55. In Spanish as 'Marxismo y la cuestion nacional: el caso de Puerto Rico', in *Revista Mensual* (Spain), vol. 1, no. 6, 1977, pp. 20–38, and in *Pensamiento Critico* (Puerto Rico), vol. 1, no. 2, 1978, pp. 1–11

—— 'Some Principles of Ethnogeography', in S. Gale and G. Olsson (eds.), *Philosophy in Geography*, Reidel, Dordrecht, 1979

—— 'The Dissenting Tradition', *Annals of the Association of American Geographers*, vol. 69, 1979, pp. 157–61

—— 'Nairn on Nationalism', *Antipode: A Radical Journal of Geography*, vol. 12, no. 3, 1980, pp. 1–17

—— 'El mito de la asimilación', *Claridad (En Rojo* supplement), 1 January 1982

—— 'Nationalism as an Autonomous Force', *Science and Society*, vol. 46, no. 1, 1982, pp. 1–23

—— 'Ghettos Are Real, Not Ideal', *Transition*, vol. 11, no. 4, 1982, pp. 10–13

—— 'Assimilation versus Ghettoization', *Antipode: A Radical Journal of Geography*, vol. 15, no. 1, 1983, pp. 35–41

—— 'Pringle on "Bourgeois Nationalist Ideology"', Etcetera', *Antipode: A Radical Journal of Geography*, vol. 14, no. 2, 1984, pp. 33–9

Blaut, J. M., Johnson, K., O'Keefe, P. and Wisner, B., 'Theses on Peasantry', *Antipode: A Radical Journal of Geography*, vol. 9, no. 3, 1977, pp. 125–7

Bloom, Solomon, *The World of Nations: A Study of the National Implications in the Work of Karl Marx*, Columbia University Press, New York, 1941

Bonilla, Frank, 'Puerto Ricans in the United States and Puerto Ricans in Puerto Rico', *Journal of Contemporary Puerto Rican Thought*, vol. 2, no. 2–3, 1975, pp. 65–9

—— 'Beyond Survival: Por que seguiremos siendo Puertorriqueños', in López and Petras (eds.), *Puerto Rico and Puerto Ricans*, pp. 439–51

—— 'Clase y nación: elementos para una discusión', unpublished essay, 1978

—— 'Ethnic Orbits: The Circulation of Capitals and Peoples', *Contemporary Marxism*, no. 10, 1985, pp. 148–67

—— and Campos, Ricardo, 'A Wealth of Poor: Puerto Ricans in the New Economic Order', *Daedalus*, Spring, 1981, pp. 133–76

—— and Campos, Ricardo, 'Imperialist Initiatives and the Puerto Rican Worker: from Foraker to Reagan', *Contemporary Marxism*, no. 5, 1982, pp. 1–18

Bottomore, T., and Goode, P., *Austro-Marxism*, Oxford University Press, Oxford, 1978

Brutents, K. N., *National Liberation Revolutions Today*, 2 vols., Progress, Moscow, 1977

Bryce-Laporte, R. S. (ed.), *Sourcebook on the New Immigration*, Transaction Books, New Brunswick, 1980

Cabral, Amilcar, *Revolution in Guinea: Selected Texts*, Monthly Review Press, New York and London, 1969

—— 'Declaration of Principles', in Cabral and others, *Portuguese Colonies: Victory or Death*, Tricontinental, La Habana, 1971

—— 'National Liberation and Culture', in *Return to the Source: Selected Speeches of Amilcar Cabral*, Monthly Review Press, New York and London, 1973

—— *Unity and Struggle: Speeches and Writings of Amilcar Cabral*, Monthly Review Press, New York and London, 1979

Campos, Ricardo, and Bonilla, Frank, 'Industrialization and Migration: Some Effects on the Puerto Rican Working Class', *Latin American Perspectives*, vol. 3, no. 3, 1976, pp. 66–108

—— and Bonilla, Frank, 'Bootstraps and Enterprise Zones: The Underside of Late Capitalism in Puerto Rico and the United States', *Review*, vol. 4, 1982, pp. 556–590

—— and Flores, Juan, 'Migración y cultura nacional Puertorriqueñas: perspectivas proletarias', in Quintero and others, *Puerto Rico: Indentidad nacional*, pp. 81–146

Cardoso, L. A., *Mexican Emigration to the United States, 1871–1931*, University of Arizona Press, Tucson, 1980

Carr, E. H., *Conditions of Peace*, Macmillan, New York, 1942

—— *A History of Soviet Russia: The Bolshevik Revolution, 1917–1923*, vol. 1, Macmillan, New York, 1951

Castells, Manuel, 'Immigrant Workers and Class Struggles in Advanced Capitalism', in R. Cohen and others (eds.), *Peasants and Proletarians: The Struggles of Third World Workers*, Monthly Review, London, 1979

Castro, Fidel, 'The Revolution in Power: From Reform to Revolution', in M. Kenner and J. Petras (eds.), *Fidel Castro Speaks*, Grove Press, New York, 1969

Centro de Estudios Puertorriqueños, *Taller de Migración: Conferencia de Historiografía, Abril 1974*, Centro de Estudios Puertorriqueños, New York, 1975

Centro de Estudos Historicos Ultramarinos, *Documents on the Portuguese in Mozambique and Central Africa, 1497–1840*, vol. 1, CEHU, Lisbon, 1962

Césaire, Aimé, *Discourse on Colonialism*, Monthly Review Press, New York and London, 1972

Chan-Cheung, John, 'The Smuggling Trade between China and Southeast Asia during the Ming Dynasty', in F. Drake (ed.) *Symposium on Historical, Archaeological, and Linguistic Studies on Southern China*, Hong Kong, 1967

Chandra, Bipan, 'Karl Marx, His Theories of Asian Societies, and Colonial Rule', in UNESCO, *Sociological Theories: Race and Colonialism*, UNESCO, Paris, 1980

Chang Chih-i, *The Party and the National Question in China*, MIT Press, Cambridge, Mass., 1966

Chang Teh-ch'ang, 'Maritime Trade at Canton During the Ming Dynasty', *Chinese Social and Political Science Review*, vol. 17, 1933–34, pp. 264–82

Chattopadhyaya, B. D., 'Trade and Urban Centers in Early Medieval North India', *Indian Historical Review*, vol. 1, 1974, pp. 203–19

Chaudhuri, K. N., 'Treasure and Trade Balances: The East India Company's Export Trade, 1660–1720', *Economic History Review*, 2nd series, vol. 21, 1968, pp. 480–503

Chaudhuri, Sushil, 'Textile Trade and Industry in Bengal Suba, 1650–1720', *Indian Historical Review*, vol. 1, 1974, pp. 262–78

Chicherov, Alexander, 'On the Multiplicity of Socio-Economic Structures in India in the 17th to the Early 19th Century', in *New Indian Studies by Soviet Scholars*, Problems of the Contemporary World, no. 33, *Social Sciences Today* Editorial Board, Moscow, 1977

Churchill, Ward (ed.), *Marxism and Native Americans*, Southend Press, Boston, 1983

Claudín, Fernando, *The Communist Movement: From Comintern to Cominform*, Part 1, Monthly Review Press, New York and London, 1975

Cobban, Alfred, *National Self-Determination*, revised edn., University of Chicago Press, Chicago, 1951

Colectivo Socialista de San Juan, 'Marxismo o independentismo socialista?' *Pensamiento Crítico*, año 5, no. 35, 1983, pp. 38–44

El Comité, Comisión Sobre Cuestión Nacional, 'Crítica a una perspectiva nacionalista de la cuestión nacional', *Pensamiento Crítico*, año 1, no. 5–6, 1978, pp. 1–12

*Congress of the Peoples of the East, Baku, September, 1920: Stenographic Report*, translated and annotated by Brian Pearce, New Park Publications, London, 1977

Cripps, L. L., *Puerto Rico: The Case for Independence*, Schenkman, Cambridge, Mass., 1974

——— *Human Rights in a United States Colony*, Schenkman, Cambridge, Mass., 1982

Cuba, Communist Party, *First Congress of the Communist Party of Cuba: Collection of Documents*, Progress, Moscow, 1976

Curtin, Philip, *The Atlantic Slave Trade*, University of Wisconsin Press, Madison, 1969

Dalberg-Acton, J. E. E., *The History of Freedom and Other Essays*, J. Figgis and R. Lawrence (eds.), London, 1922

Daniels, R. V., *The Conscience of the Revolution*, Simon and Schuster, New York, 1960

Das Gupta, A., *Malabar in Asian Trade*, Cambridge University Press, Cambridge, 1967

Davis, George, O., and Donaldson, Fred, *Blacks in the United States: A Geographic Perspective*, Houghton-Mifflin, Boston, 1975

Davis, Horace B., *Nationalism and Socialism: Marxist and Labour Theories of Nationalism to 1917*, Monthly Review Press, New York and London, 1967

——— *Toward a Marxist Theory of Nationalism*, Monthly Review Press, New York and London, 1978

Deane, Phyllis, *The First Industrial Revolution*, Cambridge University Press, Cambridge, 1969

Debray, Régis, 'Marxism and the National Question: Interview with Régis Debray', *New Left Review*, no. 105, 1977, pp. 25–41

Deerr, Noel, *A History of Sugar*, 2 vols., London, Chapman and Hall, 1949–1950

Delgado Pasapera, Germán, *Puerto Rico: sus luchas emancipadoras*, Ed. Cultural, Río Piedras, P. R., 1984

Deutsch, Karl, *Nationalism and Communication*, 2nd edn., MIT Press, Cambridge, Mass., 1966

——— *Nationalism and Its Alternatives*, Knopf, New York, 1969

Diaz Quiñones, Arcadio, *Conversación con José Luis González*, Huracán, Río Piedras, P. R., 1976

Dietz, James, 'The Puerto Rican Political Economy', *Latin American Perspectives*, vol. 3, no. 3, 1976

Di Meglio, R. R., 'Arab Trade with Indonesia and the Malay Peninsula from the 8th to the 16th Century', in D. Richards (ed.) *Islam and the Trade of Asia*, Oxford University Press, Oxford, 1970

Duyvendak, J. L. L., 'Chinese in the Dutch East Indies', *Chinese Social and Political*

*Science Review*, vol. 11, 1927, pp. 1–15

Economic Research Group, Puerto Rican Socialist Party, 'The Economic Importance of Puerto Rico for the United States', *Latin American Perspectives*, vol. 3, no. 3, 1976, pp. 46–65

Ehrenreich, John, 'The Theory of Nationalism: A Case of Underdevelopment', *Monthly Review*, vol. 27, no. 1, 1977, pp. 57–61

—— 'Socialism, Nationalism and Capitalist Development', *Review of Radical Political Economics*, vol. 15, no. 1, 1983, pp. 1–40

Elvin, Mark, *The Pattern of the Chinese Past*, Stanford University Press, Stanford, 1973

Engels, Frederick, *Anti-Dühring*, International, New York, 1939

—— 'What Have the Working Classes To Do With Poland?' in D. Fernbach (ed.) *Karl Marx: Political Writings*, vol. 3, Vintage, New York, 1974

—— Letter to K. Kautsky, Feb. 7. 1882. In B. Kautsky (ed.), *Friedrich Engels Briefwechsel mit Karl Kautsky*, Vienna, 1955

—— Letter to K. Kautsky, Sept. 12, 1882. In Marx and Engels, *Selected Correspondence*, 3 edn., Progress, Moscow, 1975

—— *Ludwig Feuerbach and the End of Classical German Philosophy*, Foreign Languages Press, Peking, 1976

—— explanatory note to the 1888 English edn., *Manifesto of the Communist Party*, in Marx and Engels *Works* (MEW), vol. 6, p. 482

—— 'The Beginning of the End in Austria', MEW, vol. 6, pp. 530–36

—— articles in the *Neue Rheinische Zeitung* on the Poland debates in the Frankfurt Assembly, 1848. In MEW, vol. 7, pp. 337–82

—— 'What Is to Become of Turkey in Europe?' MEW, vol. 12, pp. 32–5

—— 'Po and Rhine', MEW, vol. 16, pp. 211–55

Fichte, J. G., *Addresses to the German Nation*, Chicago, Open Court, 1922

Figueroa, Loida, *Historiografía de Puerto Rico*, Paraninfo, Madrid, 1975

—— *Breve historia de Puerto Rico*, Editorial, Edil, Río Piedras, 1971

—— *History of Puerto Rico, From the Beginning to 1898*, New York, 1972

Frelimo, História de Moçambique, Afrontamiento, Maputo, 1971

Galiñanes, Maria Teresa B. de (ed.), *Geovisión de Puerto Rico*, Editorial Universitaria, University of Puerto Rico, Río Piedras, 1977

Gellner, Ernest, *Thought and Change*, Weidenfeld and Nicolson, London, 1964

—— 'Nationalism', *Theory and Society*, vol. 10, 1981

—— *Nations and Nationalism*, Cornell University Press, Ithaca, 1983

Goblet, Y. M., *Political Geography and the World Map*, Praeger, New York, 1955

Godelier, Maurice, *Sobre el modo de producción asiático*, Ediciones Martínez Roca, Barcelona, 1969

Gómez-Quiñones, Juan, and Ríos-Bustamente, Antonio, 'La comunidad mexicana al norte del Río Bravo' in D. Maciel (ed.), *La otra cara de México: El pueblo chicano*, Ediciones El Caballito, México, D. F., 1977

González, José Luis, *El país de cuatro pisos, y otros ensayos*, Ediciones Huracán, Río Piedras, 1980

Gopal, Lallanji, 'Quasi-Manorial Rights in Ancient India', *Journal of the Economic and Social History of the Orient*, vol. 6, 1963, pp. 296–308

Gramsci, Antonio, *Prison Notebooks*, Lawrence and Wishart, London, 1971

Habib, Irfan, 'Structure of Agrarian Society in Mughal India', in B. N. Ganguli (ed.), *Readings in Indian Economic History*, Asia Publishing House, Bombay, 1964

—— 'Problems of Marxist Historical Analysis', *Enquiry*, new series vol. 3, 1969, pp. 52–67

Harris, Nigel, *Beliefs in Society*, Penguin, Harmondsworth, 1971

Hasan, Aziza, 'Silver Currency Output of the Mughal Empire and Prices in India during the 16th and 17th Centuries', *Indian Economic and Social History Review*, vol. 6, 1969, pp. 85–116

Haupt, George, 'Rosa Luxemburg y la cuestión nacional', *Cuadernos políticos*, no. 21, 1979, pp. 75–90

Hayes, C. J. H., 'Nationalism', in E. Seligman (ed.), *Encyclopedia of the Social Sciences*, Vol. 11, Macmillan, New York, 1933, pp. 231–49

—— *Nationalism: A Religion*, Macmillan, New York, 1960

Hegel, G. W. F., *Philosophy of Right*, Oxford University Press, Oxford, 1952

—— *The Philosophy of History*, Dover, New York, 1956

Herder, J. G. von, *Reflections on the Philosophy of the History of Mankind*, abridged and translated by T. Manuel, University of Chicago, Chicago, 1968

History Task Force, Centro de Estudios Puertorriqueños, *Labor Migration Under Capitalism: The Puerto Rican Experience*, Monthly Review Press, New York, 1979

Hobsbawm, Eric, *The Age of Revolution: 1789–1848*, World, New York, 1962

—— 'The Attitude of Popular Classes towards National Movements for Independence', in *Mouvements Nationaux d'Independance et Classes Populaires*, vol. 1, Armand Colin, Paris, 1971

—— 'Some Reflections on Nationalism', in T. Nossiter and others (eds.), *Imagination and Precision in the Social Sciences*, Faber and Faber, London, 1972

—— *The Age of Capital: 1848–1875*, Scribner's New York, 1975

—— 'Some Reflections on "The Break-Up of Britain"', *New Left Review*, no. 105, 1977

—— *The History of Marxism*, vol. 1, Indiana University Press, Bloomington, 1982

—— *Workers: Worlds of Labour*, Pantheon, New York, 1984

—— and T. Ranger (eds.), *The Invention of Tradition*, Cambridge University Press, Cambridge, 1983

Ho Chi Minh, *Ho Chi Minh, Selected Articles and Speeches: 1920–1967*, ed. J. Woddis, International, New York, 1970

Hopkins, A. G., *An Economic History of West Africa*, Columbia University Press, New York, 1973

International Working-Men's Association, *The General Council of the First International, 1871–1872: Minutes*, Progress Publishers, Moscow, 1968

Isayev, M. I., *National Languages in the USSR: Problems and Solutions*, Progress, Moscow, 1977

Ismagilova, R. N., *Ethnic Problems of Tropical Africa*, Progress, Moscow, 1978

James, C. L. R., *The Black Jacobins*, 2nd edn., Vintage, New York, 1963

Jha, S. C., *Studies in the Development of Capitalism in India*, Mukhopadhyay, Calcutta, 1963

Johnson, Dale, 'Economism and Determinism in Marxist Theory', *Latin American Perspectives*, vol. 8, nos. 3–4, 1981, pp. 108–118

Kaltajchian, Suren, 'El concepto de "nación"', *Historia y sociedad*, 2nd series, no. 8, 1975, pp. 20–37

Kamenka, Eugene (ed.), *Nationalism, the Nature and Evolution of an Idea*, Edward Arnold, London, 1976

Kautsky, Karl, 'La nacionalidad moderna' ('Die moderne Nationalität'), in K.

Kautsky and others (anthology), *La segunda internacional y el problema nacional y colonial*, part 1, Cuadernos de pasado y presente no. 73, México, D. F., 1978

Kedourie, Elie, *Nationalism*, Hutchinson, London, 1960

—— *Nationalism in Asia and Africa*, World, New York, 1970

Kim, Yong Mok, 'The Korean Minority in Japan and Their Dilemma of Cultural Identity', in T. S. Kang (ed.), *Nationalism and the Crises of Ethnic Minorities in Asia*, Greenwood, Westport and London, 1979

Kohn, Hans, 'Nationalism', *International Encyclopedia of the Social Sciences*, 2nd edn., vol. 11, Macmillan, New York, 1968, pp. 63–70

Kosambi, D. D., *Ancient India*, Meridian, New York, 1969

Laclau, Ernesto, *Politics and Ideology in Marxist Theory*, New Left Books, London, 1977

Lane, Frederic, *Venice: A Maritime Republic*, Johns Hopkins University Press, Baltimore, 1973

*Latin American Perspectives*, special issue, *Puerto Rico: Class Struggle and National Liberation*, vol. 3, no. 3, 1976

Le Duan, *This Nation and Socialism Are One*, Vanguard, Chicago, 1976

Lenin, V. I., *Collected Works* (cited here as *Works*), Progress, Moscow, various dates

—— 'The "Vexed Questions" of Our Party: The "Liquidationist" and "National" Questions', *Works*, vol. 18, pp. 405–12

—— Letter to S. G. Shahumyan, December 6, 1913, *Works*, vol. 19, pp. 499–502

—— 'The National Programme of the R.S.D.L.P.', *Works*, vol. 19, pp. 539–45

—— 'Critical Remarks on the National Question', *Works*, vol. 20, pp. 17–51

—— 'The Right of Nations to Self-Determination', *Works*, vol. 20, pp. 393–455

—— 'The Question of Peace', *Works*, vol. 21, pp. 290–94

—— 'Socialism and War', *Works*, vol. 21, pp. 295–338

—— 'The Revolutionary Proletariat and the Right of Nations to Self-Determination', *Works*, vol. 21, pp. 407–14

—— 'The Socialist Revolution and the Right of Nations to Self-Determination: Theses', *Works*, vol. 22, pp. 150–52

—— 'Imperialism: The Highest Stage of Capitalism', *Works*, vol. 22, pp. 185–304

—— 'The Discussion of Self-Determination Summed Up', *Works*, vol. 22, pp. 320–60

—— 'The Nascent Trend of Imperialist Economism', *Works*, vol. 23, pp. 13–21

—— 'Reply to P. Kievsky (Y. Pyatakov)', *Works*, vol. 23, pp. 22–27

—— 'A Caricature of Marxism and Imperialist Economism', *Works*, vol. 23, pp. 28–76

—— 'Imperialism and the Split in Socialism', *Works*, vol. 23, pp. 105–120

—— 'War and Revolution', *Works*, vol. 24, pp. 400–421

—— 'Revision of the Party Programme', *Works*, vol. 26, pp. 149–78

—— 'The State', *Works*, vol. 29, pp. 470–88

—— '"Left-Wing" Communism – an Infantile Disorder', *Works*, vol. 31, pp. 17–118

—— 'Preliminary Draft Theses on the National and Colonial Questions', *Works*, vol. 31, pp. 144–51

—— 'Terms of Admission into the Communist International', *Works*, vol. 31, pp. 206–11

—— 'Report on the International Situation', *Works*, vol. 31, pp. 215–34

—— 'Report of the Commission on the National and the Colonial Questions',

*Works*, vol. 31, pp. 240–45

—— 'The Question of Nationalities or "Autonomisation"', *Works*, vol. 36, pp. 605–11

—— Notes for a lecture on 'imperialism and the right of nations to self-determination' given in Geneva, October, 1915, *Works*, vol. 39, pp. 735–42

—— 'Theses for a Lecture on the National Question', *Works*, vol. 41, pp. 313–23

Lerner, Warren, *Karl Radek: The Last Internationalist*, Stanford University Press, Stanford, 1970

Lewis, Archibald, 'Maritime Skills in the Indian Ocean, 1368–1500', *Journal of Economic and Social History of the Orient*, vol. 16, 1973, pp. 238–64

Lewis, Gordon, *Puerto Rico: Freedom and Power in the Caribbean*, Monthly Review Press, New York and London, 1963

——*Notes on the Puerto Rican Revolution*, Monthly Review Press, New York and London, 1974

Lewis, W. Arthur (ed.), *Tropical Development: 1880–1913*, Northwestern University Press, Evanston, 1970

Liceria, M. A. A., 'Emergence of Brahmanas as Landed Intermediaries in Karnataka, c. A.D. 1000–1300', *Indian Historical Review*, vol. 1, 1974

Lidin, Harold, *History of the Puerto Rican Independence Movement*, vol. 1 (19th Century), San Juan, 1981

López, Adelberto, and Petras, James (eds.), *Puerto Rico and Puerto Ricans*, Wiley, New York, 1974

López, José A. (ed.), *Puerto Rican Nationalism: A Reader*, Editorial Coquí, Chicago, 1977

Löwith, Karl, *From Hegel to Nietzsche*, Doubleday, Garden City, 1964

Löwy, Michael, 'Marxism and the National Question', in R. Blackburn (ed.) *Revolution and Class Struggle: A Reader in Marxist Politics*, Fontana, Glasgow, 1977

Luxemburg, Rosa, *The National Question: Selected Writings of Rosa Luxemburg*, edited and with an introduction by Horace B. Davis, Monthly Review Press, New York and London, 1976

—— Foreword to the anthology, *The Polish Question and the Socialist Movement* (1905). In her *The National Question . . .* , pp. 60–100

—— 'The National Question and Autonomy', In her *The National Question . . .* , pp. 101–288

—— 'The Crisis of Social Democracy', (the 'Junius pamphlet'), in *Rosa Luxemburg Speaks*, ed. Mary-Alice Waters, Pathfinder Press, New York, 1970

Macartney, C. A., *National States and National Minorities*, 2nd edn., Russell and Russell, New York, 1968

Ma Huan, *The Overall Survey of the Ocean's Shores*, Cambridge University Press, Cambridge, 1970

Maldonado-Denis, Manuel, *Puerto Rico: A Socio-Historic Interpretation*, 4th edn., Vintage, New York, 1972

——'Prospects for Latin American Nationalism: The Case of Puerto Rico', *Latin American Perspectives*, vol. 3, no. 3, 1976, pp. 36–45

—— 'El nacionalismo en Puerto Rico: una approximación crítica', *Historia y Sociedad*, no. 13, 2nd series, 1977, pp. 47–69

—— *Hacia una interpretación marxista de la historia de Puerto Rico, y otros ensayos*, Editorial Antillana, Río Piedras, 1977

——*The Emigration Dialectic: Puerto Rico and the USA*, International, New York, 1980

—— 'En torno a "el pais de cuatro pisos": approximación crítica a la obra sociológica de José Luis González', *Casa de las Américas*, no. 135, 1982, pp. 151–159

—— 'Puerto Rican Emigration: Proposals for its Study', *Contemporary Marxism*, no. 5, 1982, pp. 19–26

—— *Pedro Albizu Campos: la conciencia nacional Puertorriqueña*, Ediciones Compromisos, San Juan, 1984

—— 'Puerto Rico: The National and Social Struggle during the 20th Century', in López and Petras (eds.), *Puerto Rico and Puerto Ricans*

Mao Tse-Tung, 'On New Democracy', in his *Selected Works*, vol. 2, Foreign Languages Press, Peking, 1967

Mari Brás, Juan, 'Albizu Campos: His Historical Significance', in I. Zavala and R. Rodríguez (eds.), *The Intellectual Roots of Independence: An Anthology of Political Essays*, Monthly Review Press, London, 1980

—— *Puerto Rico: el otro colonialismo: intervenciones en la Organización de Naciones Unidas y el Movimiento de Paises No-Alineados (1973–1981)*, San Juan, Partido Socialista Puertorriqueño, 1982

—— *El independentismo: su pasado, su presente, y su futuro*, Editorial Cepa, San Juan, 1984

Marx, Karl, *Contribution to the Critique of Hegel's Philosophy of Law*, MEW, vol. 13, pp. 3–129

—— *Capital*, 3 vols., Fowkes translation, Random House, New York, 1977–1981

—— and Engels, Frederick, *Collected Works* (cited here as MEW), International Publishers, New York, various dates

—— —— *The German Ideology*, MEW, vol. 5, pp. 19–450

—— —— *Manifesto of the Communist Party*, MEW, vol. 6, pp. 477–519

—— —— 'Demands of the Communist Party of Germany', MEW, vol. 7, pp. 3–7

—— —— *Ireland and the Irish Question* (anthology), Progress, Moscow, 1971

—— —— *Marx and Engels on Proletarian Internationalism* (anthology), Progress, Moscow, 1972

—— —— *Marx and Engels: Selected Correspondence*, 3rd edn., Progress, Moscow, 1975

Merced Rosa, Florencio, 'One Nation, One Party', *Journal of Contemporary Puerto Rican Thought*, vol. 2, no. 2–3, 1975, pp. 49–63

Miliband, Ralph, *Marxism and Politics*, Oxford University Press, Oxford, 1977

Minchinton, W. E., *The Growth of English Overseas Trade in the 17th and 18th Centuries*, Methuen, London, 1969

Minogue, K. R., *Nationalism*, Penguin, Harmondsworth, 1970

Nairn, Tom, *The Break-Up of Britain*, New Left Books, London, 1977

Needham, Joseph, *Science and Civilization in China*, vol. 4, part 3, Cambridge University Press, Cambridge, 1970

Nettl, J. P., *Rosa Luxemburg*, 2 vols., Oxford University Press, London, 1966

Nguyen Khac Vien, *Traditional Vietnam: Some Historical Stages*, Vietnamese Studies, no. 21, Hanoi, c. 1970

Nicholas, D. M., 'Town and Countryside: Social and Economic Tensions in 14th-Century Flanders', *Comparative Studies in Society and History* col. 10, 1967–1968, pp. 458–485

Novak, V. J. A., 'The Principle of Sociogenesis, Real Socialism, and the Problem of Lasting Peace', *Antipode: A Radical Journal of Geography*, vol. 16, no. 1, 1984, pp. 5–11

—— *The Principle of Sociogenesis*, Academia Publishing House, Czechoslovak Academy of Sciences, Prague, 1982

Palumbo, M., and Shanahan, W. (eds.), *Nationalism: Essays in Honor of Louis L. Snyder*, Greenwood, Westport, 1981

Partido Socialista Puertorriqueño, Seccional de Estados Unidos, *Desde las entrañas, Nueva Lucha* (Puerto Rico), special number, 1974

Peet, J. R. (ed.), *Radical Geography*, Maaroufa, Chicago, 1977

Perrons, Diane, 'Ireland and the Break-Up of Britain', *Antipode: A Radical Journal of Geography*, vol. 12, no. 2, 1980

Piore, Michael, *Birds of Passage: Migrant Labour and Industrial Societies*, Cambridge University Press, Cambridge, 1979

Poulantzas, Nicos, *State, Power, Socialism*, New Left Books, London, 1978

Pringle, Dennis, 'Marxism, the National Question, and the Conflict in Northern Ireland: A Response to Blaut', *Antipode: A Radical Journal of Geography*, vol. 14, no. 2, 1982, pp. 21–32

Purcell, Victor, *The Chinese in Southeast Asia*, Oxford University Press, London, 1951

Quintero-Rivera, Angel, 'Background to the Emergence of Imperialist Capitalism to Puerto Rico', in López and Petras (eds.), *Puerto Rico and Puerto Ricans*

—— 'The Development of Social Classes and Political Conflicts in Puerto Rico', in López and Petras (eds.), *Puerto Rico and Puerto Ricans*

—— (ed.), *Workers' Struggles in Puerto Rico: A Documentary History*, Monthly Review Press, New York and London, 1976

—— *Conflictos de clase y política en Puerto Rico*, Ediciones Huracán, Río Piedras, 1977

—— 'Imperialism and Class Struggle in Puerto Rico', *Two Thirds*, vol. 2, no. 1, 1979, pp. 4–11

—— 'Notes on Puerto Rican National Development: Class and Nation in a Colonial Context', *Marxist Perspectives*, vol. 3, no. 1, 1980, pp. 10–31

—— González, José Luis, Campos, Ricardo, and Flores, Juan, *Puerto Rico: Identidad nacional y clases sociales (coloquio de Princeton)*, Ediciones, Huracán, Río Piedras, 1981

Ramos Mattei, Andrés, *La hacienda azucarera: Su crecimiento y crisis en Puerto Rico* (Siglo 19), CEREP, San Juan, 1981

Rawski, Evelyn, *Agricultural Change and the Peasant Economy of South China*, MIT Press, Cambridge, Mass., 1972

Renner, Karl, *Der Kampf der österreichischen Nationen um der Staat*, Vienna, 1903

Ríos-Bustamante, Antonio, *Mexicans in the United States and the National Question: Current Polemics and Organizational Positions*, Editorial La Causa, Santa Barbara, 1978

Rodinson, Maxime, *Islam and Capitalism*, Pantheon, New York, 1974

Royal Institute of International Affairs, *Nationalism*, Oxford University Press, 1939

Santiago, Kelvin Antonio, 'Puerto Rico: la cuestión nacional', *Historia y Sociedad*, no. 16, 2nd series, 1977, pp. 24–38

—— 'La cuestión nacional: Algunas tesis ignoradas', *Proceso* (Puerto Rico), no. 4, 1981

Searle, Chris, *Grenada: The Struggle Against Destabilization*, Writers and Readers, London, 1983

Shafer, Boyd, *Nationalism: Myth and Reality*, Harcourt Brace, New York, 1955

Sharma, R. S., *Indian Feudalism: c. 300–1200*, University of Calcutta, Calcutta, 1965

——— *Light on Early Indian Society and Economy*, Manaktalas, Bombay, 1966
——— 'Indian Feudalism Retouched', *Indian Historical Review*, vol. 1, 1974, pp. 320–330
Silén, Juan Angel, 'Aspectos sobresalientes del problema nacional puertorriqueño y la nueva lucha de independencia', *Journal of Contemporary Puerto Rican Thought*, vol. 2, no. 2–3, 1975, pp. 14–20
——— *Pedro Albizu Campos*, Editorial Antillana, 1976
Simonsen, Roberto, *História Económica do Brasil, 1500–1820*, Editora Nacional, Sao Paulo, 1944
Smith, Abdullahi, 'The Early States of the Central Sudan', in J. F. A. Ajayi and M. Crowder (eds.), *History of West Africa*, vol. 1, Columbia University Press, 1972
Smith, Anthony D., *Theories of Nationalism*, Harper and Row, London, 1971
——— *Nationalism in the Twentieth Century*, New York University Press, New York, 1979
——— *State and Nation in the Third World*, Harvester Press, Brighton, 1983
Smith, C. T., *An Historical Geography of Western Europe before 1800*, Longmans, London, 1967
Snyder, Louis L., *The Meaning of Nationalism*, Rutgers University Press, New Brunswick, 1954
——— *The Dynamics of Nationalism: A Reader*, Princeton University Press, Princeton, 1964
——— 'Nationalism and the Territorial Imperative', *Canadian Review of Studies in Nationalism*, vol. 3, no. 1, 1975, pp. 1–21
So Kwan-wei, *Japanese Piracy in Ming China during the 16th Century*, Michigan State University Press, East Lansing, 1975
Stalin, Joseph, *Foundations of Leninism*, International, New York, 1939
——— 'The October Revolution and the National Question', *Collected Works*, vol. 4, Progress, Moscow, 1953–1955, p. 170
——— 'Marxism and the National Question', *Collected Works*, vol. 3, Progress, Moscow, 1953–1955, pp. 300–384
——— *Marxism and the National-Colonial Question* (anthology), Proletarian, San Francisco, 1975
Stover, C. A., 'Tropical Exports', in W. A. Lewis (ed.), *Tropical Development, 1880–1913*
Suret-Canale, Jean, *French Colonialism in Tropical Africa, 1900–1945*, Pica Press, New York, 1971
Taller de Formación Política, *La cuestión nacional: el Partido Nacionalista y el moviemiento obrero puertorriqueño*, Ediciones Huracán, Río Piedras, 1982
——— Talleres Socialistas, and Pensamiento Crítico, 'Crítica a la ponencia del Colectivo Socialista de San Juan', *Pensamiento Crítico*, año 7, no. 36, 1984
Talmon, J. L., *The Myth of the Nation and the Vision of Revolution*, Secker and Warburg, London, 1981
Taylor, P. J. 'Geographical Scales Within the World-Economy Approach', *Review*, vol. 5, 1981, pp. 3–11
Thapar, Romila, 'Ideology and the Interpretation of Early Indian History', *Review*, vol. 5, 1982, pp. 389–412
Thompson, E. P., *The Poverty of Theory and Other Essays*, Monthly Review Press, London, 1978
Titow, J. Z., *English Rural Society, 1200–1350*, Allen and Unwin, London, 1969
Tivey, L., (ed.), *The Nation-State*, St. Martin's, London, 1981

Townsend, Mary Evelyn, 'Hitler and the Revival of German Colonialism', in E. M. Earle (ed.), *Nationalism and Internationalism*, Columbia University Press, New York, 1950

Toynbee, Arnold, *A Study of History*, 11 vols., Oxford University Press, London, 1954

Trotsky, Leon, *Stalin*, Stein and Day, New York, 1967

Ts'ao Yung Ho, 'Chinese Overseas Trade in the Late Ming Period', *Proceedings, 2nd Biennial Conference, International Association of Historians of Asia*, Taipei, 1962

Turner, Bryan, *Marx and the End of Orientalism*, Allen and Unwin, London, 1978

United States Commission on Civil Rights, *Puerto Ricans in the Continental United States: An Uncertain Future*, U.S. Commission on Civil Rights, Washington D.C., 1976

United States Department of Commerce, *Economic Study of Puerto Rico*, 2 vols., U.S. Government Printing Office, Washington, 1979

Vázquez Calzada, José L., 'La población de Puerto Rico', in M. Galiñanes (ed.), *Geovisión de Puerto Rico*

Vilar, Pierre, 'On Nations and Nationalism', *Marxist Perspectives*, vol. 2, no. 1, 1979, pp. 8–29

Villamil, José, 'The Puerto Rican Model: The Limits of Dependent Growth', *Two Thirds*, vol. 1, no. 2, 1979, pp. 12–24

—— (ed.), *Transnational Capitalism and National Development*, Humanities, Atlantic Highlands, N.J., 1979

Volkov, Mai, 'The "Interdependence of Nations" and Neocolonialism', *Social Sciences*, vol. 13, no. 1, 1982, pp. 126–136

Wallerstein, Immanuel, 'The Future of the World Economy', in T. Hopkins and I. Wallerstein (eds.), *Processes of the World-System*, Sage, Beverly Hills, 1980

—— 'Crisis as Transition', in S. Amin, G. Arrighi, A. G. Frank, and I. Wallerstein, *Dynamics of World Crisis*, Monthly Review, London, 1983

——'Patterns and Prospectives of the Capitalist World-Economy', *Contemporary Marxism*, no. 9, 1984, pp. 59–70

Wang Gung-Wu, 'Early Ming Relations with Southeast Asia', in J. K. Fairbanks (ed.), *The Chinese World Order*, MIT Press, Cambridge, Mass., 1967

Weber, Max, *The Protestant Ethic and the Spirit of Capitalism*, Scribner's, New York, 1958

Wiens, Herold, *China's March into the Tropics*, Yale, New Haven, 1954

Wiethoff, Bodo, *Die chinesische Seeverbotspolitik und der private Überseehandel von 1868 bis 1567*, Gesellschaft für Natur- und Völkerkunde Ostasiens, Hamburg, 1963

Wheatley, Paul, *The Golden Khersonese*, University of Malaya Press, Kuala Lumpur, 1961

White, Lynn Jr., *Medieval Technology and Social Change*, Oxford University Press, London, 1962

—— *Machina ex Deo: Essays in the Dynamism of Western Culture*, MIT Press, Cambridge, Mass., 1968

Wu Yu Kan, 'Chinese Overseas Intercourse and Trade in Ancient Times', *Eastern Horizon*, vol. 4, no. 2, 1965, pp. 6–17

Yadav, B. N. S., 'Immobility and Subjugation of Indian Peasantry in Early Medieval Complex', *Indian Historical Review*, vol. 1, 1974, pp. 18–27

Zavala, Iris M., and Rodríguez, Rafael, *The Intellectual Roots of Independence: An*

*Anthology of Political Essays*, Monthly Review Press, New York and London, 1980

Zubaida, Sami, 'Theories of Nationalism', in G. Littlejohn and others (eds.), *Power and the State*, St. Martin's, London, 1978

# Index